nakaba suzuki presents

37

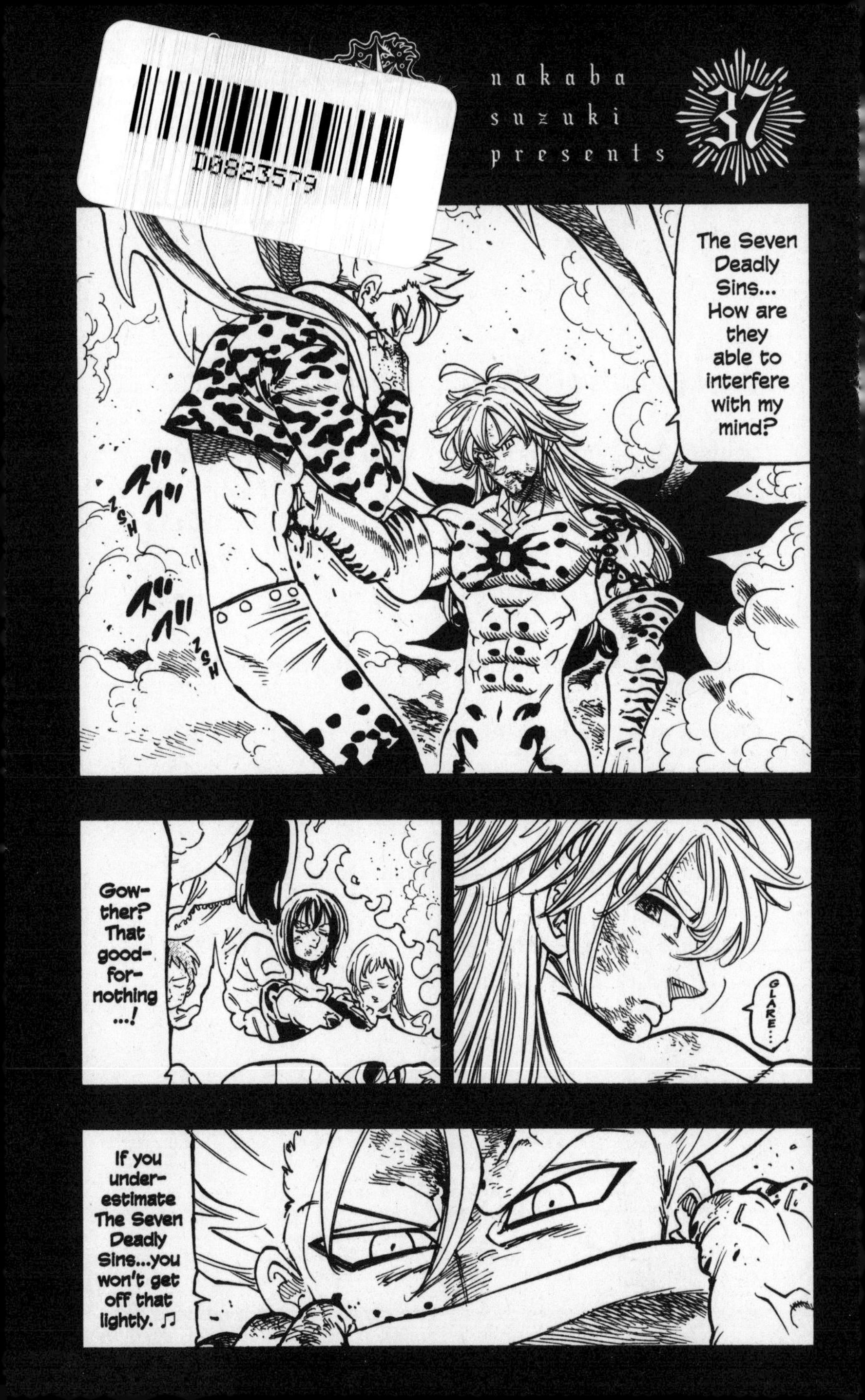

The Seven Deadly Sins... How are they able to interfere with my mind?
ZSH
ZSH
GLARE...
Gow-ther? That good-for-nothing ...!
If you under-estimate The Seven Deadly Sins...you won't get off that lightly. ♫

# CONTENTS

**Chapter 303 - We'll All Be Your Strength**     003

**Chapter 304 - The Executioner's Wish**     023

**Chapter 305 - Death Throes**     043

**Chapter 306 - The End of a Long Journey**     063

**Chapter 307 - Until We're Shrouded in Happiness**     083

**Chapter 308 - Meliodas Disappears**     103

**Chapter 309 - This is the Path I Live**     123

**Chapter 310 - Farewell, Seven Deadly Sins**     143

**Chapter 311 - It's Not Over Yet**     163

BOAR HAT
The Seven Deadly Sins

# Chapter 303 - We'll All Be Your Strength

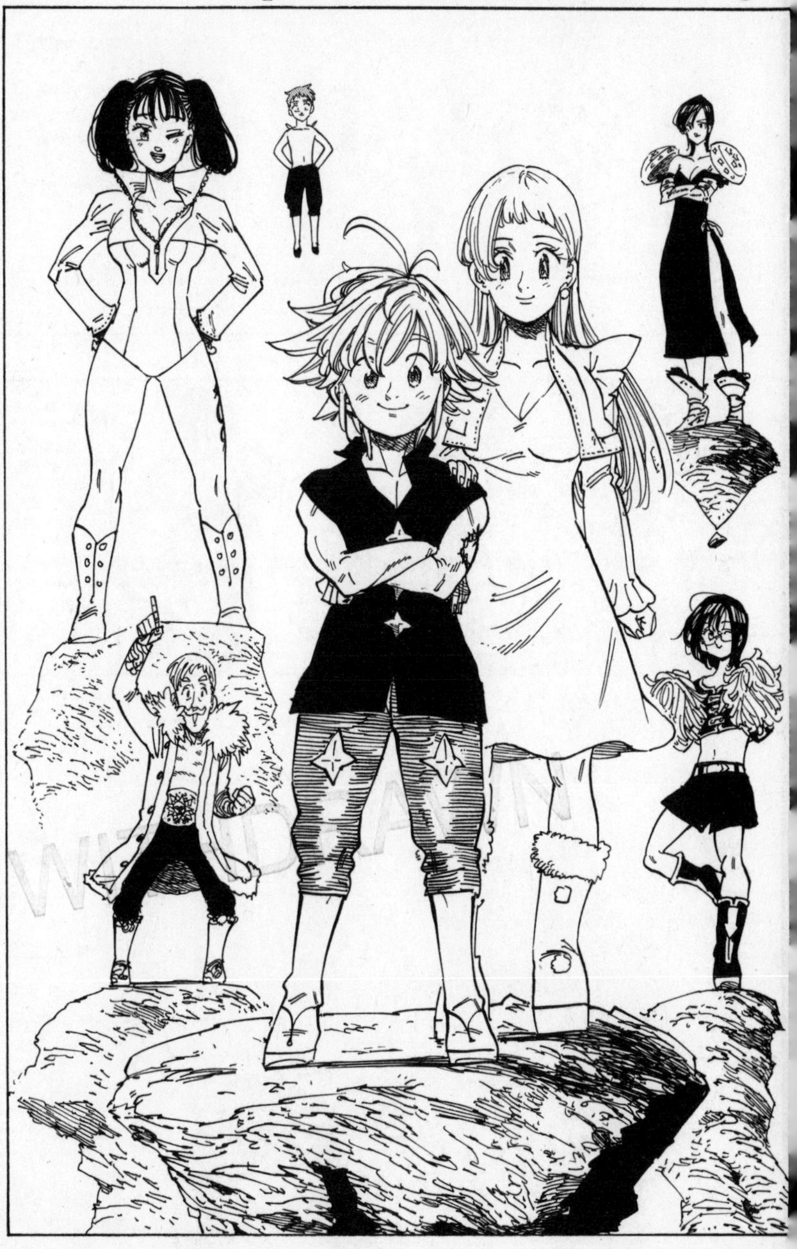

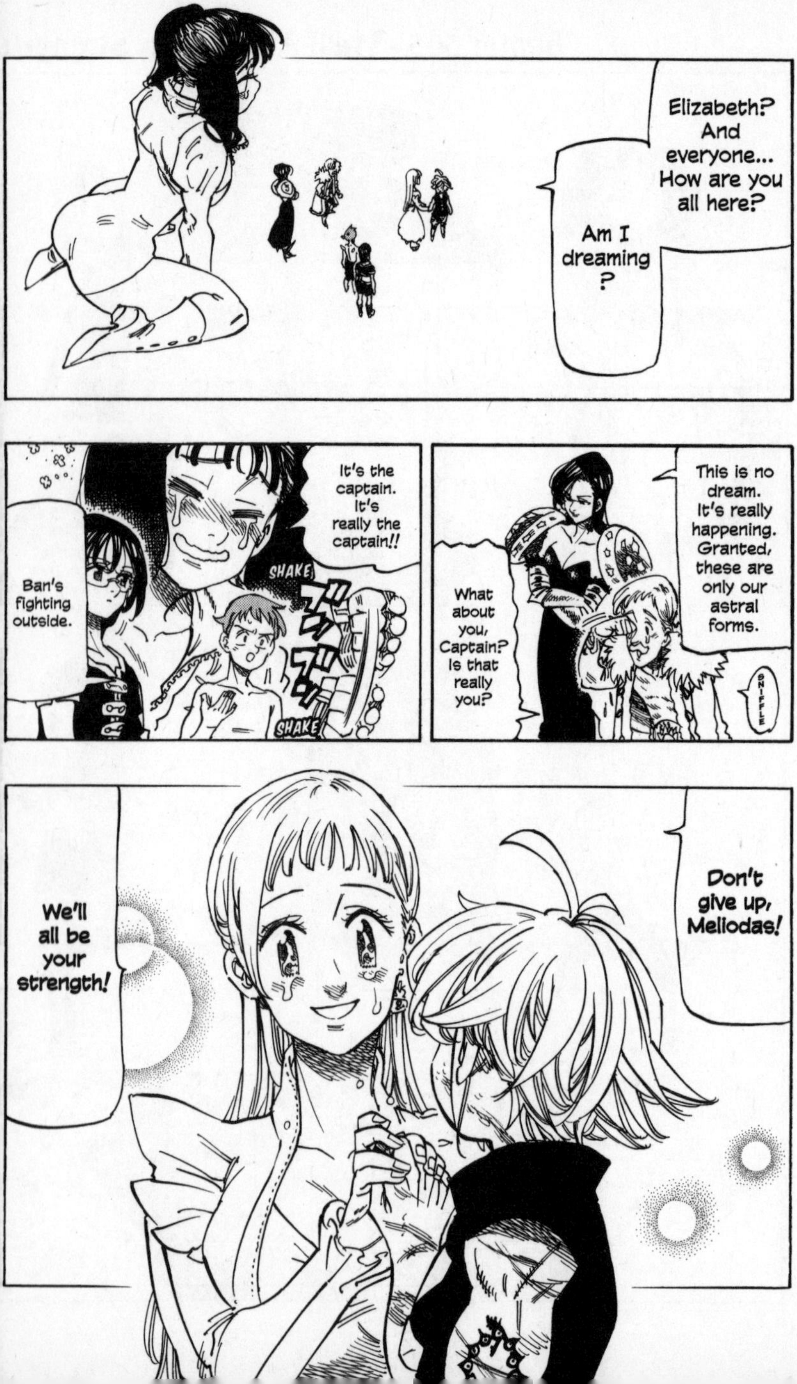
Elizabeth? And everyone... How are you all here?
Am I dreaming?
This is no dream. It's really happening. Granted, these are only our astral forms.
What about you, Captain? Is that really you?
SNIFFLE
It's the captain. It's really the captain!!
SHAKE
SHAKE
Ban's fighting outside.
Don't give up, Meliodas!
We'll all be your strength!

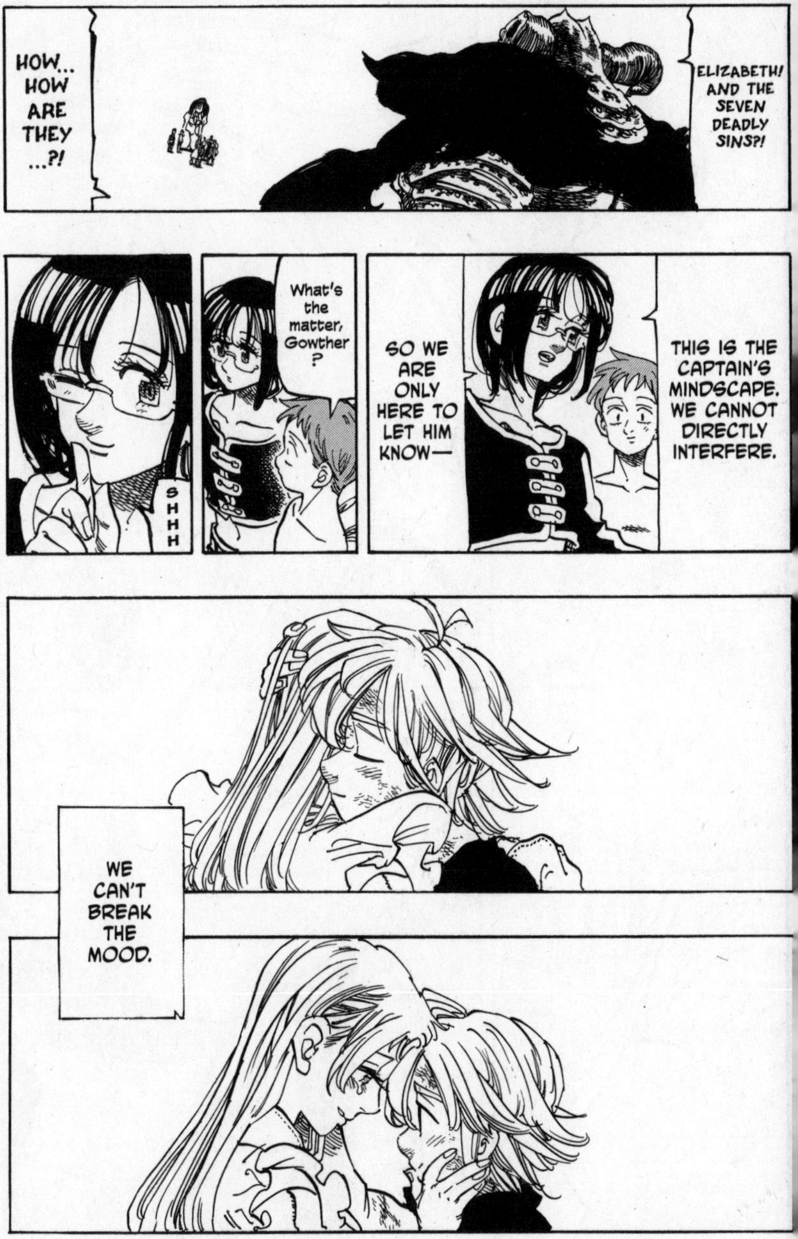
ELIZABETH! AND THE SEVEN DEADLY SINS?!
HOW... HOW ARE THEY ...?!
THIS IS THE CAPTAIN'S MINDSCAPE. WE CANNOT DIRECTLY INTERFERE.
SO WE ARE ONLY HERE TO LET HIM KNOW—
What's the matter, Gowther?
SHHH
WE CAN'T BREAK THE MOOD.

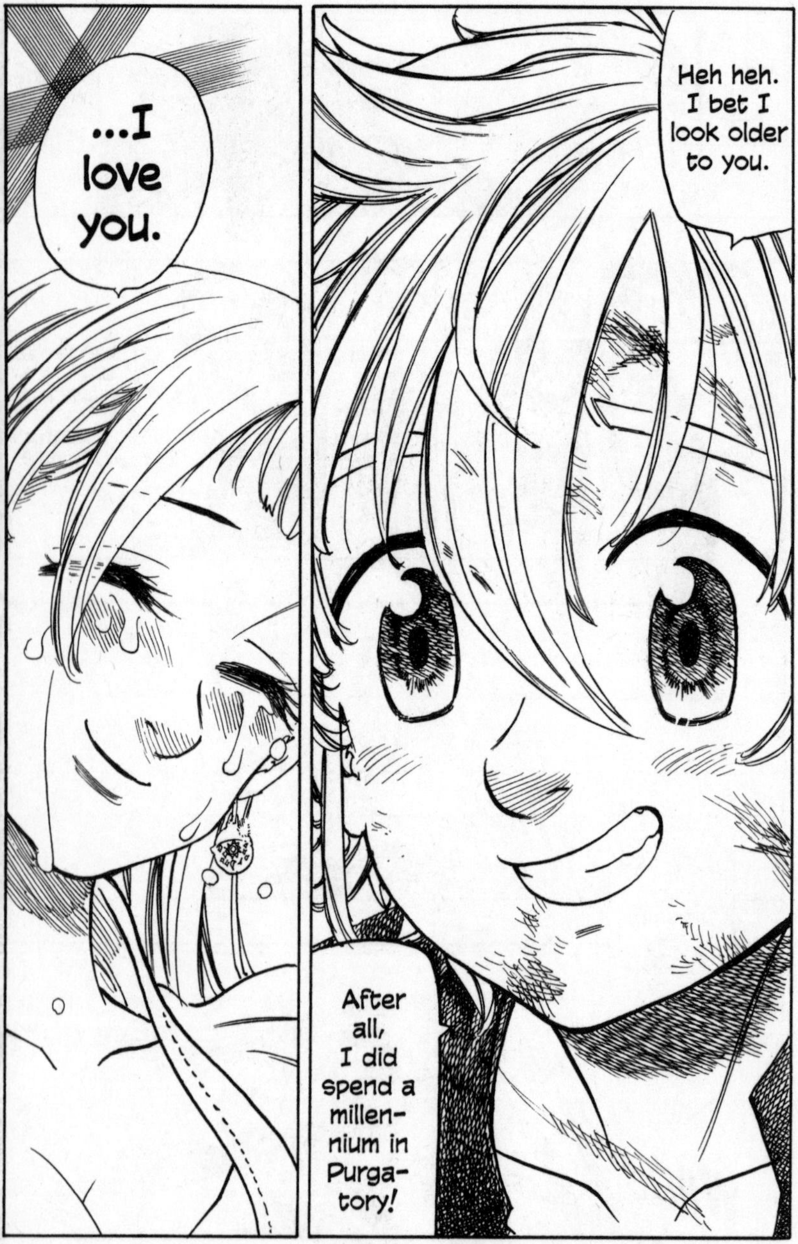
Heh heh. I bet I look older to you.
After all, I did spend a millennium in Purgatory!
...I love you.

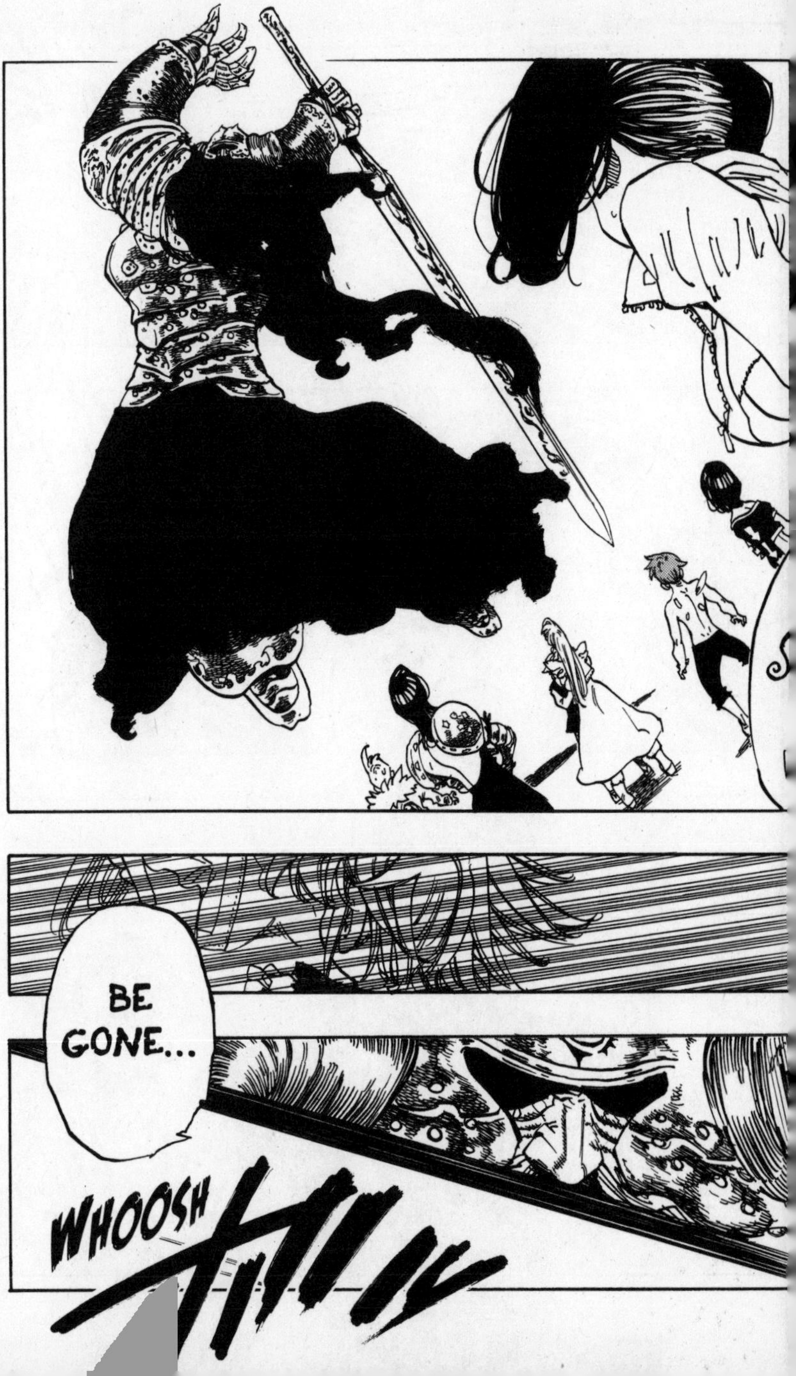
BE GONE...
WHOOSH

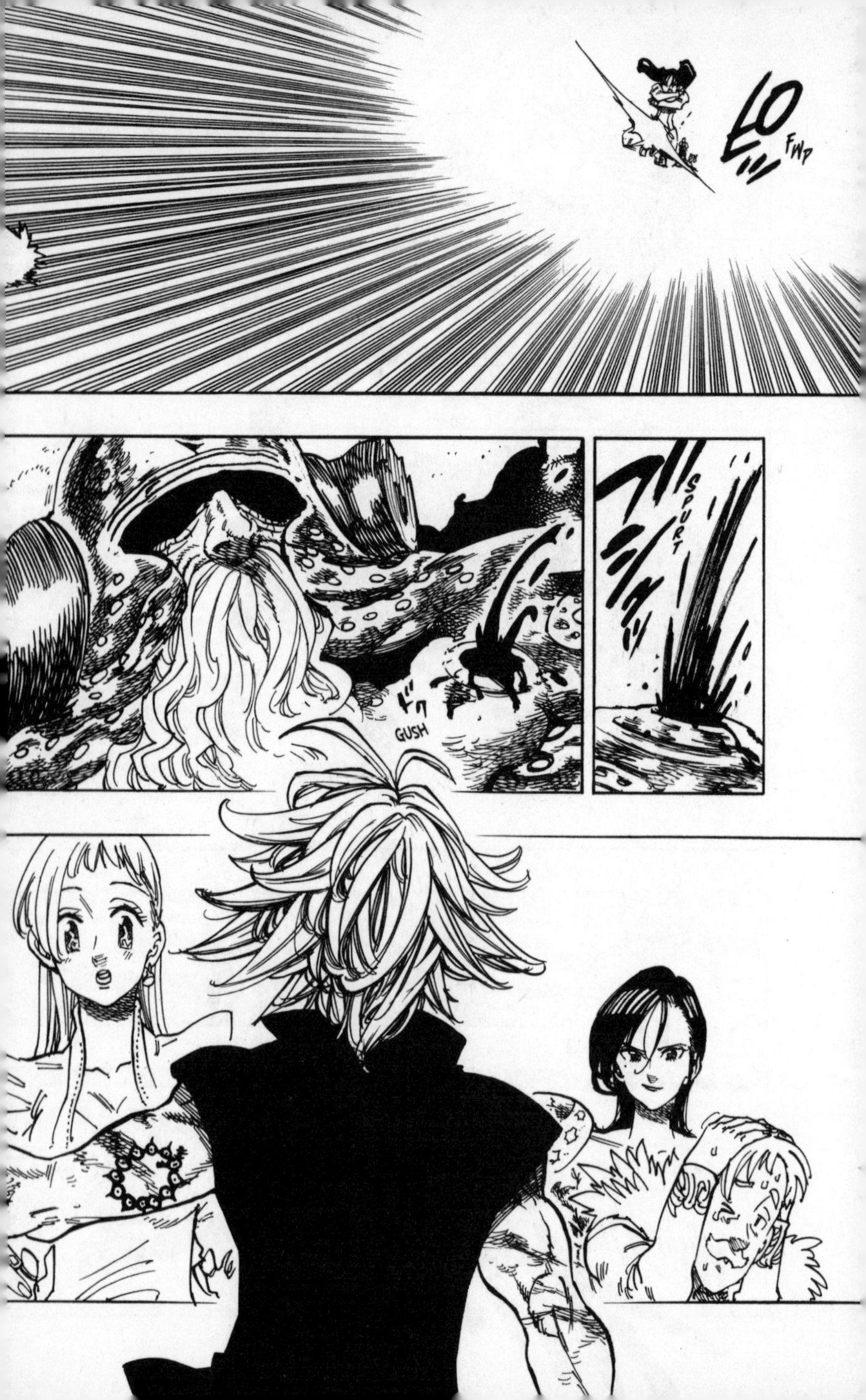
FWP
SPURT
GUSH

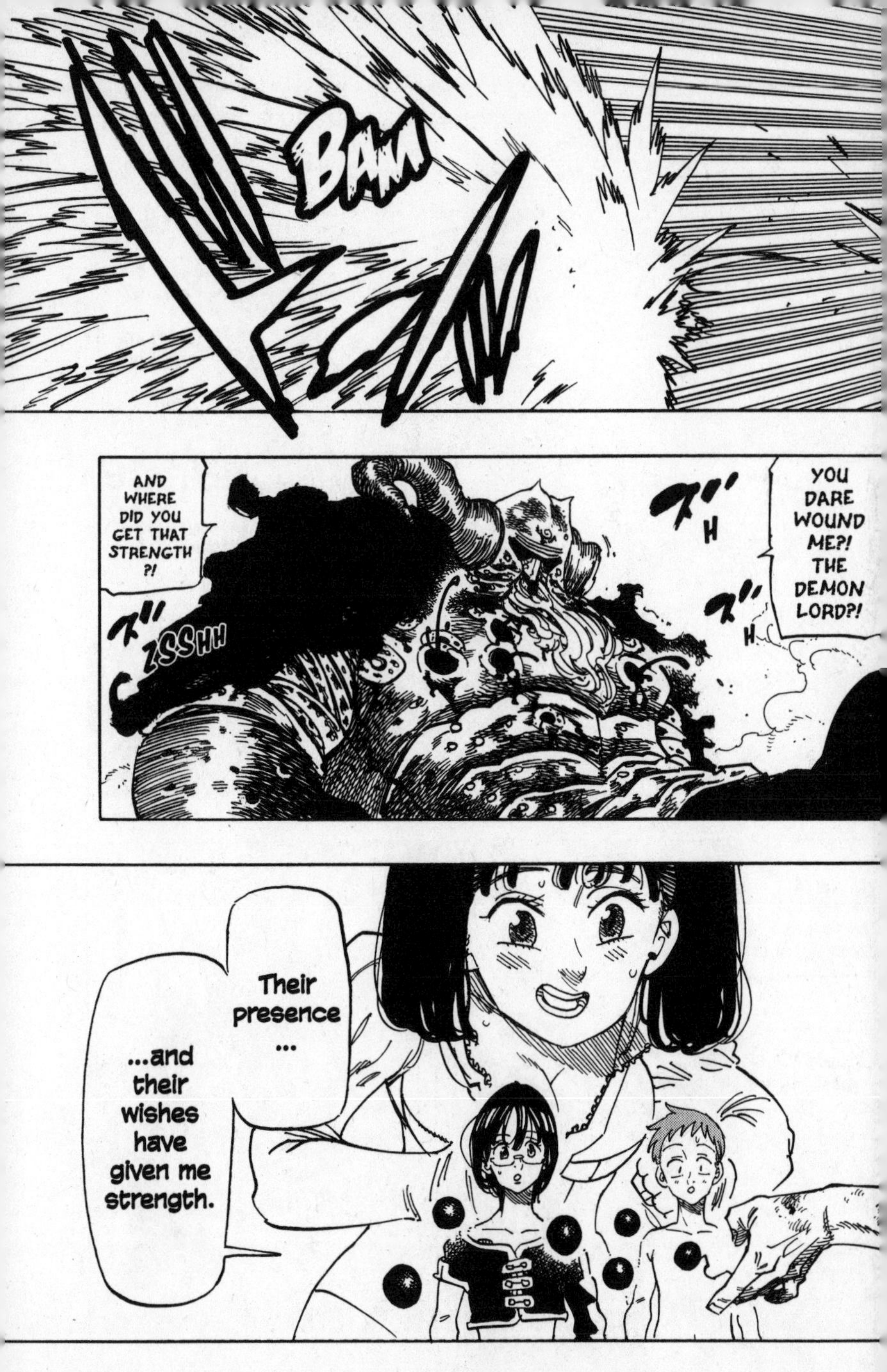
BAM
YOU DARE WOUND ME?! THE DEMON LORD?!
AND WHERE DID YOU GET THAT STRENGTH ?!
ZSSHH
Their presence ...
...and their wishes have given me strength.

You don't stand a chance now!

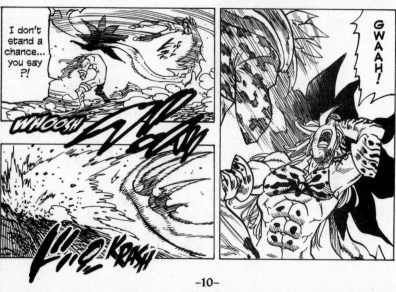

I don't stand a chance... you say?!

WHOOSH

KRASH

GWAAH!

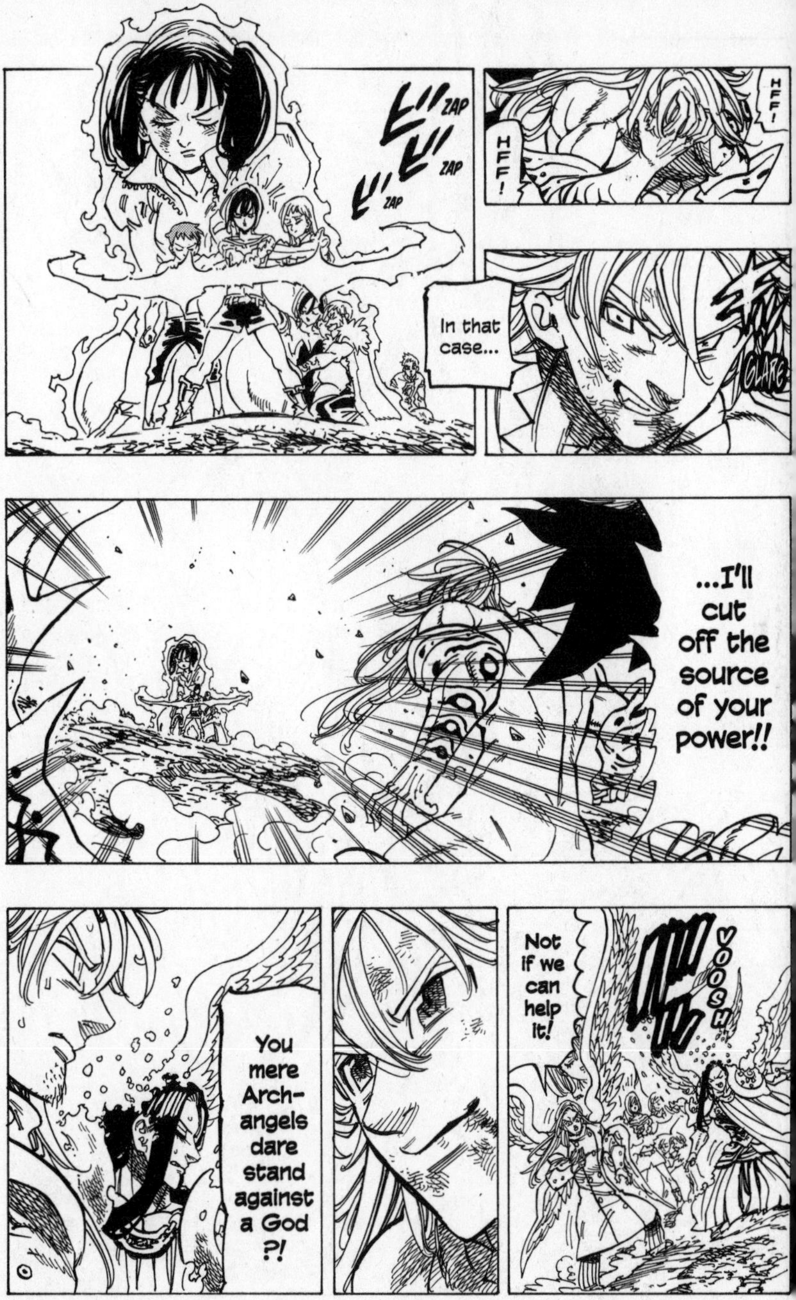
HFF!
HFF!
In that case...
GLARE
ZAP
ZAP
ZAP
...I'll cut off the source of your power!!
VOOSH
Not if we can help it!
You mere Arch-angels dare stand against a God?!

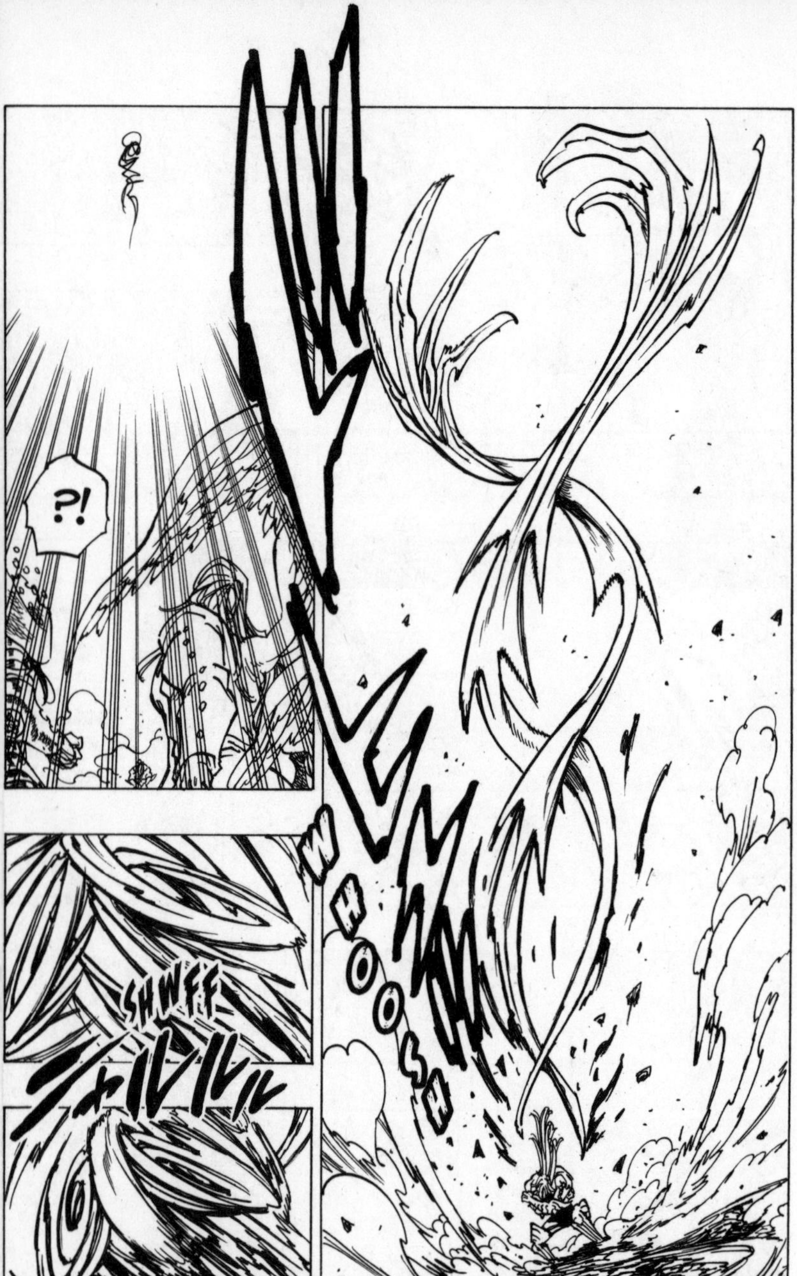
WHOOSH
?!
SHWFF
シャルルル

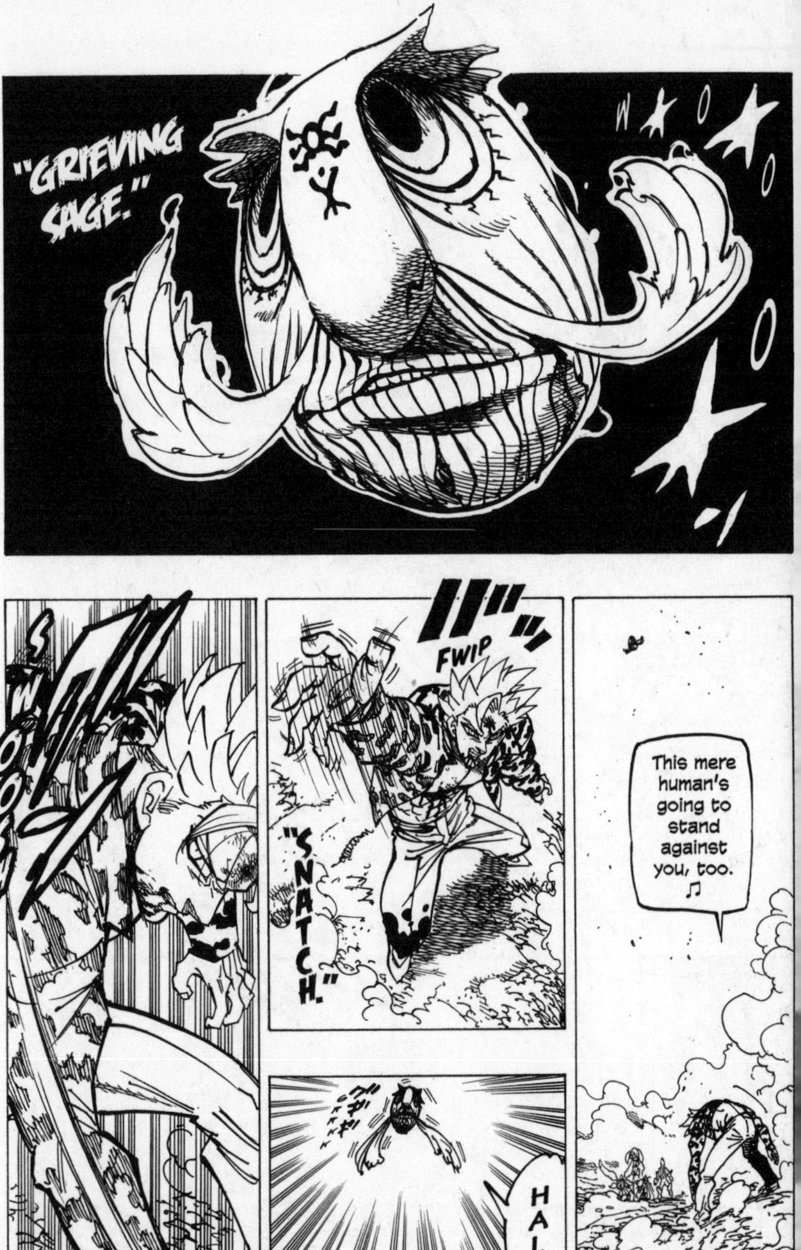
"GRIEVING SAGE."
This mere human's going to stand against you, too. ♫
FWIP
"SNATCH."
HALT

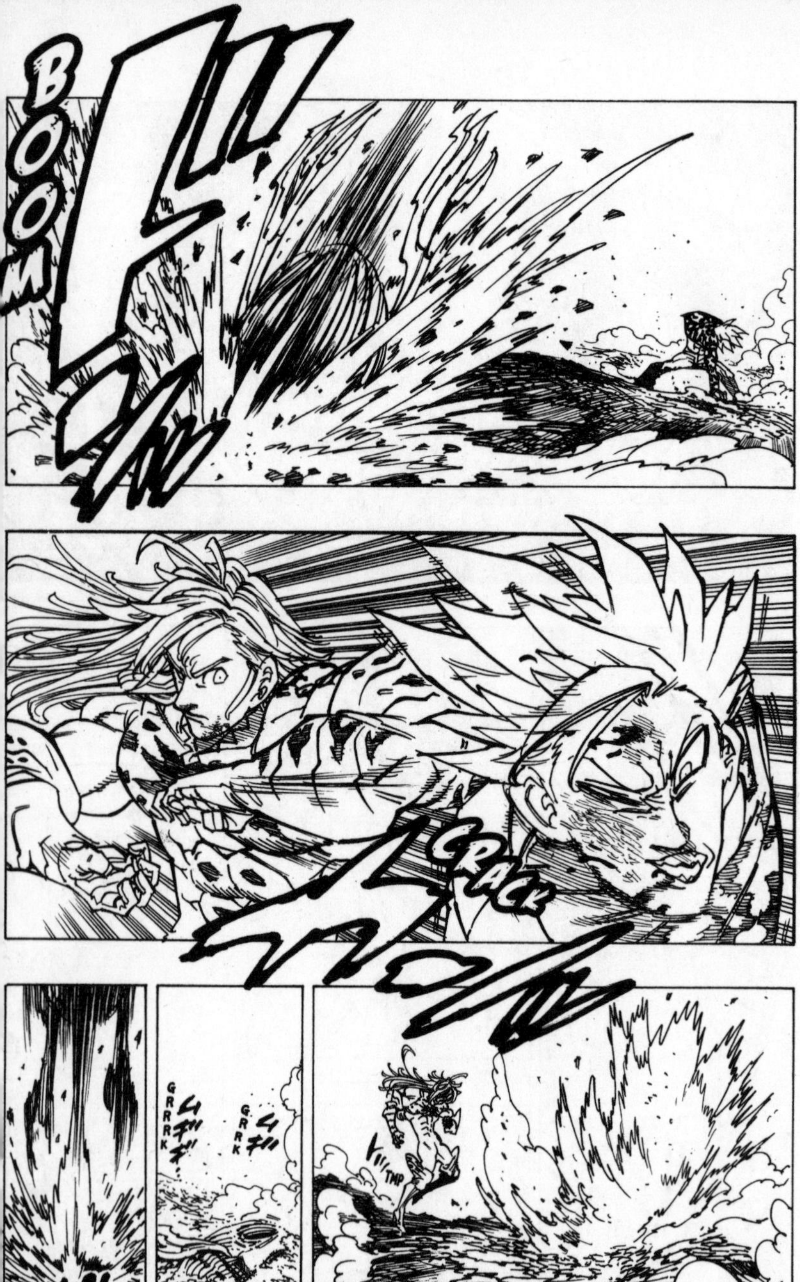
BOOM
CRACK
TMP
GRRRK
GRRRK
WOOSH

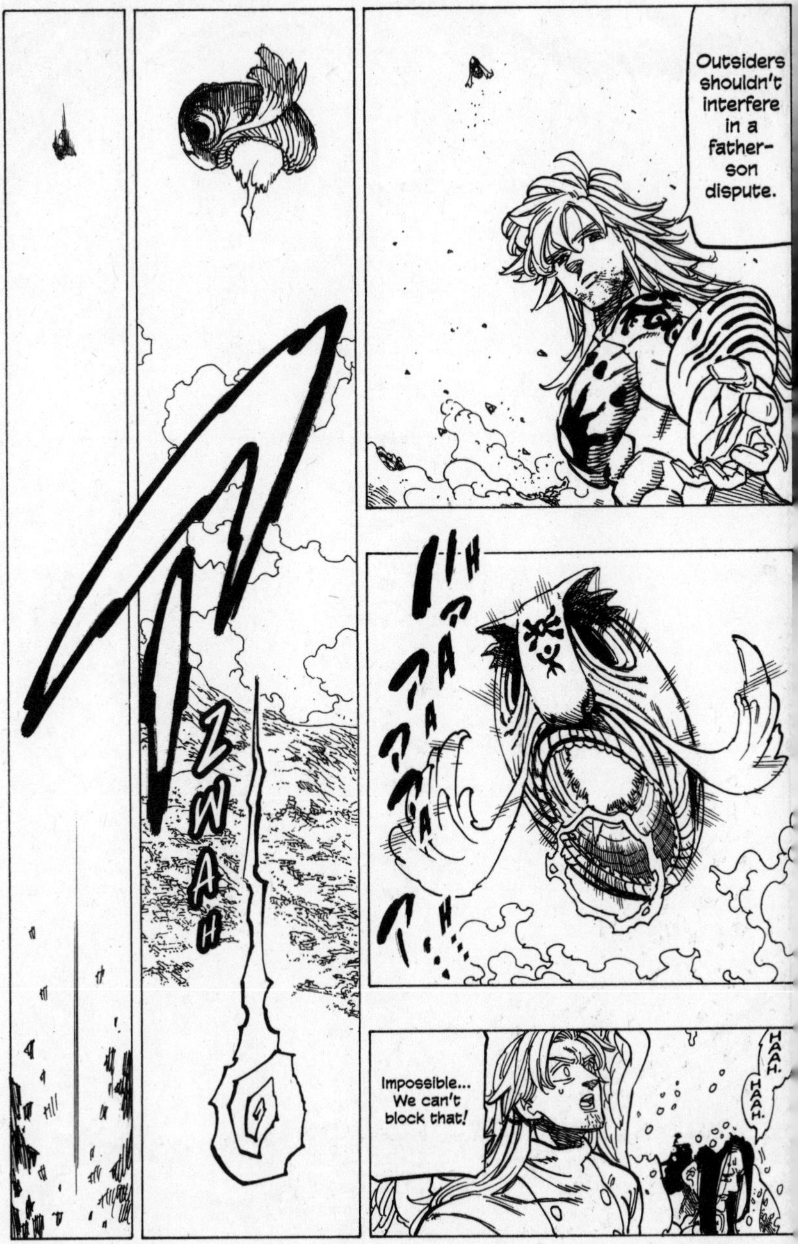

Outsiders shouldn't interfere in a father-son dispute.
HAAAAAH...
ZWAH
HAAH. HAAH.
Impossible... We can't block that!

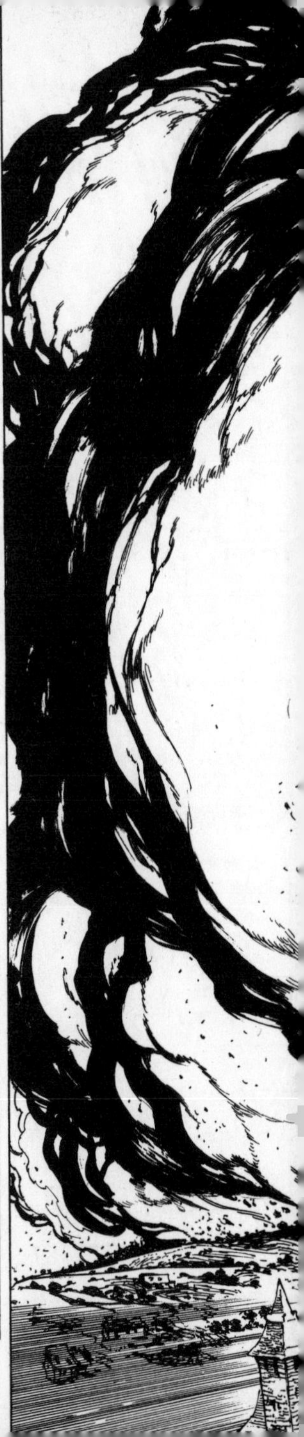

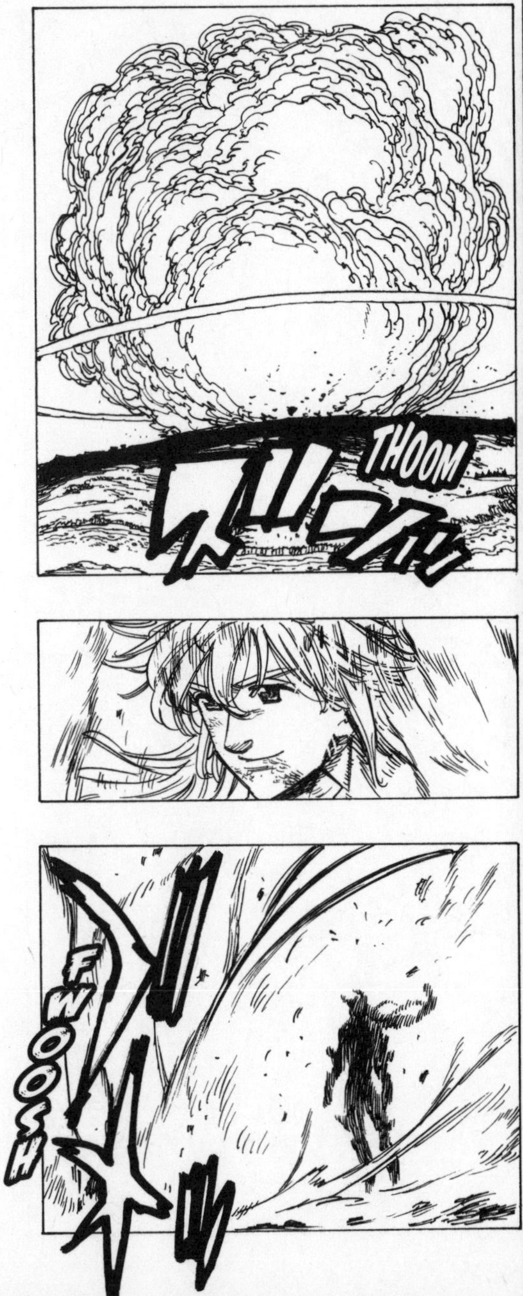
THOOM
FWOOOSH

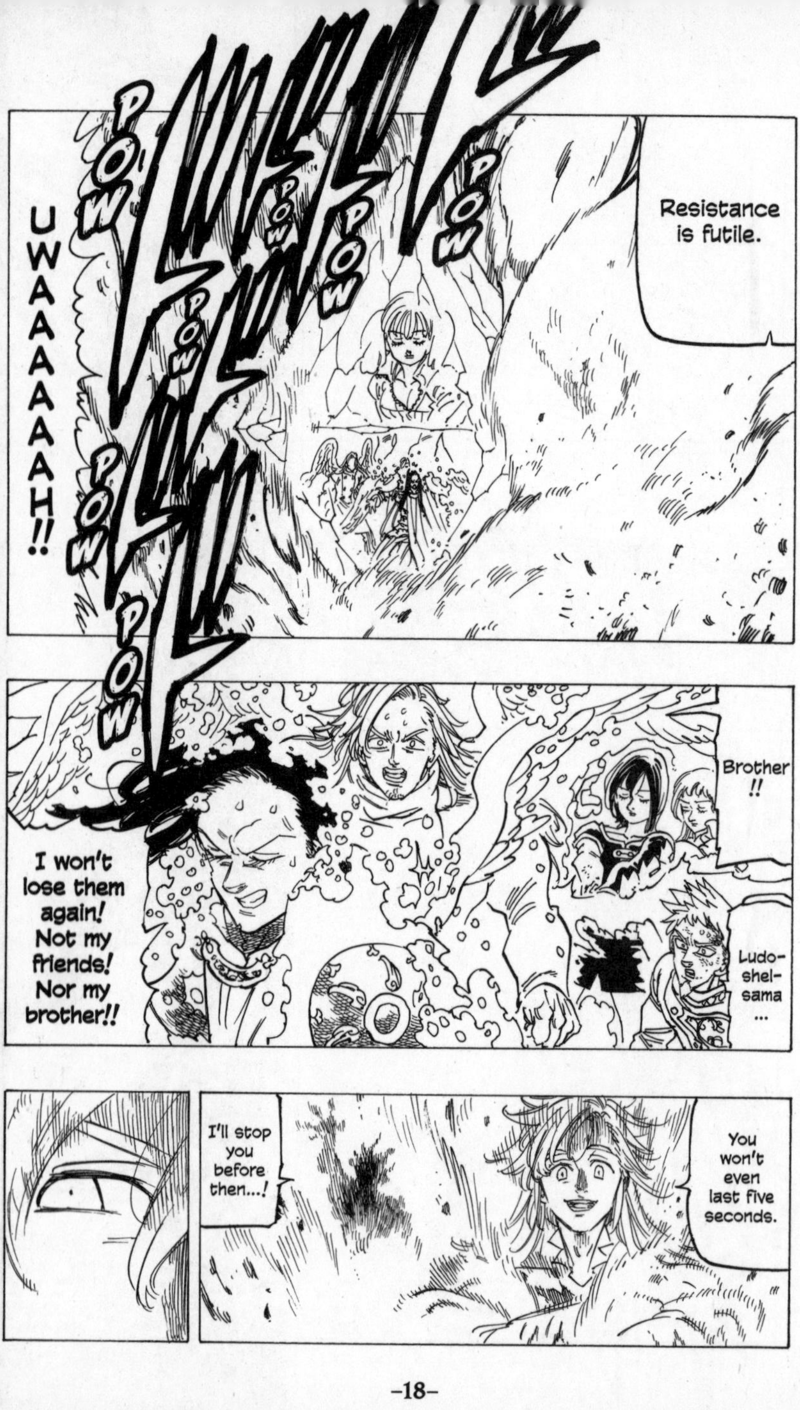
Resistance is futile.
POW
POW
POW
POW
POW
POW
POW
UWAAAAAAH!!
Brother!!
Ludo-shel-sama...
I won't lose them again! Not my friends! Nor my brother!!
You won't even last five seconds.
I'll stop you before then...!

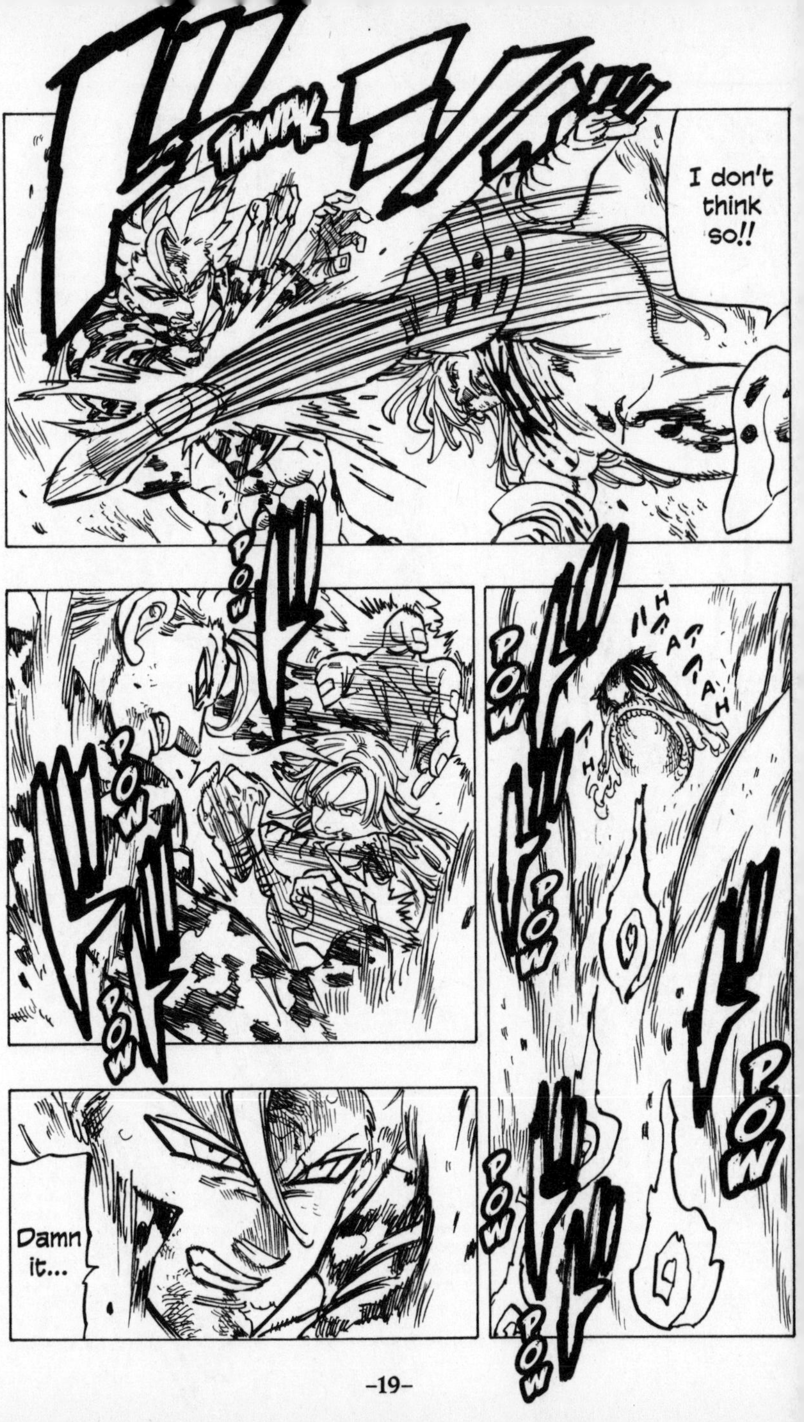
THWAK
I don't think so!!
POW POW
HAAAAH
POW POW
POW POW
POW POW
POW
POW POW
POW POW
Damn it...

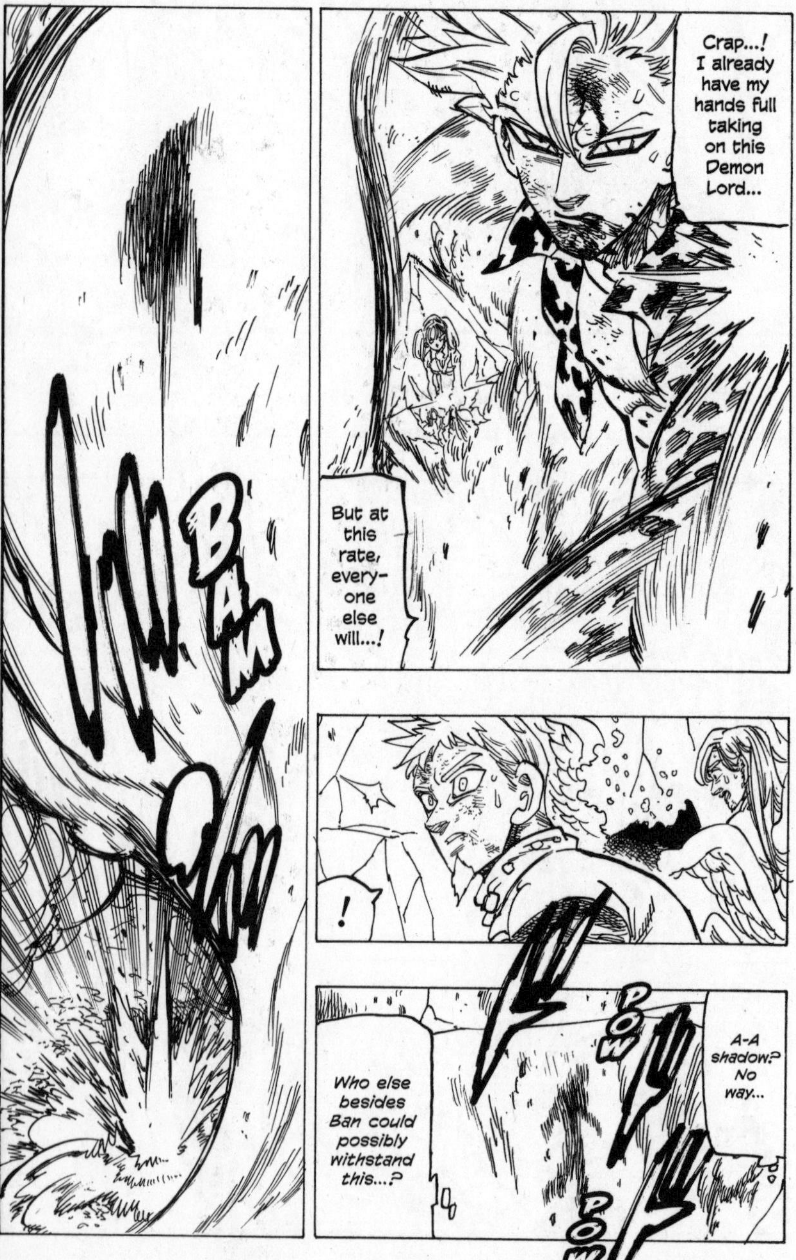
Crap...! I already have my hands full taking on this Demon Lord...
But at this rate, every-one else will...!
!
A-A shadow? No way...
POW
POW
Who else besides Ban could possibly withstand this...?
BAM

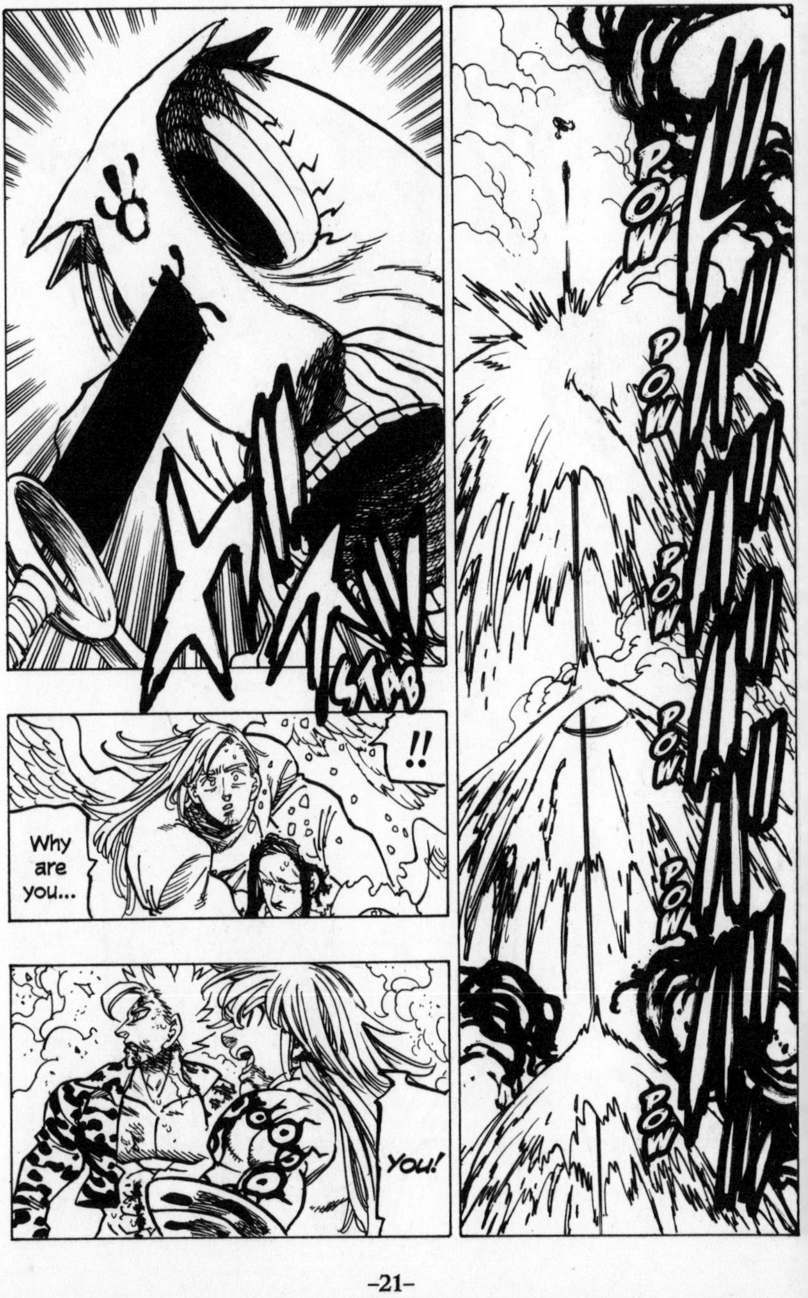
POW
POW POW
POW POW
POW POW
POW POW
POW POW
STAB
!!
Why are you...
YOU!

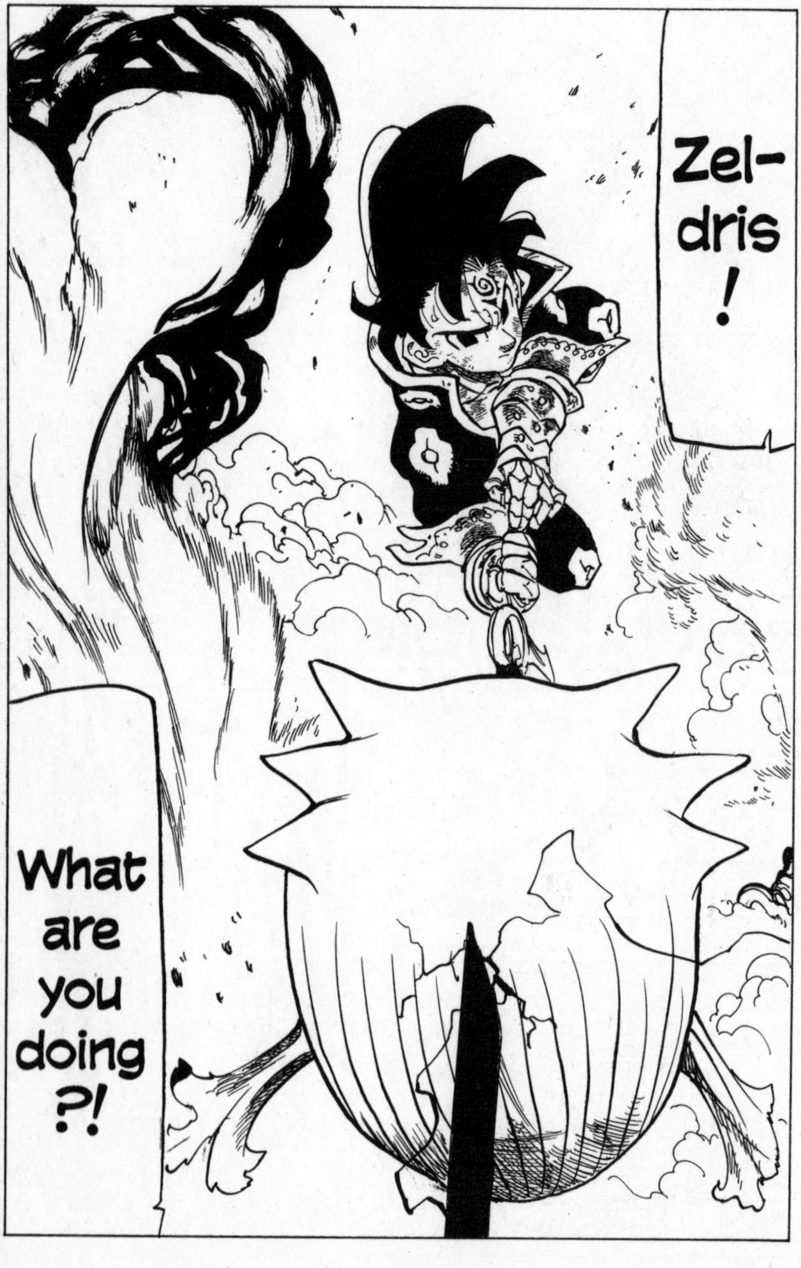
Zel-dris!
What are you doing?!

## Chapter 304 - The Executioner's Wish

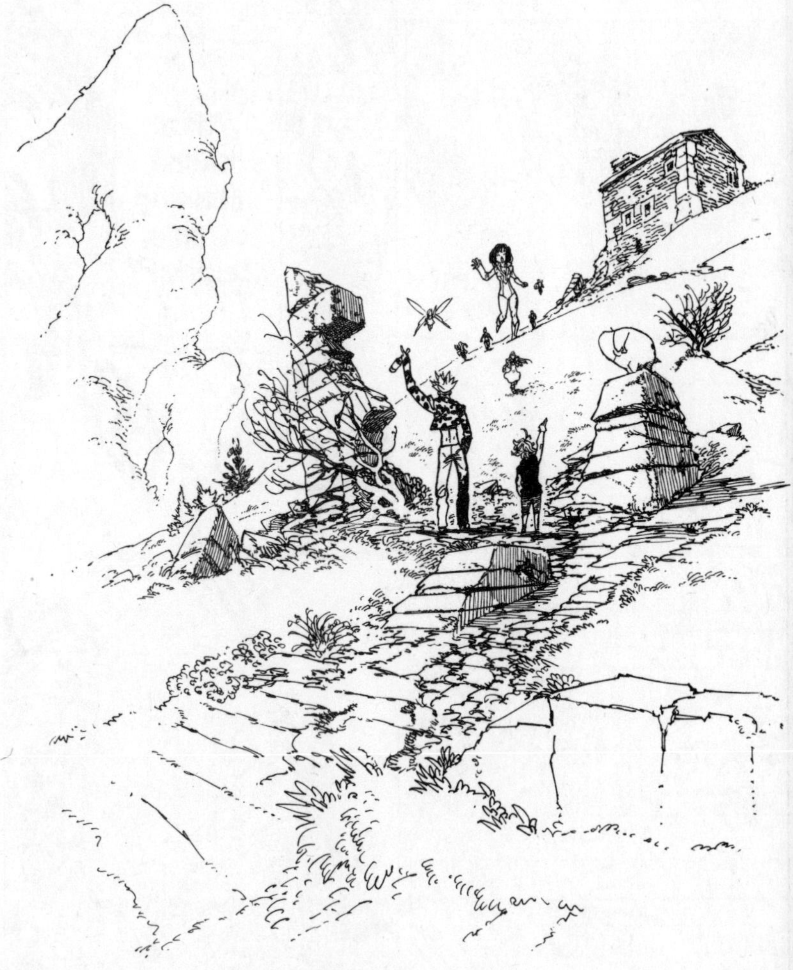

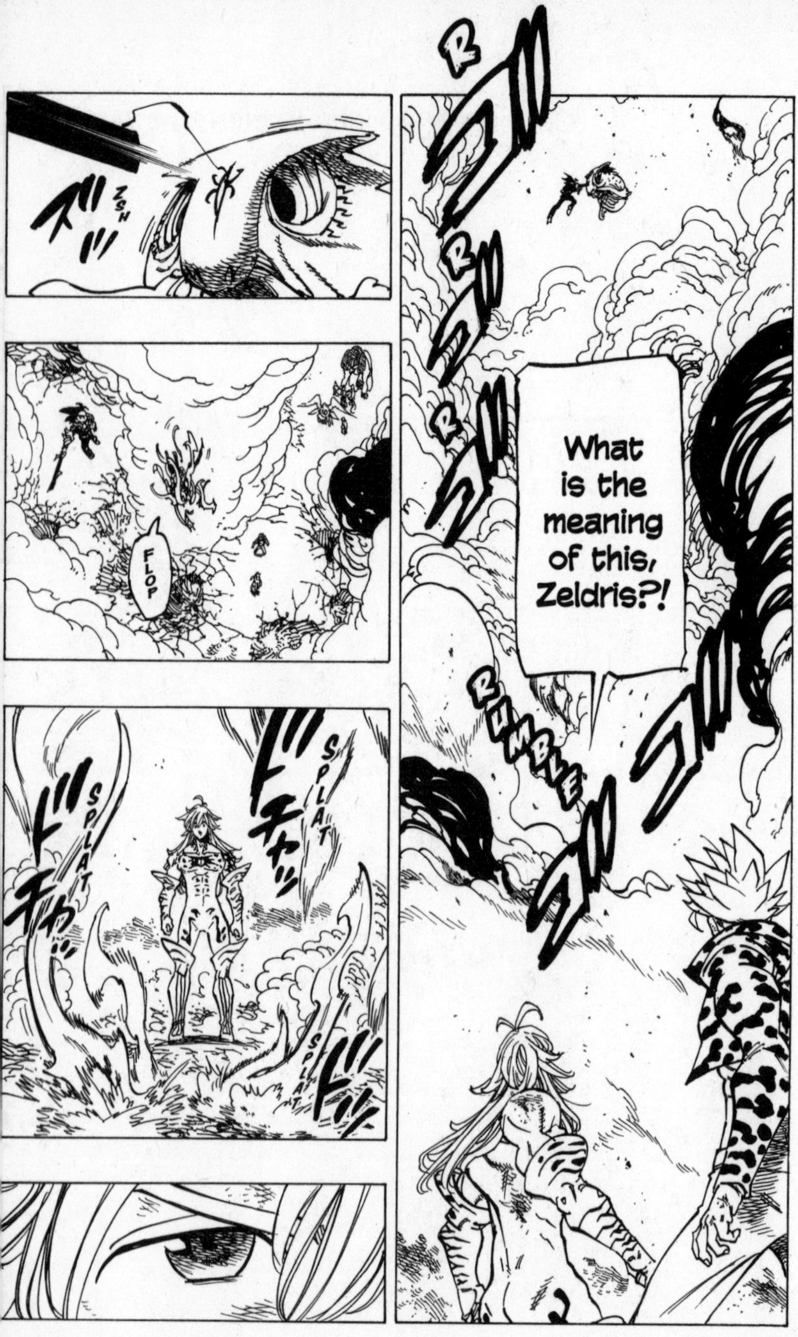
RRR
What is the meaning of this, Zeldris?!
RUMBLE
ZSH
FLOP
SPLAT
SPLAT
SPLAT

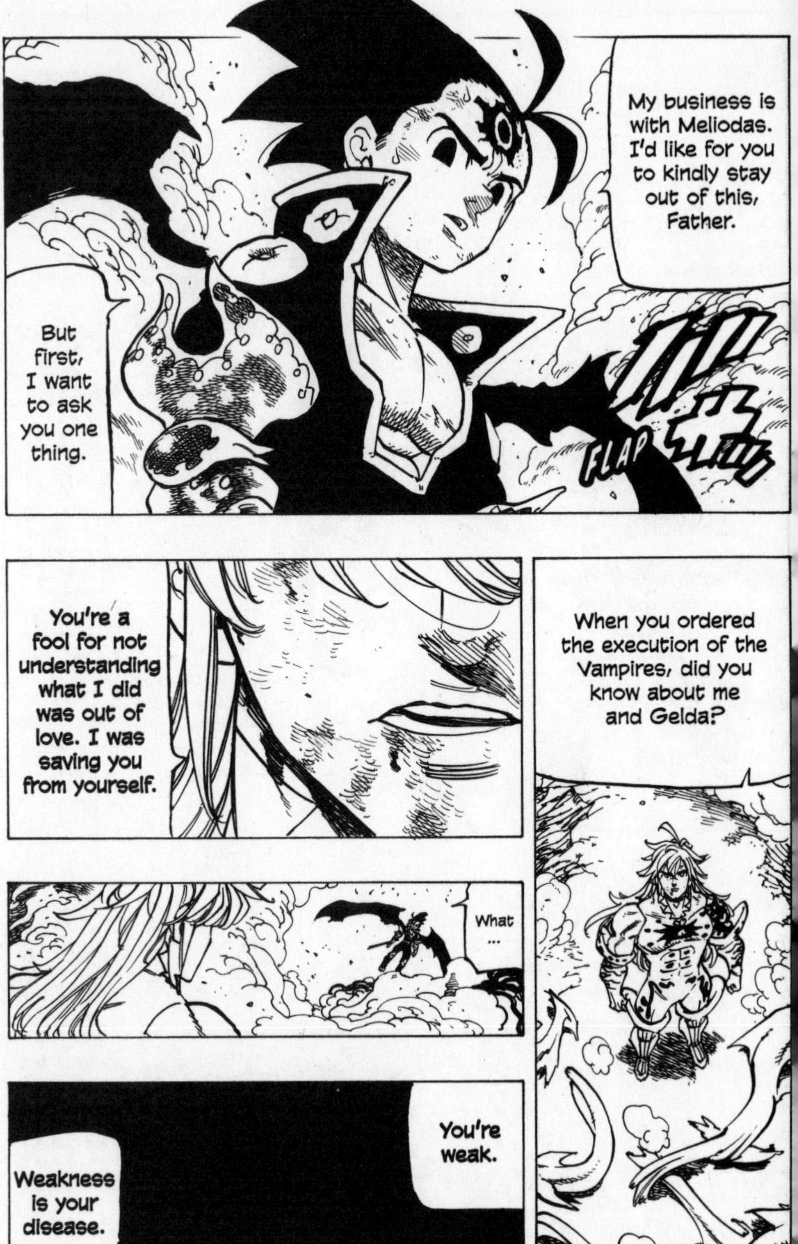
My business is with Meliodas. I'd like for you to kindly stay out of this, Father.
FLAP
But first, I want to ask you one thing.
When you ordered the execution of the Vampires, did you know about me and Gelda?
You're a fool for not understanding what I did was out of love. I was saving you from yourself.
What ...
You're weak.
Weakness is your disease.

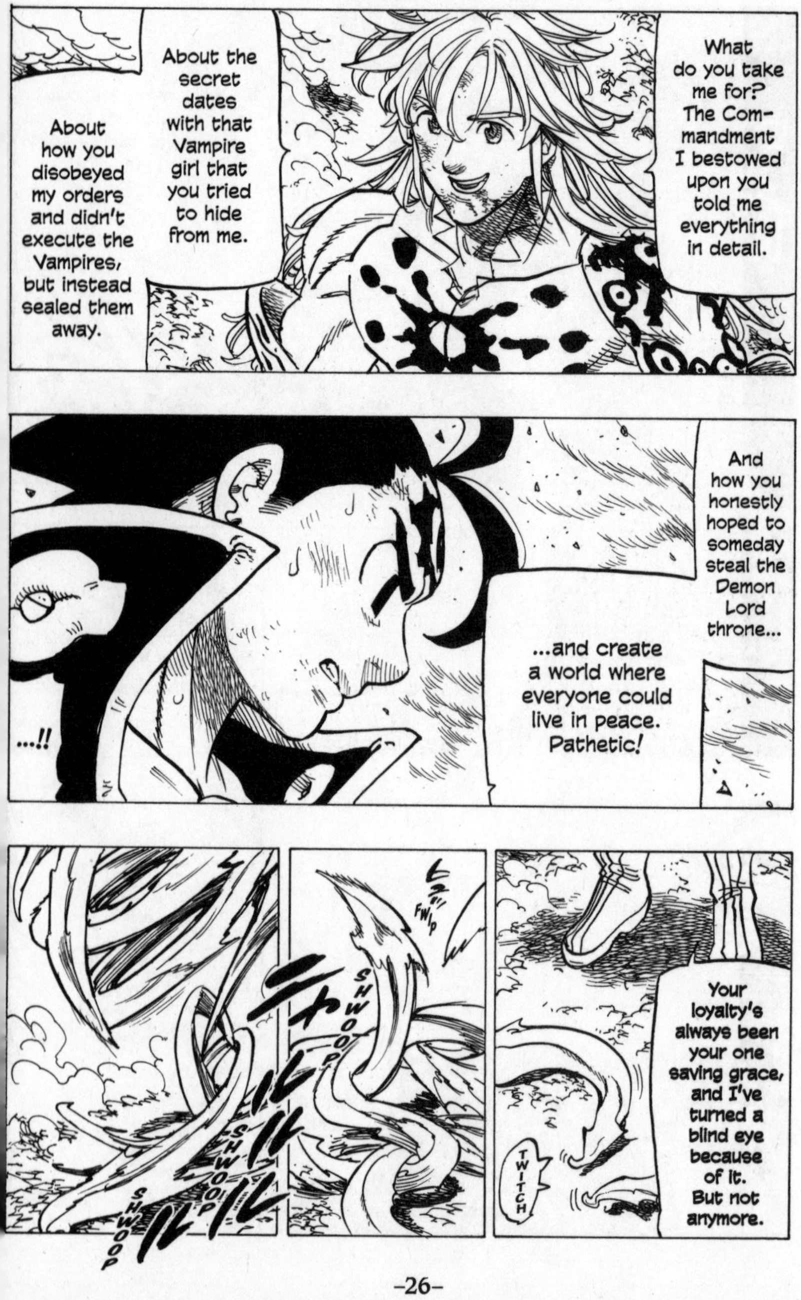
What do you take me for? The Commandment I bestowed upon you told me everything in detail.
About the secret dates with that Vampire girl that you tried to hide from me.
About how you disobeyed my orders and didn't execute the Vampires, but instead sealed them away.
And how you honestly hoped to someday steal the Demon Lord throne...
...and create a world where everyone could live in peace. Pathetic!
...!!
Your loyalty's always been your one saving grace, and I've turned a blind eye because of it. But not anymore.
TWITCH
FWIP
SHWOOOP
SHWOOP
SHWOOP

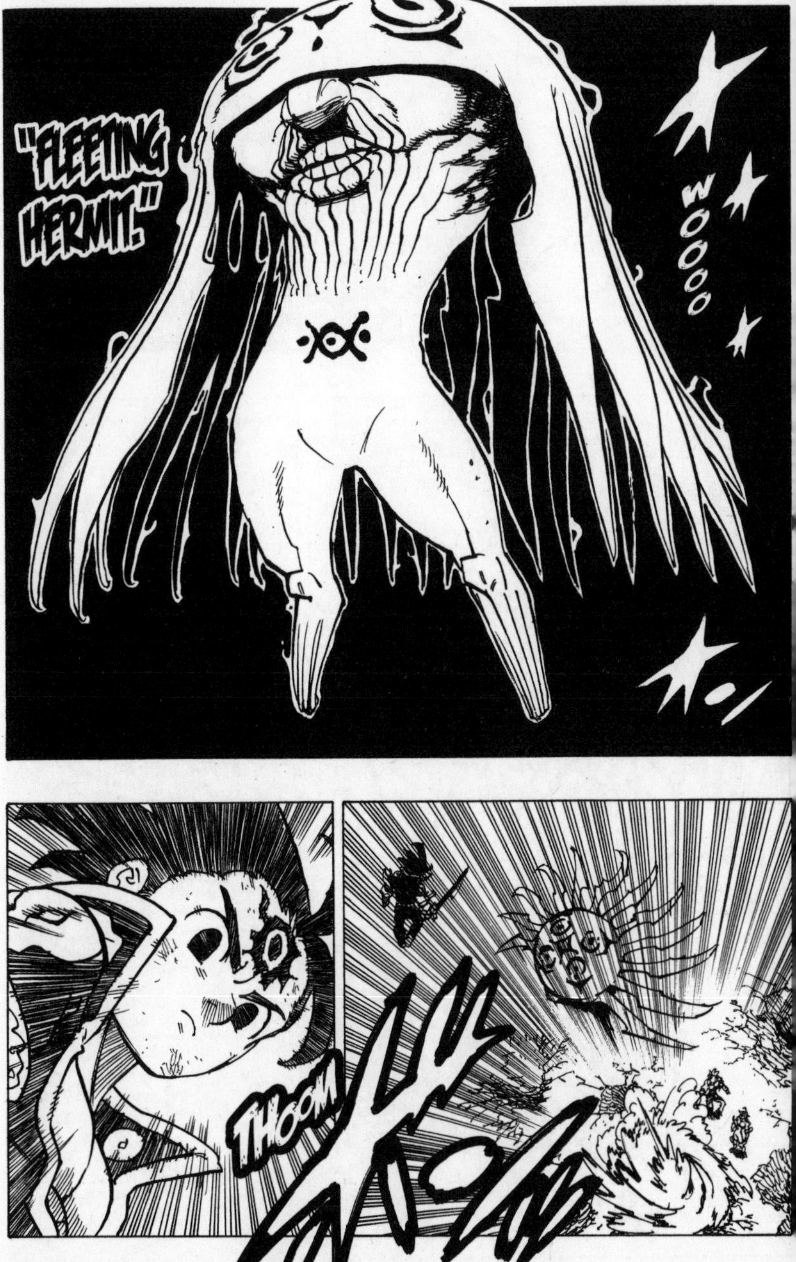
"FLEETING HERMIT."
WOOOOO
THOOM

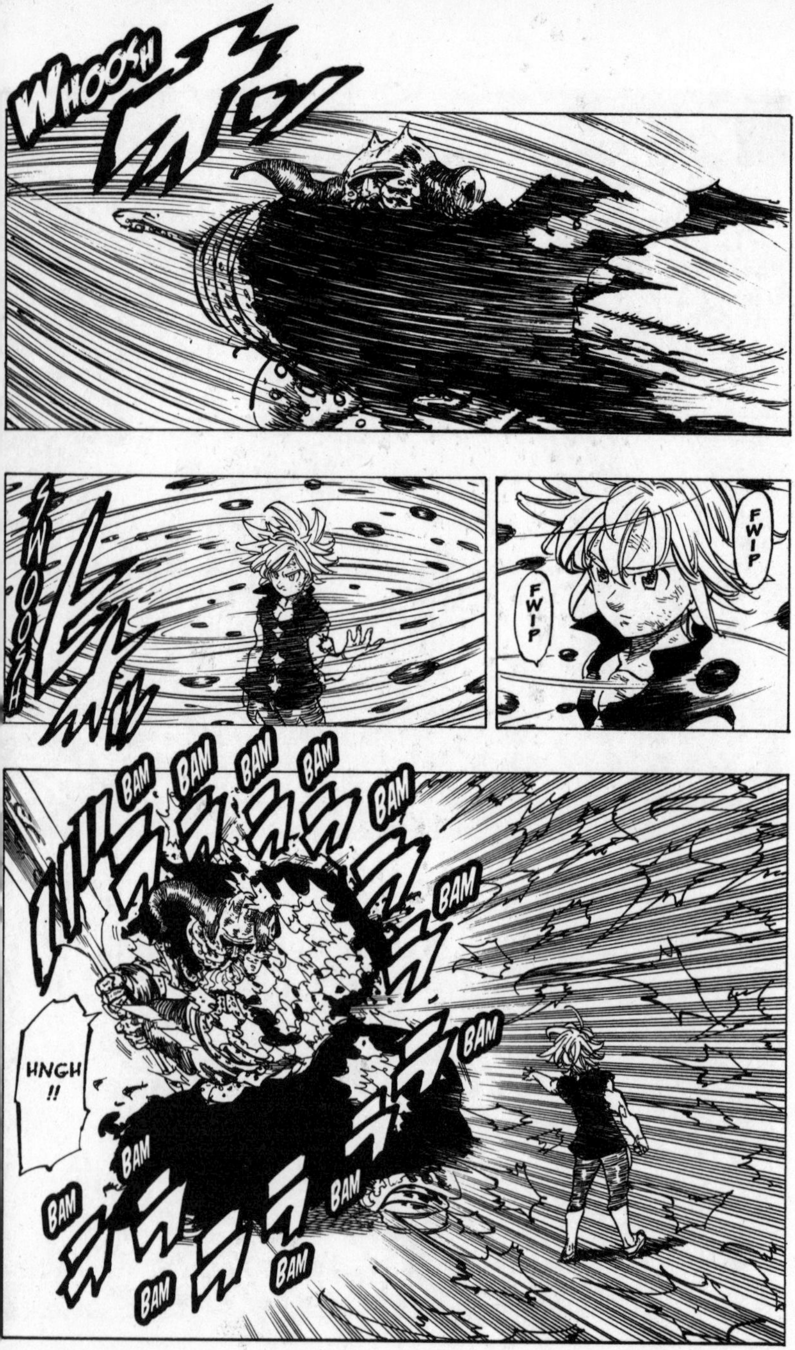
WHOOSH
FWIP
FWIP
SWOOSH
BAM
BAM
BAM
BAM
BAM
BAM
BAM
HNGH !!
BAM
BAM
BAM
BAM
BAM

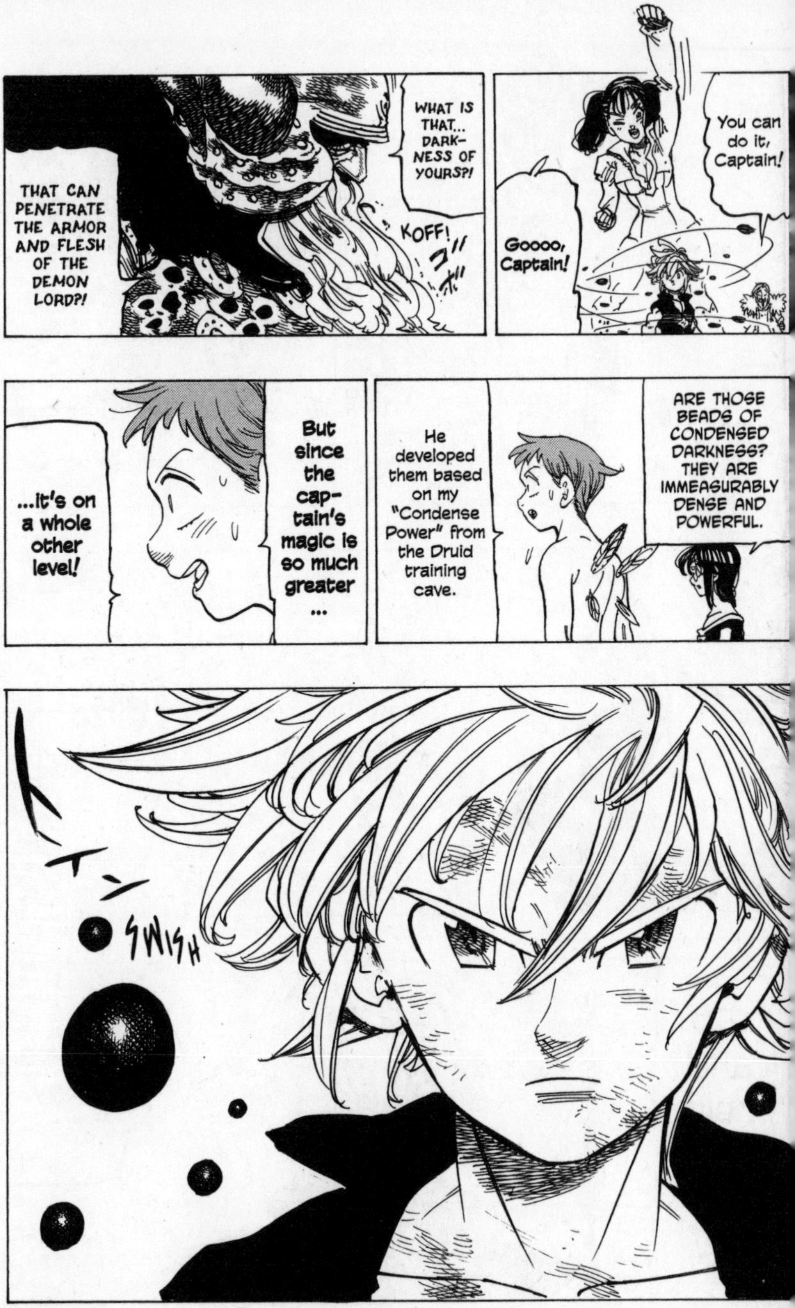
You can do it, Captain!
Goooo, Captain!
WHAT IS THAT... DARKNESS OF YOURS?!
KOFF!
THAT CAN PENETRATE THE ARMOR AND FLESH OF THE DEMON LORD?!
ARE THOSE BEADS OF CONDENSED DARKNESS? THEY ARE IMMEASURABLY DENSE AND POWERFUL.
He developed them based on my "Condense Power" from the Druid training cave.
But since the captain's magic is so much greater...
...it's on a whole other level!
SWISH

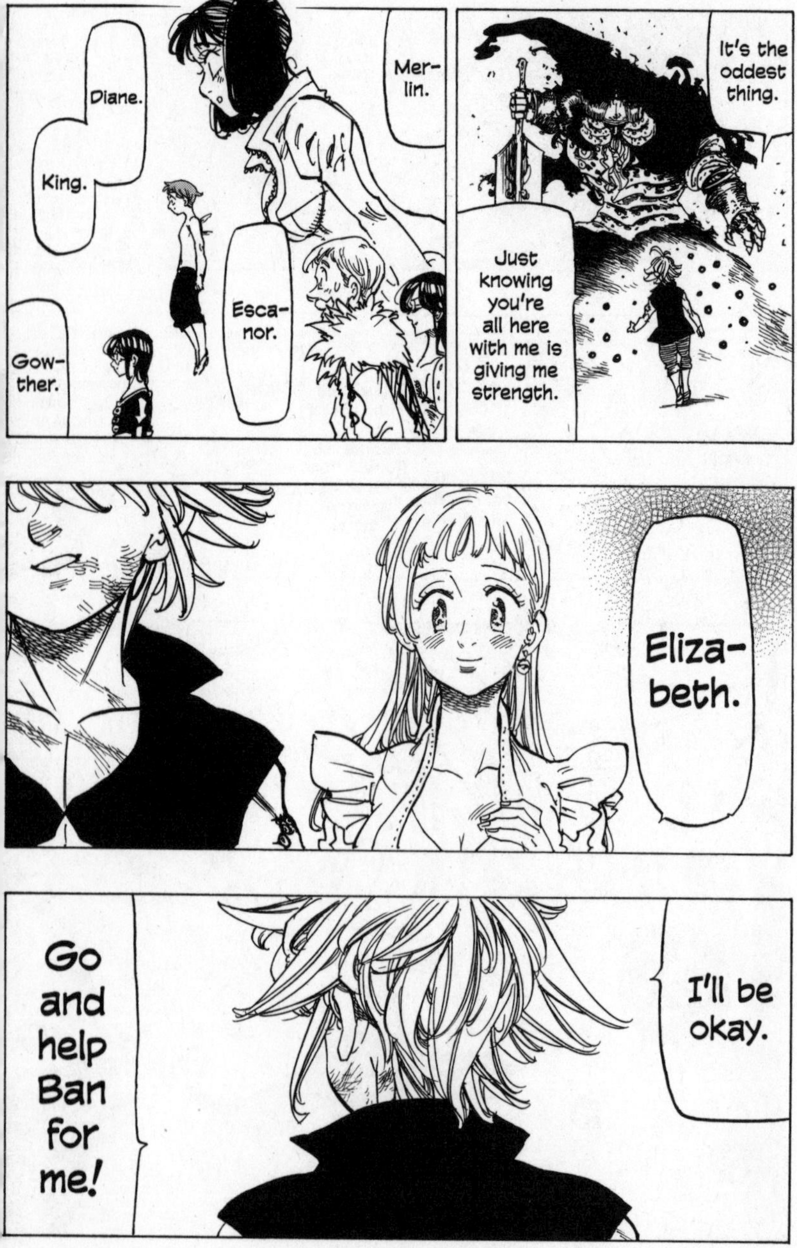
It's the oddest thing.
Just knowing you're all here with me is giving me strength.
Mer-lin.
Diane.
King.
Esca-nor.
Gow-ther.
Eliza-beth.
I'll be okay.
Go and help Ban for me!

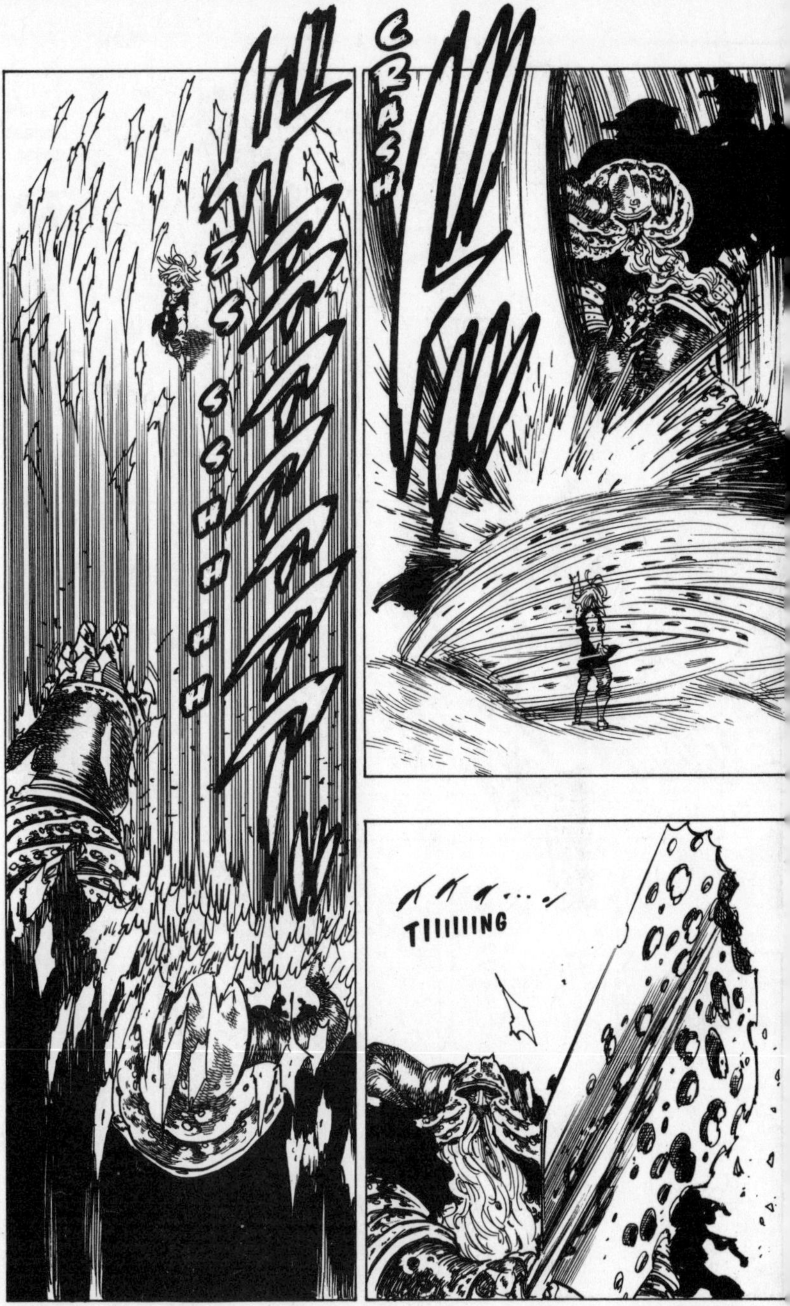
CRASH
ZSSSHHHH
TIIIIIING

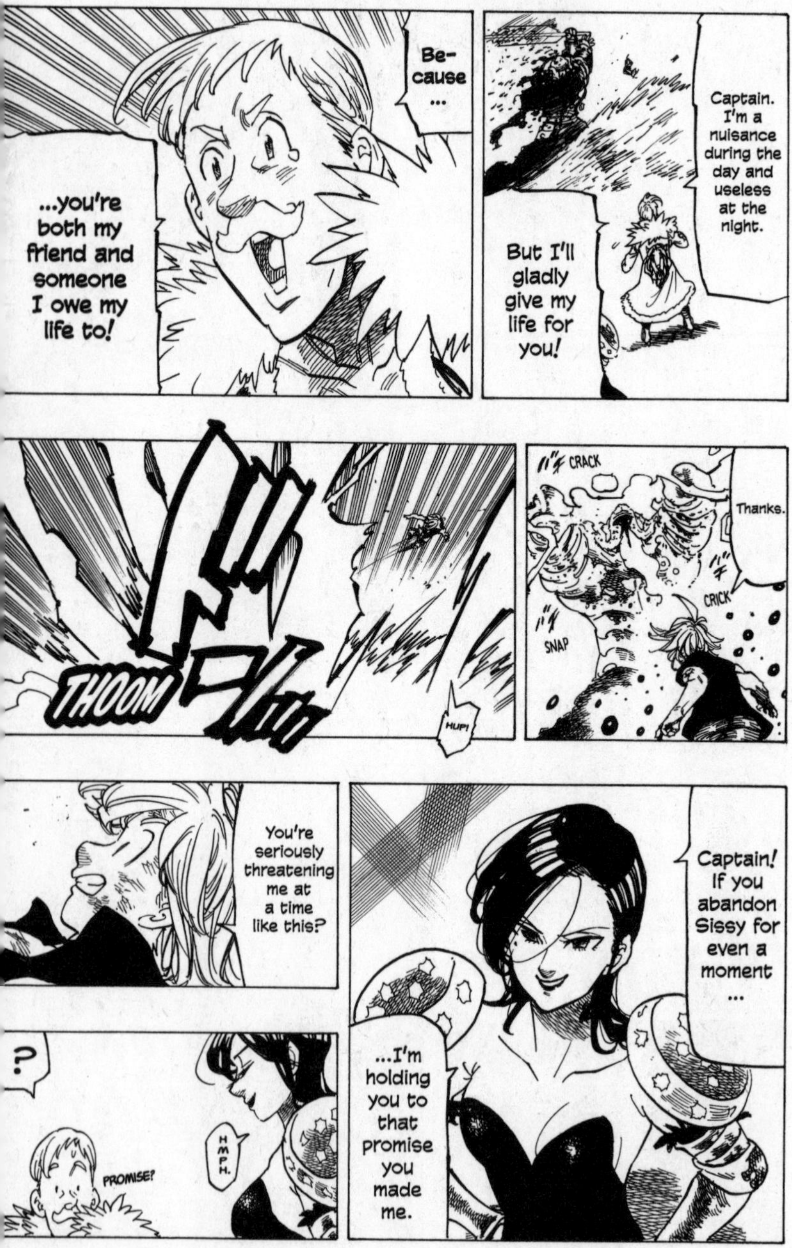
Captain. I'm a nuisance during the day and useless at the night.
But I'll gladly give my life for you!
Be- cause ...
...you're both my friend and someone I owe my life to!
Thanks.
CRACK
CRICK
SNAP
HUP!
THOOM
Captain! If you abandon Sissy for even a moment ...
...I'm holding you to that promise you made me.
You're seriously threatening me at a time like this?
?
HMPH.
PROMISE?

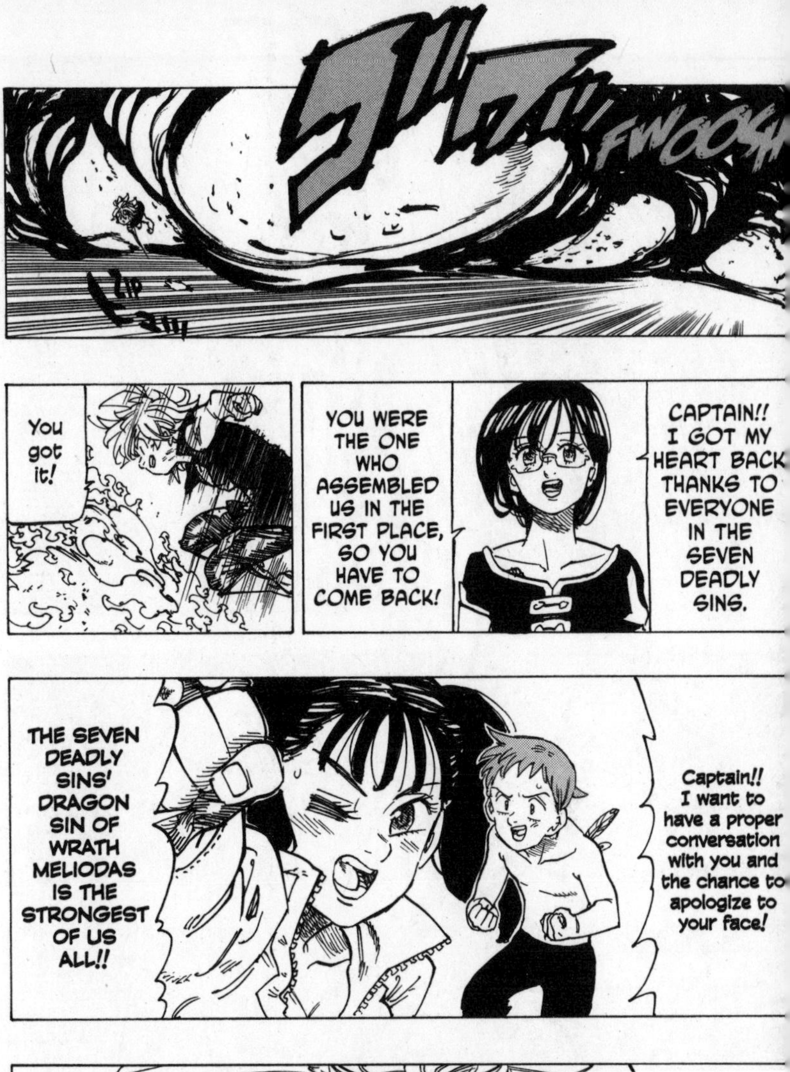
FWOOSH
CAPTAIN!! I GOT MY HEART BACK THANKS TO EVERYONE IN THE SEVEN DEADLY SINS.
YOU WERE THE ONE WHO ASSEMBLED US IN THE FIRST PLACE, SO YOU HAVE TO COME BACK!
You got it!
Captain!! I want to have a proper conversation with you and the chance to apologize to your face!
THE SEVEN DEADLY SINS' DRAGON SIN OF WRATH MELIODAS IS THE STRONGEST OF US ALL!!
SURE! WHEN I GET BACK, LET'S TALK ALL NIGHT OVER SOME DRINKS!
ALL OF US!!

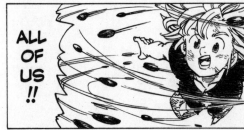

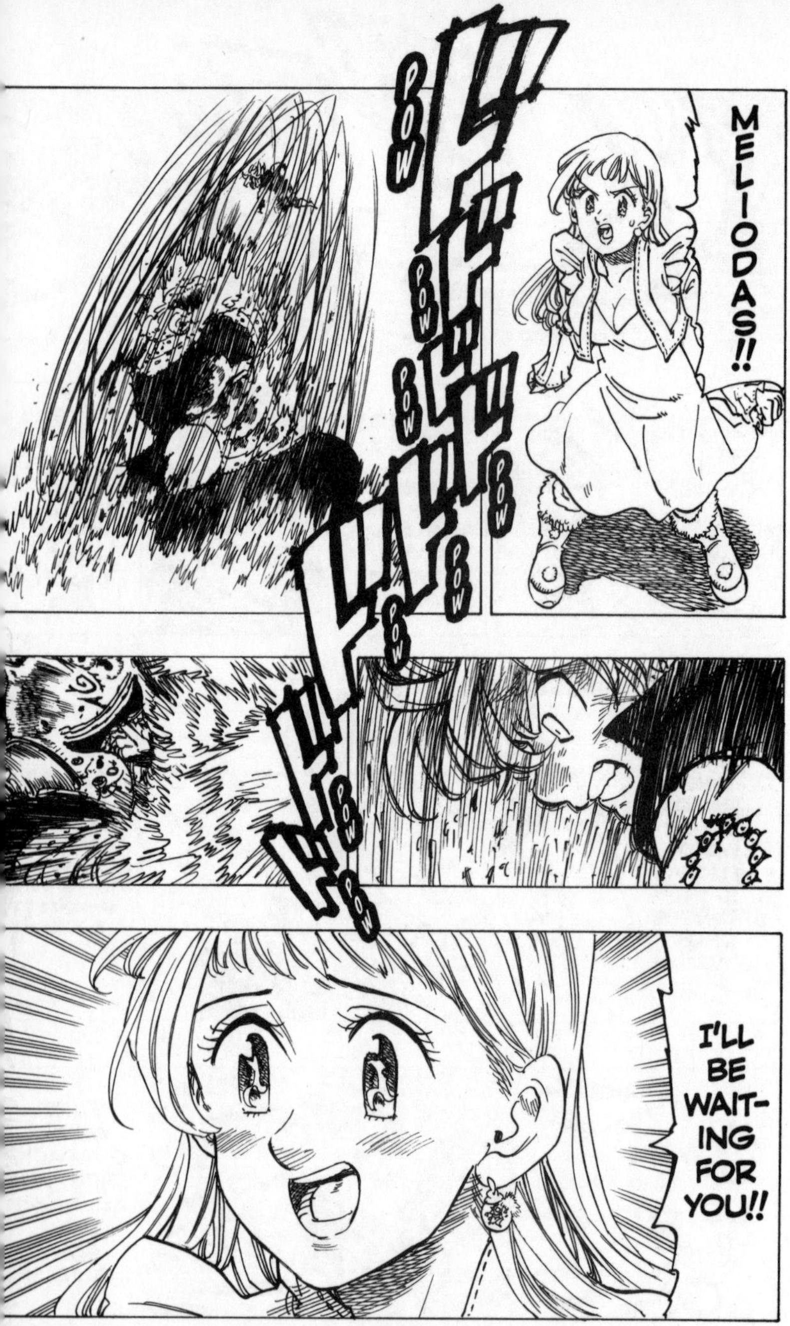
MELIODAS!!
POW POW
POW POW
POW POW
POW
POW POW
POW POW
POW POW
I'LL BE WAITING FOR YOU!!

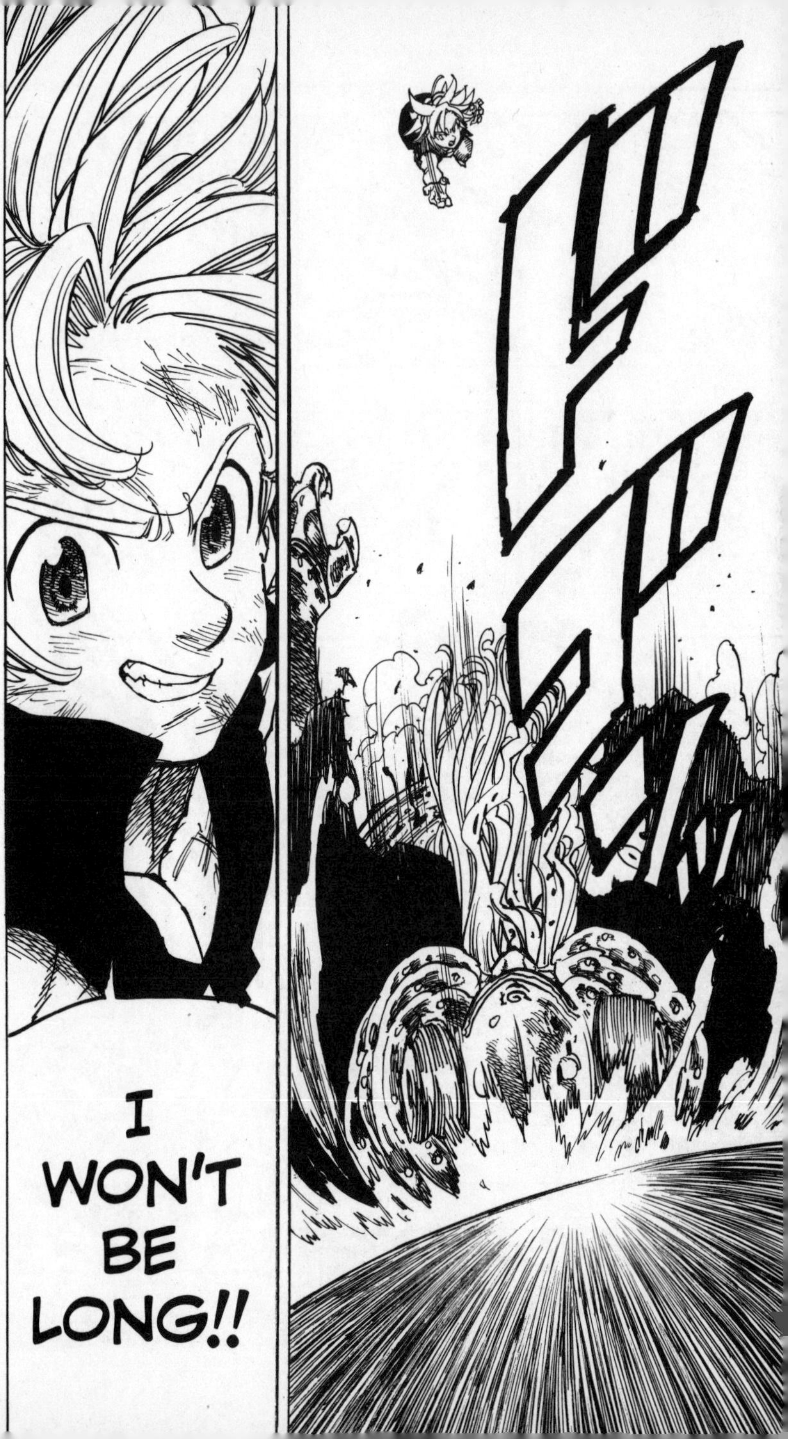
I WON'T BE LONG!!

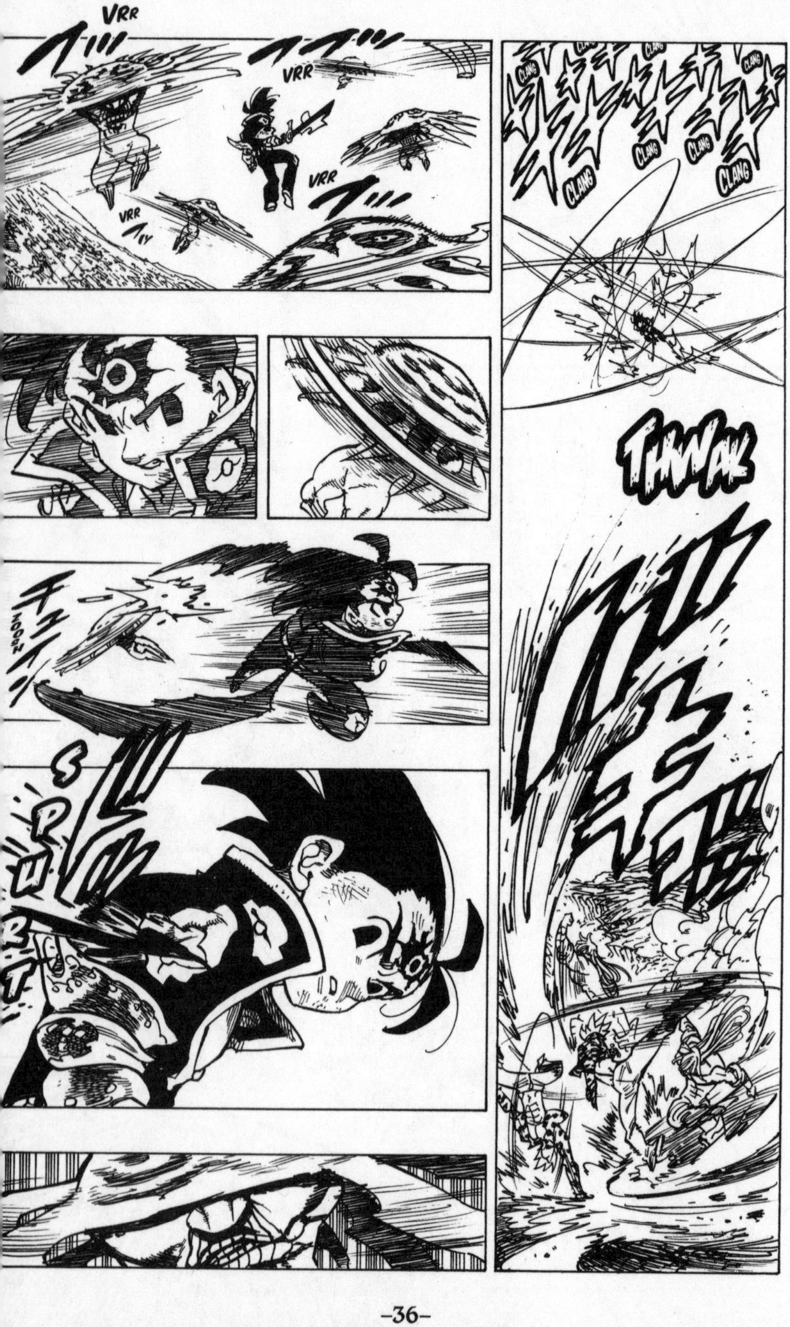
CLANG
CLANG
CLANG
CLANG
CLANG
CLANG
CLANG
CLANG
THWAK
VRR
VRR
VRR
VRR
ZOOM
SPURT

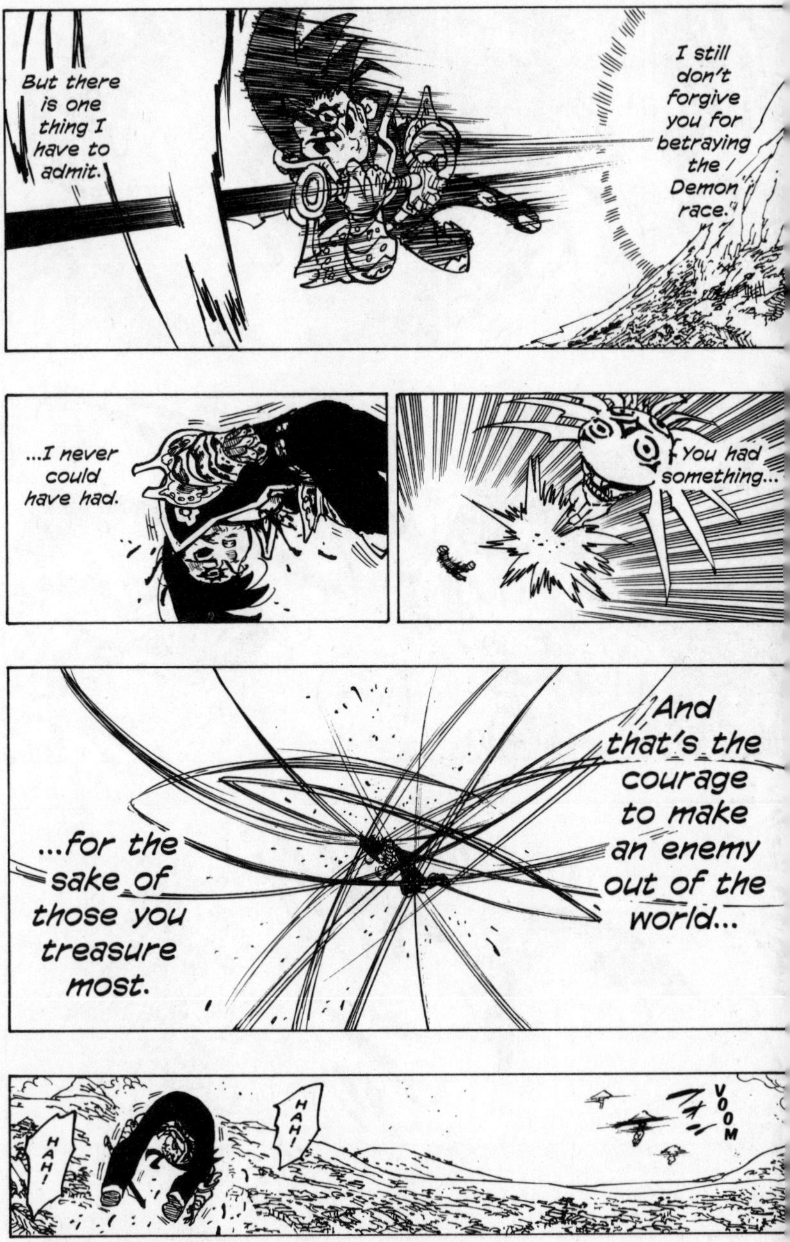
I still don't forgive you for betraying the Demon race.
But there is one thing I have to admit.
You had something...
...I never could have had.
And that's the courage to make an enemy out of the world...
...for the sake of those you treasure most.
VOOM
HAH!
HAH!

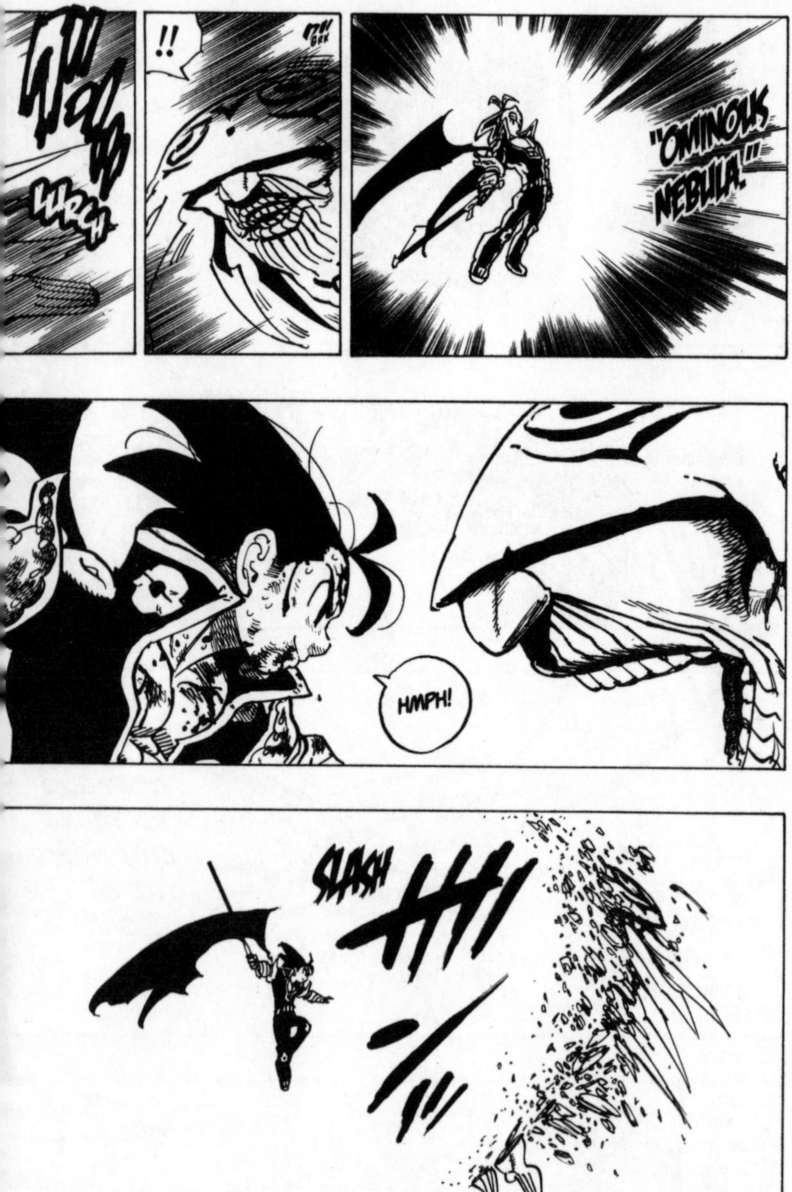
"OMINOUS NEBULA."
!!
BRK
LURCH
HMPH!
SLASH

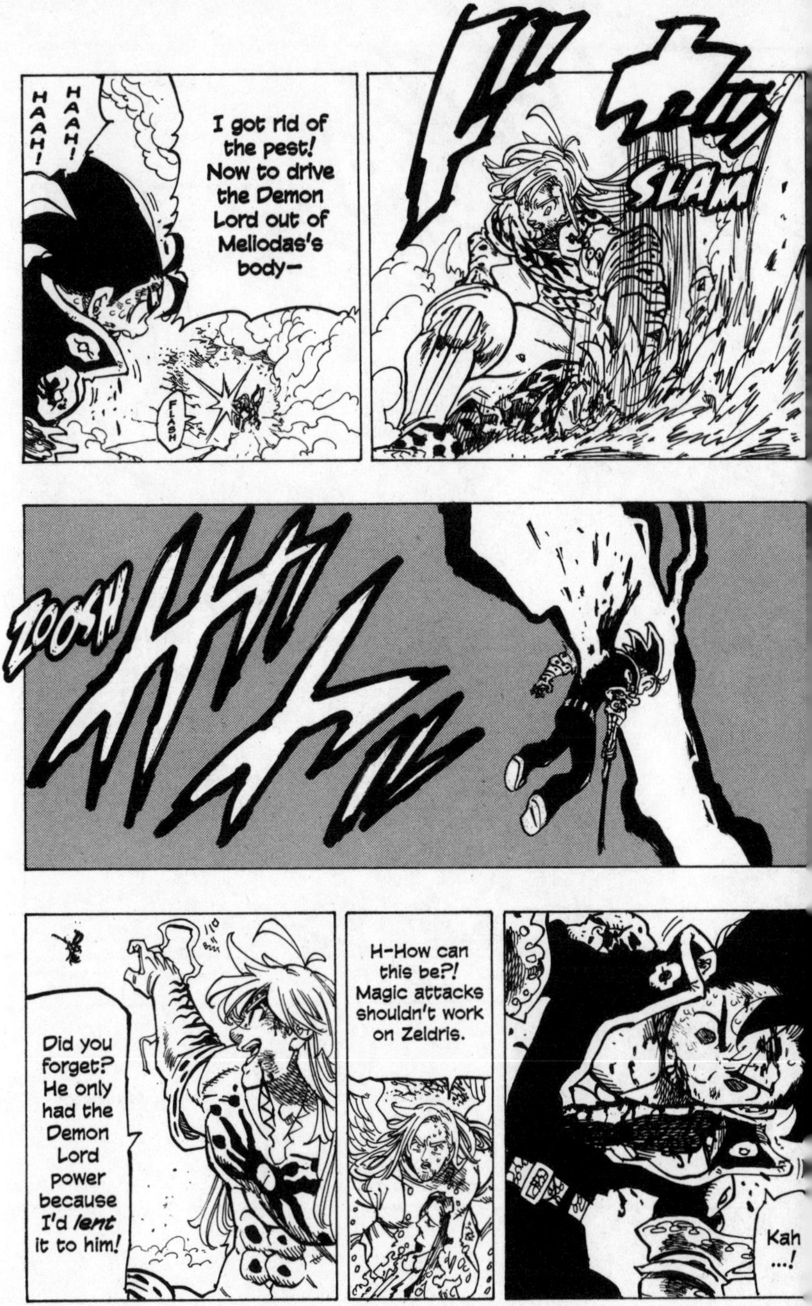
SLAM
I got rid of the pest! Now to drive the Demon Lord out of Meliodas's body—
HAAAH! HAAAH!
FLASH
ZOOSH
Kah...!
H-How can this be?! Magic attacks shouldn't work on Zeldris.
Did you forget? He only had the Demon Lord power because I'd *lent* it to him!

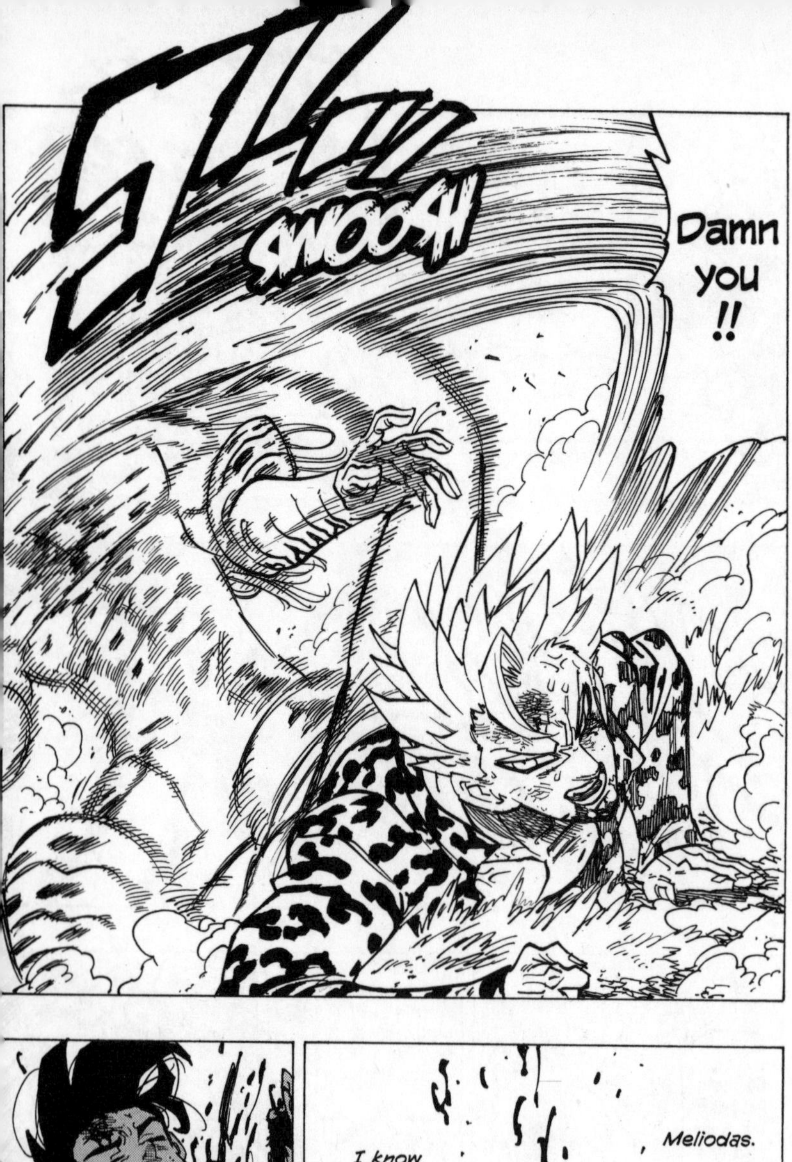
SWOOSH
Damn you!!
Meliodas.
I know that...you, if anybody... can change everything.

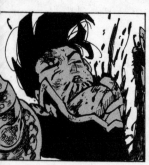

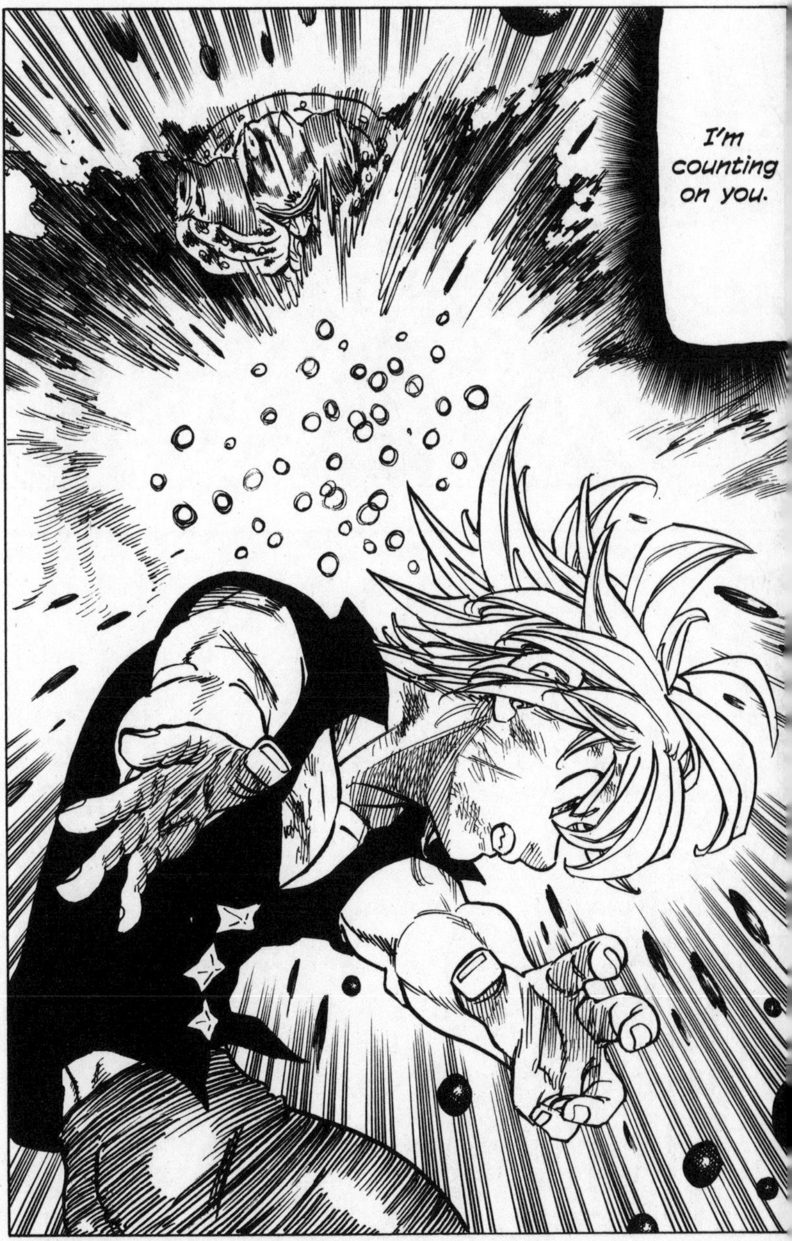
I'm counting on you.

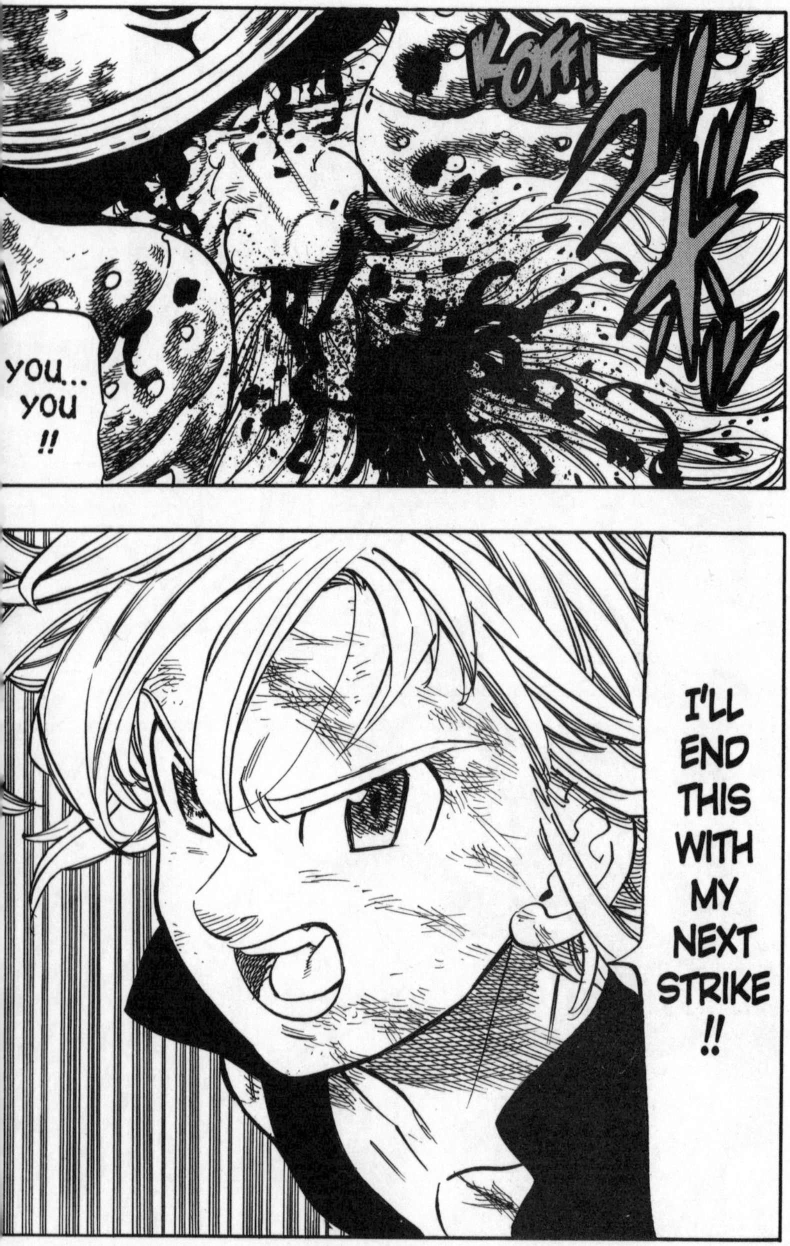
KOFF!
YOU... YOU !!
I'LL END THIS WITH MY NEXT STRIKE !!

# Chapter 305 - Death Throes

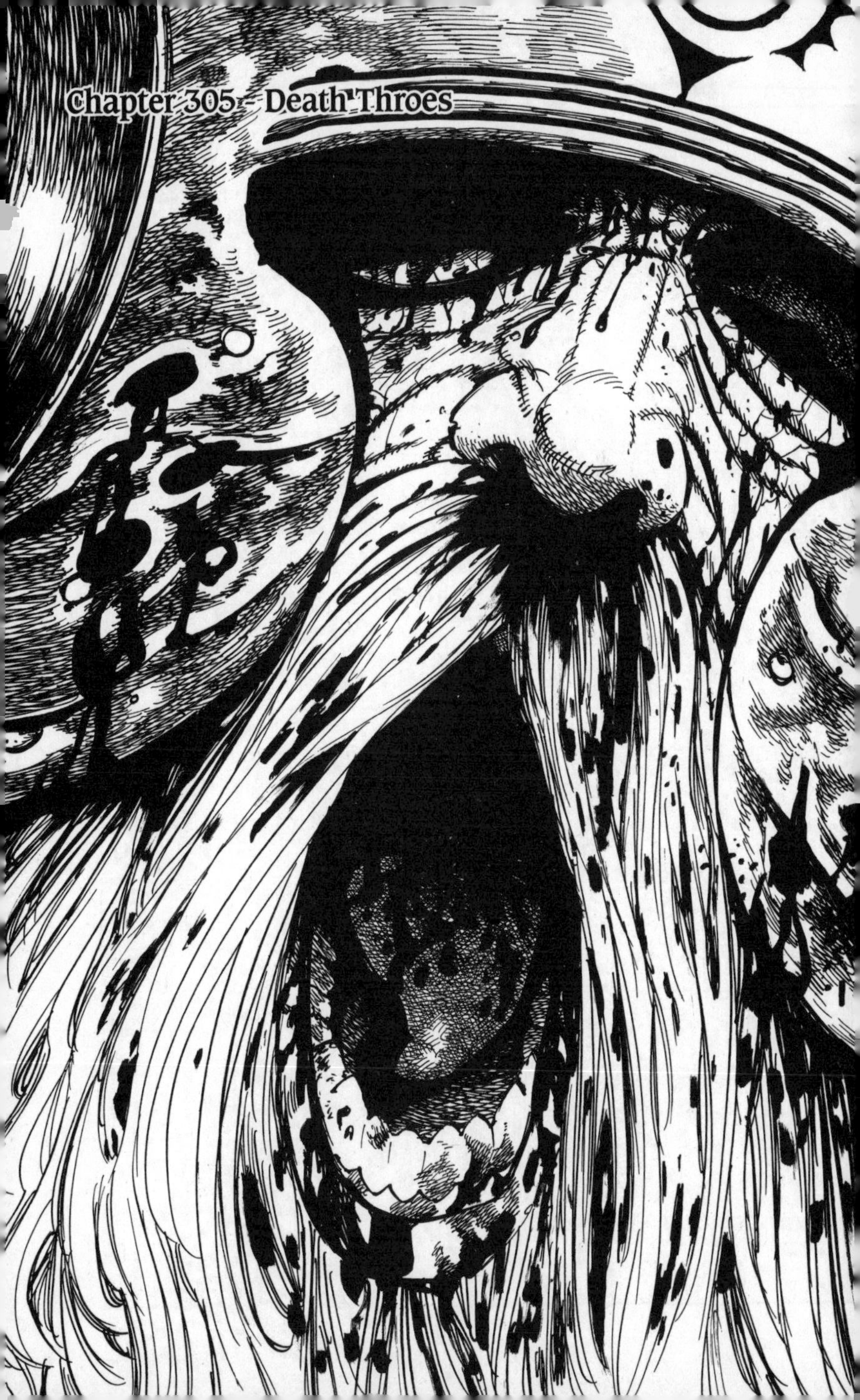

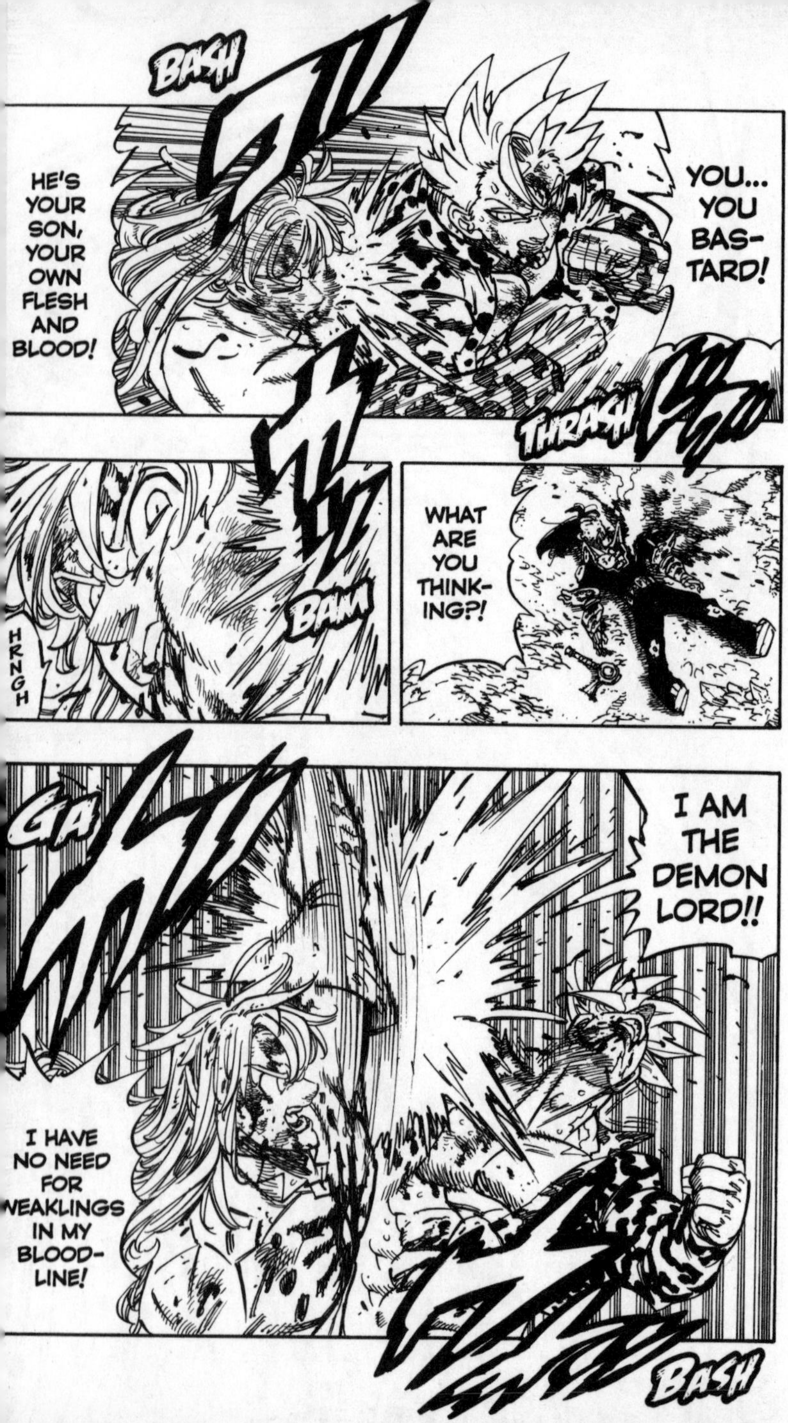
BASH
YOU... YOU BAS-TARD!
HE'S YOUR SON, YOUR OWN FLESH AND BLOOD!
THRASH
WHAT ARE YOU THINKING?!
BAM
HRNGH
I AM THE DEMON LORD!!
GA
I HAVE NO NEED FOR WEAKLINGS IN MY BLOOD-LINE!
BASH

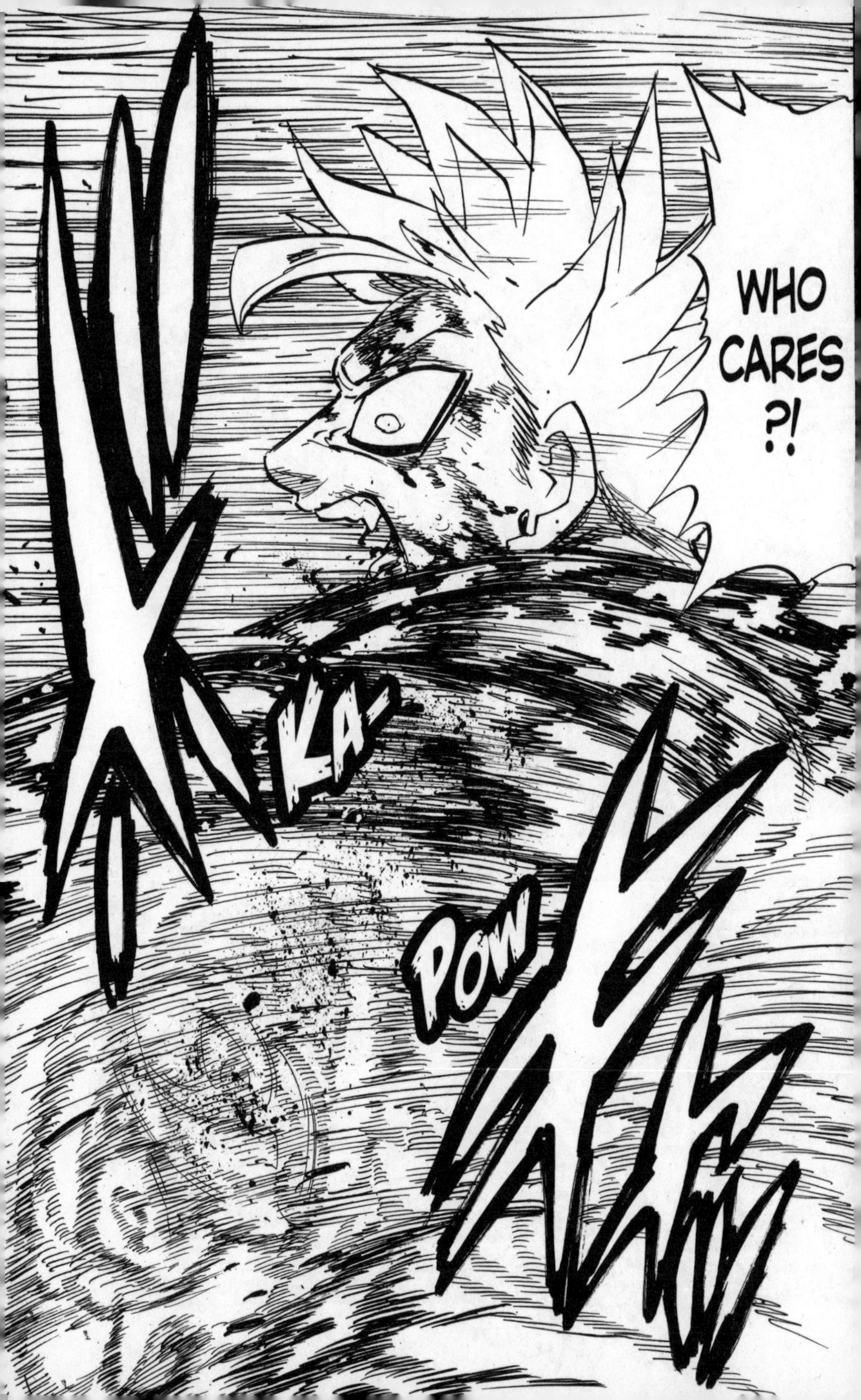
WHO CARES ?!
KA-
POW

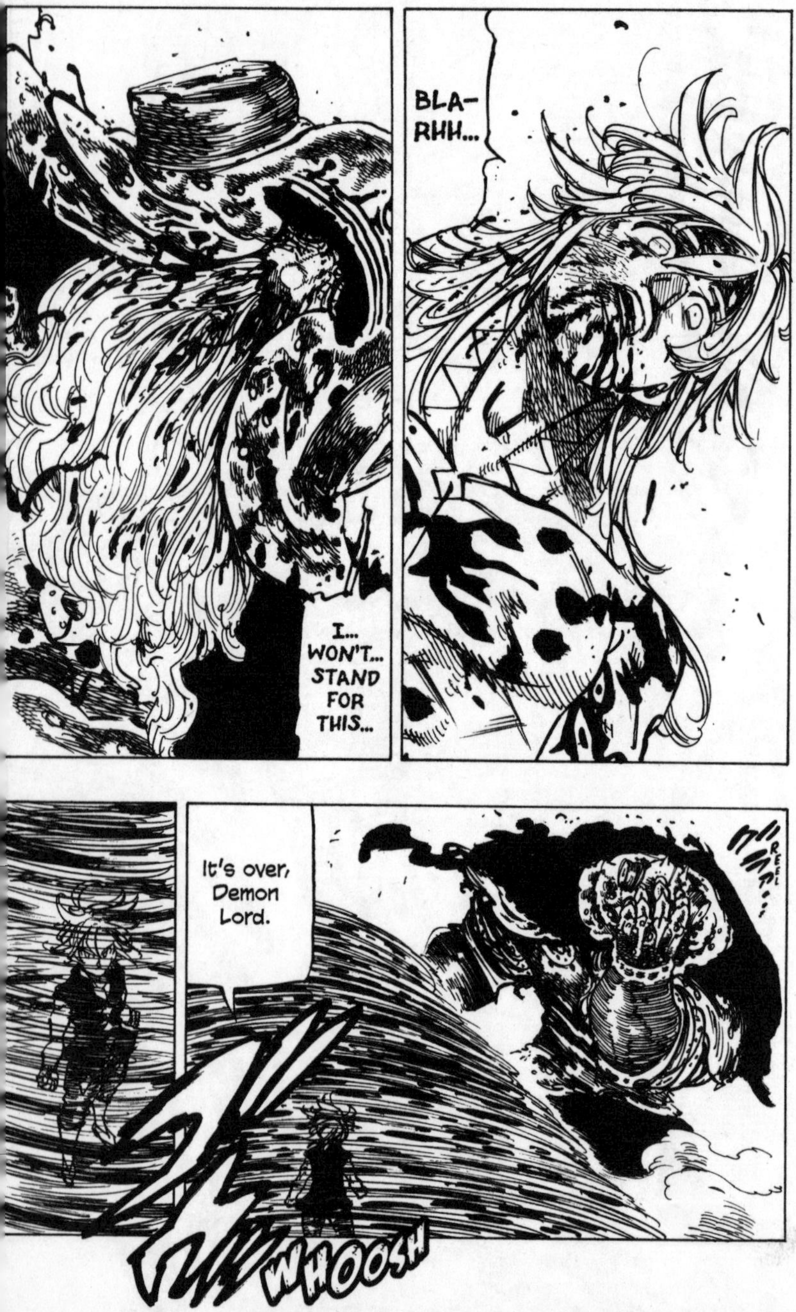
BLA-RHH...
I... WON'T... STAND FOR THIS...
REEL
It's over, Demon Lord.
WHOOSH

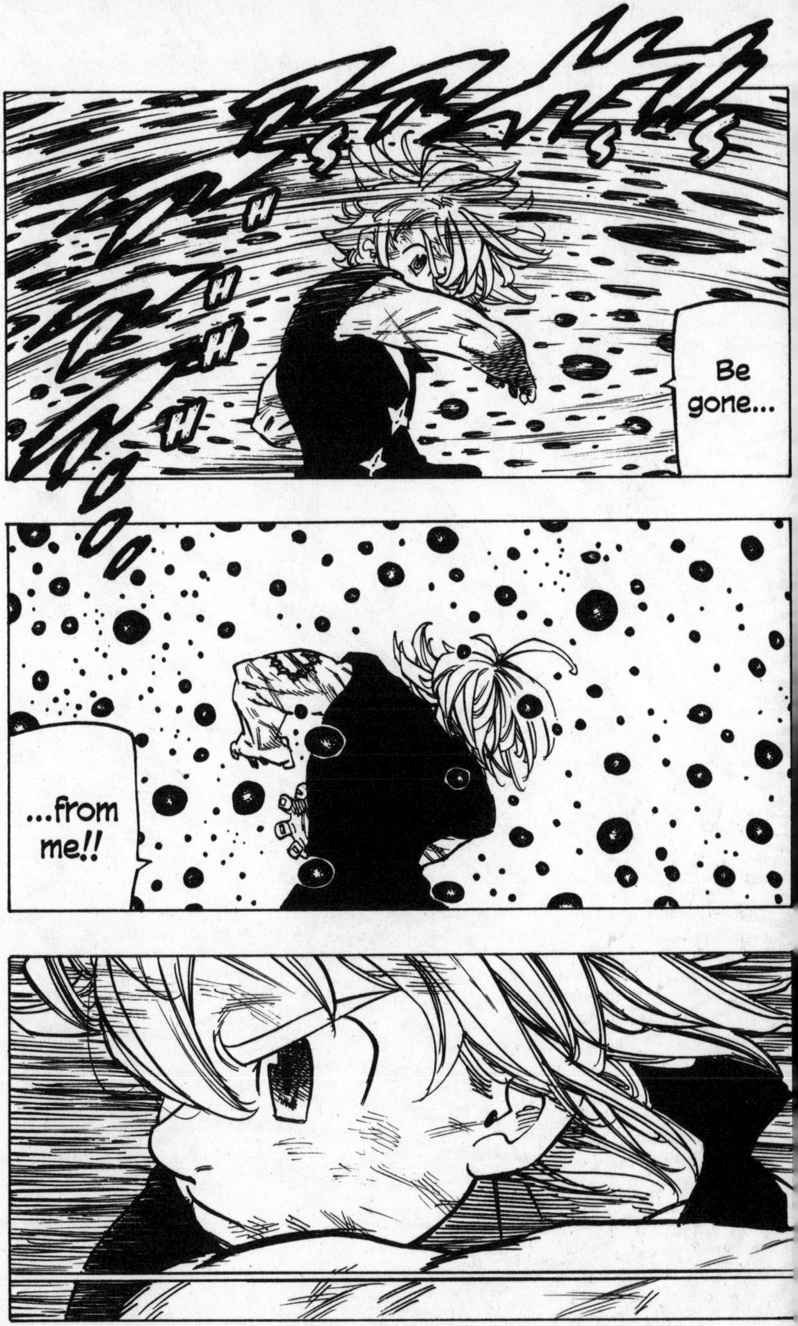
Be gone...
...from me!!

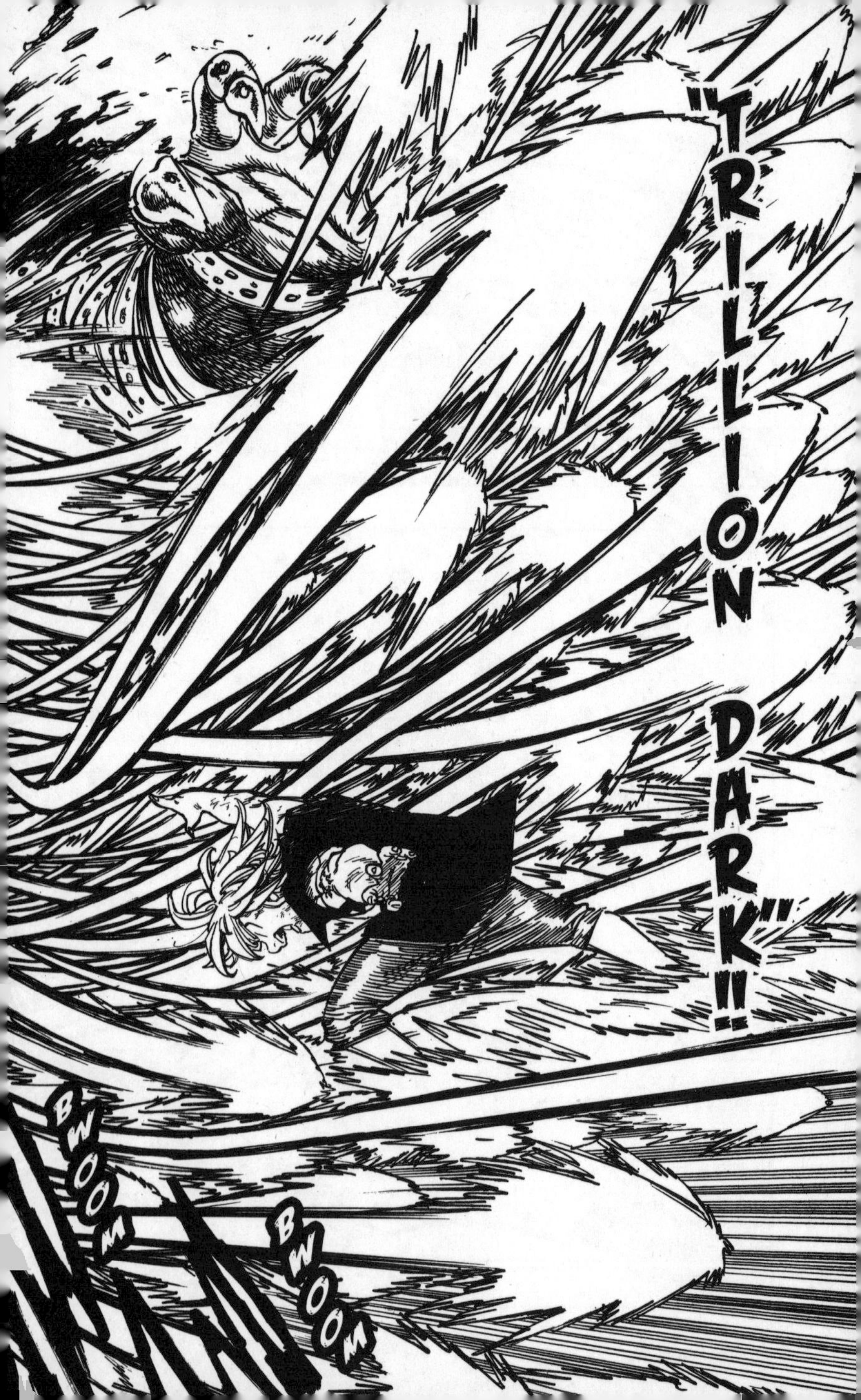
"TRILLION DARK"!!
BWOOM
BWOOM

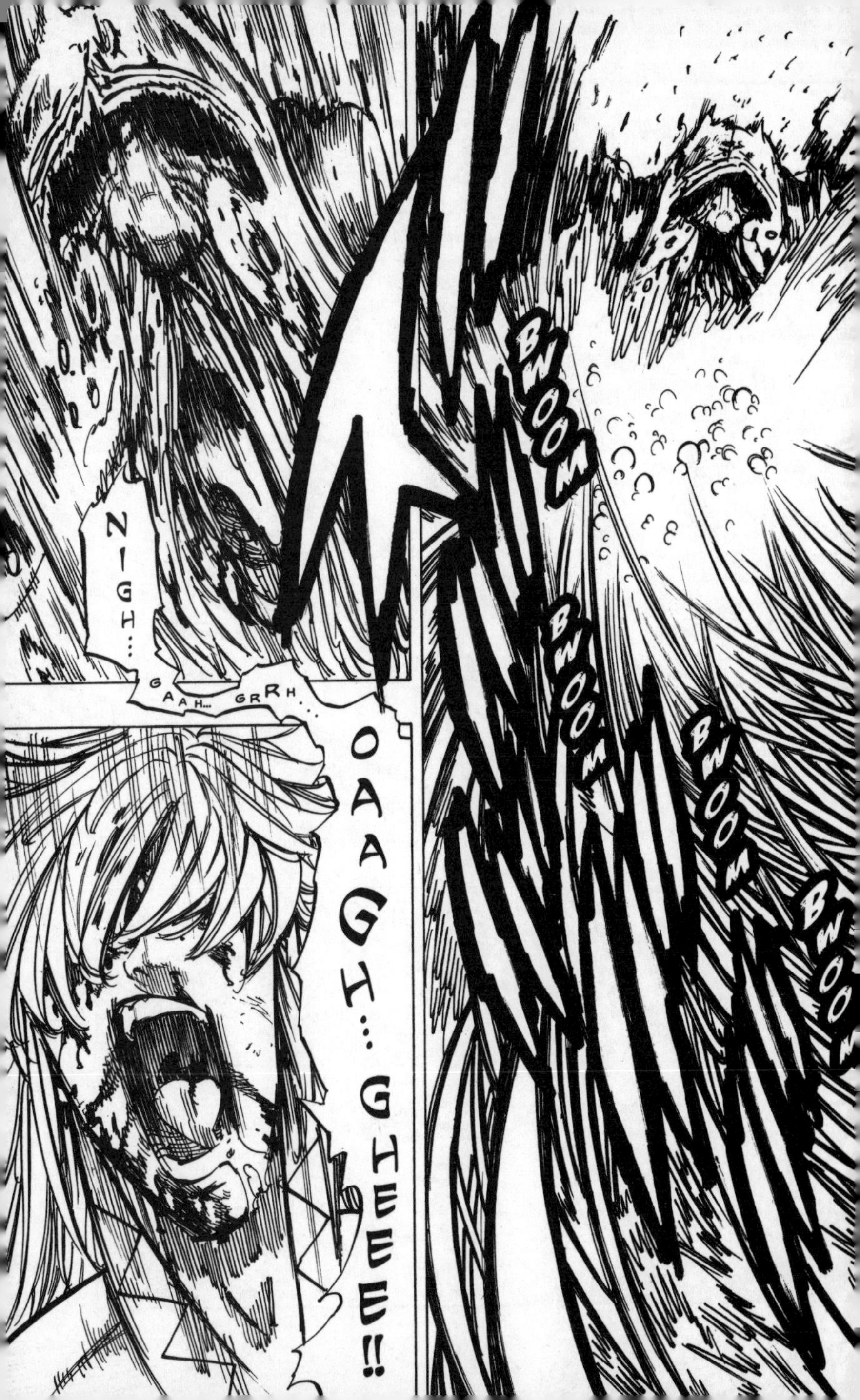
BWOOM
BWOOM
BWOOM
BWOOM
NIGH...
GAAH... GRRH...
OAAGH... GHEEE!!

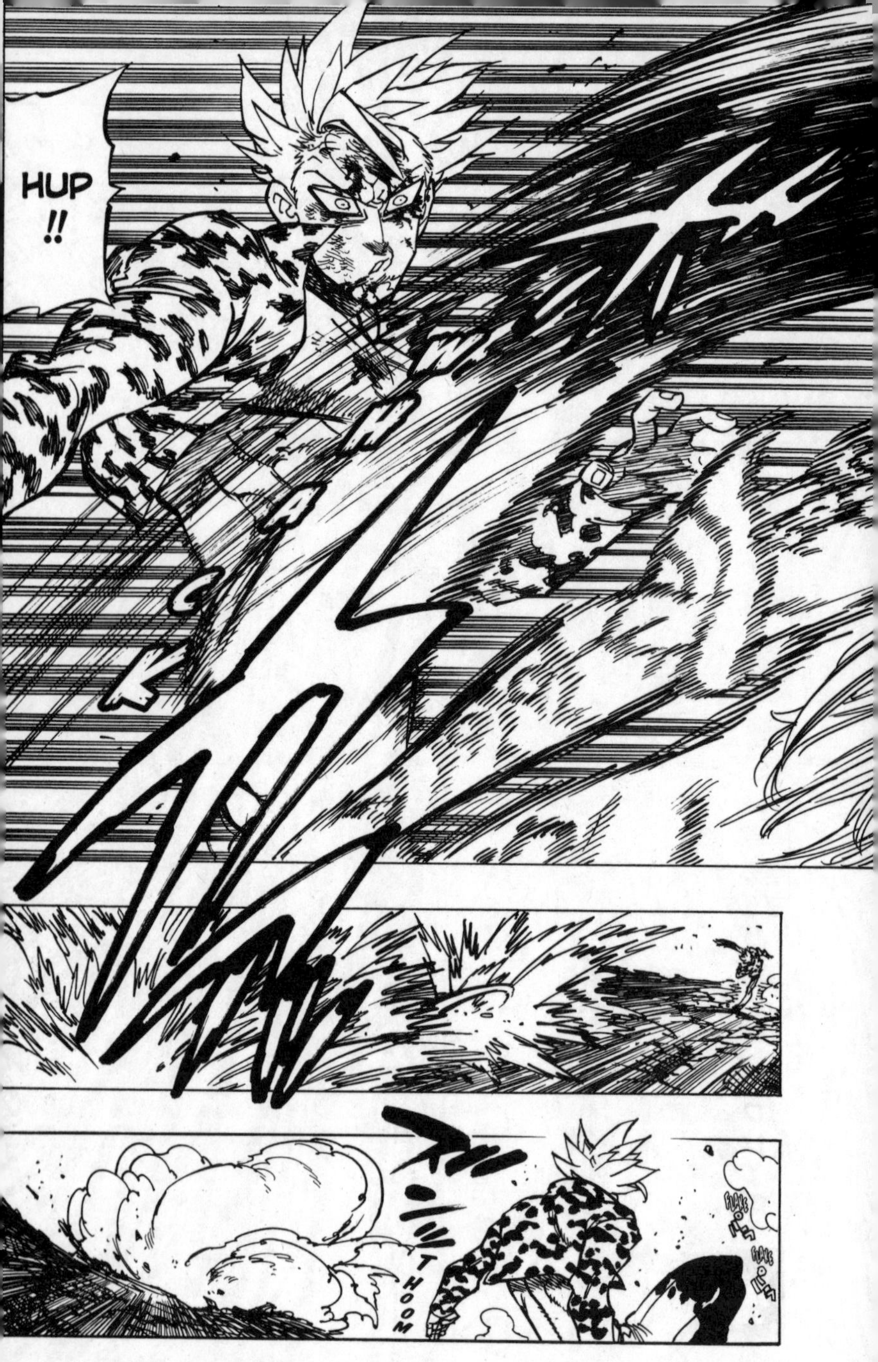
HUP !!
FLAKE
FLAKE
THOOM

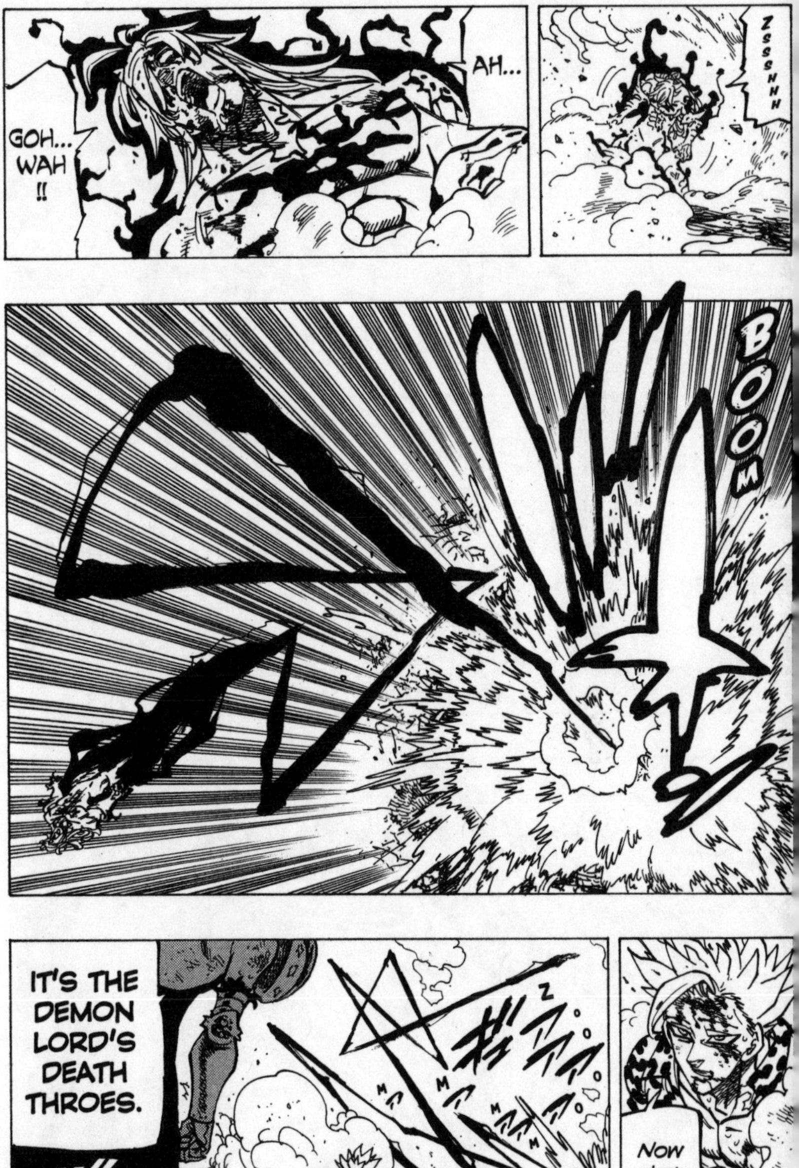
ZSSSHHH
AH...
GOH... WAH !!
BOOM
Now what ?!
IT'S THE DEMON LORD'S DEATH THROES.
ZSH

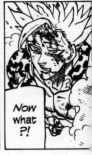

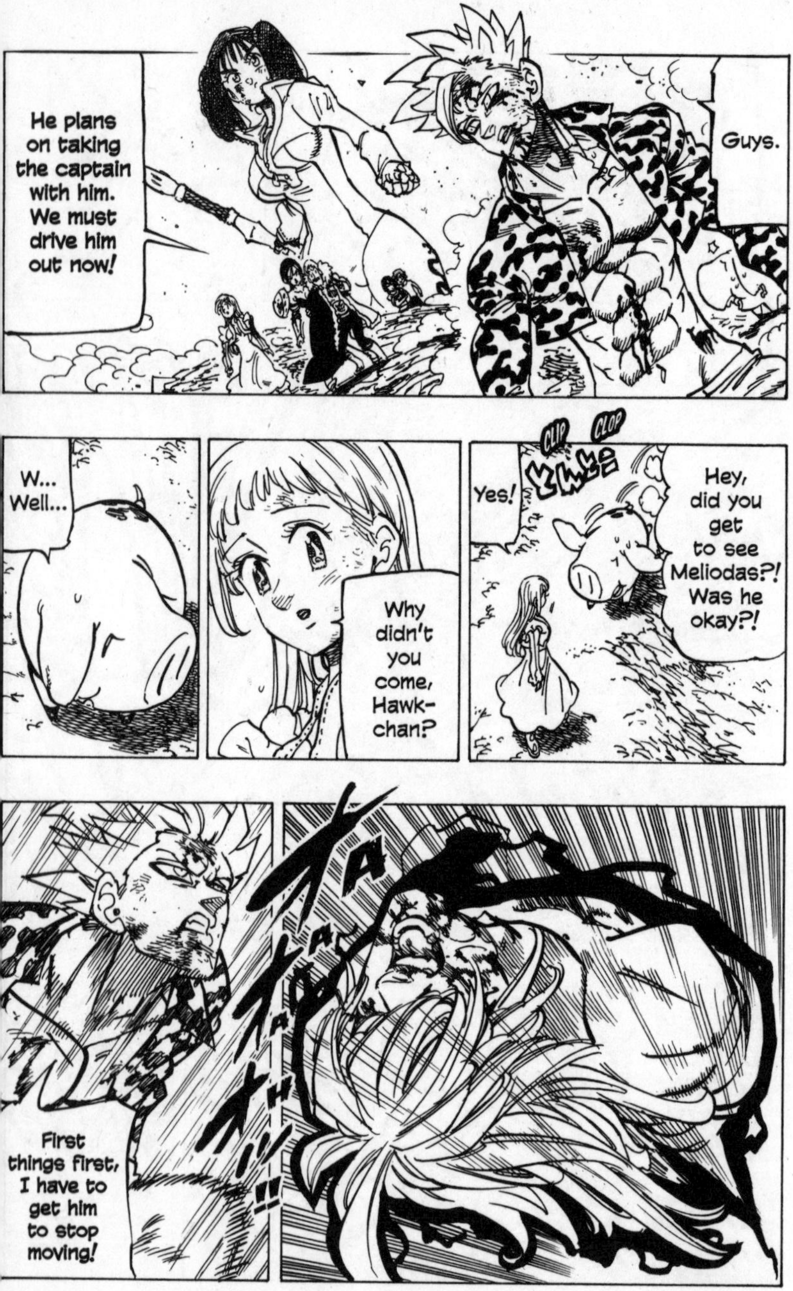
Guys.
He plans on taking the captain with him. We must drive him out now!
CLIP CLOP
Hey, did you get to see Meliodas?! Was he okay?!
Yes!
Why didn't you come, Hawk-chan?
W... Well...
First things first, I have to get him to stop moving!

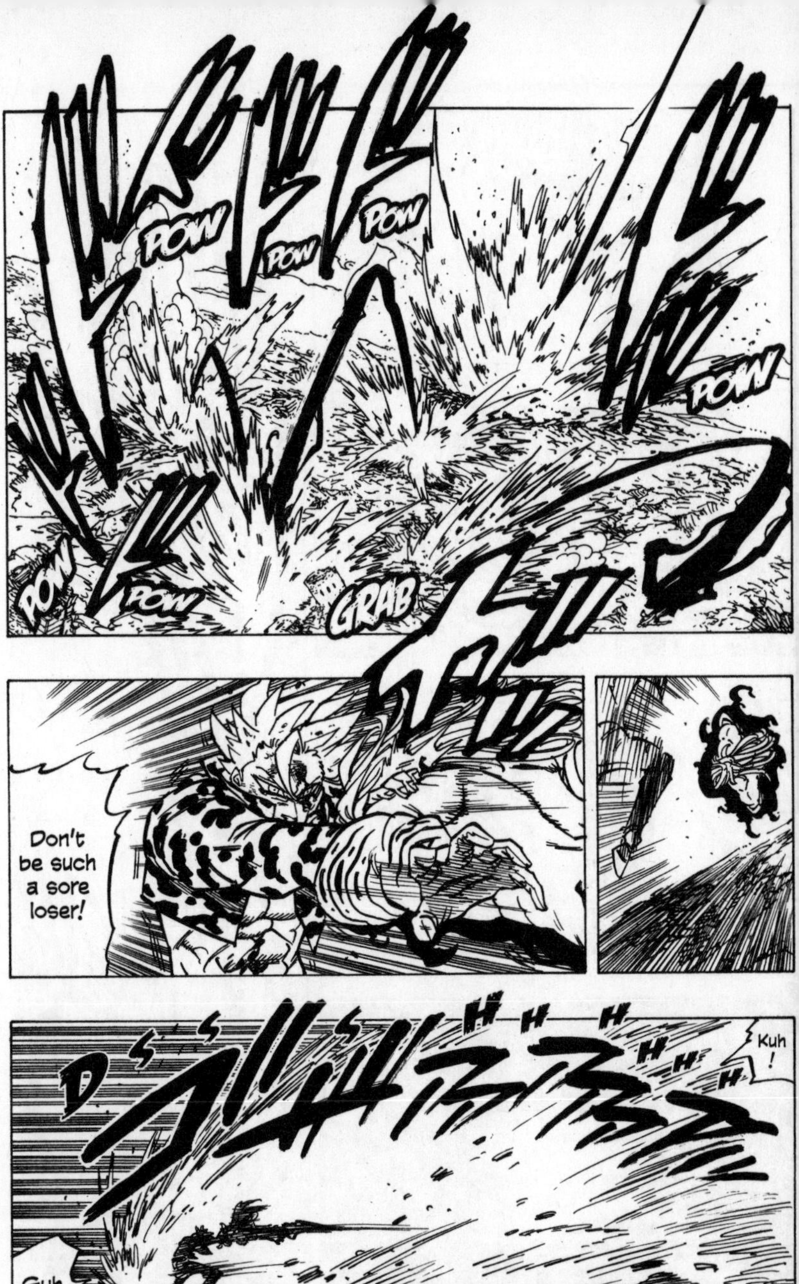
POW
POW
POW
POW
GRAB
POW
POW
Don't be such a sore loser!
Kuh!
Guh!

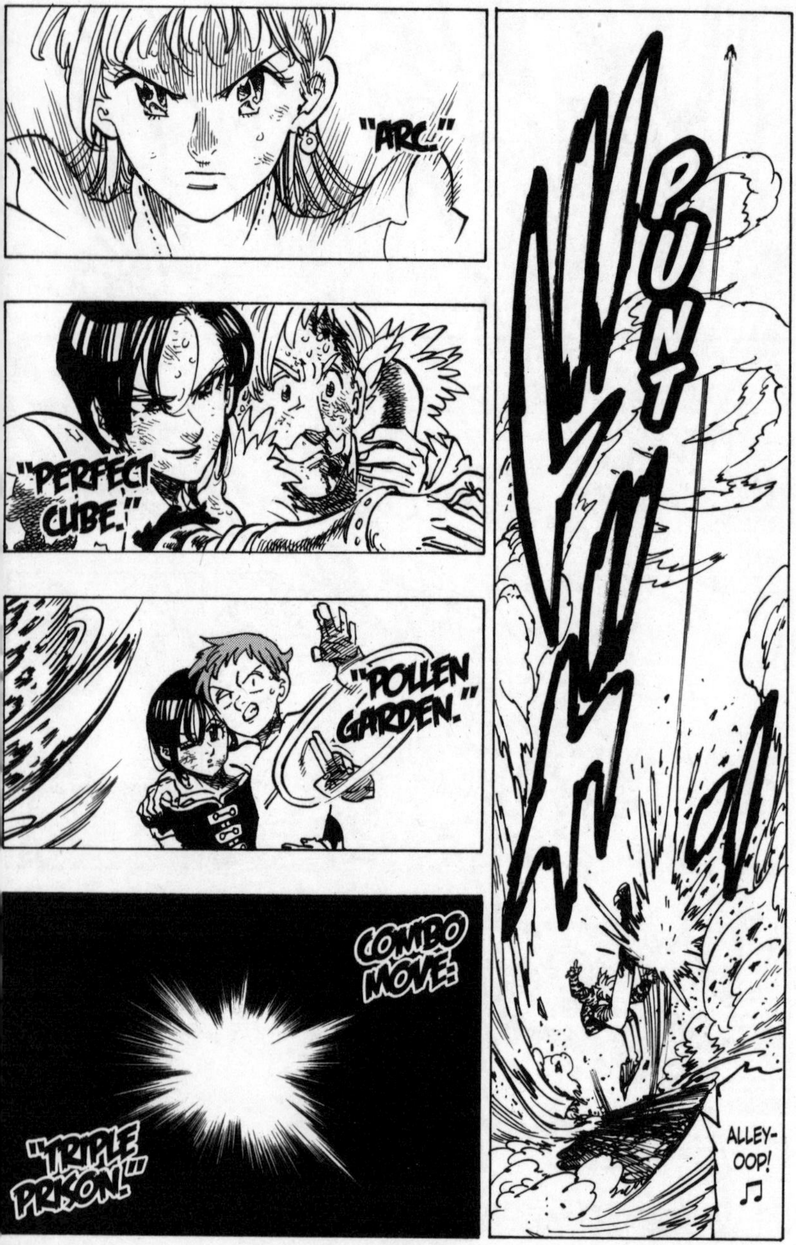
PUNT
ALLEY-OOP! ♫
"ARC."
"PERFECT CUBE."
"POLLEN GARDEN."
COMBO MOVE:
"TRIPLE PRISON."

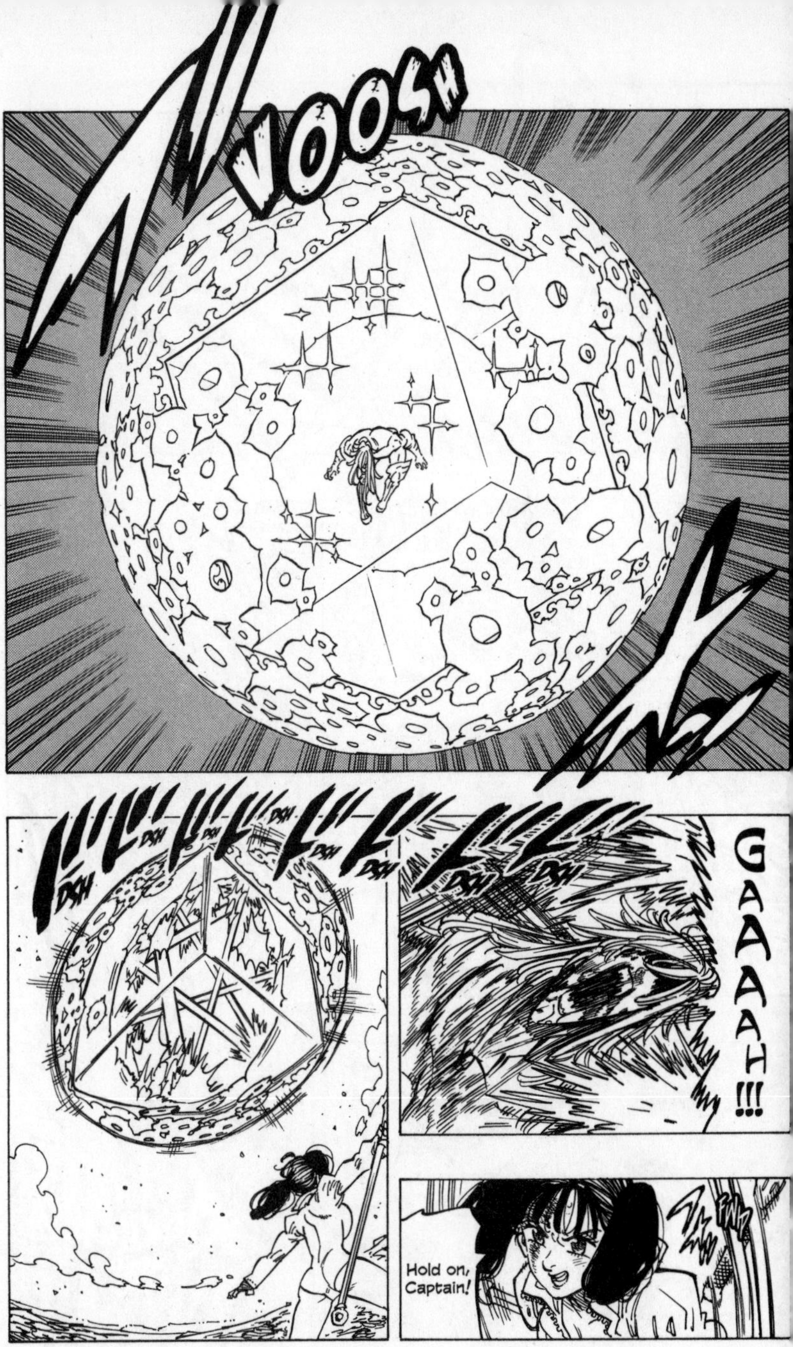
VOOSH
DSH DSH DSH DSH DSH DSH DSH
GAAAAH!!!
Hold on, Captain!

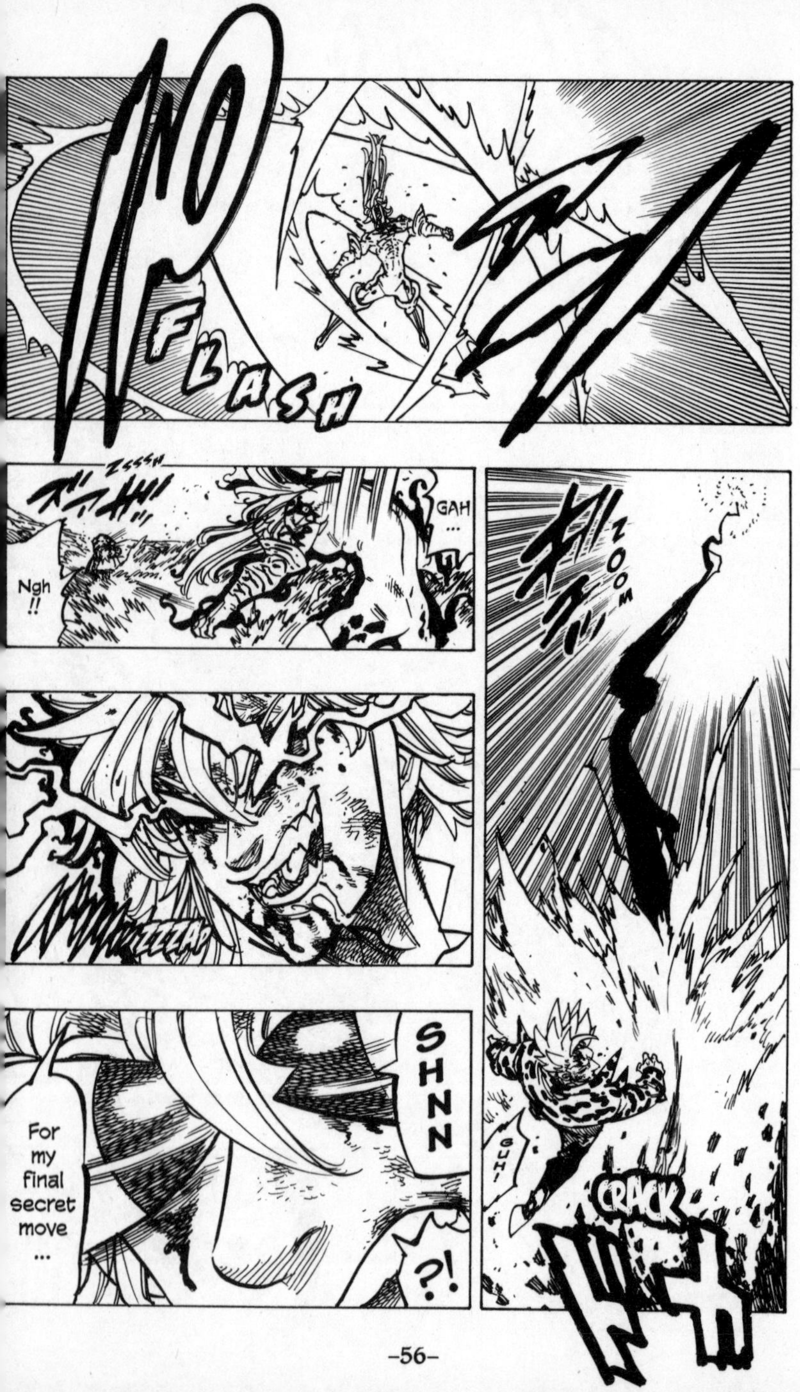
FLASH
ZOOM
GUH!
CRACK
GAH ...
ZSSSH
Ngh !!
ZZZZAP
SHNN
?!
For my final secret move ...

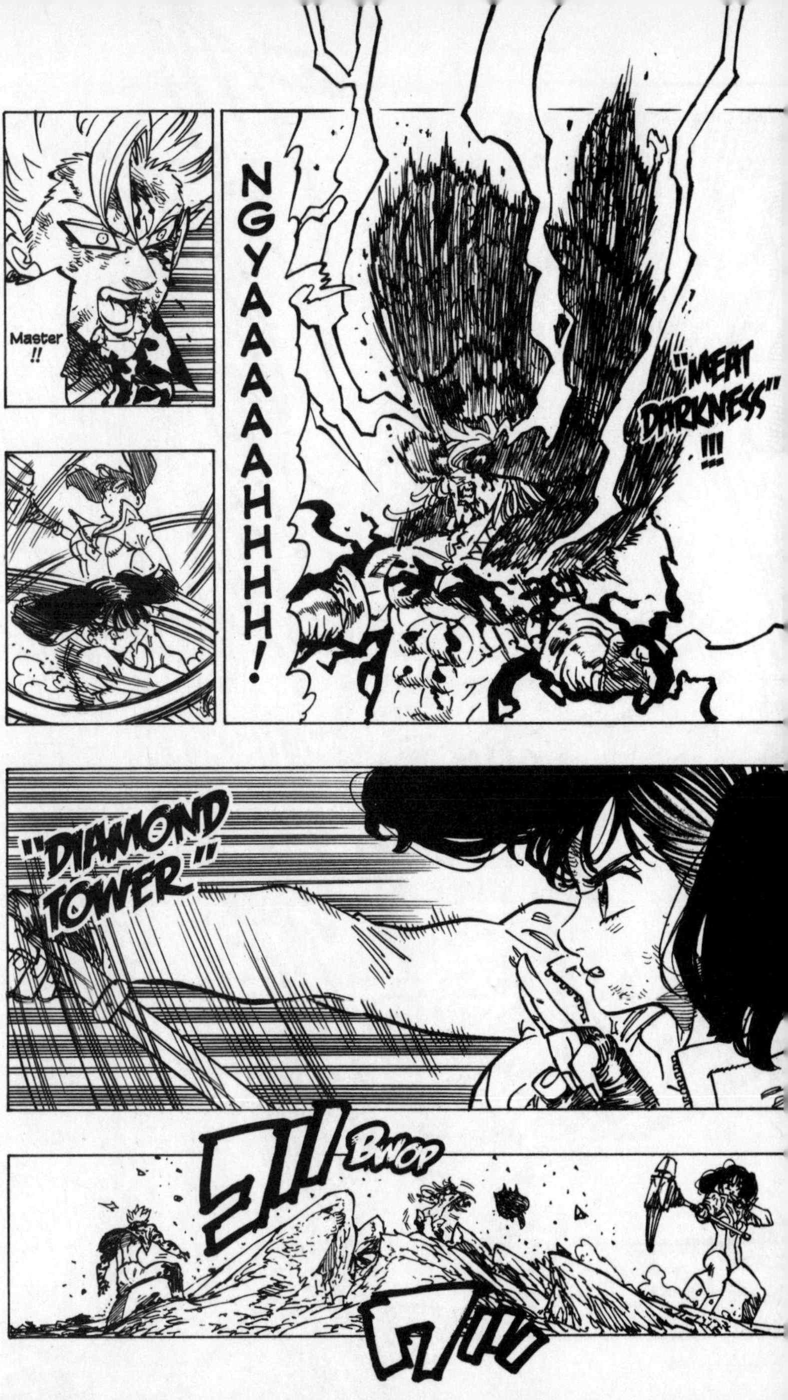
"MEAT DARKNESS" !!!
NGYAAAAAHHHH!
Master !!
"DIAMOND TOWER"
BWOP

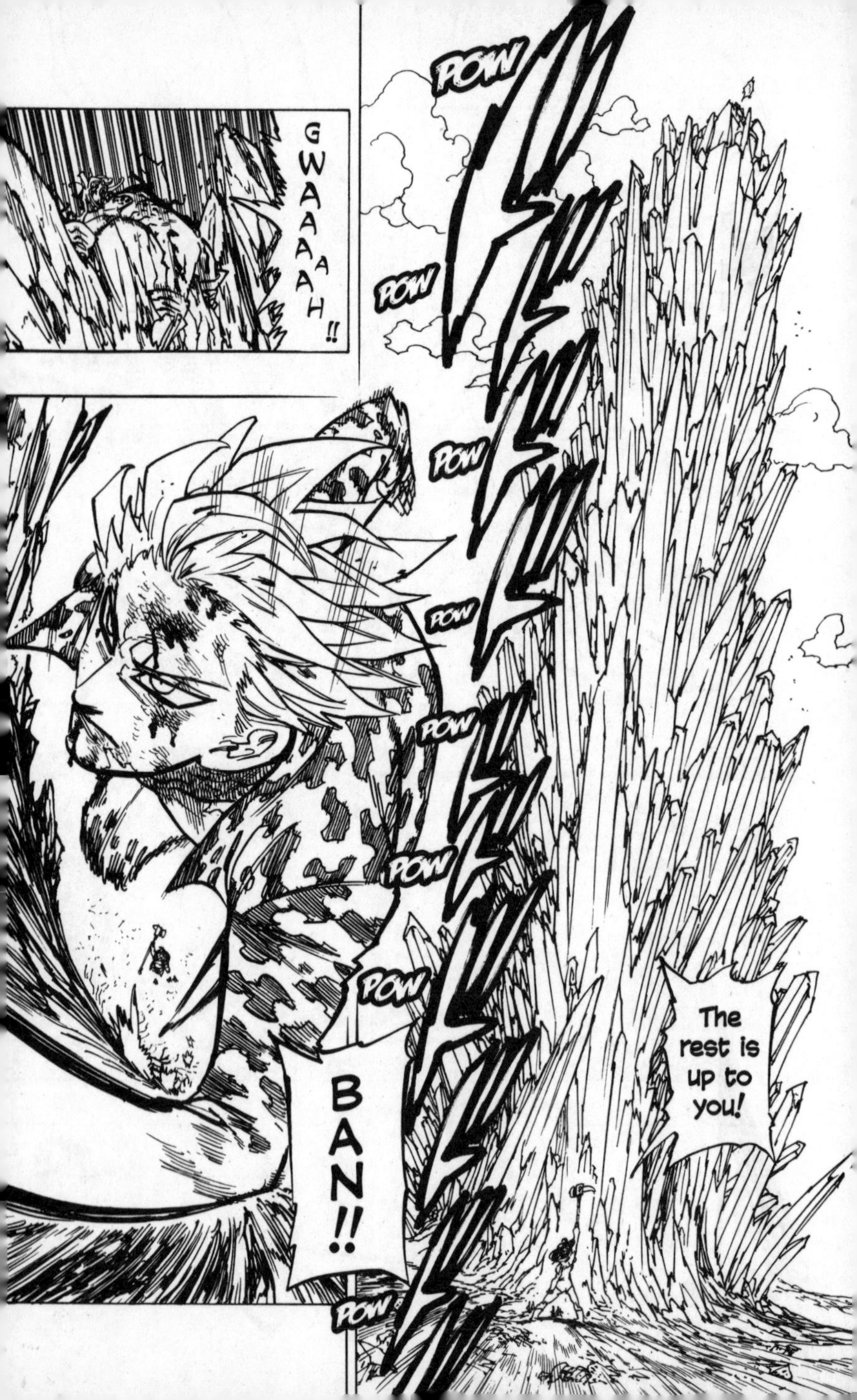
POW
POW
POW
POW
POW
POW
POW
POW
The rest is up to you!
GWAAAAAH!!
BAN!!

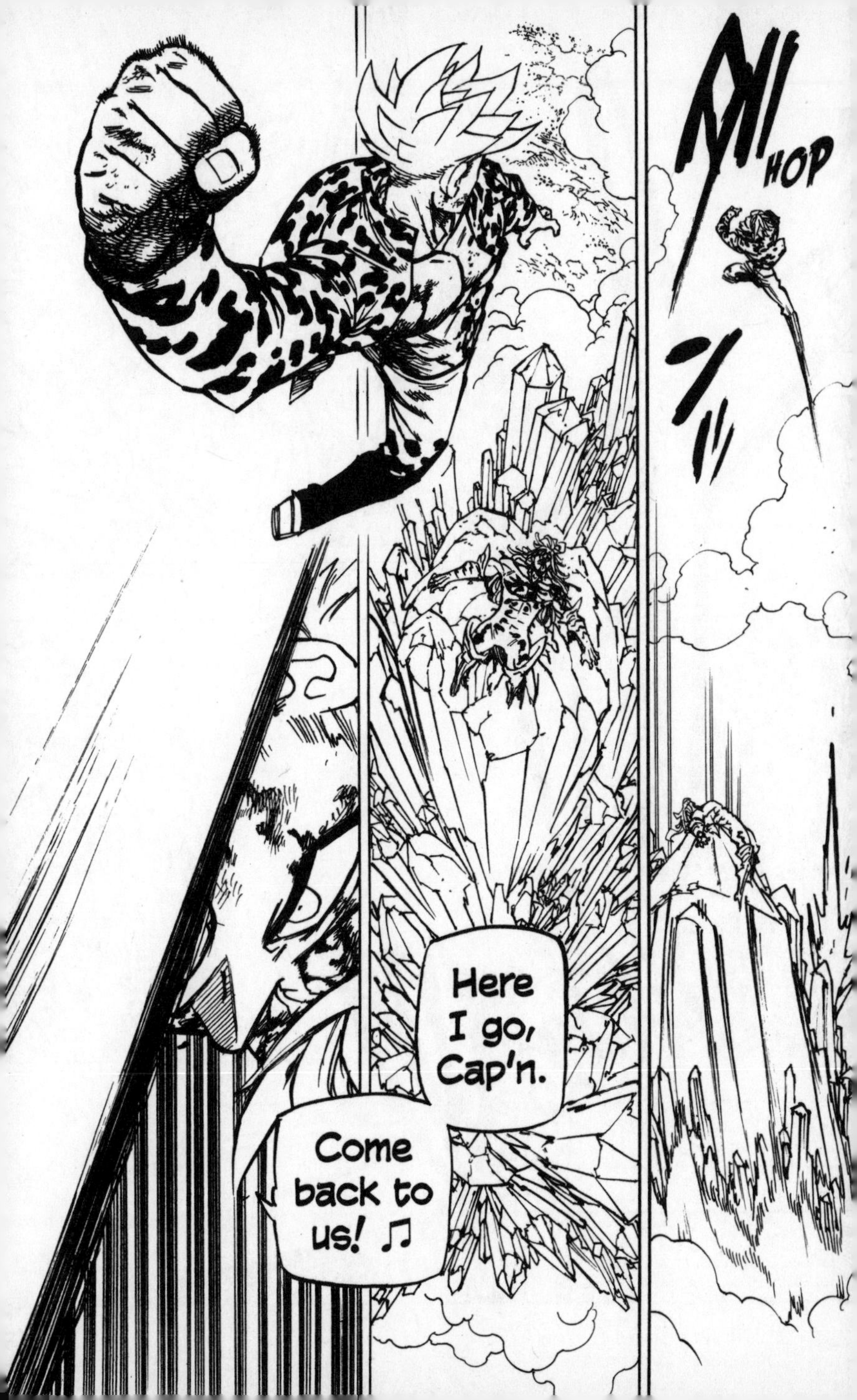
HOP
Here I go, Cap'n.
Come back to us! ♫

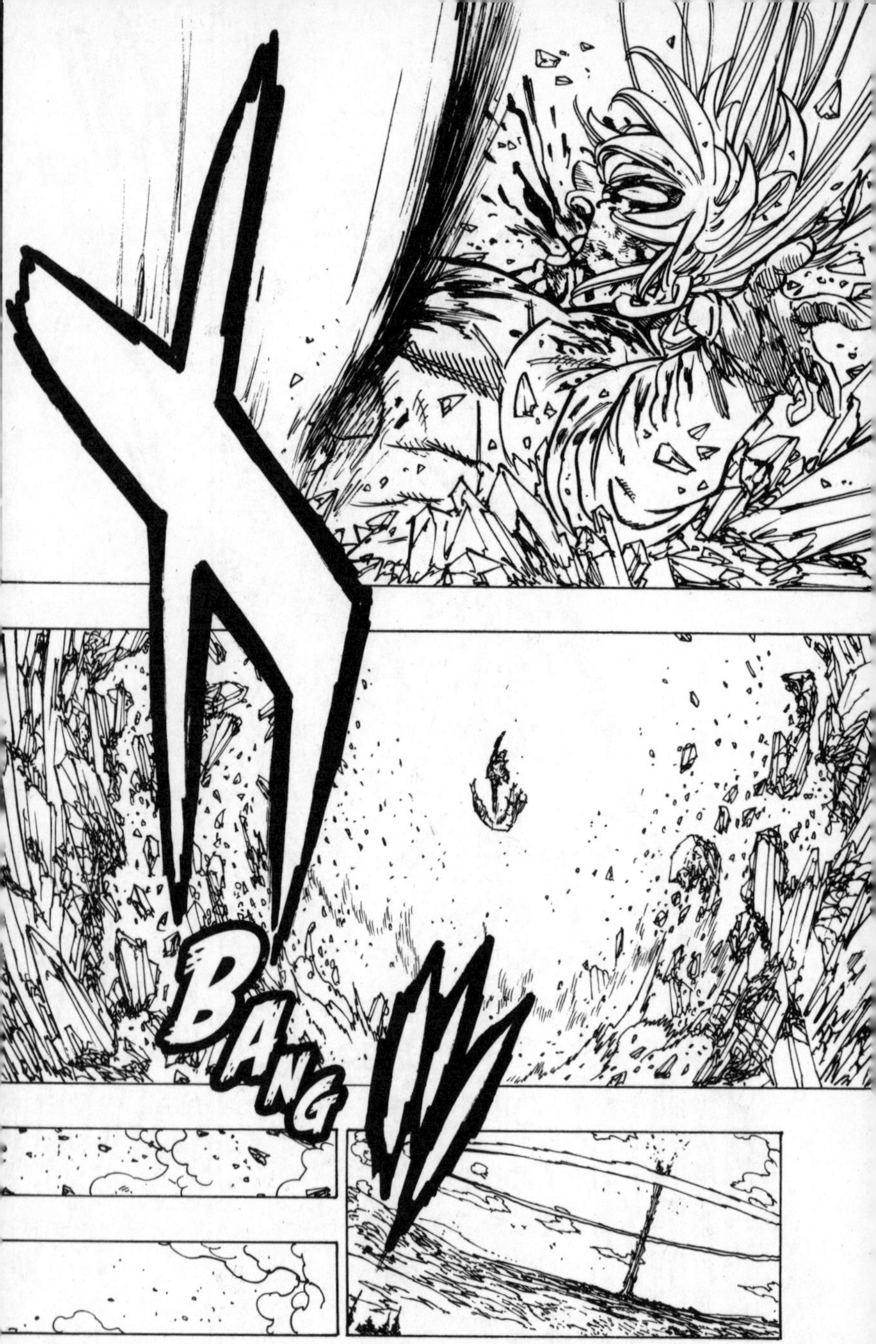
BANG

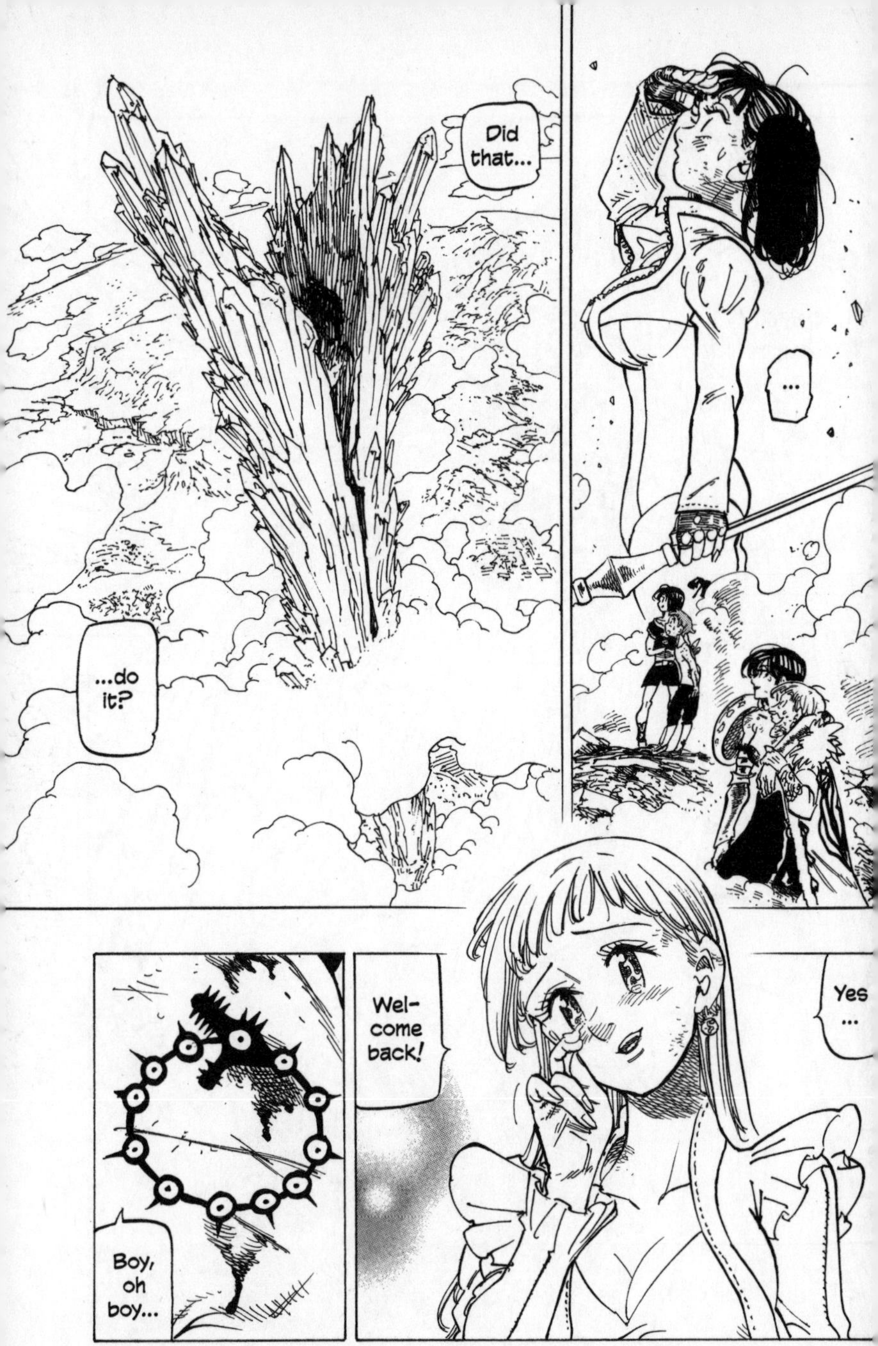
...
Did that...
...do it?
Yes ...
Wel-come back!
Boy, oh boy...

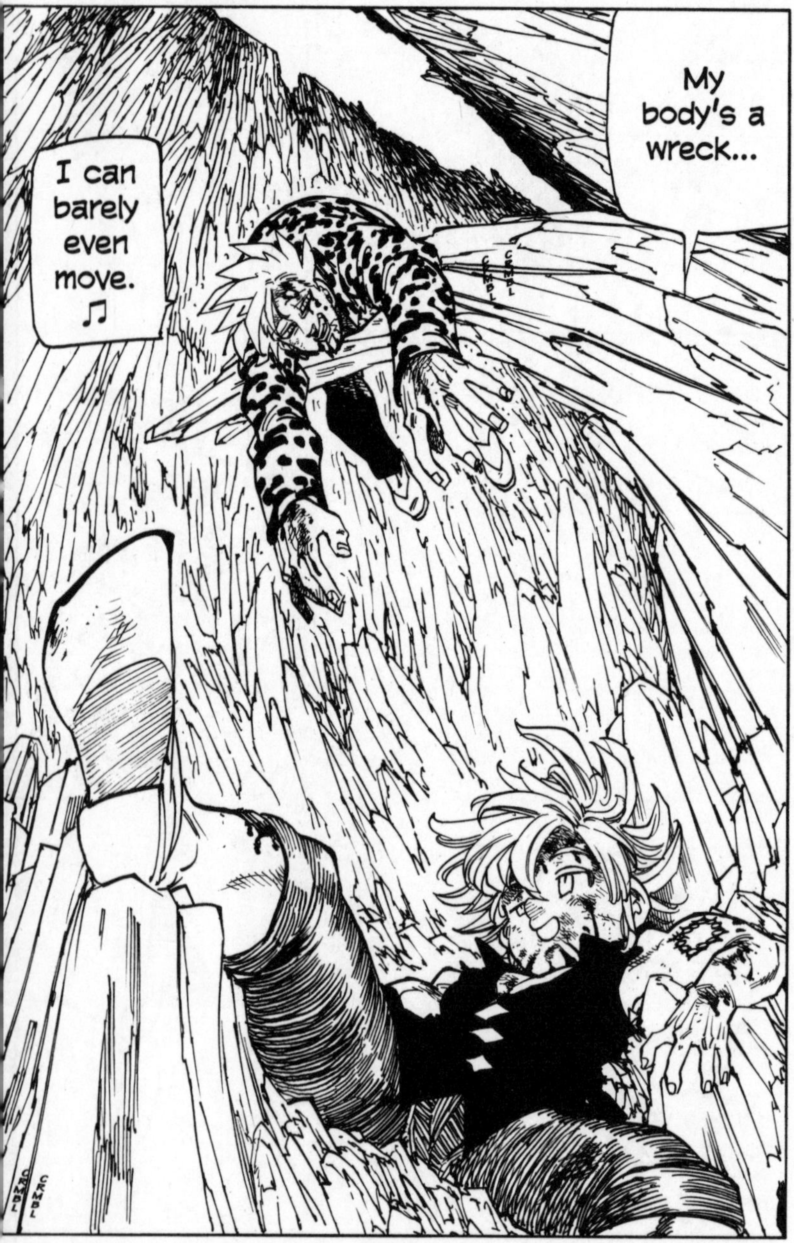
My body's a wreck...
CRMBL CRMBL
I can barely even move. ♫
CRMBL CRMBL

# Chapter 306 - The End of a Long Journey

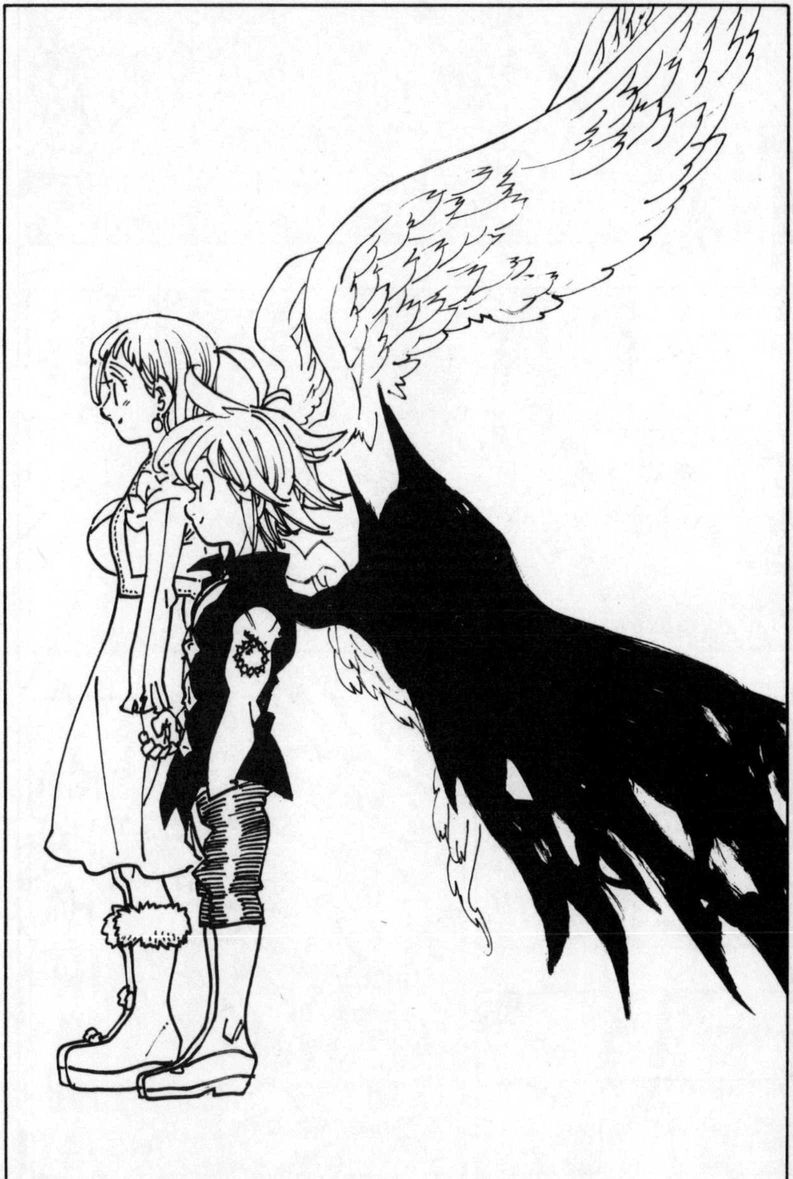

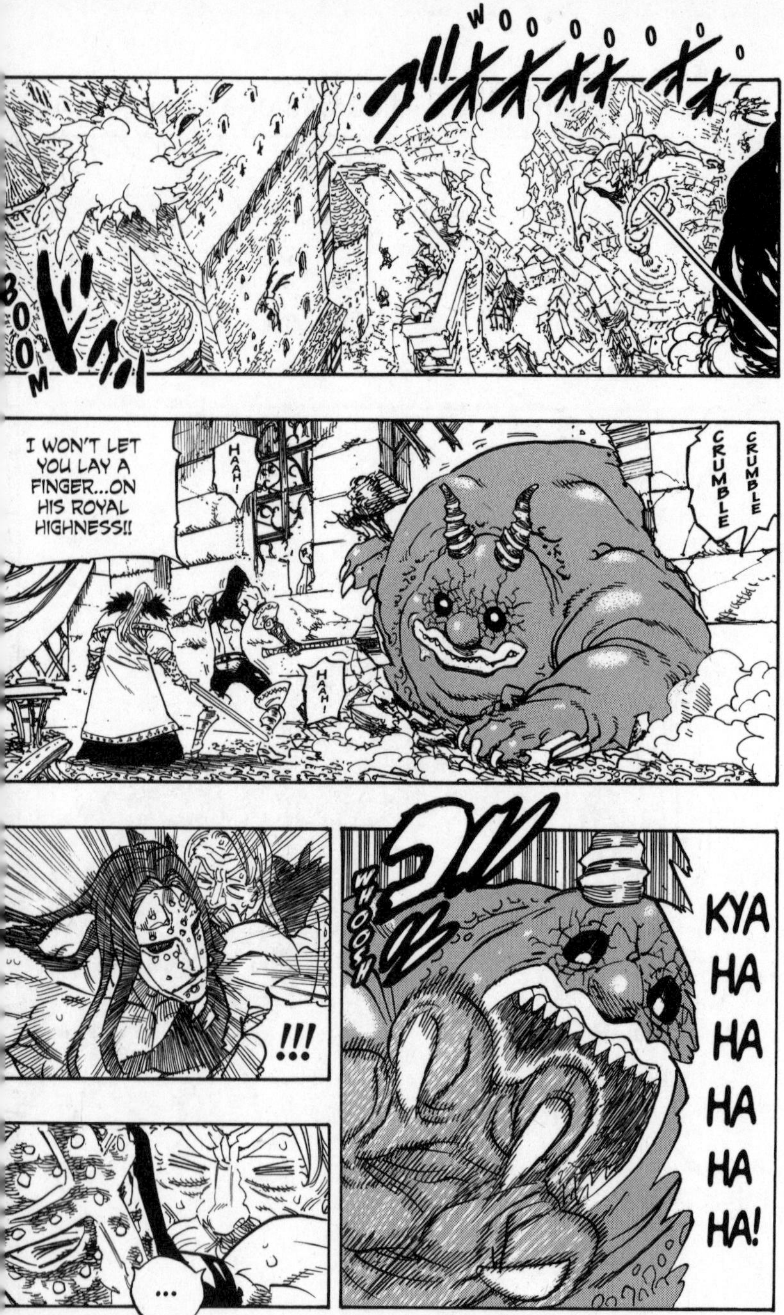
WOOOOOOOO
BOOM
CRUMBLE
CRUMBLE
HAAH!
I WON'T LET YOU LAY A FINGER...ON HIS ROYAL HIGHNESS!!
HAAH!
WHOOOM
KYA HA HA HA HA HA HA!
!!!
...

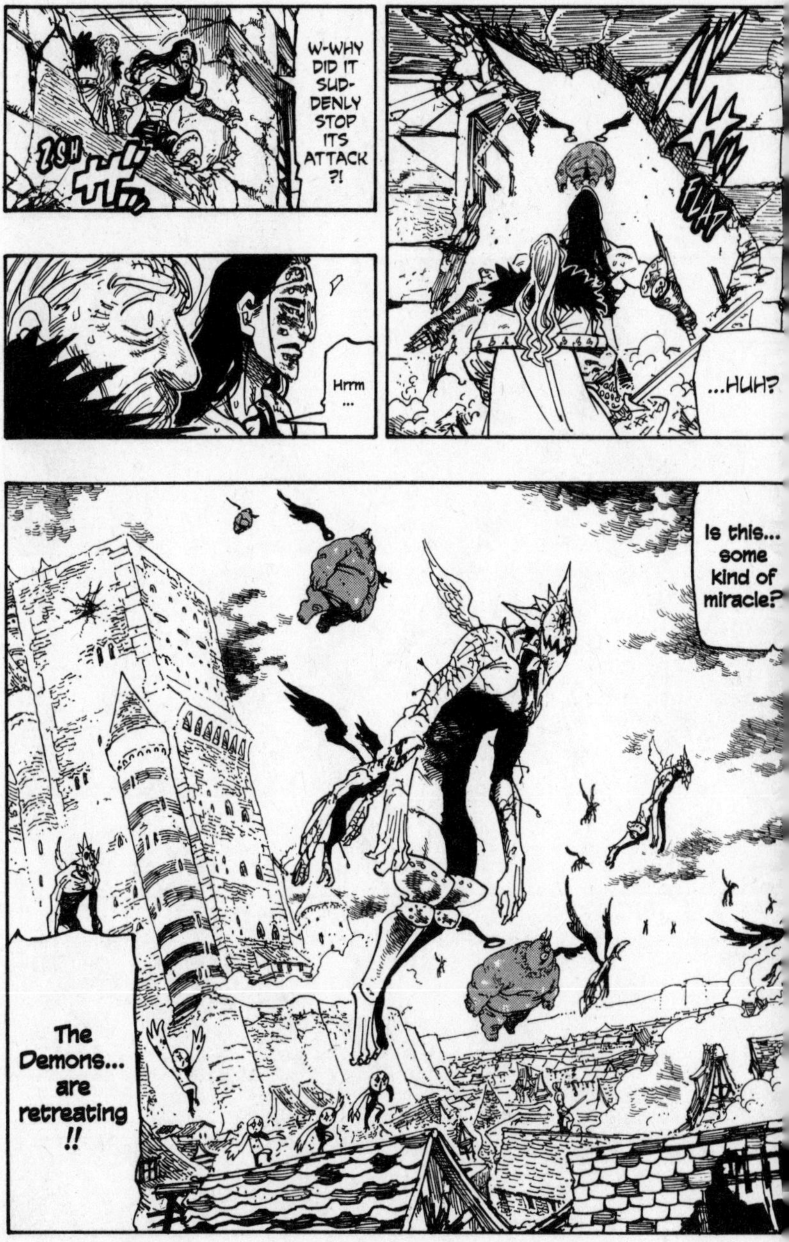
FLAP
...HUH?
W-WHY DID IT SUD-DENLY STOP ITS ATTACK ?!
ZSH
Hrrm ...
Is this... some kind of miracle?
The Demons... are retreating !!

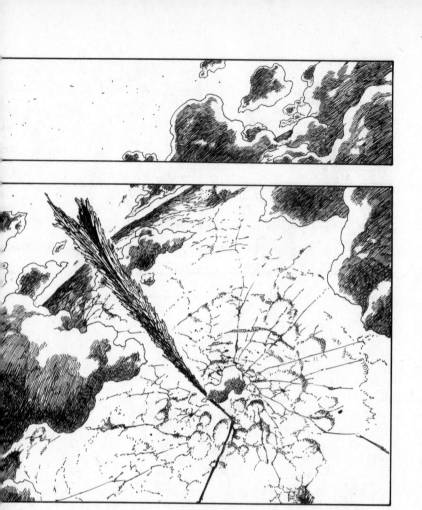

It's
so...
quiet.

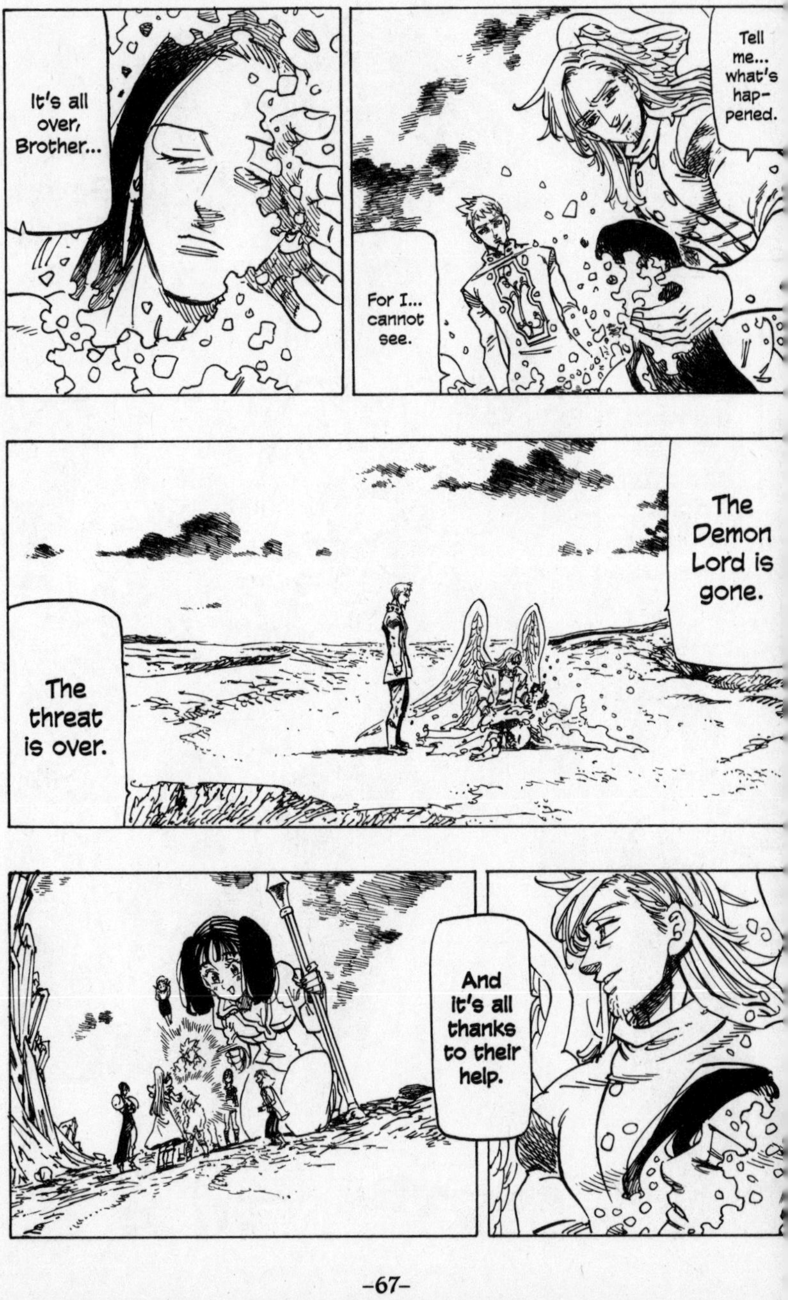
Tell me... what's hap-pened.
For I... cannot see.
It's all over, Brother...
The Demon Lord is gone.
The threat is over.
And it's all thanks to their help.

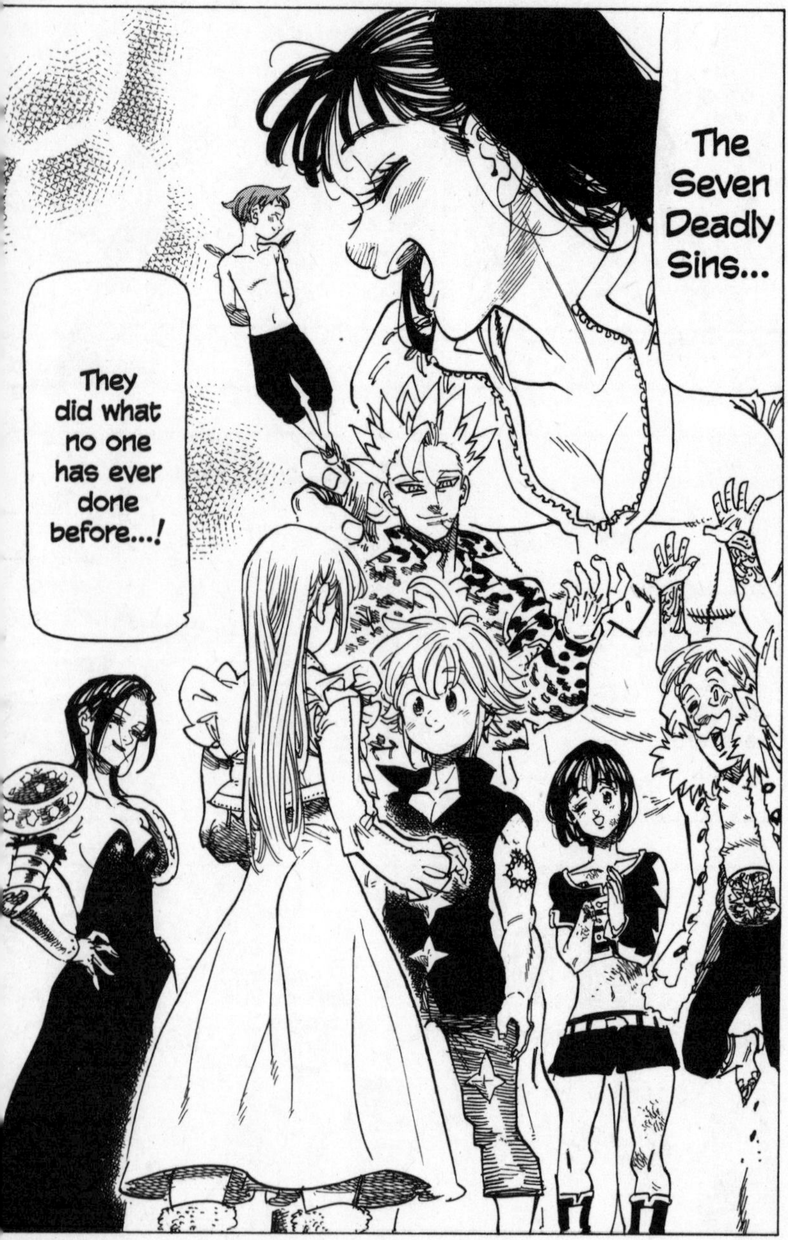
The Seven Deadly Sins...
They did what no one has ever done before...!

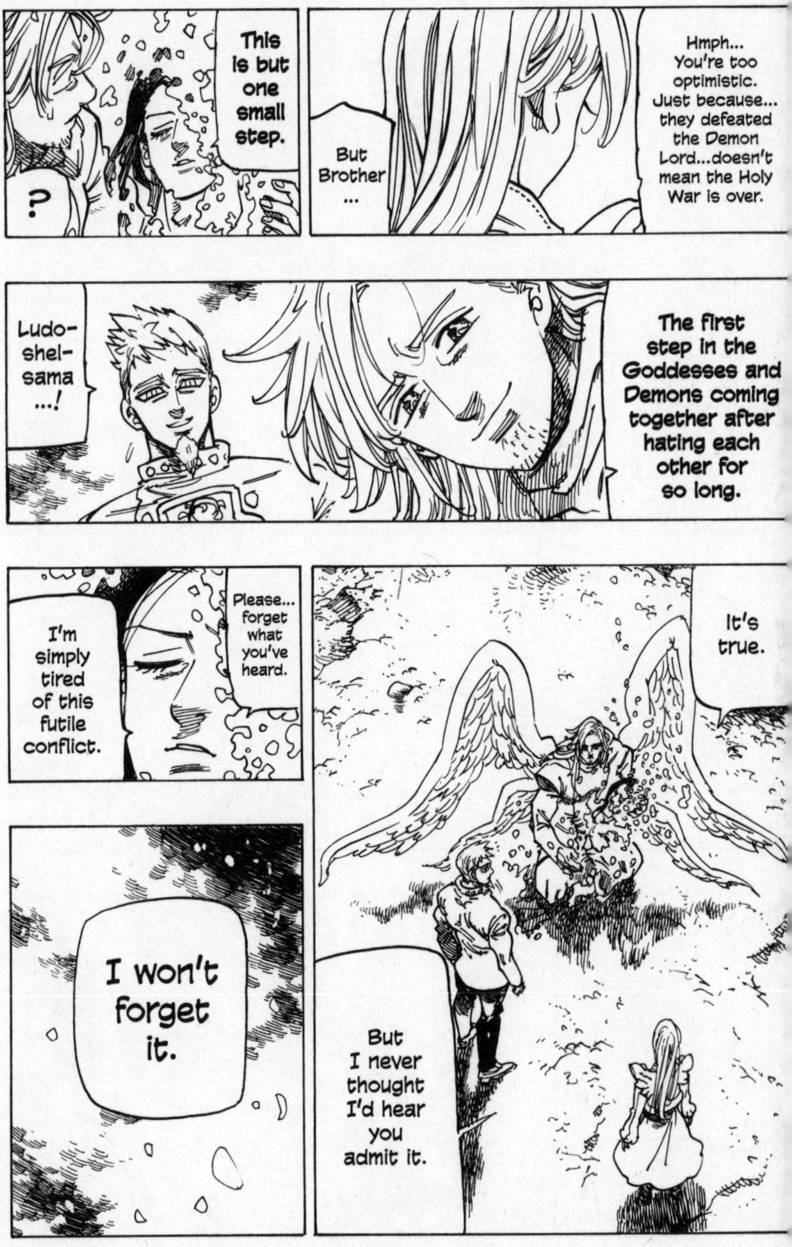
Hmph... You're too optimistic. Just because... they defeated the Demon Lord...doesn't mean the Holy War is over.
But Brother ...
This is but one small step.
?
The first step in the Goddesses and Demons coming together after hating each other for so long.
Ludo-shel-sama ...!
It's true.
But I never thought I'd hear you admit it.
Please... forget what you've heard.
I'm simply tired of this futile conflict.
I won't forget it.

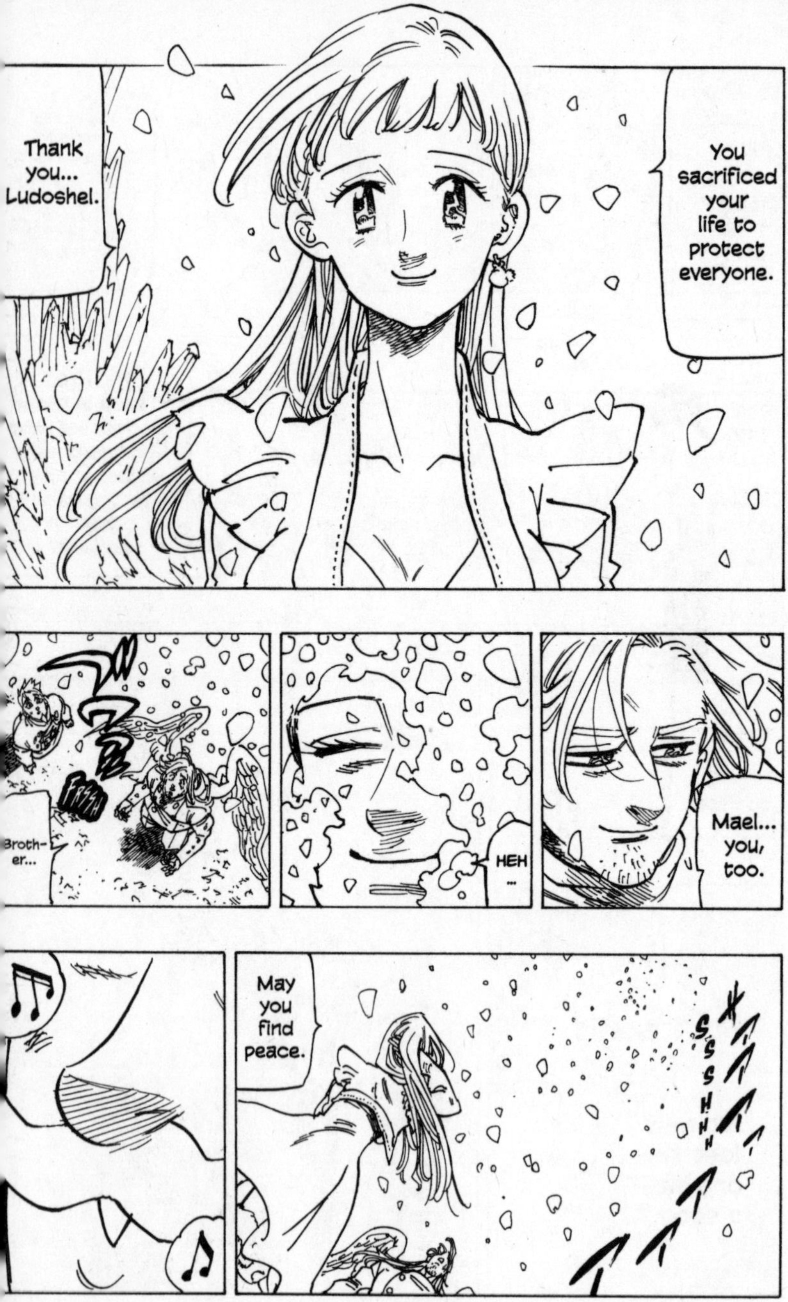
You sacrificed your life to protect everyone.
Thank you... Ludoshel.
Mael... you, too.
HEH ...
FRSSH
Brother...
SSSHHH
May you find peace.

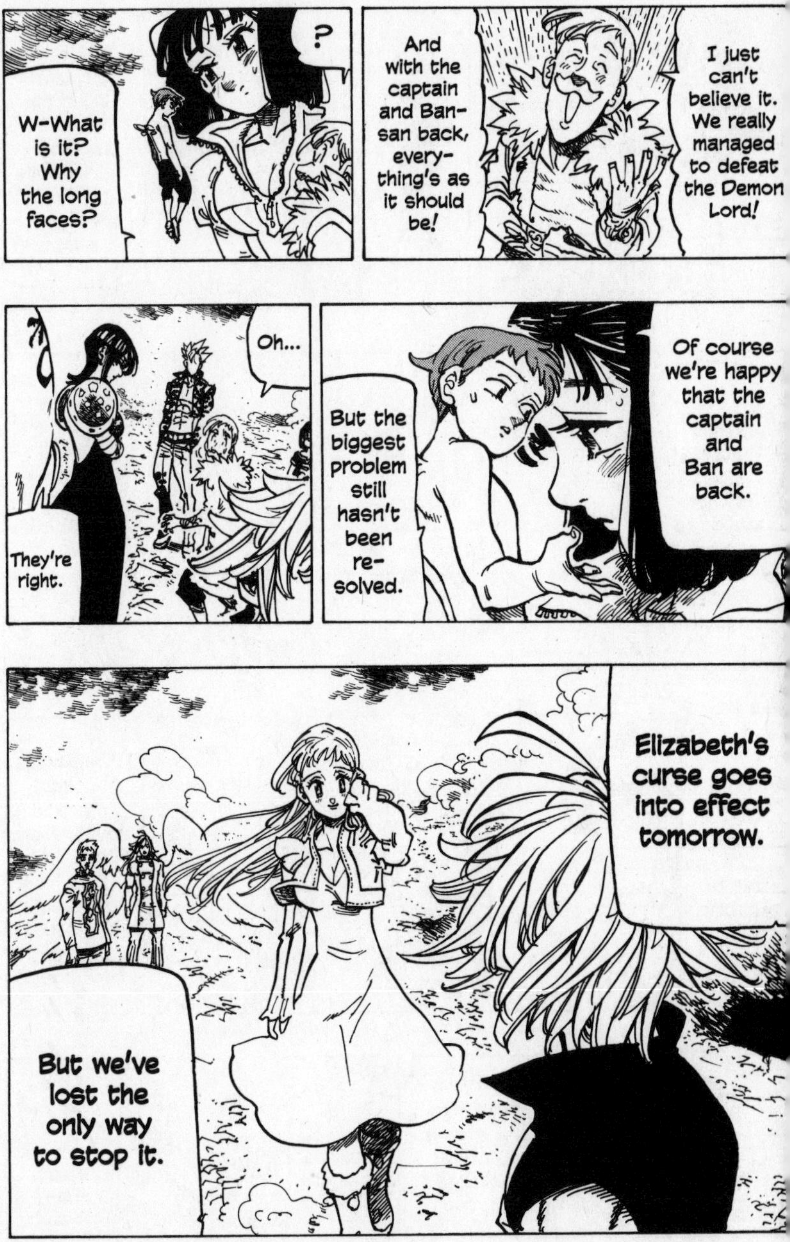
I just can't believe it. We really managed to defeat the Demon Lord!
And with the captain and Ban-san back, everything's as it should be!
?
W-What is it? Why the long faces?
Of course we're happy that the captain and Ban are back.
But the biggest problem still hasn't been resolved.
Oh...
They're right.
Elizabeth's curse goes into effect tomorrow.
But we've lost the only way to stop it.

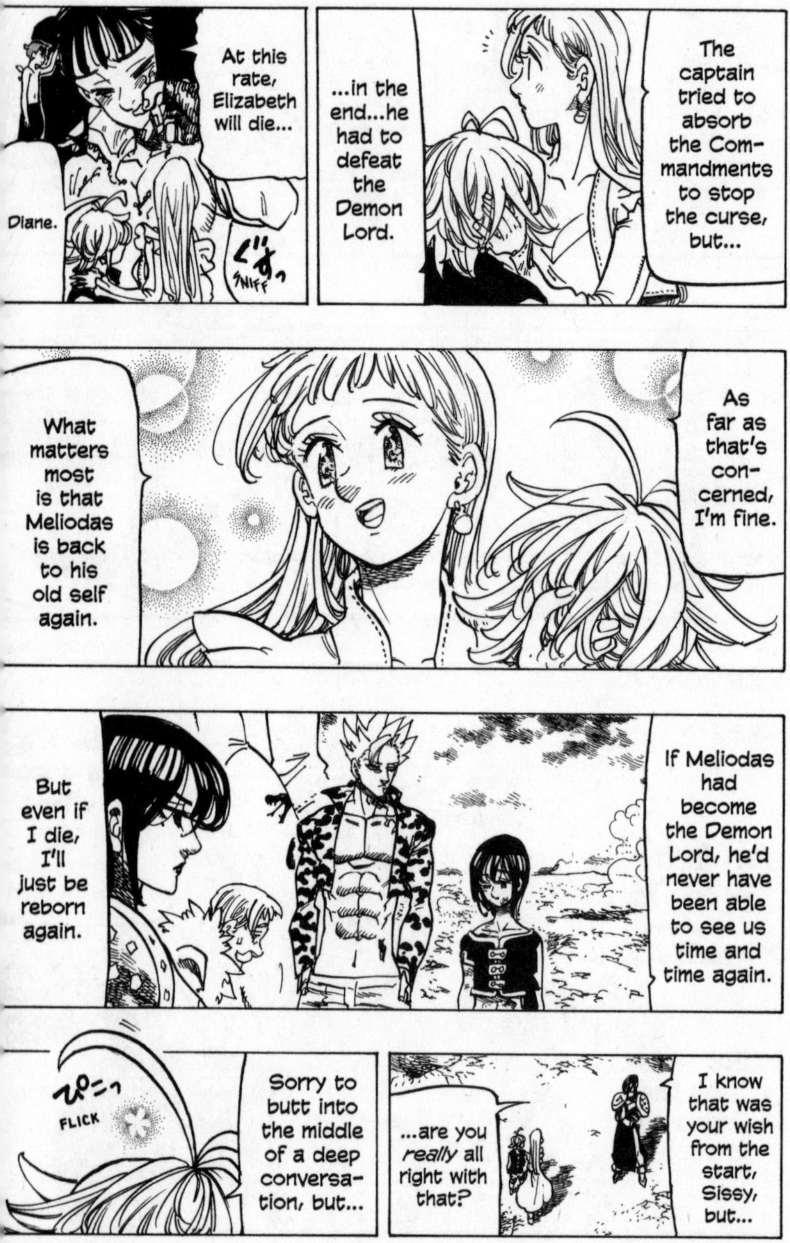
The captain tried to absorb the Commandments to stop the curse, but...
...in the end...he had to defeat the Demon Lord.
At this rate, Elizabeth will die...
ぐすっ
SNIFF
Diane.
As far as that's concerned, I'm fine.
What matters most is that Meliodas is back to his old self again.
If Meliodas had become the Demon Lord, he'd never have been able to see us time and time again.
But even if I die, I'll just be reborn again.
I know that was your wish from the start, Sissy, but...
...are you *really* all right with that?
Sorry to butt into the middle of a deep conversation, but...
ぴこっ
FLICK

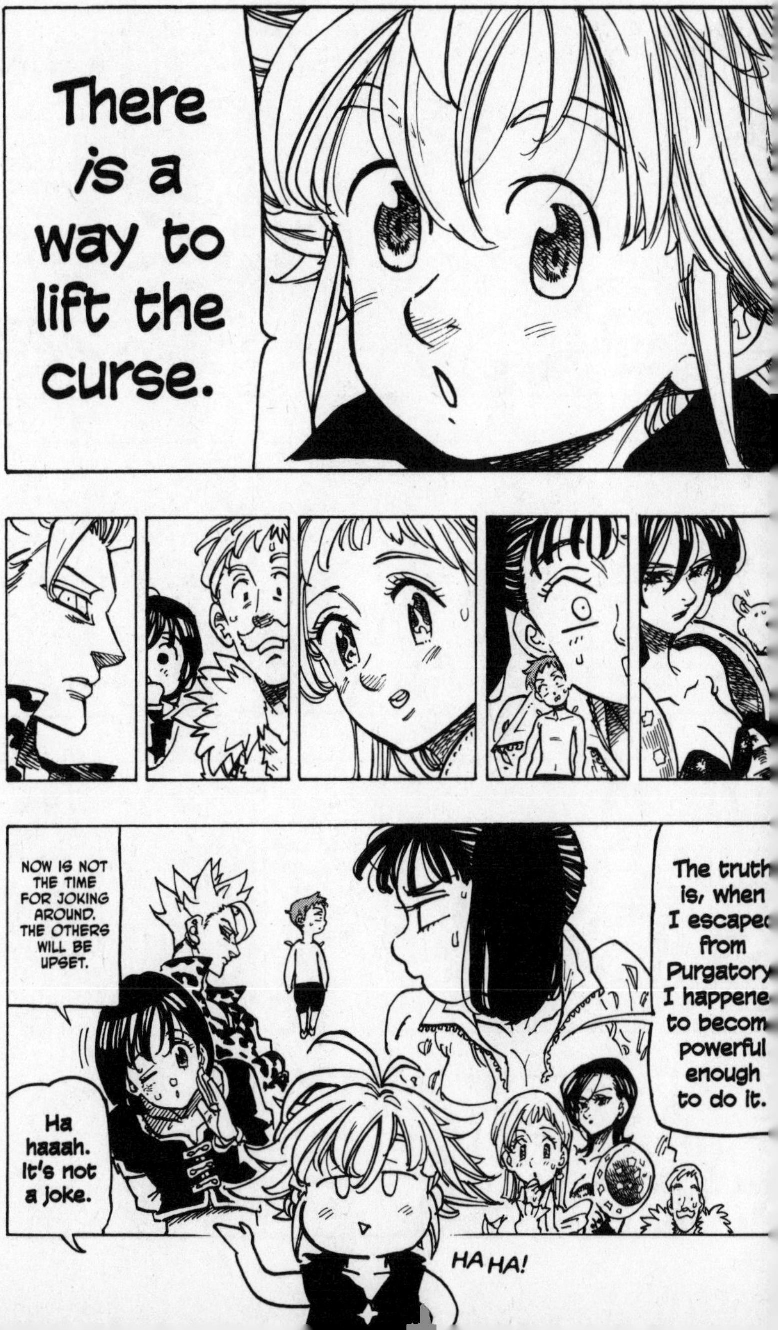

There is a way to lift the curse.
The truth is, when I escape from Purgatory I happene to becom powerful enough to do it.
NOW IS NOT THE TIME FOR JOKING AROUND. THE OTHERS WILL BE UPSET.
Ha haaah. It's not a joke.
HA HA!

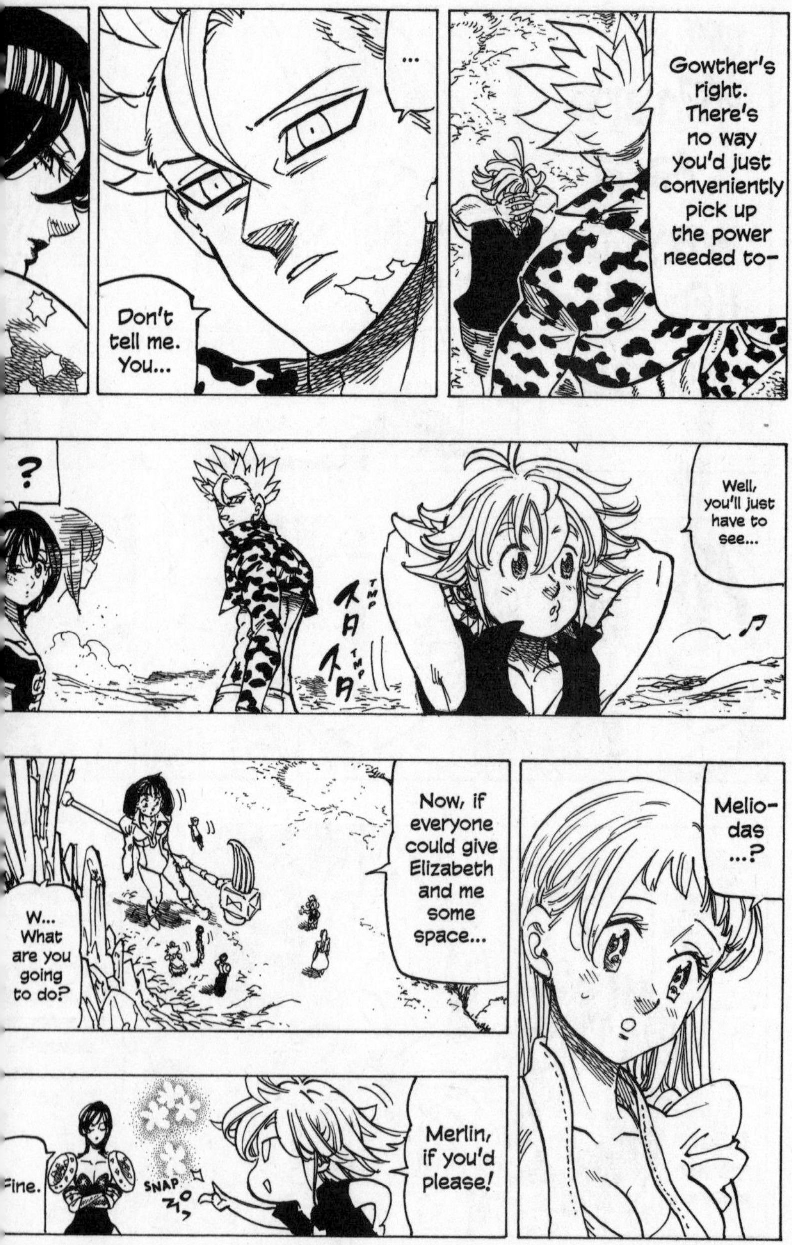
Gowther's right. There's no way you'd just conveniently pick up the power needed to-
...
Don't tell me. You...
Well, you'll just have to see...
♪
TMP
TMP
?
Melio-das ...?
Now, if everyone could give Elizabeth and me some space...
W... What are you going to do?
Merlin, if you'd please!
SNAP
Fine.

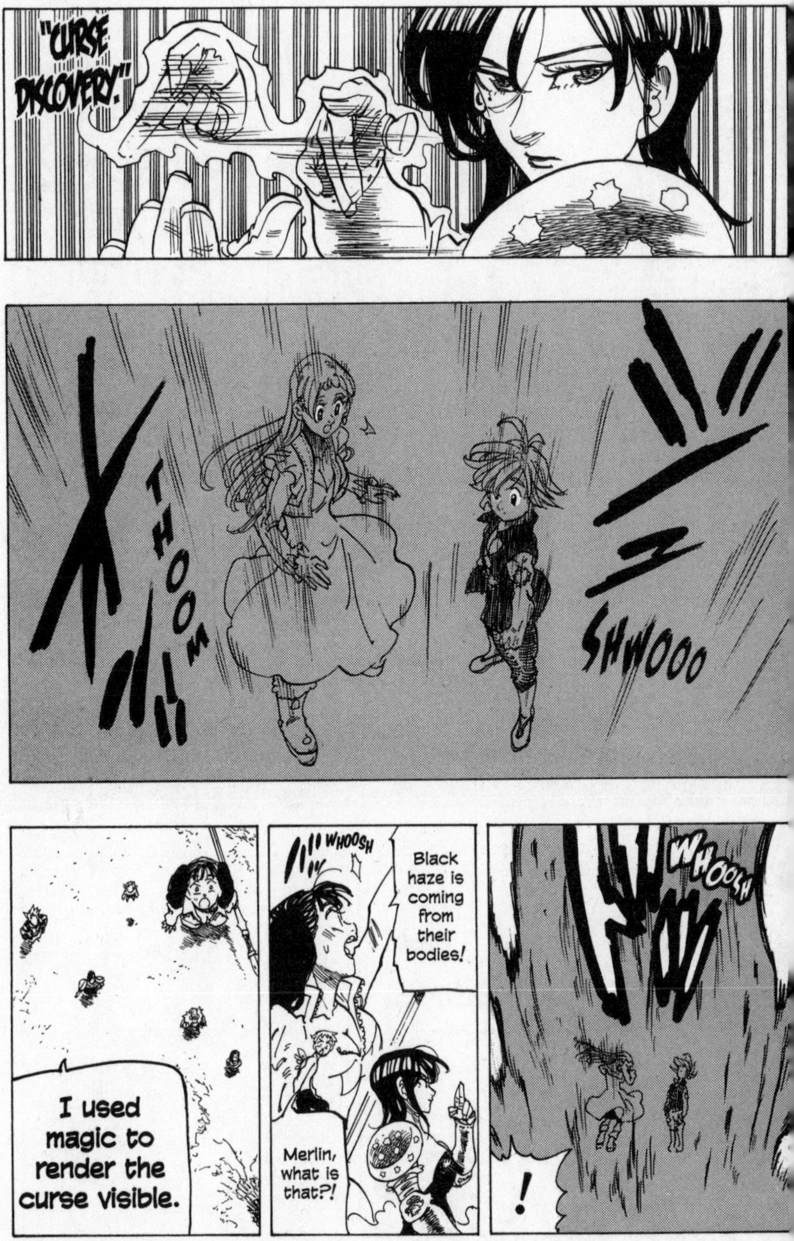
"CURSE DISCOVERY."
SHWOOO
THOOM
WHOOSH
!
WHOOSH
Black haze is coming from their bodies!
Merlin, what is that?!
I used magic to render the curse visible.

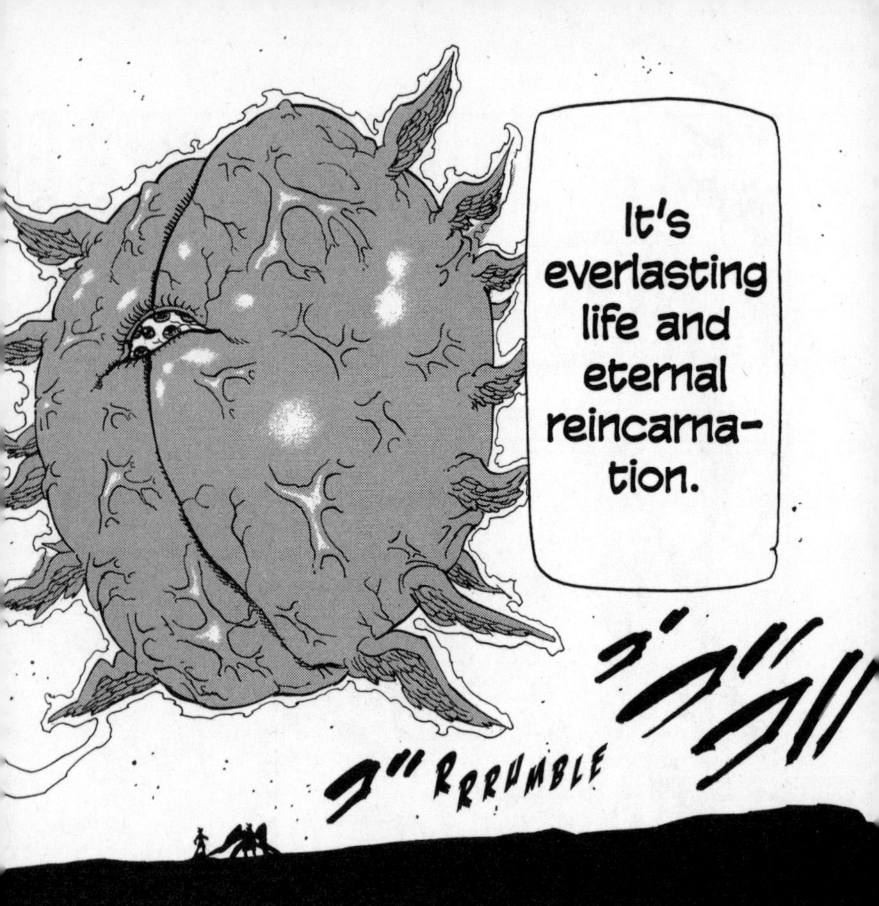
It's everlasting life and eternal reincarnation.
RRRUMBLE

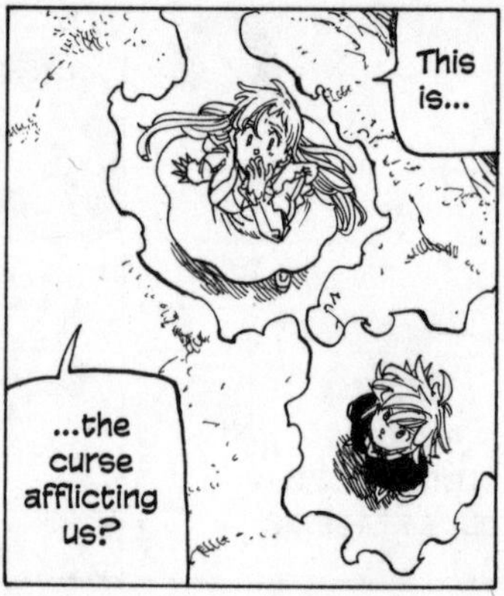
This is...
...the curse afflicting us?

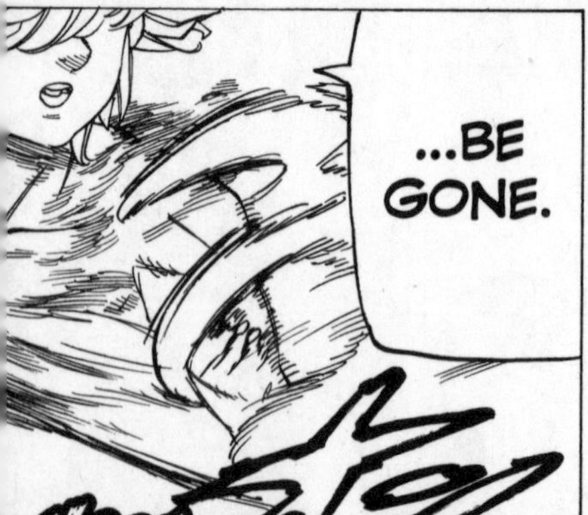
...BE GONE.
VOOM

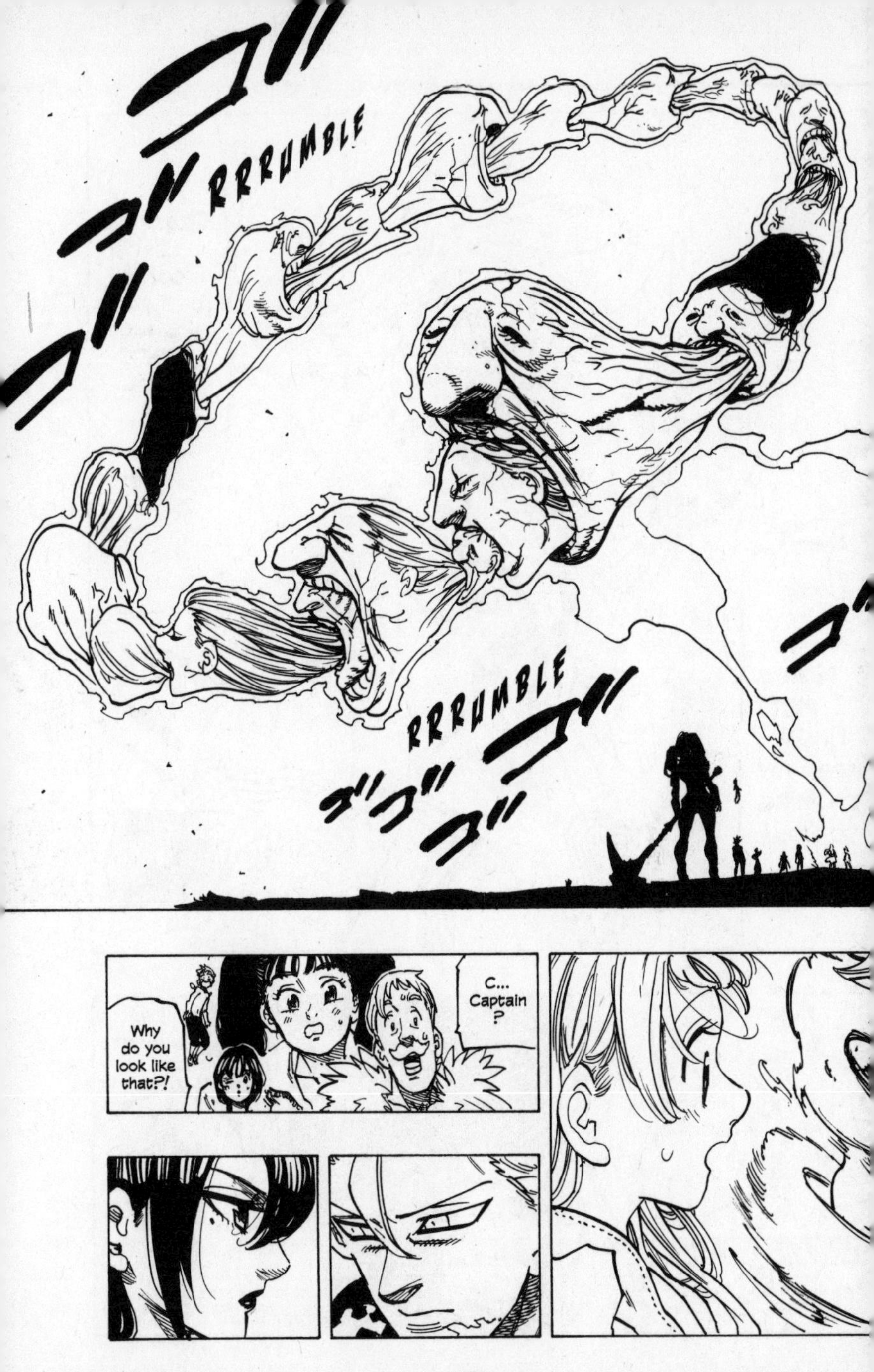
RRRUMBLE
RRRUMBLE
C... Captain?
Why do you look like that?!

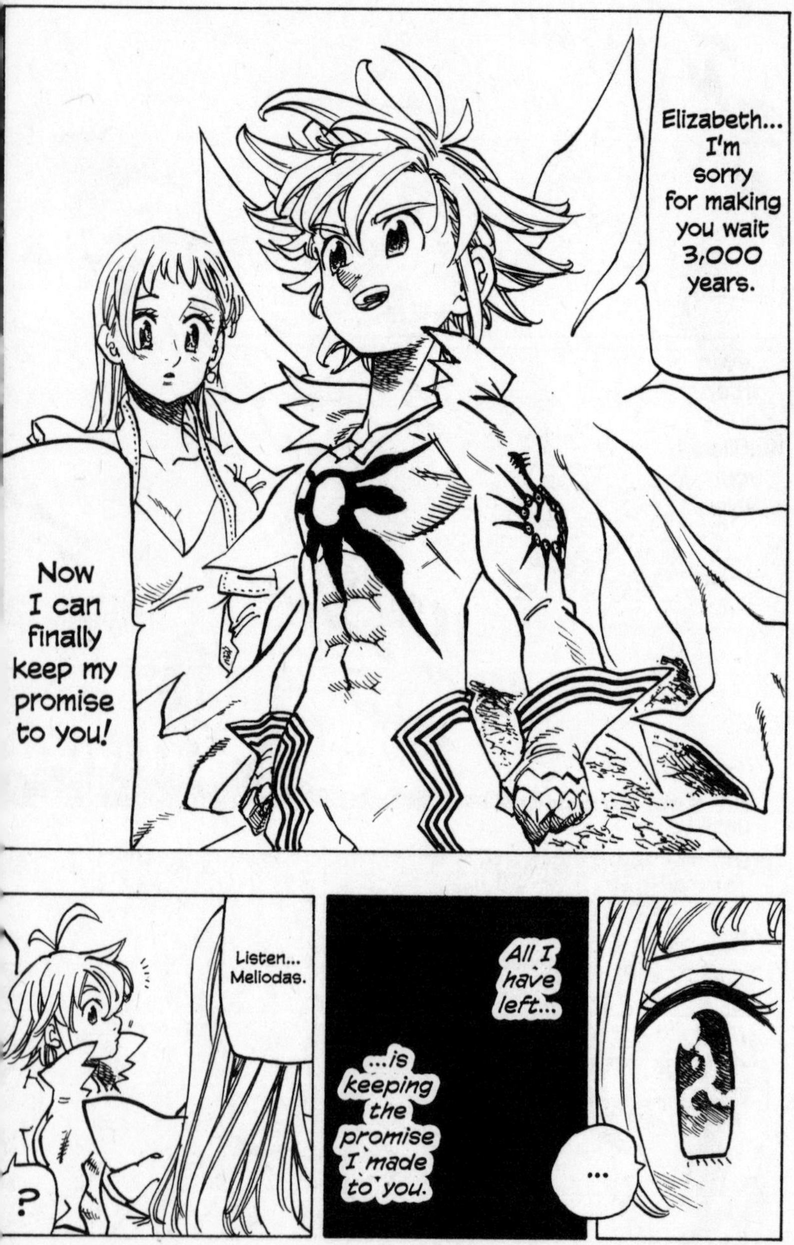
Elizabeth... I'm sorry for making you wait 3,000 years.
Now I can finally keep my promise to you!
...
All I have left...
...is keeping the promise I made to you.
Listen... Meliodas.
?

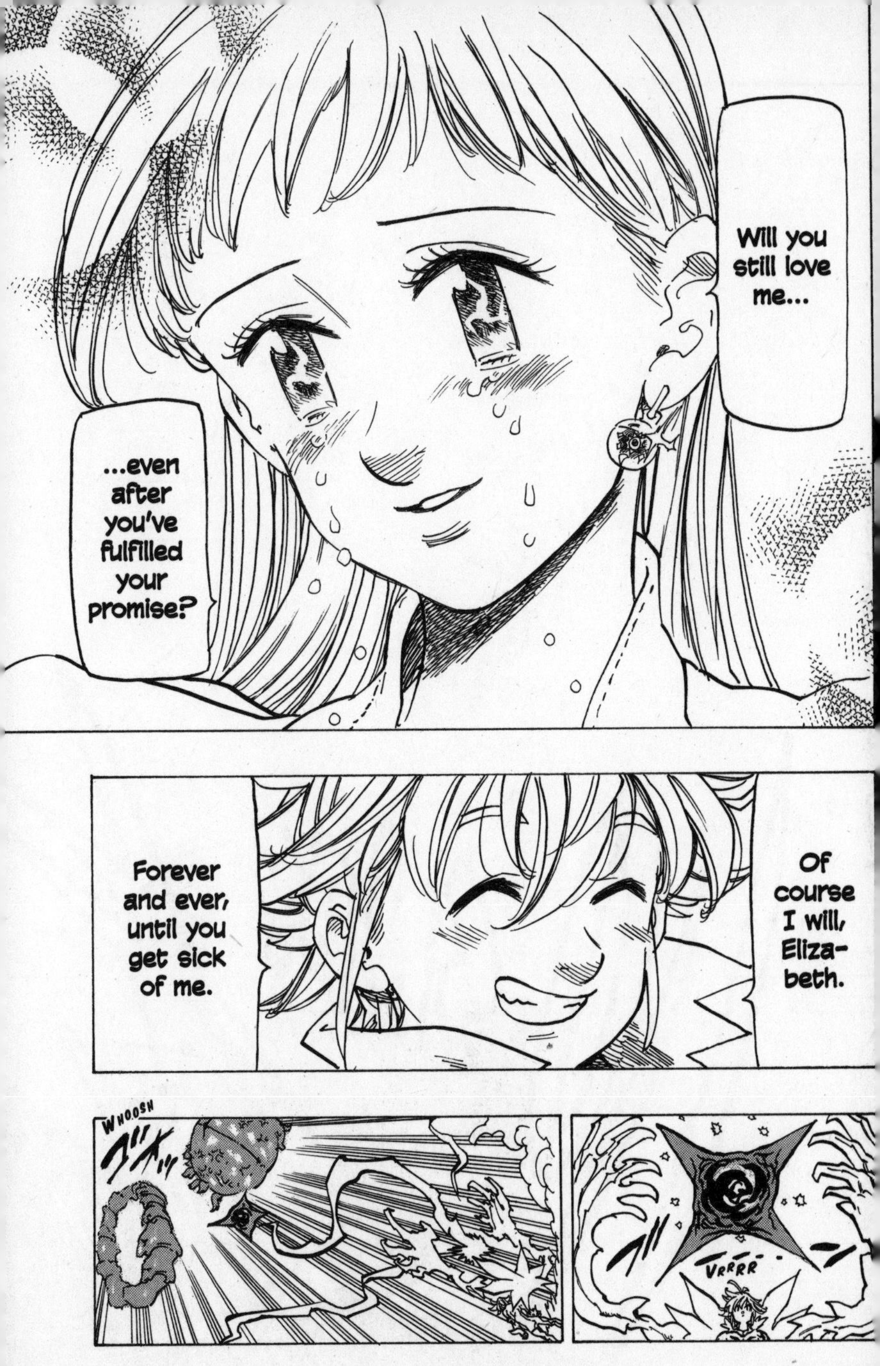
Will you still love me...
...even after you've fulfilled your promise?
Of course I will, Eliza-beth.
Forever and ever, until you get sick of me.
VRRRR
WHOOSH

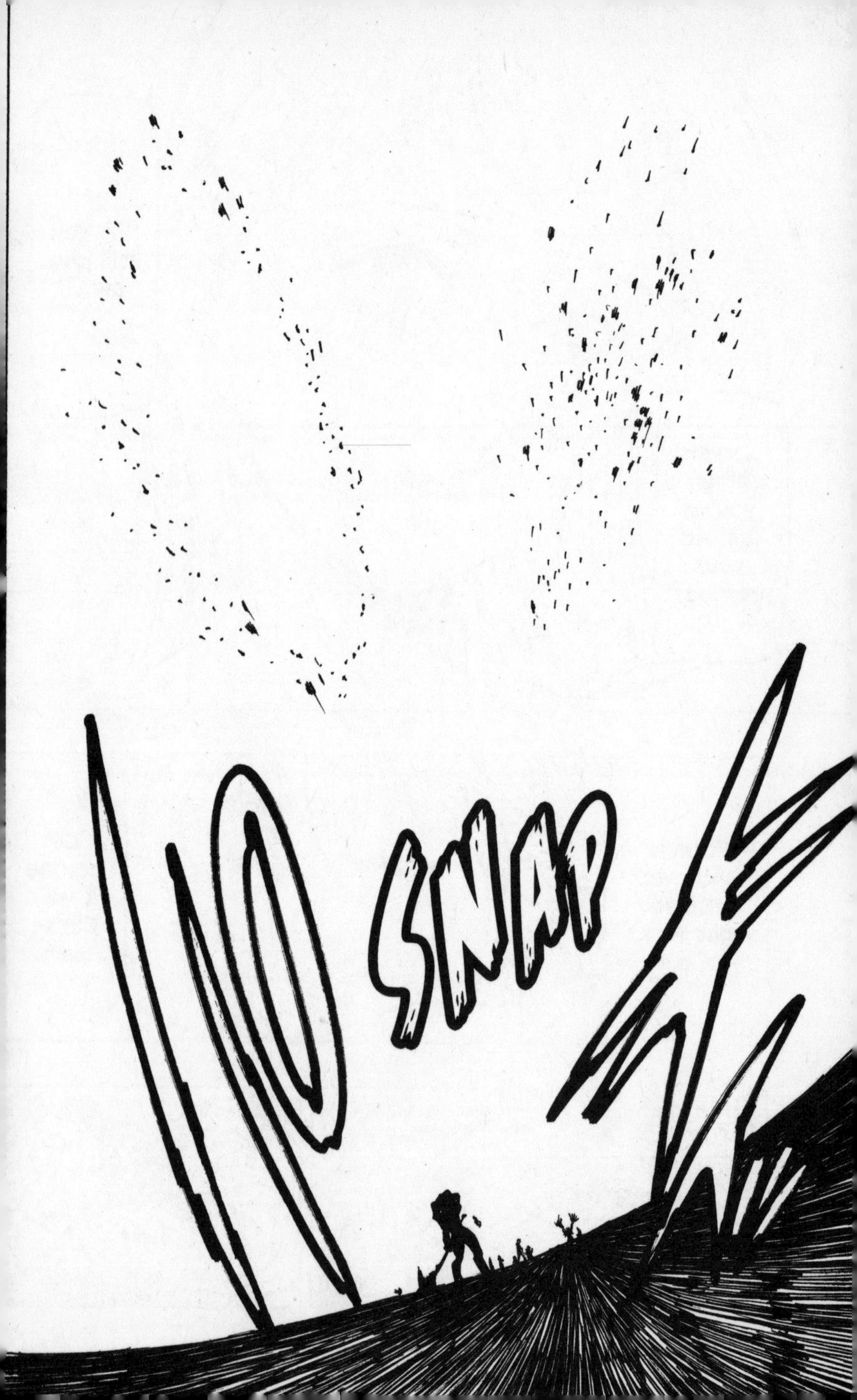
SNAP

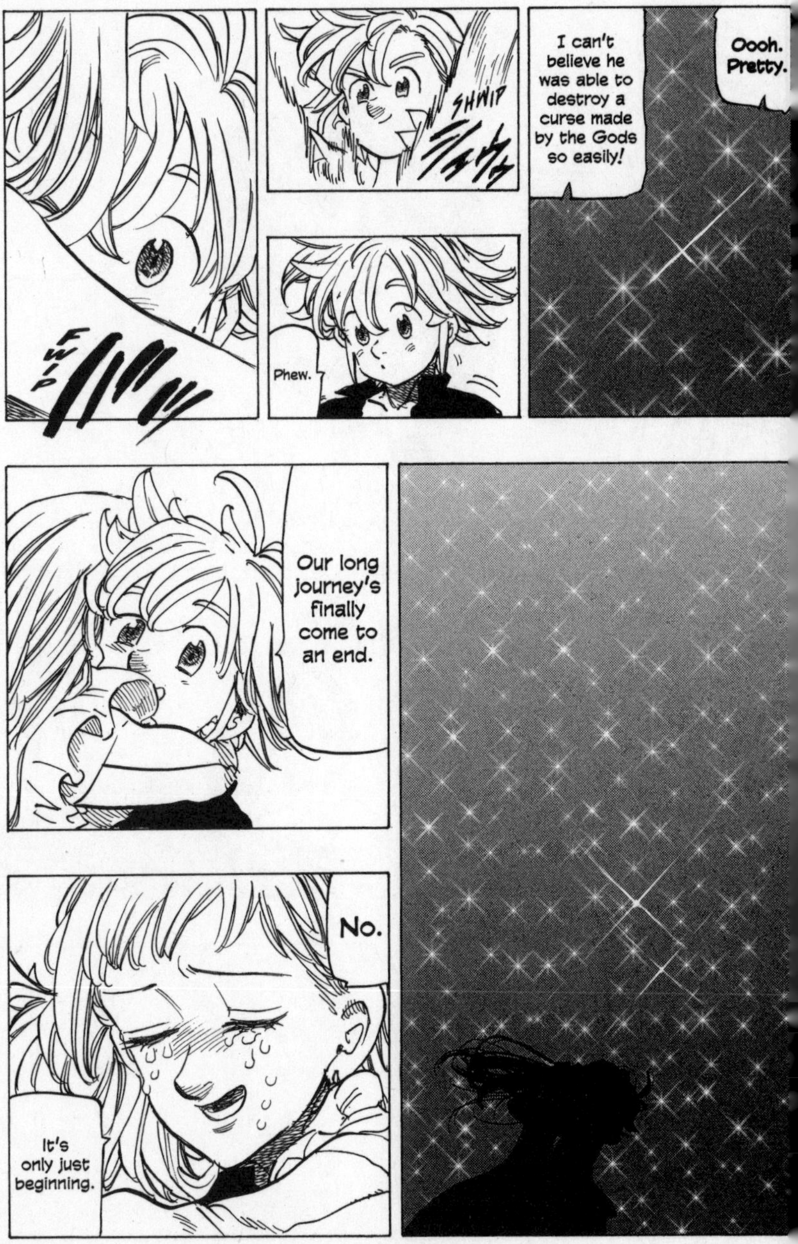
Oooh. Pretty.
I can't believe he was able to destroy a curse made by the Gods so easily!
SHWIP
Phew.
FWIP
Our long journey's finally come to an end.
No.
It's only just beginning.

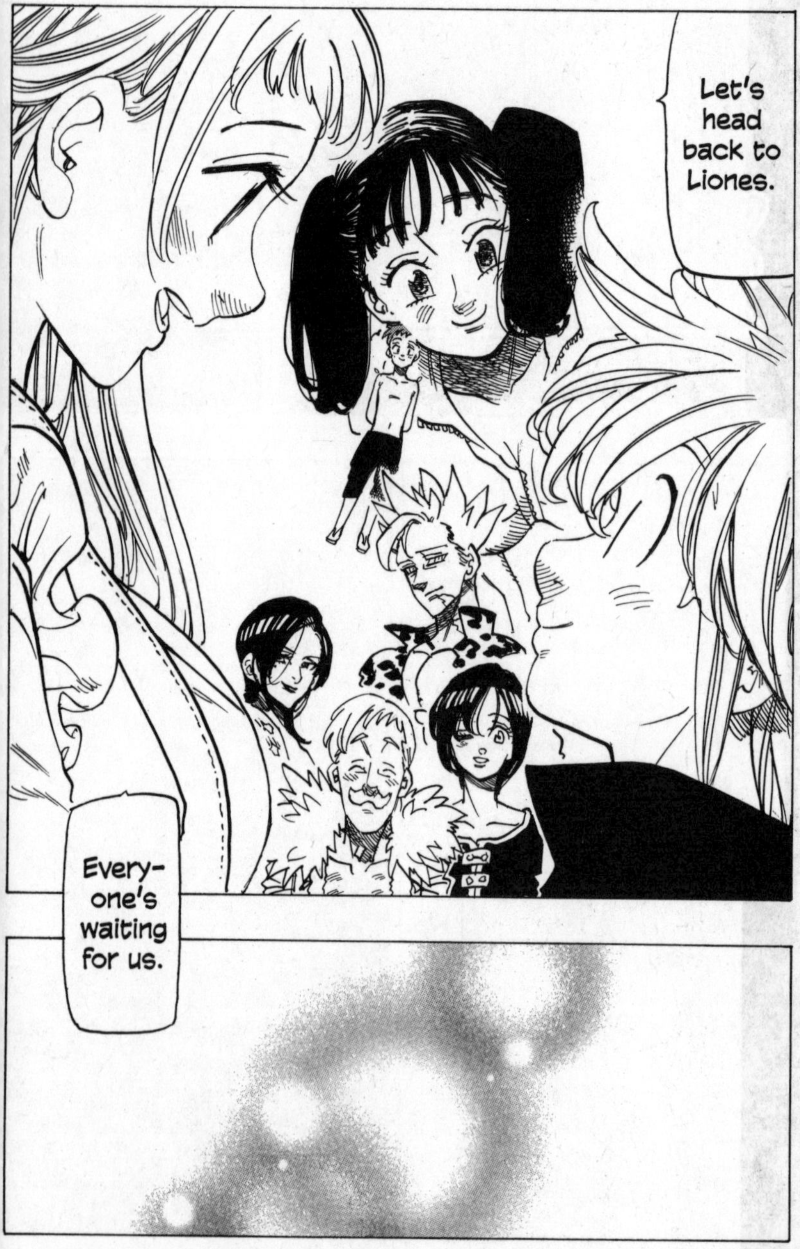
Let's head back to Liones.
Every-one's waiting for us.

# THE SEVEN DEADLY SINS

Chapter 307 - Until We're Shrouded in Happiness

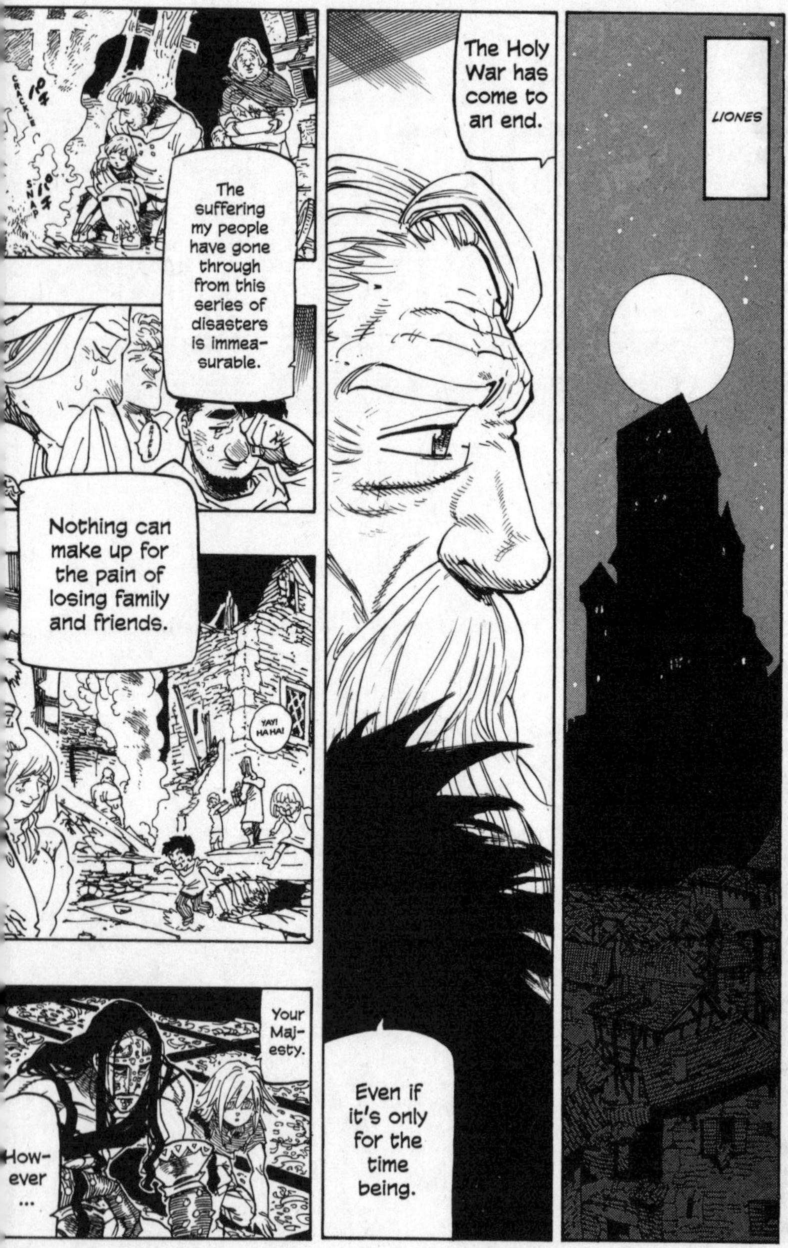
LIONES
The Holy War has come to an end.
Even if it's only for the time being.
CRACKLE
SNAP
The suffering my people have gone through from this series of disasters is immeasurable.
Nothing can make up for the pain of losing family and friends.
YAY! HAHA!
Your Majesty.
However...

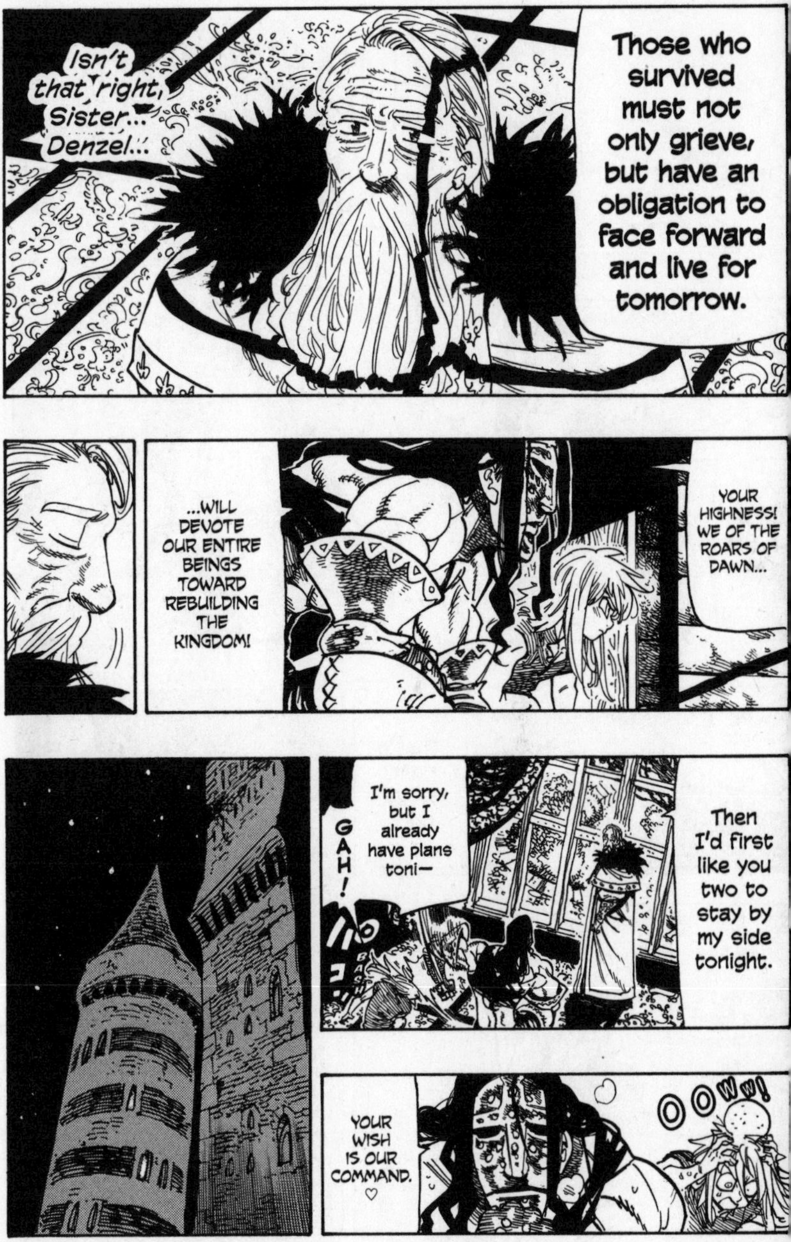
Those who survived must not only grieve, but have an obligation to face forward and live for tomorrow.
Isn't that right, Sister... Denzel...
YOUR HIGHNESS! WE OF THE ROARS OF DAWN...
...WILL DEVOTE OUR ENTIRE BEINGS TOWARD REBUILDING THE KINGDOM!
Then I'd first like you two to stay by my side tonight.
I'm sorry, but I already have plans toni—
GAH!
BASH
OOWW!
YOUR WISH IS OUR COMMAND. ♡

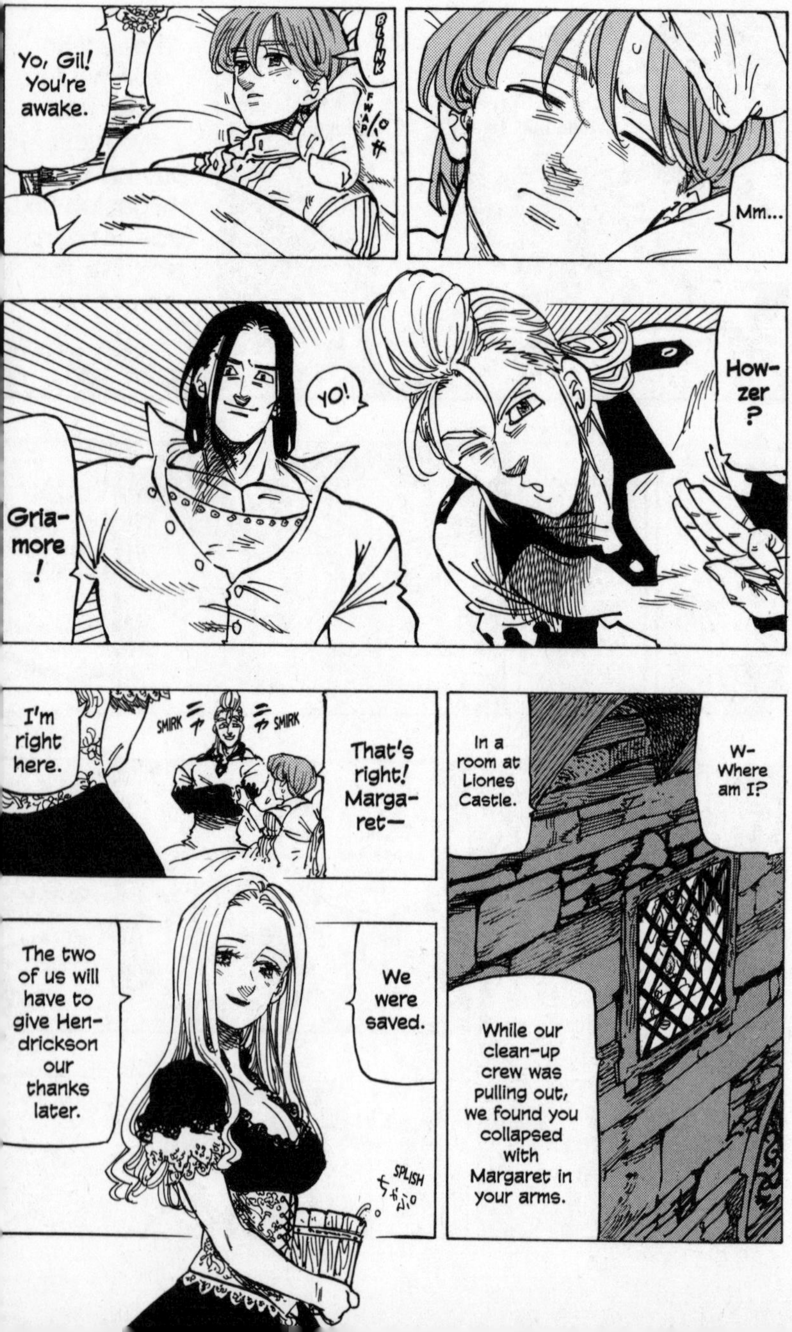
Mm...
BLINK
FWAP
Yo, Gil! You're awake.
Howzer?
YO!
Griamore!
W-Where am I?
In a room at Liones Castle.
While our clean-up crew was pulling out, we found you collapsed with Margaret in your arms.
That's right! Margaret—
SMIRK
SMIRK
I'm right here.
We were saved.
The two of us will have to give Hendrickson our thanks later.
SPLISH

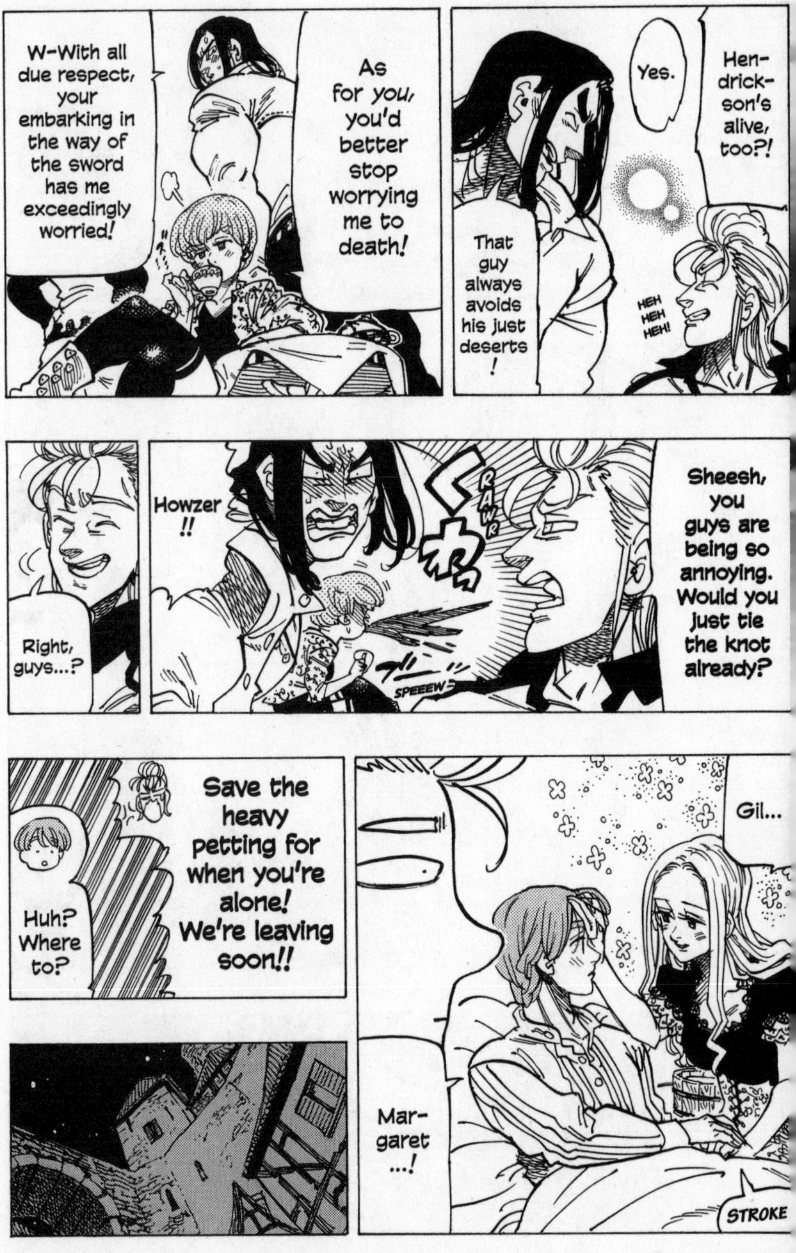
Hen-drickson's alive, too?!
Yes.
HEH HEH HEH!
That guy always avoids his just deserts!
As for you, you'd better stop worrying me to death!
W-With all due respect, your embarking in the way of the sword has me exceedingly worried!
Sheesh, you guys are being so annoying. Would you just tie the knot already?
RAWR
SPEEEW
Howzer!!
Right, guys...?
Gil...
STROKE
Mar-garet...!
Save the heavy petting for when you're alone! We're leaving soon!!
Huh? Where to?

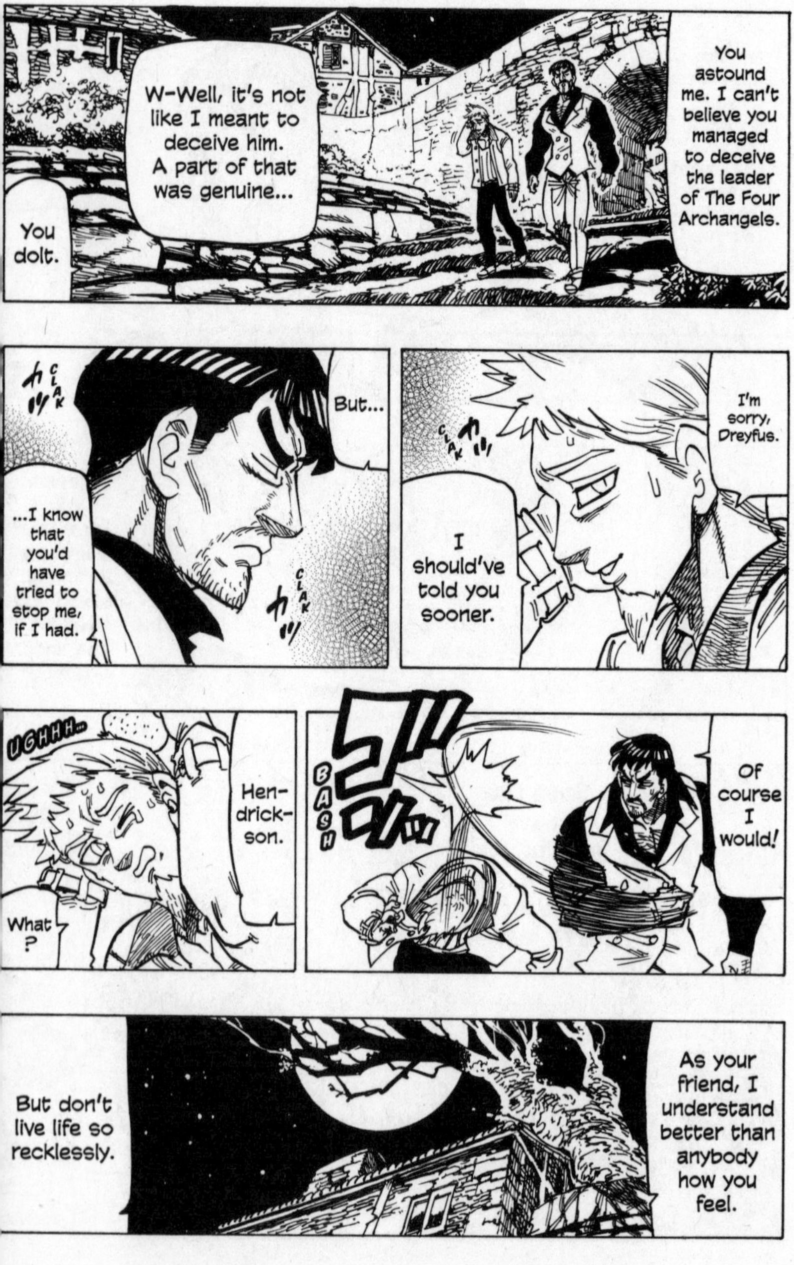
You astound me. I can't believe you managed to deceive the leader of The Four Archangels.
W-Well, it's not like I meant to deceive him. A part of that was genuine...
You dolt.
I'm sorry, Dreyfus.
CLAK
I should've told you sooner.
But...
CLAK
...I know that you'd have tried to stop me, if I had.
CLAK
Of course I would!
BASH
Hen-drick-son.
UGHHH...
What?
As your friend, I understand better than anybody how you feel.
But don't live life so recklessly.

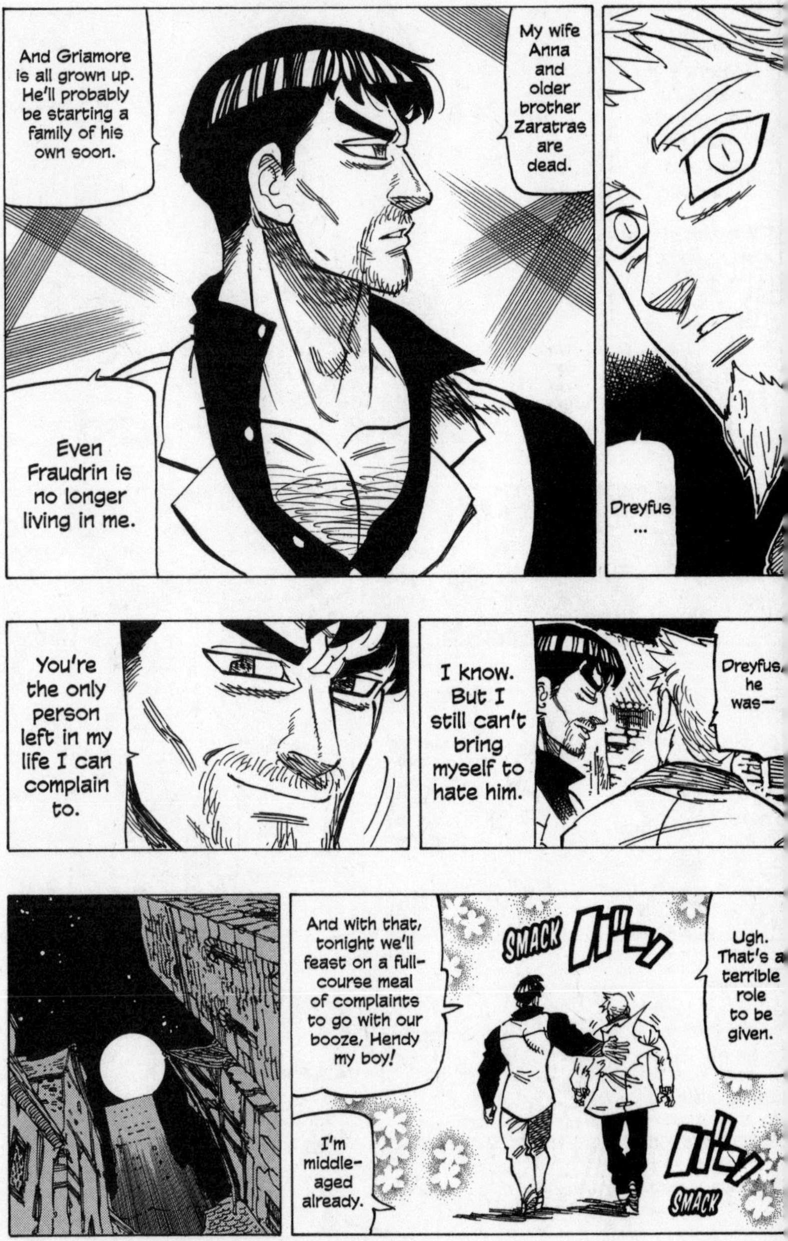
Dreyfus ...
My wife Anna and older brother Zaratras are dead.
And Griamore is all grown up. He'll probably be starting a family of his own soon.
Even Fraudrin is no longer living in me.
Dreyfus, he was—
I know. But I still can't bring myself to hate him.
You're the only person left in my life I can complain to.
Ugh. That's a terrible role to be given.
SMACK
And with that, tonight we'll feast on a full-course meal of complaints to go with our booze, Hendy my boy!
SMACK
I'm middle-aged already.

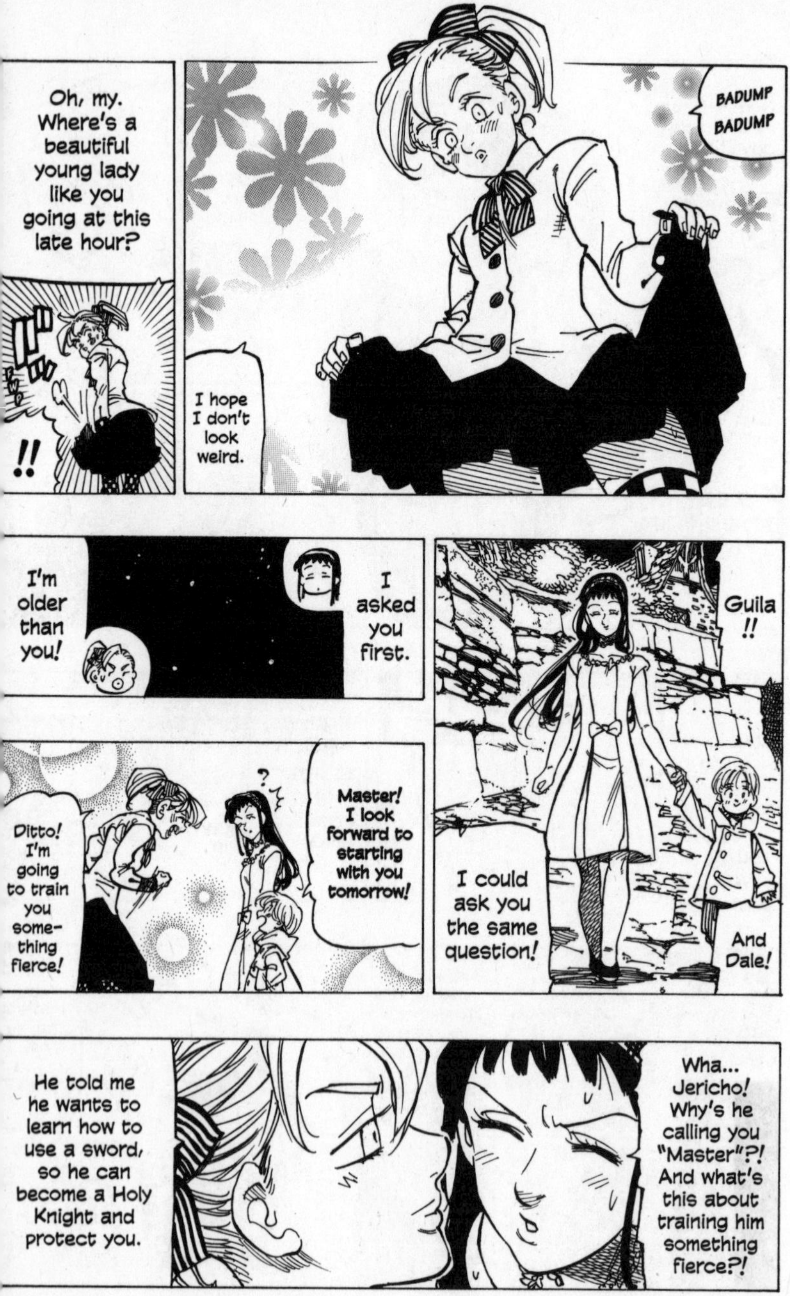
BADUMP BADUMP
I hope I don't look weird.
Oh, my. Where's a beautiful young lady like you going at this late hour?
!!
Guila !!
And Dale!
I could ask you the same question!
I asked you first.
I'm older than you!
Master! I look forward to starting with you tomorrow!
?
Ditto! I'm going to train you some-thing fierce!
Wha... Jericho! Why's he calling you "Master"?! And what's this about training him something fierce?!
He told me he wants to learn how to use a sword, so he can become a Holy Knight and protect you.

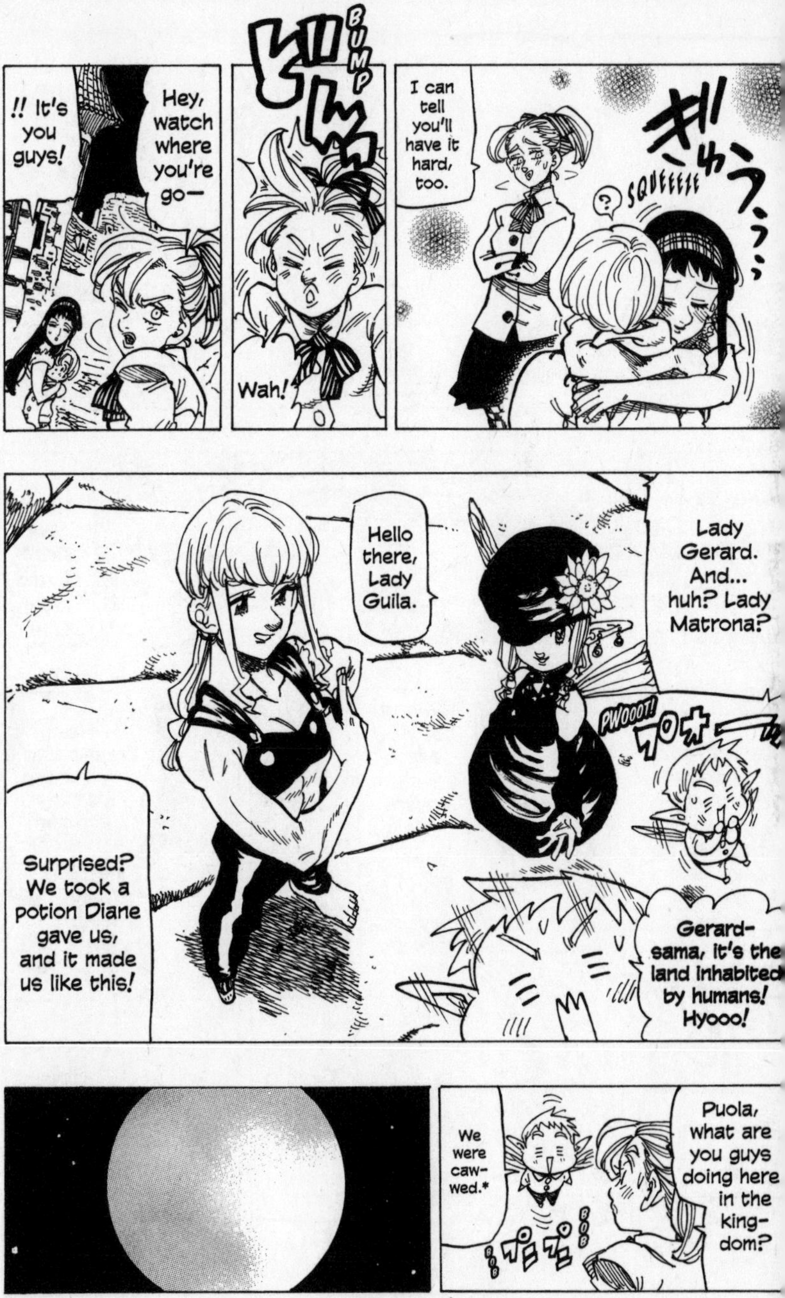
SQUEEEEE
I can tell you'll have it hard, too.
BUMP
Wah!
Hey, watch where you're go—
!! It's you guys!
Lady Gerard. And... huh? Lady Matrona?
Hello there, Lady Guila.
PWOOOT!
Gerard-sama, it's the land inhabited by humans! Hyooo!
Surprised? We took a potion Diane gave us, and it made us like this!
Puola, what are you guys doing here in the kingdom?
We were caw-wed.*
BOB
BOB

*CALLED.

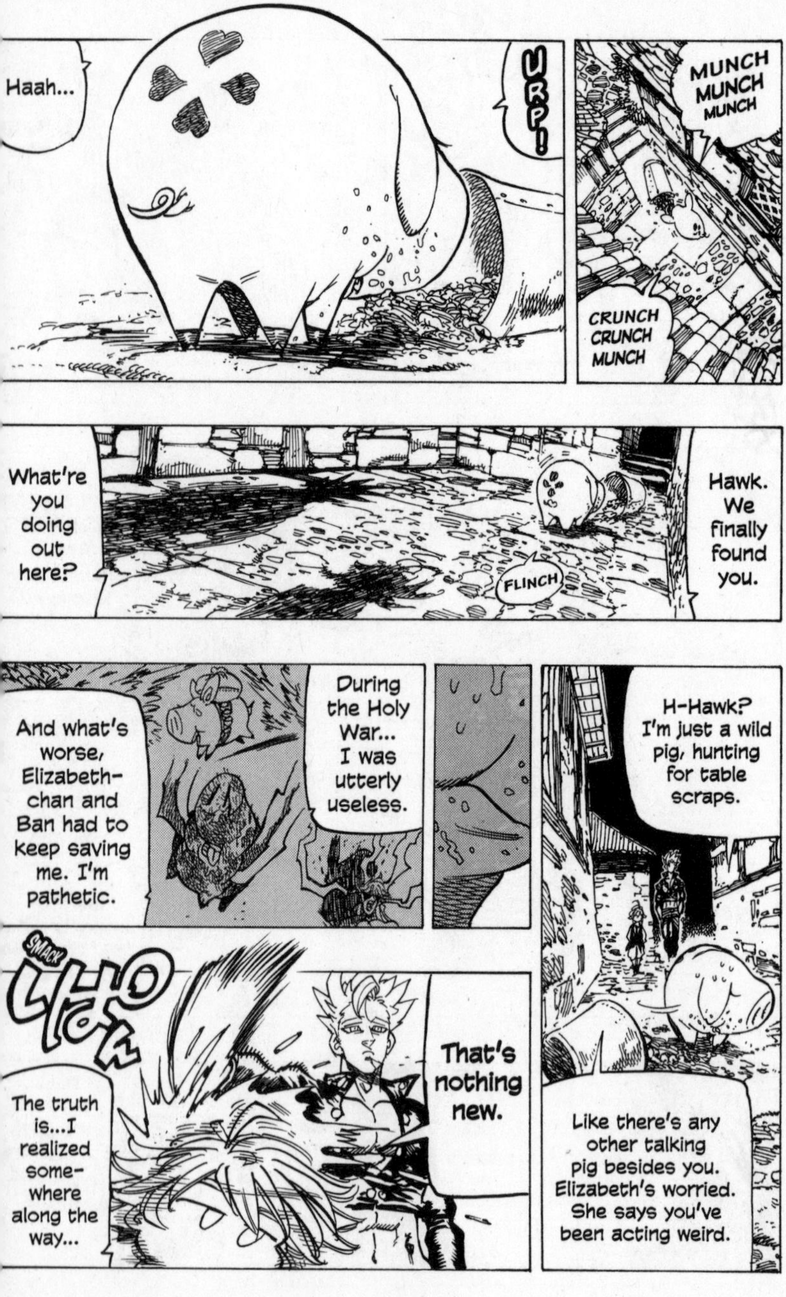
MUNCH MUNCH MUNCH
CRUNCH CRUNCH MUNCH
URP!
Haah...
Hawk. We finally found you.
FLINCH
What're you doing out here?
H-Hawk? I'm just a wild pig, hunting for table scraps.
Like there's any other talking pig besides you. Elizabeth's worried. She says you've been acting weird.
During the Holy War... I was utterly useless.
And what's worse, Elizabeth-chan and Ban had to keep saving me. I'm pathetic.
That's nothing new.
SMACK
The truth is...I realized some-where along the way...

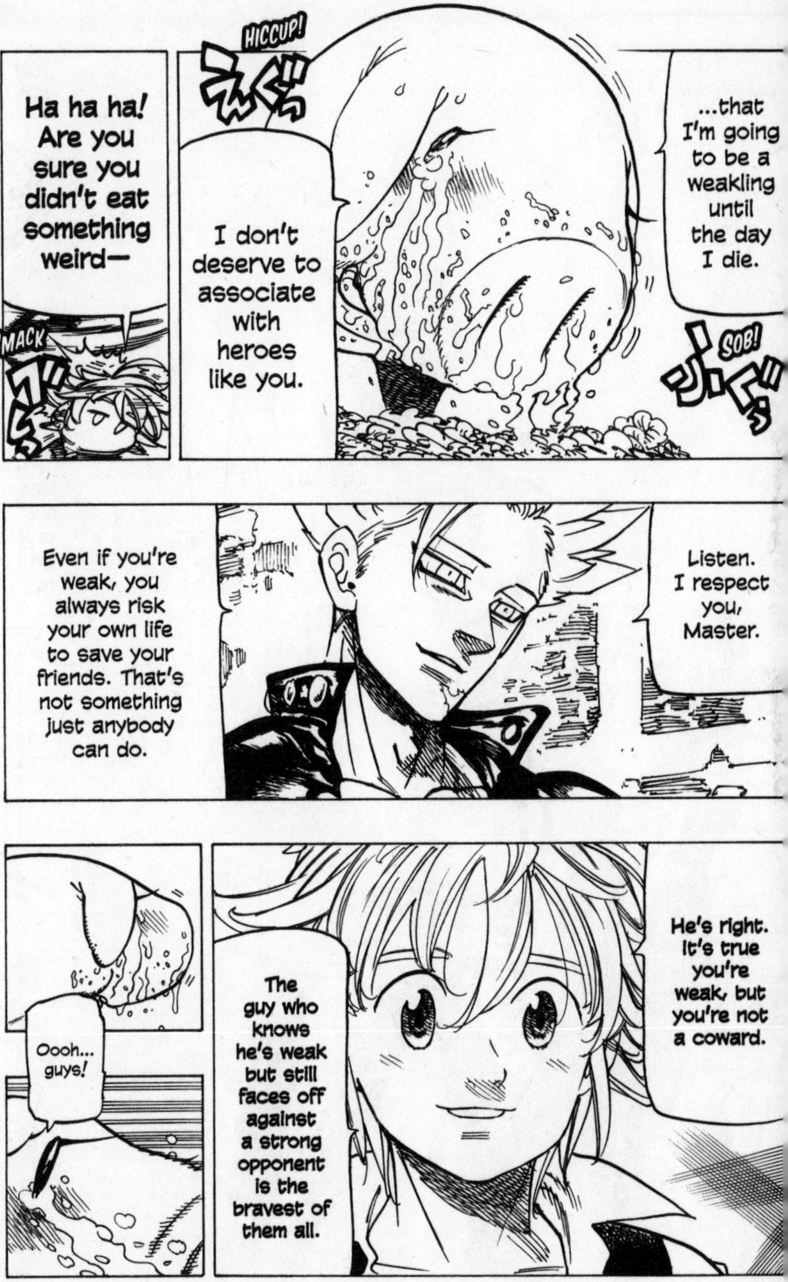
...that I'm going to be a weakling until the day I die.
SOB!
HICCUP!
I don't deserve to associate with heroes like you.
Ha ha ha! Are you sure you didn't eat something weird—
SMACK
Listen. I respect you, Master.
Even if you're weak, you always risk your own life to save your friends. That's not something just anybody can do.
He's right. It's true you're weak, but you're not a coward.
The guy who knows he's weak but still faces off against a strong opponent is the bravest of them all.
Oooh... guys!

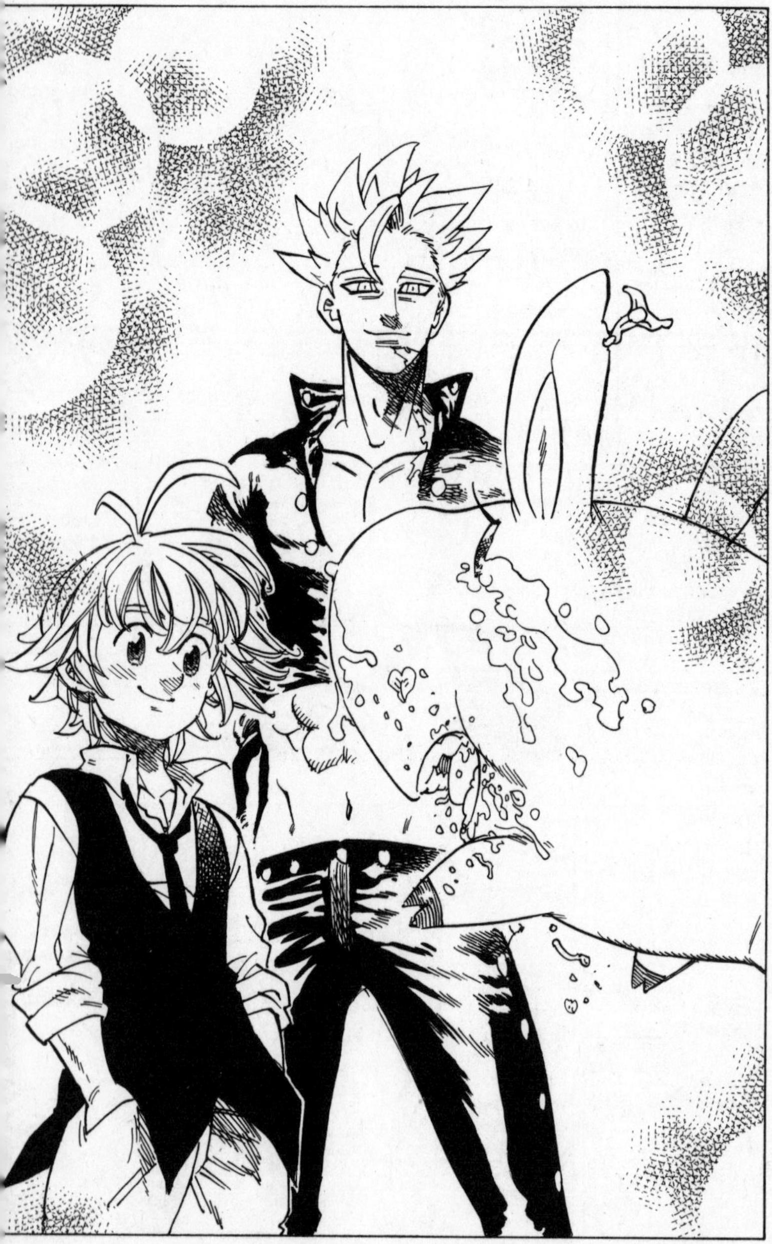

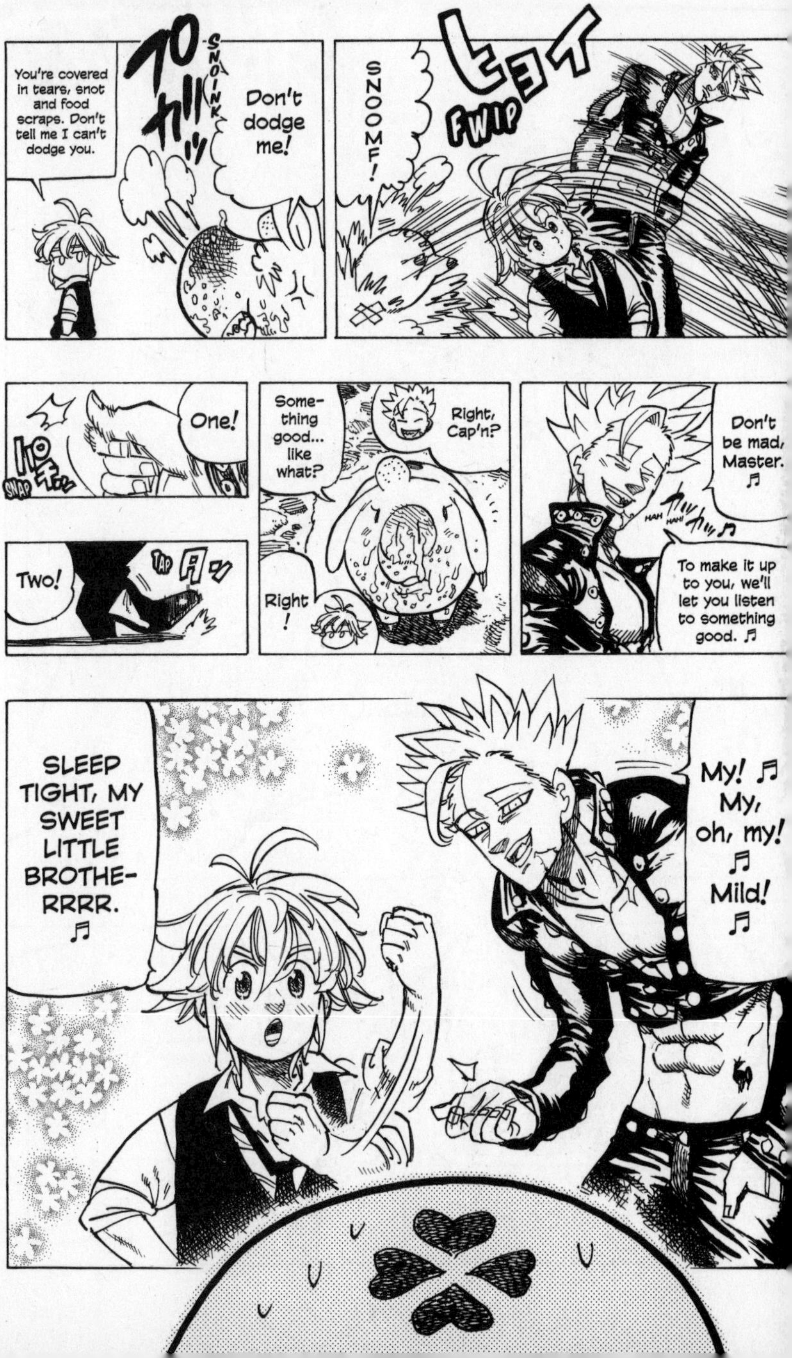
FWIP
SNOOMF!
SNOINK
Don't dodge me!
You're covered in tears, snot and food scraps. Don't tell me I can't dodge you.
Don't be mad, Master. ♫
HAH HAH
To make it up to you, we'll let you listen to something good. ♫
Right, Cap'n?
Something good... like what?
Right!
One!
SNAP
Two!
TAP
My! ♫ My, oh, my! ♫ Mild! ♫
SLEEP TIGHT, MY SWEET LITTLE BROTHE-RRRR. ♫

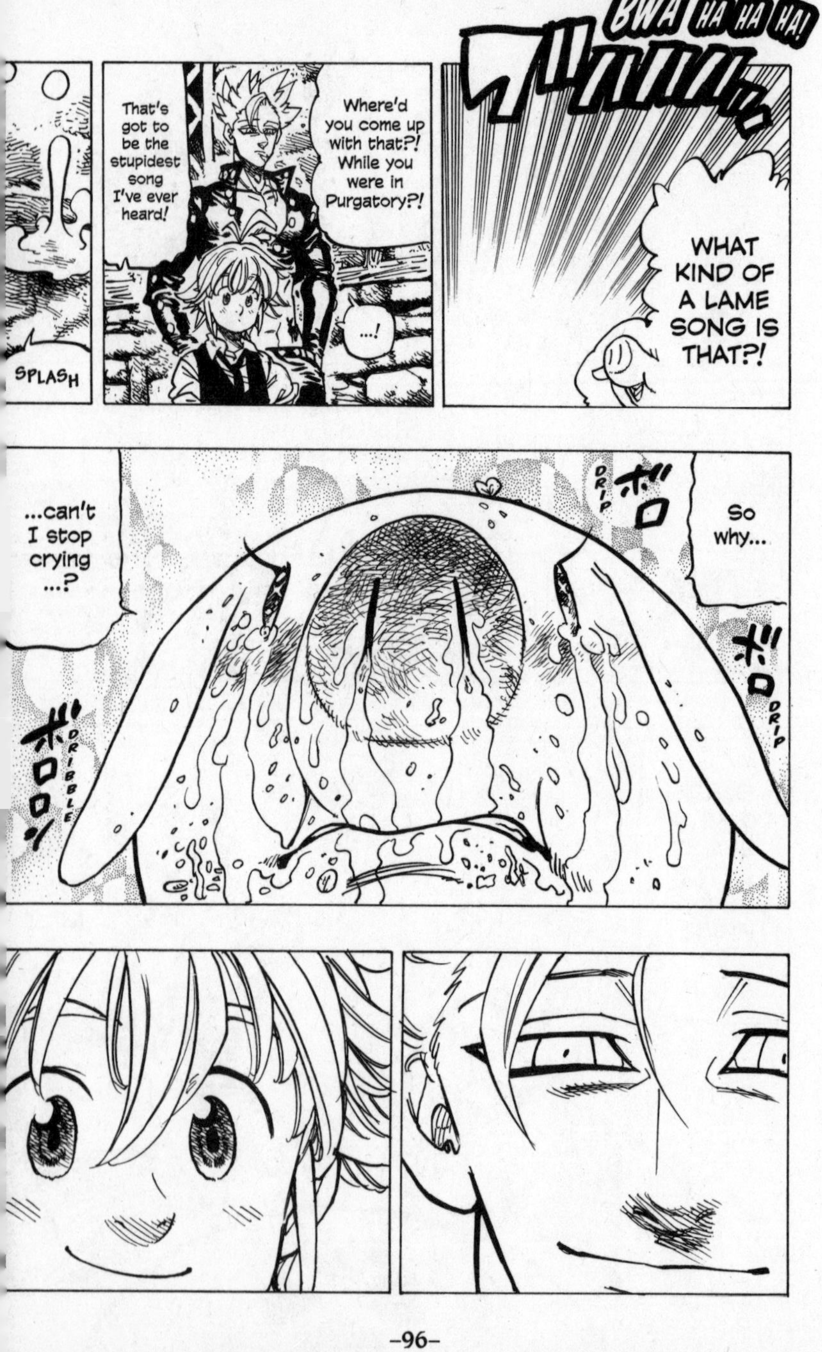
BWA HA HA HA!
WHAT KIND OF A LAME SONG IS THAT?!
Where'd you come up with that?! While you were in Purgatory?!
That's got to be the stupidest song I've ever heard!
...!
SPLASH
DRIP
So why...
DRIP
...can't I stop crying ...?
DRIBBLE

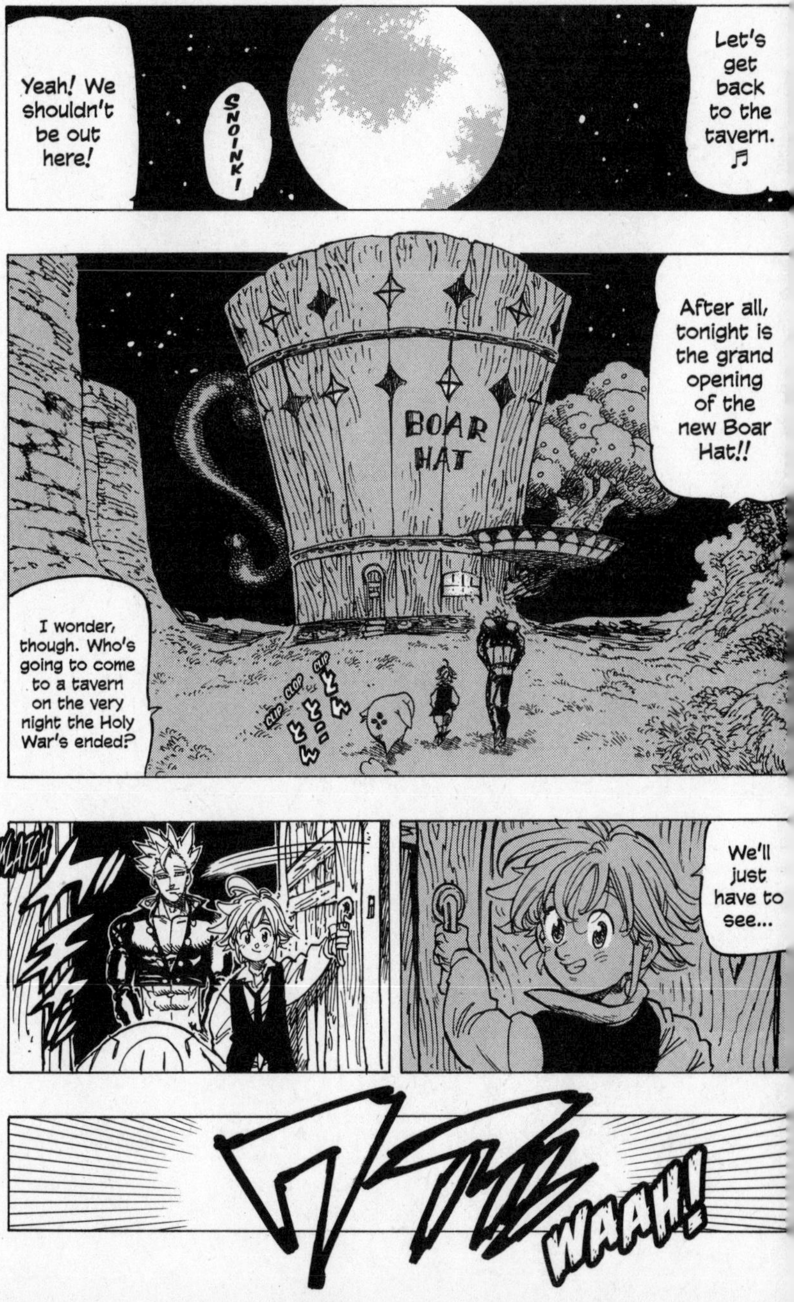
Let's get back to the tavern. ♬
SNOINK!
Yeah! We shouldn't be out here!
After all, tonight is the grand opening of the new Boar Hat!!
BOAR HAT
I wonder, though. Who's going to come to a tavern on the very night the Holy War's ended?
CLIP CLOP CLIP
We'll just have to see...
KLATCH
WAAH!

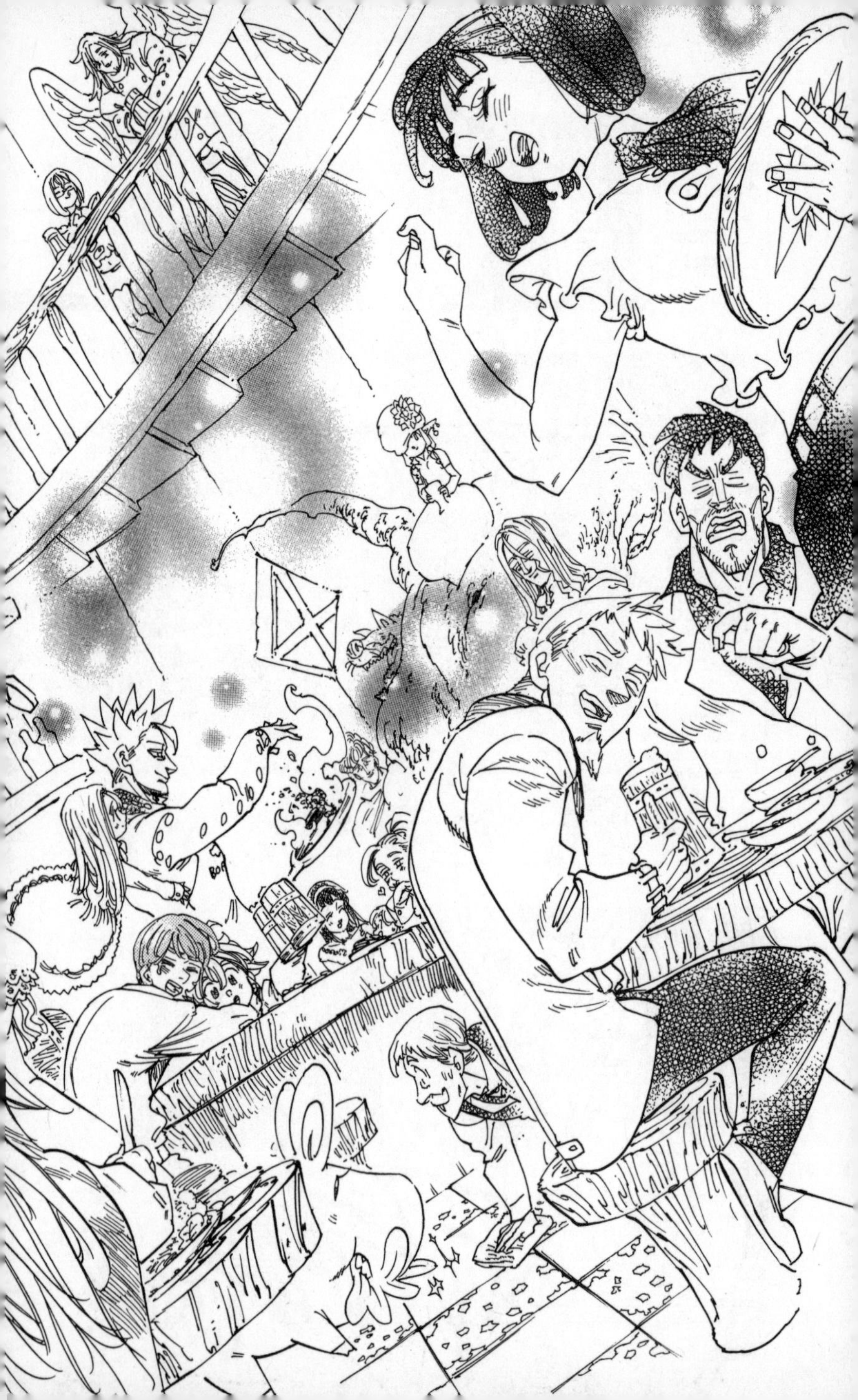

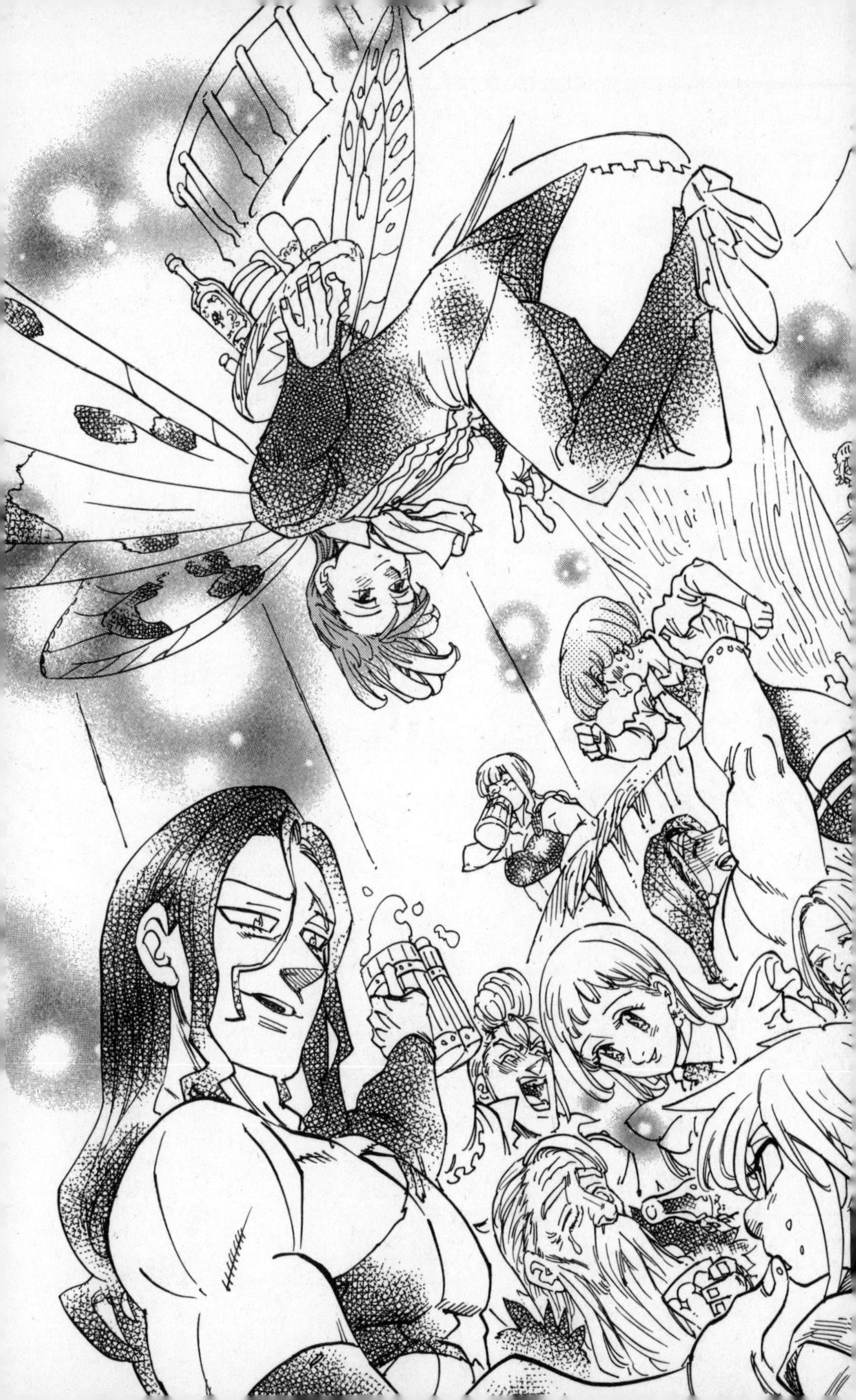

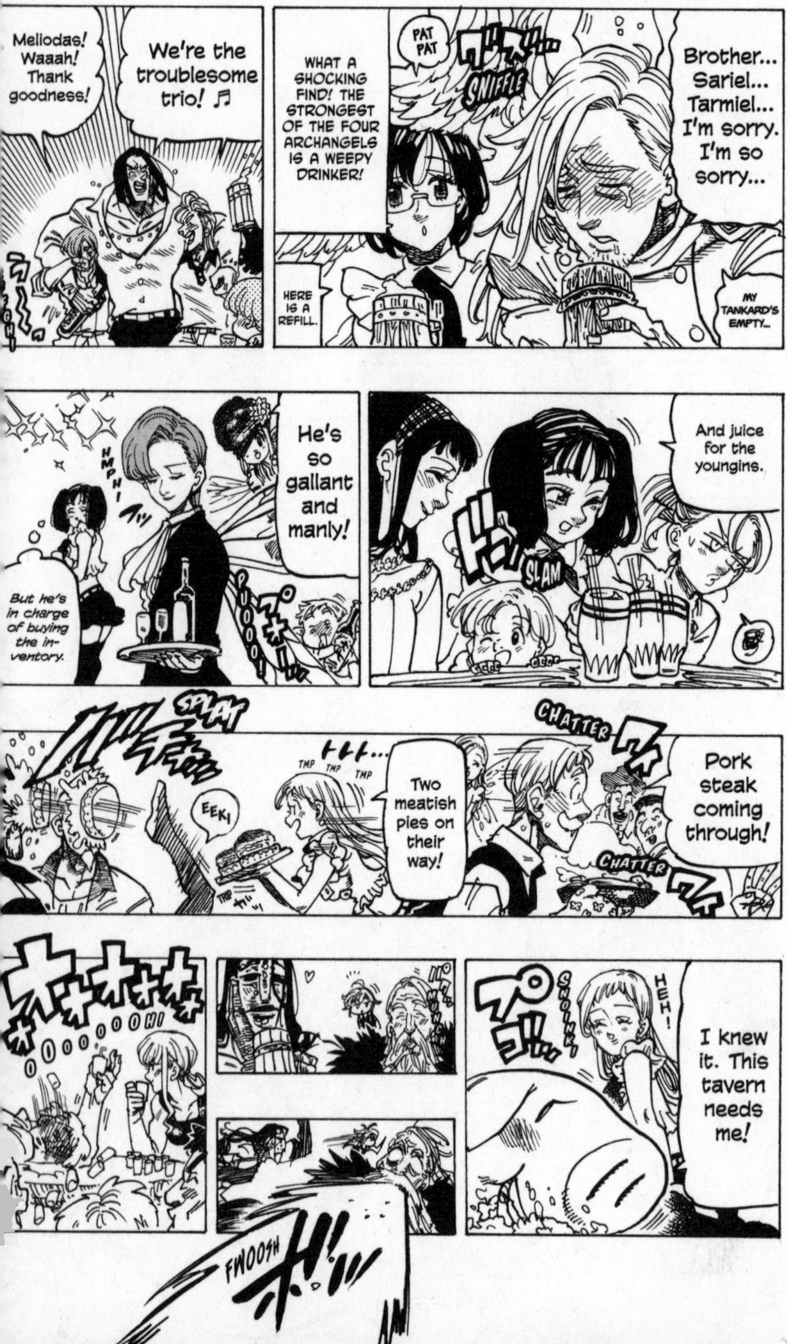
Brother... Sariel... Tarmiel... I'm sorry. I'm so sorry...
SNIFFLE
PAT PAT
WHAT A SHOCKING FIND! THE STRONGEST OF THE FOUR ARCHANGELS IS A WEEPY DRINKER!
MY TANKARD'S EMPTY...
HERE IS A REFILL.
We're the troublesome trio! ♫
Meliodas! Waaah! Thank goodness!
And juice for the youngins.
SLAM
He's so gallant and manly!
HMPH!
But he's in charge of buying the inventory.
Pork steak coming through!
CHATTER
CHATTER
Two meatish pies on their way!
TMP TMP TMP
EEK!
TRIP
SPLAT
I knew it. This tavern needs me!
HEH!
SNOINK!
FWOOSH
OOOOOOOOOH!

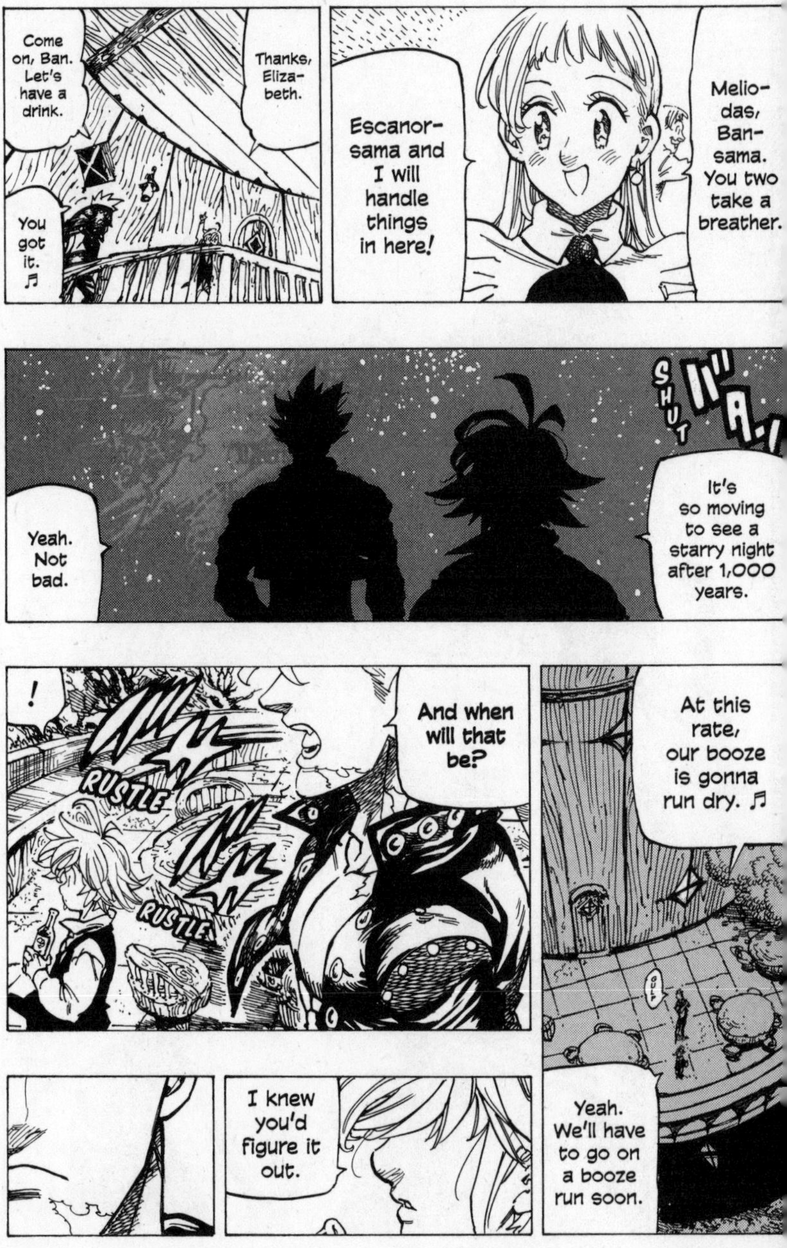
Melio-
das,
Ban-
sama.
You two
take a
breather.
Escanor-
sama and
I will
handle
things
in here!
Thanks,
Eliza-
beth.
Come
on, Ban.
Let's
have a
drink.
You
got
it.
♪
SHUT
It's
so moving
to see a
starry night
after 1,000
years.
Yeah.
Not
bad.
At this
rate,
our booze
is gonna
run dry. ♪
Yeah.
We'll have
to go on
a booze
run soon.
And when
will that
be?
!
RUSTLE
RUSTLE
I knew
you'd
figure it
out.

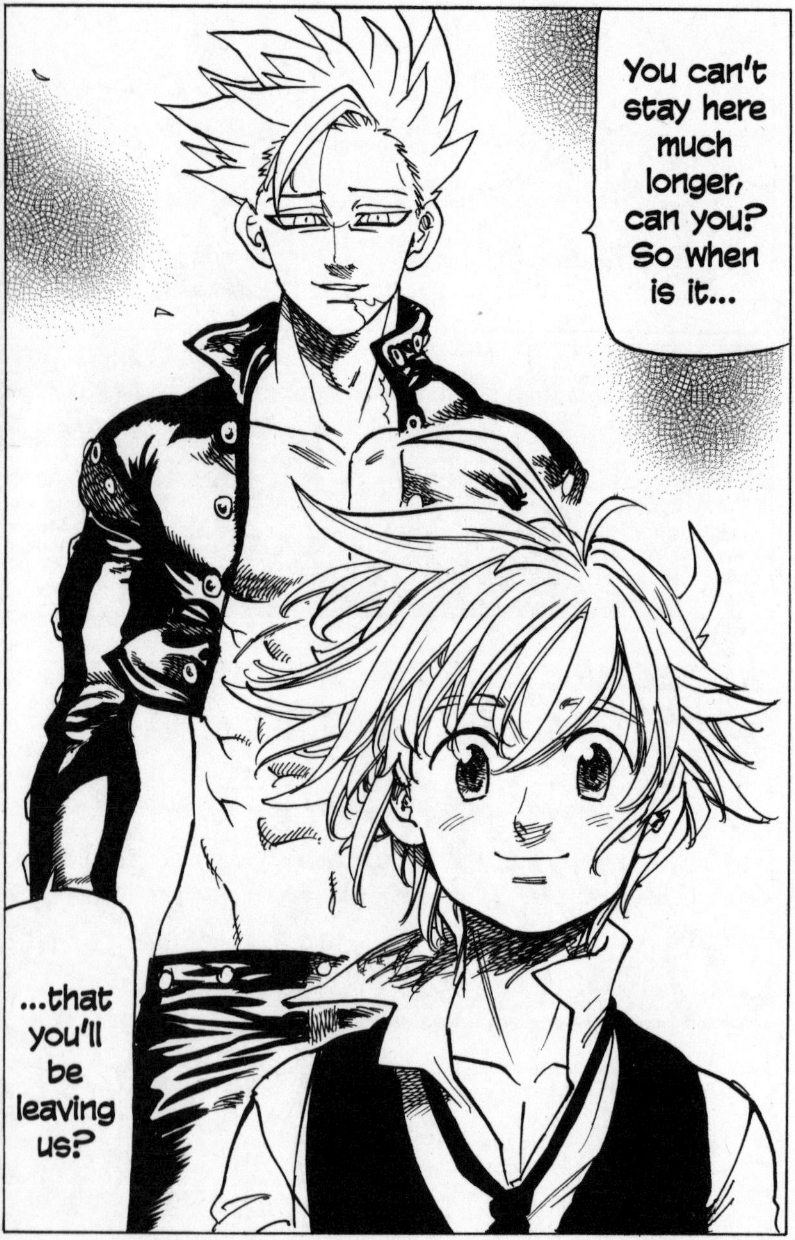
You can't stay here much longer, can you? So when is it...
...that you'll be leaving us?

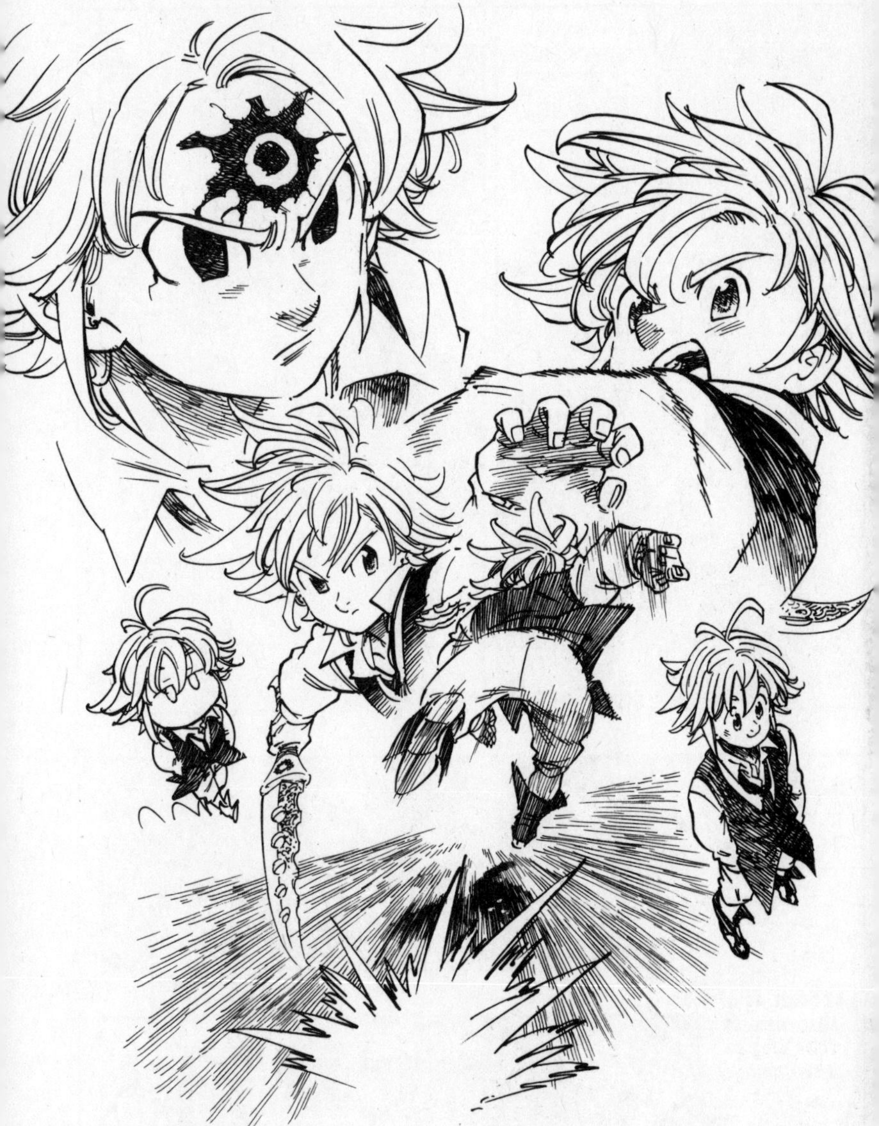

Chapter 308 - Meliodas Disappears

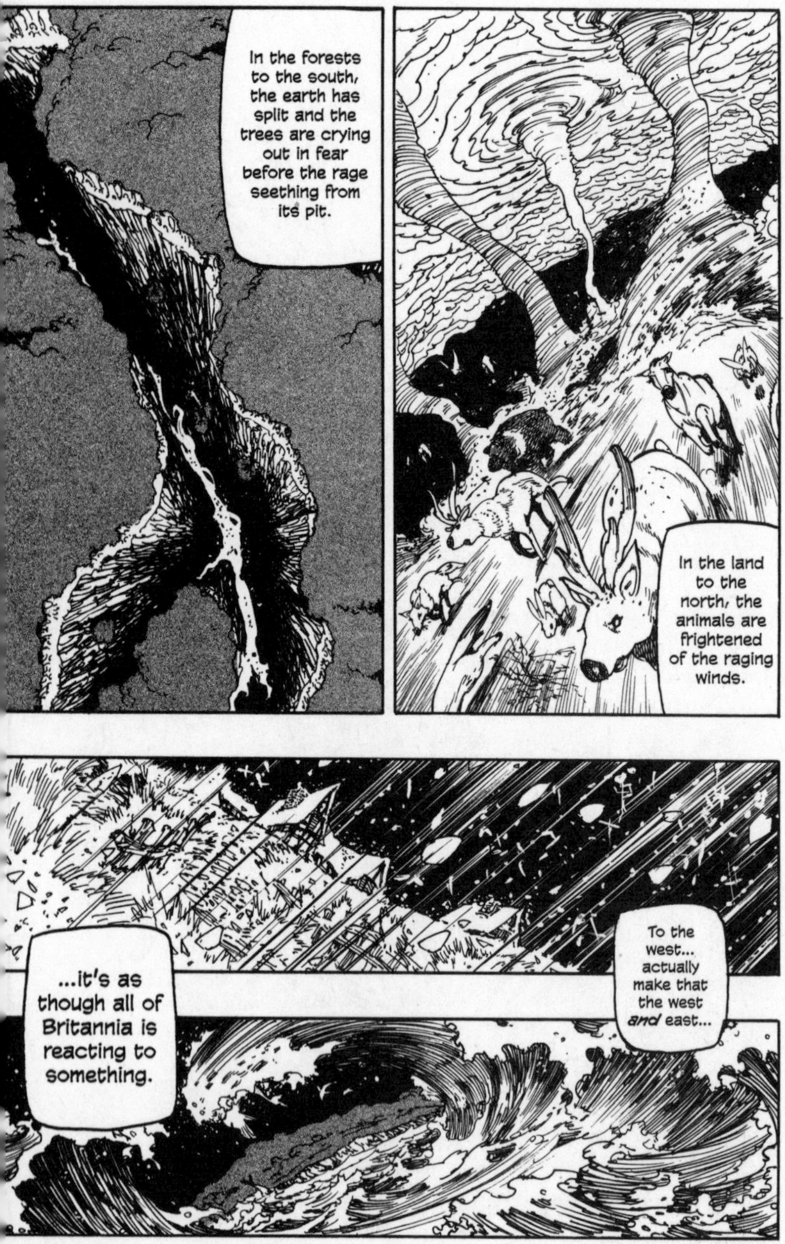
In the land to the north, the animals are frightened of the raging winds.
In the forests to the south, the earth has split and the trees are crying out in fear before the rage seething from its pit.
To the west... actually make that the west *and* east...
...it's as though all of Britannia is reacting to something.

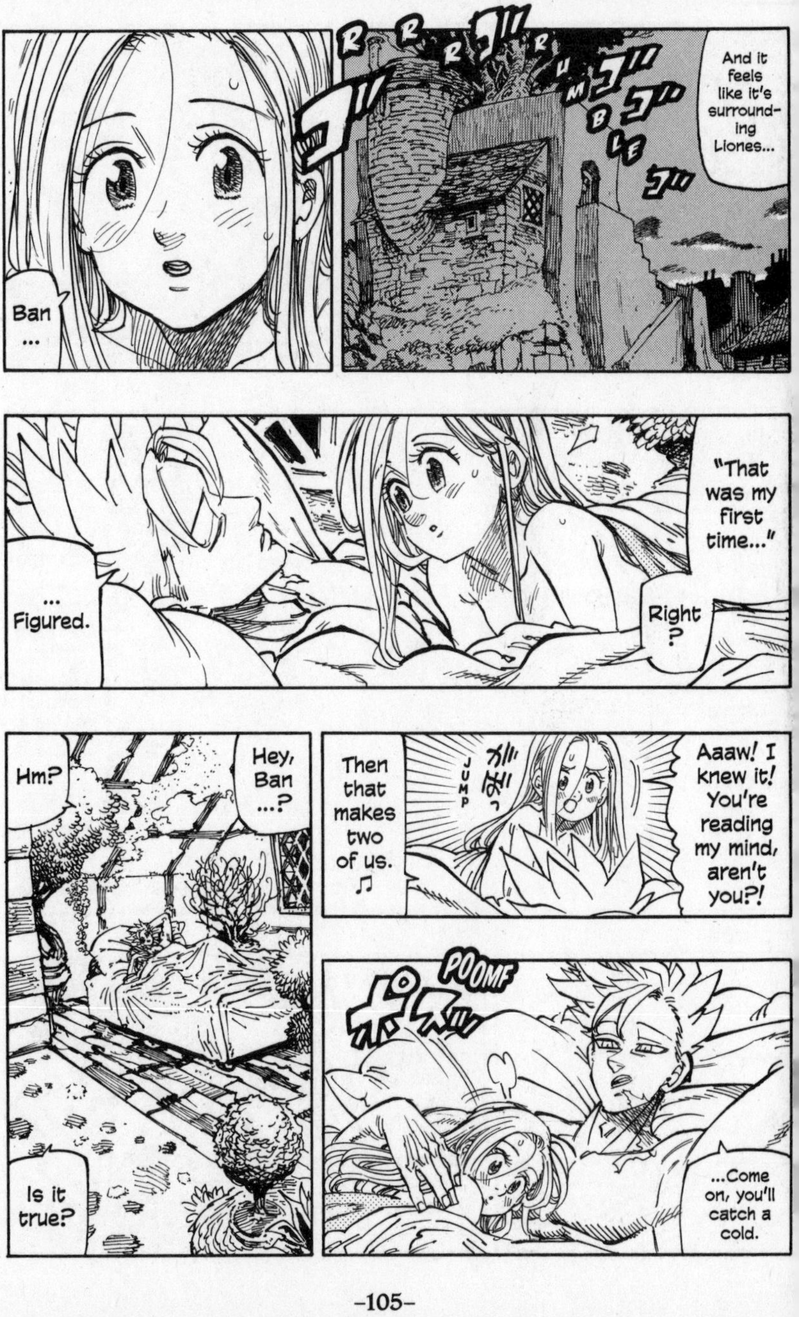
RRRRUMBLE
And it feels like it's surround-ing Liones...
Ban ...
"That was my first time..."
Right?
... Figured.
Aaaw! I knew it! You're reading my mind, aren't you?!
JUMP
Then that makes two of us. ♫
POOMF
...Come on, you'll catch a cold.
Hey, Ban ...?
Hm?
Is it true?

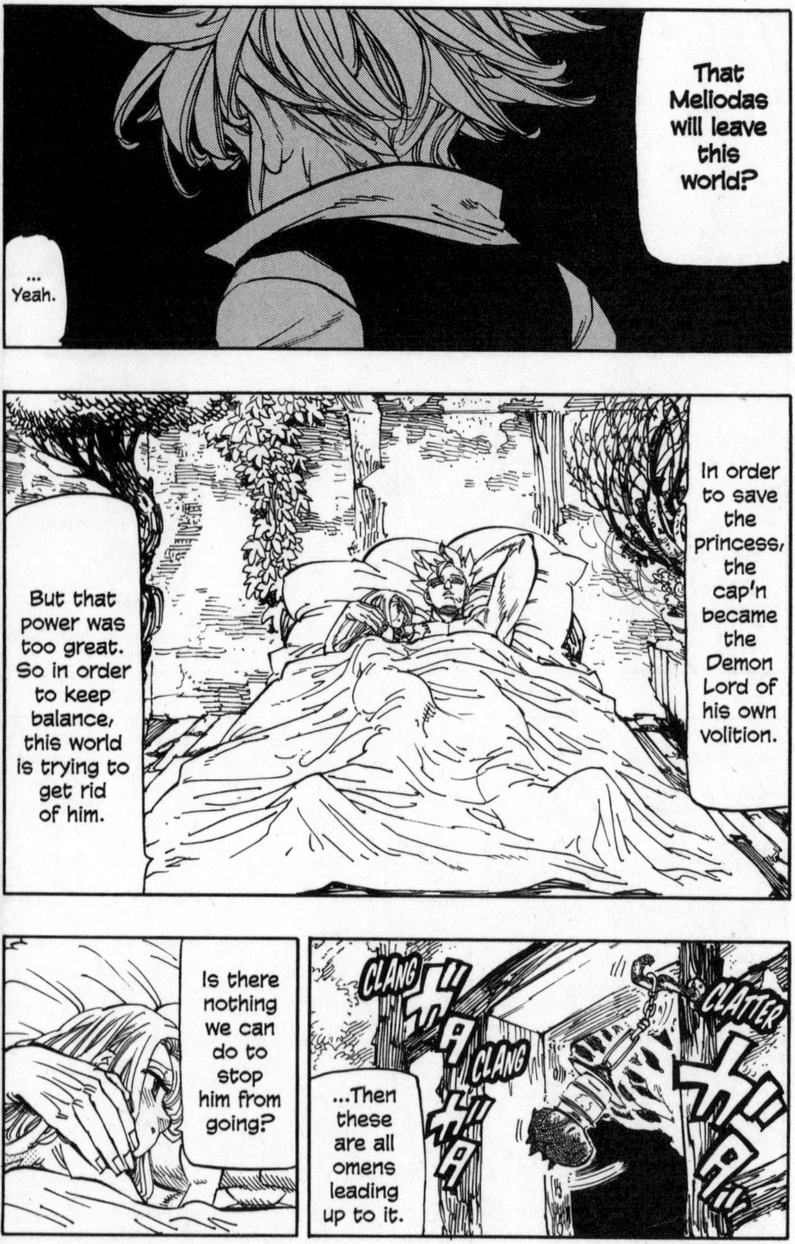
That Meliodas will leave this world?
...Yeah.
In order to save the princess, the cap'n became the Demon Lord of his own volition.
But that power was too great. So in order to keep balance, this world is trying to get rid of him.
CLATTER
CLANG
CLANG
...Then these are all omens leading up to it.
Is there nothing we can do to stop him from going?

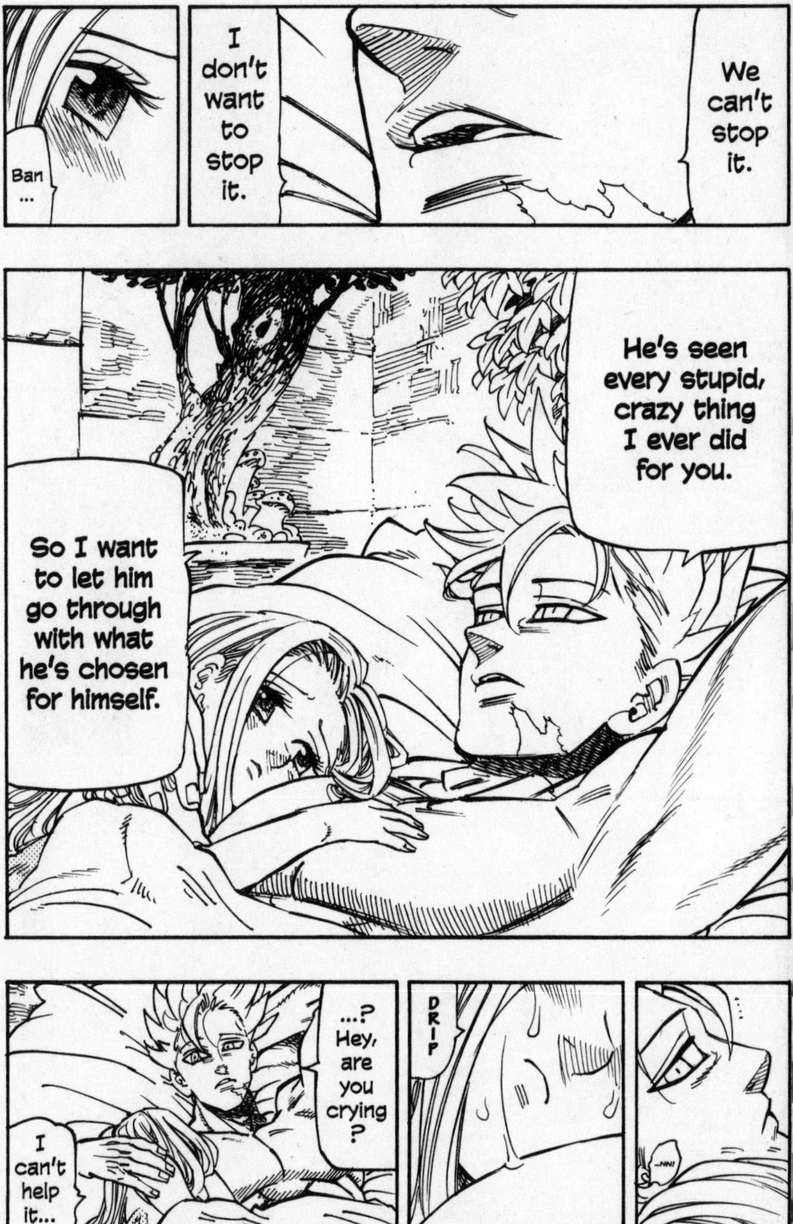
We can't stop it.
I don't want to stop it.
Ban ...
He's seen every stupid, crazy thing I ever did for you.
So I want to let him go through with what he's chosen for himself.
...
...NN!
DRIP
...? Hey, are you crying?
I can't help it...

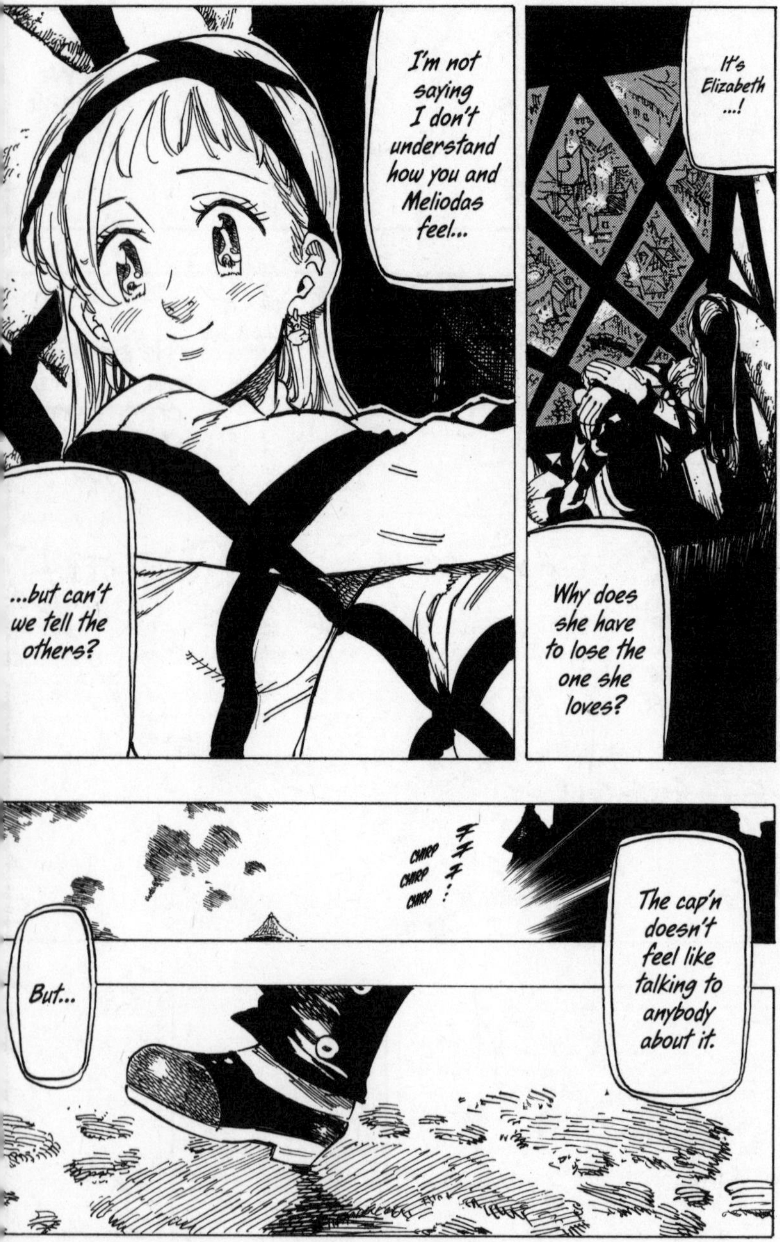
It's Elizabeth ...!
Why does she have to lose the one she loves?
I'm not saying I don't understand how you and Meliodas feel...
...but can't we tell the others?
The cap'n doesn't feel like talking to anybody about it.
チチチ…
CHIRP CHIRP CHIRP
But...

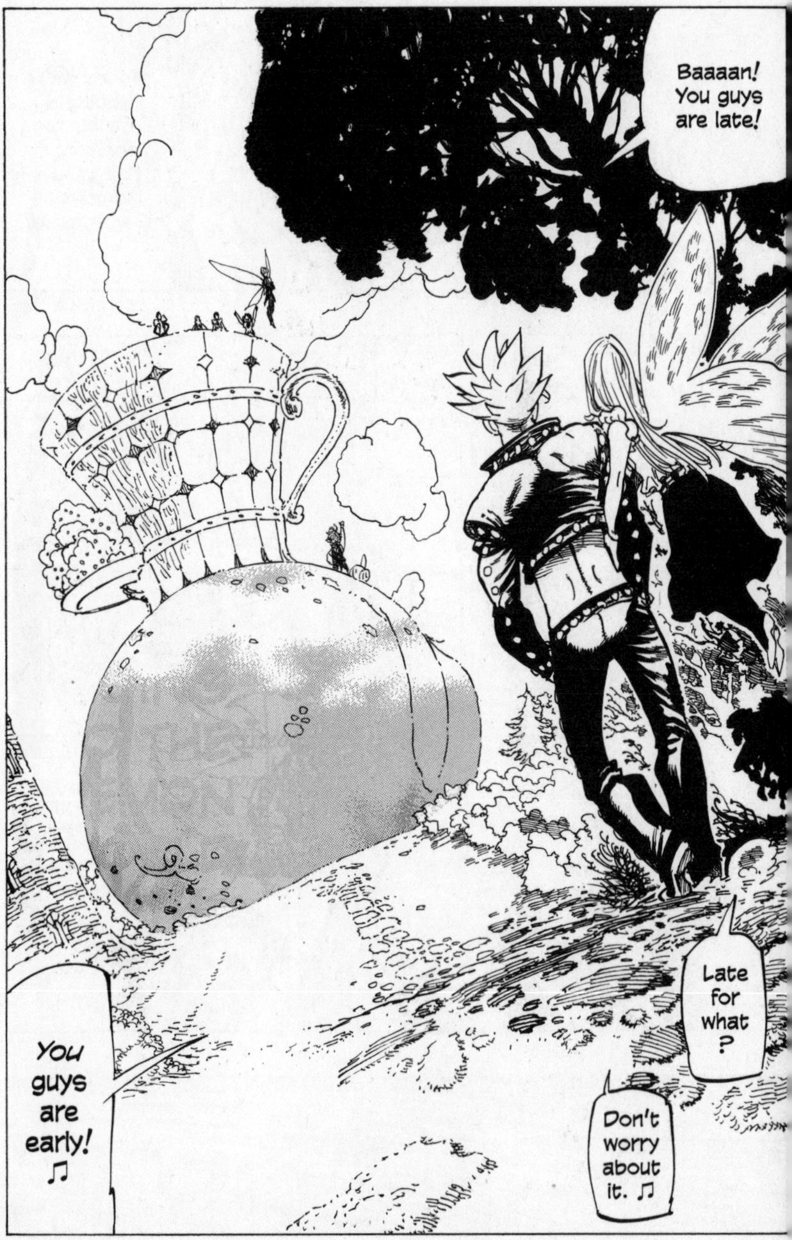
Baaaan! You guys are late!
Late for what?
Don't worry about it. ♫
You guys are early! ♫

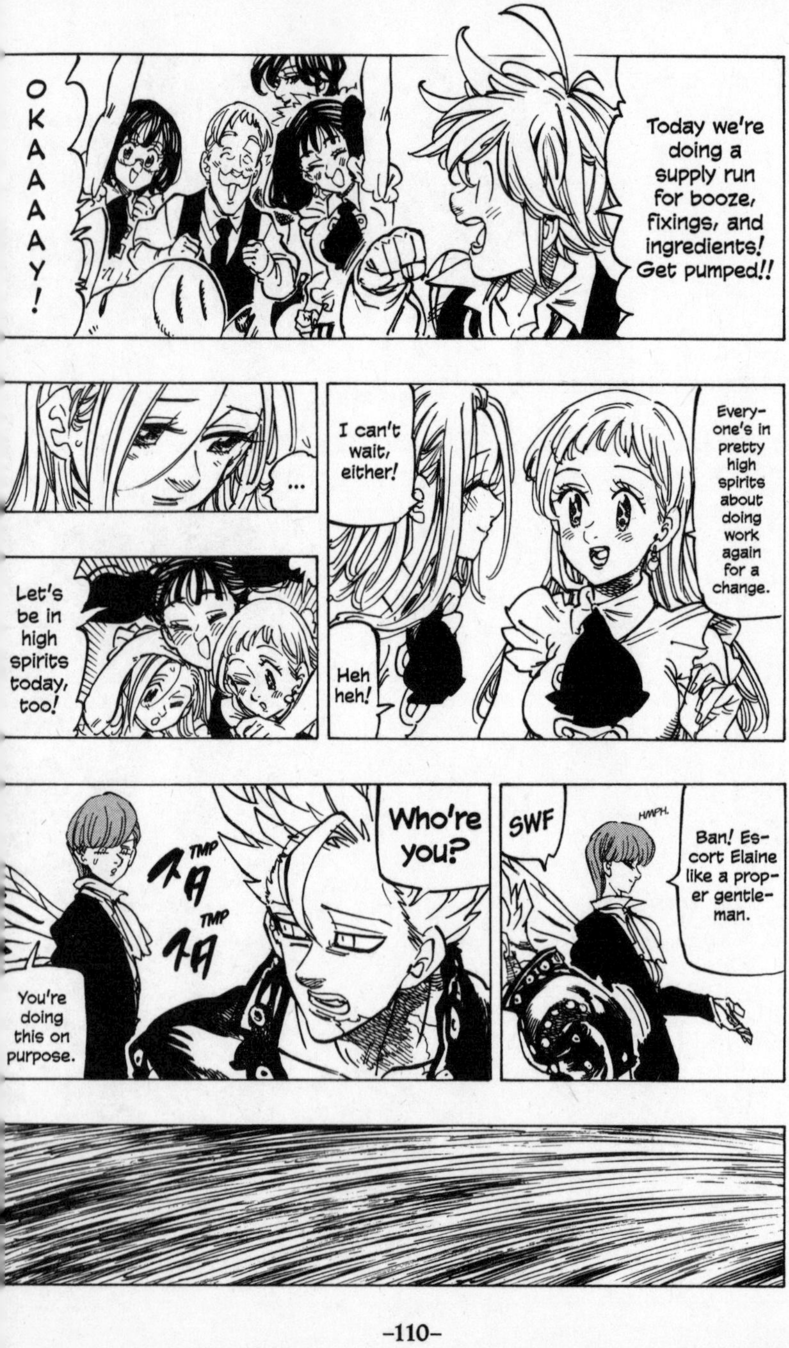
Today we're doing a supply run for booze, fixings, and ingredients! Get pumped!!
OKAAAAY!
Every-one's in pretty high spirits about doing work again for a change.
I can't wait, either!
Heh heh!
...
Let's be in high spirits today, too!
HMPH.
Ban! Es-cort Elaine like a prop-er gentle-man.
SWF
Who're you?
TMP
TMP
You're doing this on purpose.

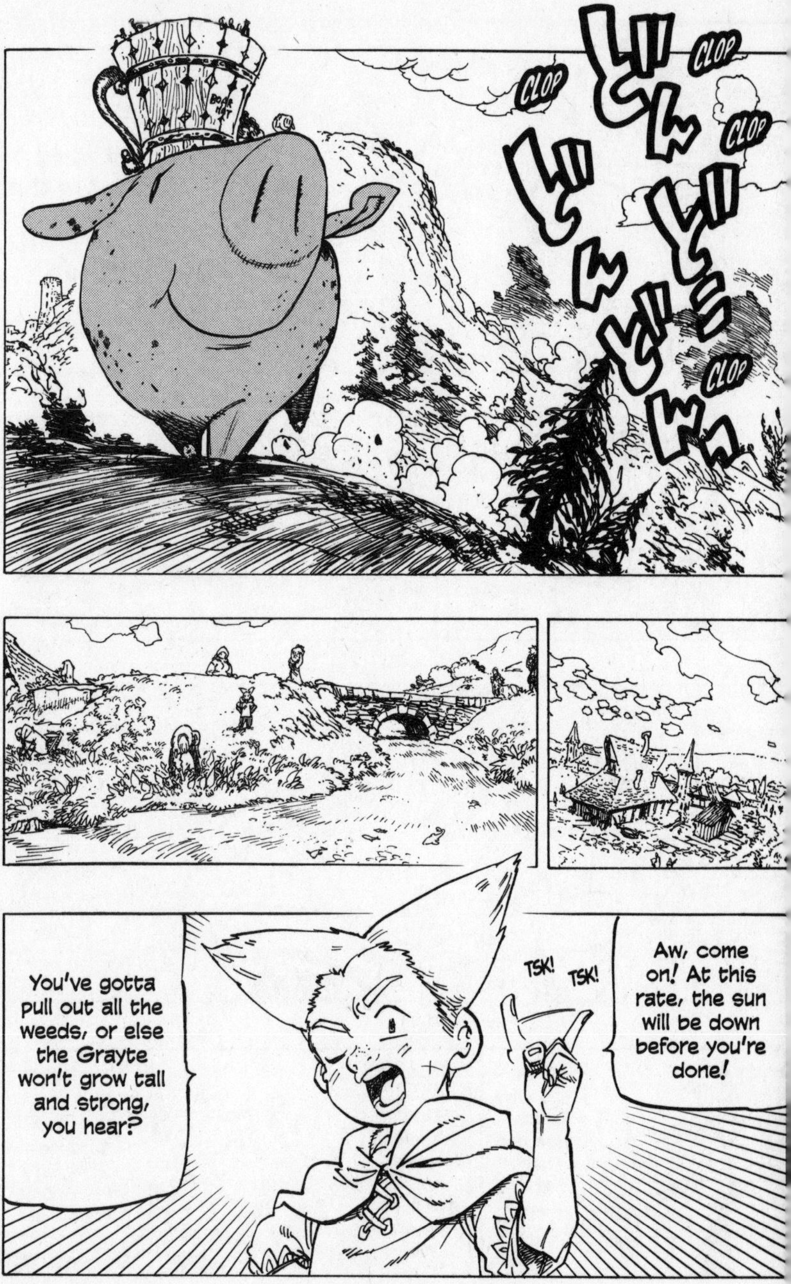
CLOP
CLOP
CLOP
CLOP
Aw, come on! At this rate, the sun will be down before you're done!
TSK!
TSK!
You've gotta pull out all the weeds, or else the Grayte won't grow tall and strong, you hear?

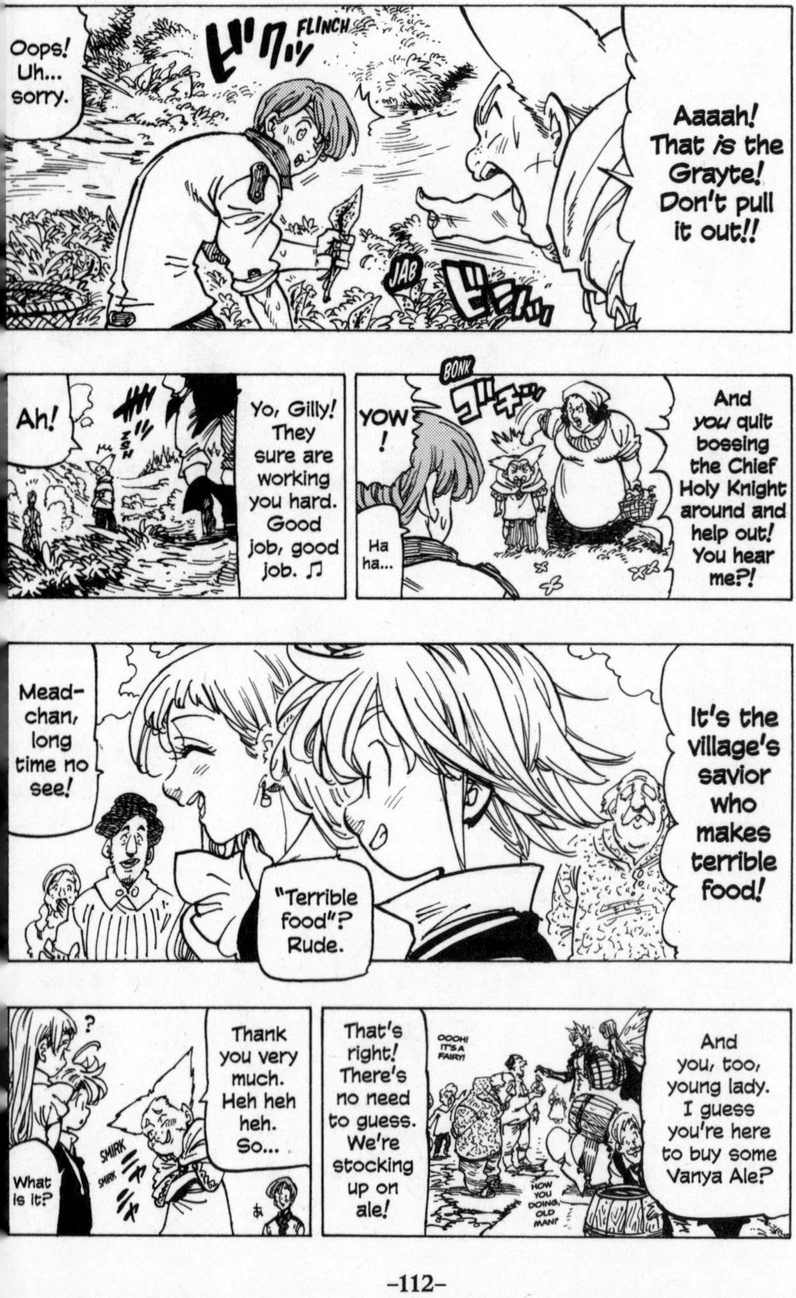
Aaaah! That *is* the Grayte! Don't pull it out!!
FLINCH
JAB
Oops! Uh... sorry.
And *you* quit bossing the Chief Holy Knight around and help out! You hear me?!
BONK
YOW!
Ha ha...
Yo, Gilly! They sure are working you hard. Good job, good job. ♫
ZSH
Ah!
It's the village's savior who makes terrible food!
Mead-chan, long time no see!
"Terrible food"? Rude.
And you, too, young lady. I guess you're here to buy some Vanya Ale?
OOOH! IT'S A FAIRY!
HOW YOU DOING, OLD MAN?
That's right! There's no need to guess. We're stocking up on ale!
Thank you very much. Heh heh heh. So...
?
SMIRK
SMIRK
What is it?

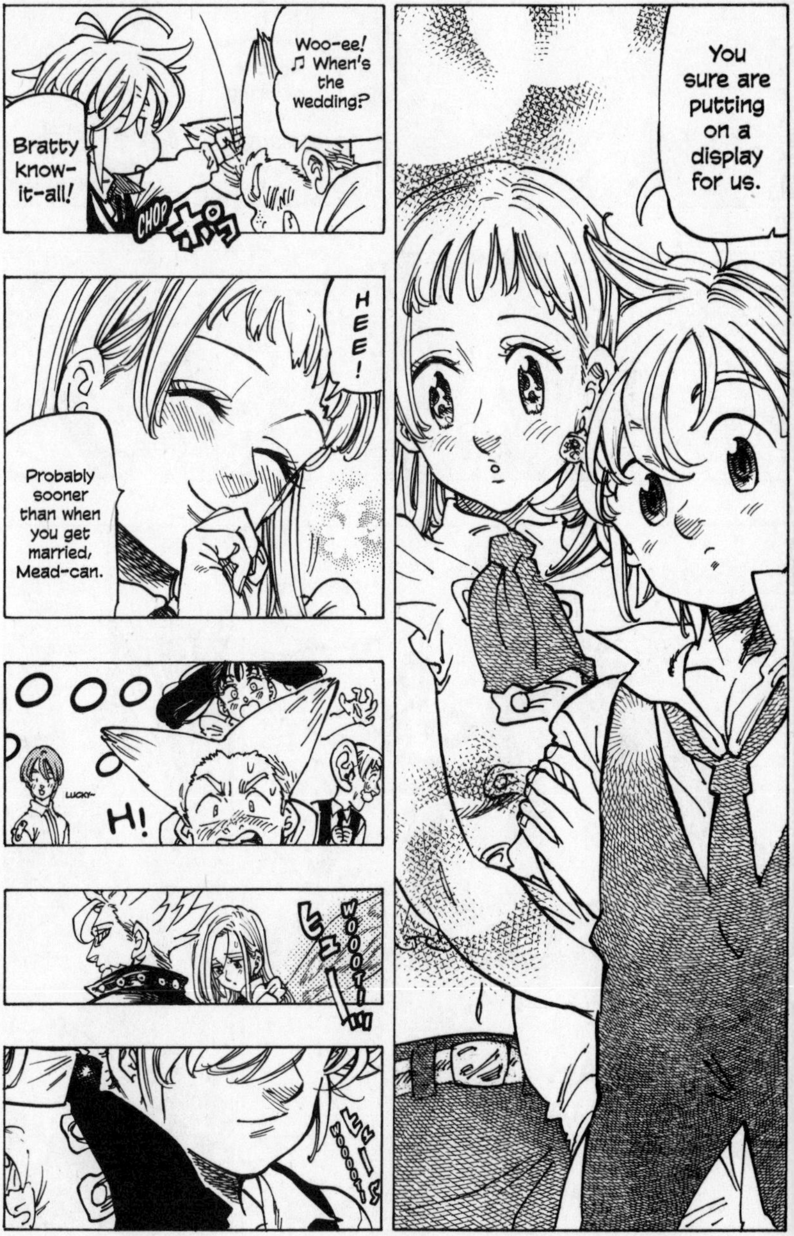
You sure are putting on a display for us.
Woo-ee! ♫ When's the wedding?
Bratty know-it-all!
CHOP
HEE!
Probably sooner than when you get married, Mead-can.
OOOOH!
LUCKY~
WOOOOT!!!
WOOOOT!

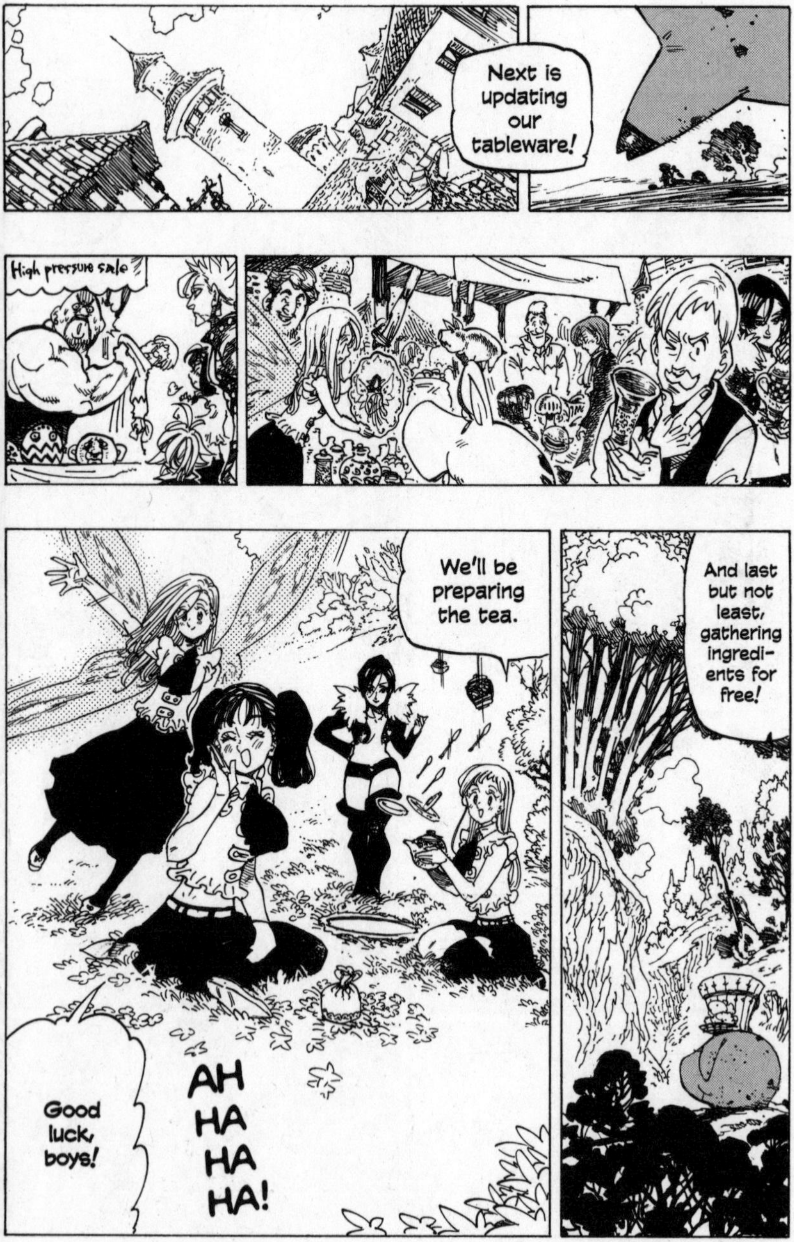
Next is updating our tableware!
High pressure sale
And last but not least, gathering ingredi-ents for free!
We'll be preparing the tea.
AH HA HA HA!
Good luck, boys!

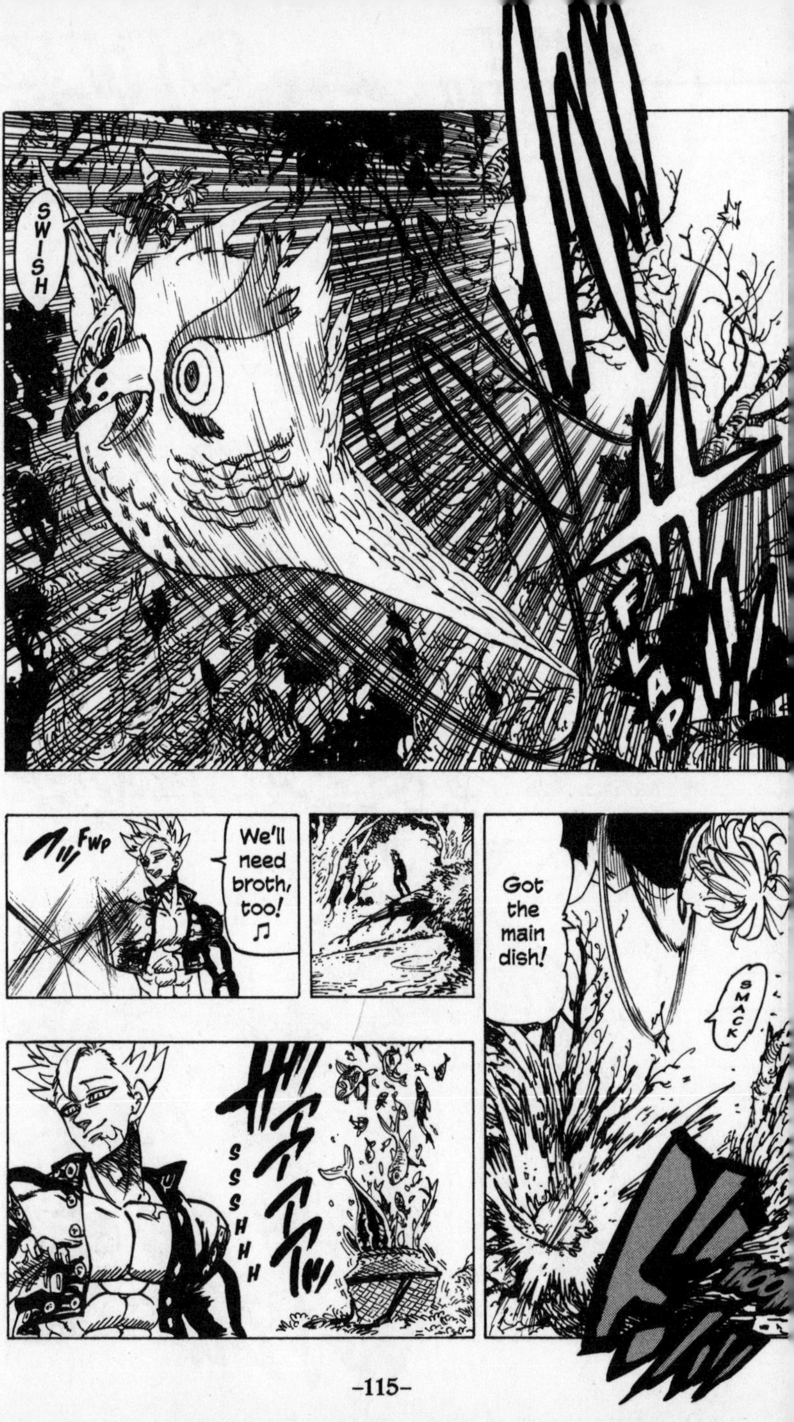
FLAP
SWISH
Got the main dish!
SMACK
FWP
We'll need broth, too! ♫
SSSHHH

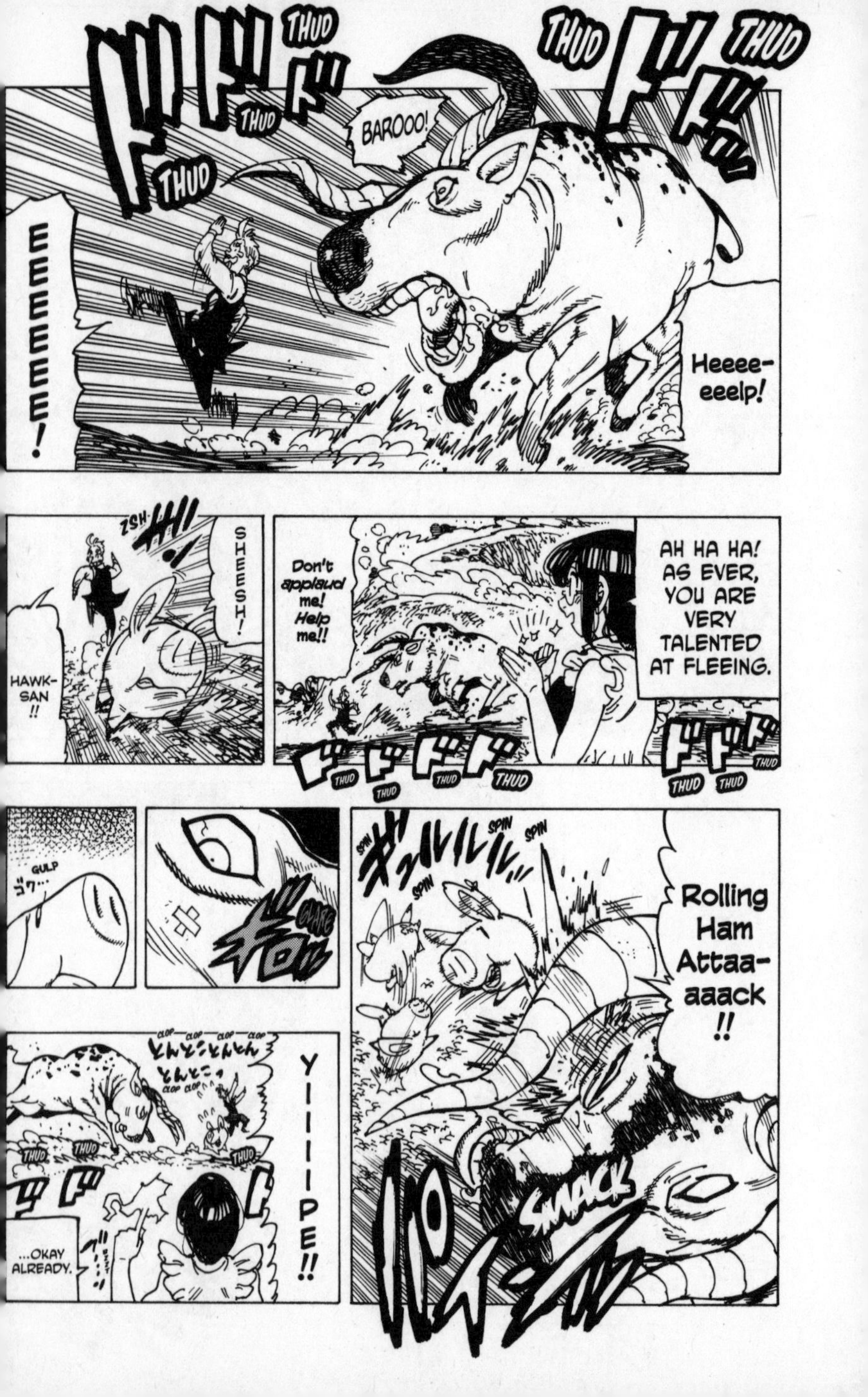
THUD
THUD
BAROOO!
Heeee-eeelp!
THUD
THUD
THUD
EEEEEEEE!
AH HA HA! AS EVER, YOU ARE VERY TALENTED AT FLEEING.
Don't applaud me! Help me!!
THUD THUD THUD
THUD THUD THUD THUD
SHEESH!
ZSH
HAWK-SAN!!
Rolling Ham Attaaa-aaack!!
SPIN SPIN SPIN SPIN
SMACK
GLARE
GULP
ゴク…
YIIIIPE!!
CLOP CLOP CLOP CLOP
とんとことんとん
CLOP CLOP
とんとこっ
THUD THUD THUD
...OKAY ALREADY.

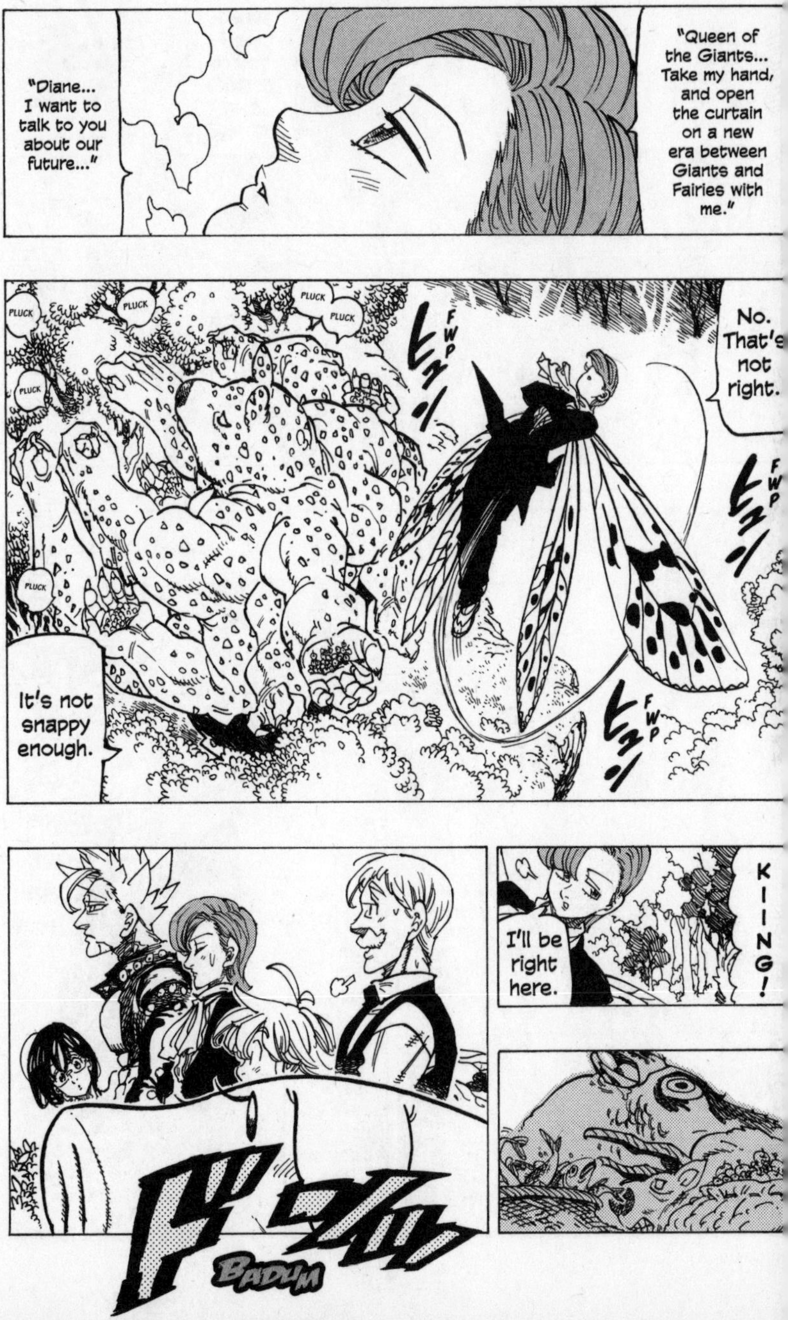
"Queen of the Giants... Take my hand, and open the curtain on a new era between Giants and Fairies with me."
"Diane... I want to talk to you about our future..."
No. That's not right.
FWP
FWP
FWP
PLUCK
PLUCK
PLUCK
PLUCK
PLUCK
PLUCK
It's not snappy enough.
KIIING!
I'll be right here.
BADUM

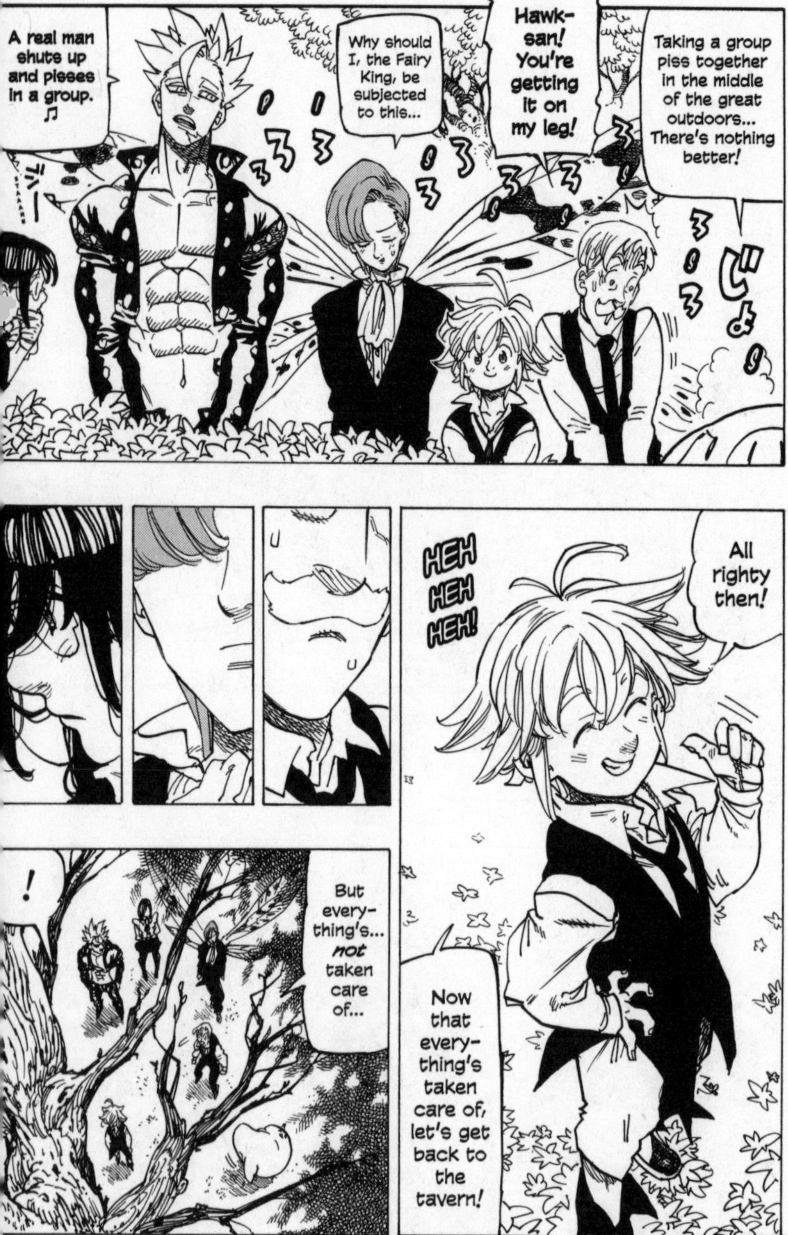

Taking a group piss together in the middle of the great outdoors... There's nothing better!
Hawk-san! You're getting it on my leg!
Why should I, the Fairy King, be subjected to this...
A real man shuts up and pisses in a group. ♫
All righty then!
HEH HEH HEH!
Now that every-thing's taken care of, let's get back to the tavern!
But every-thing's... *not* taken care of...
!

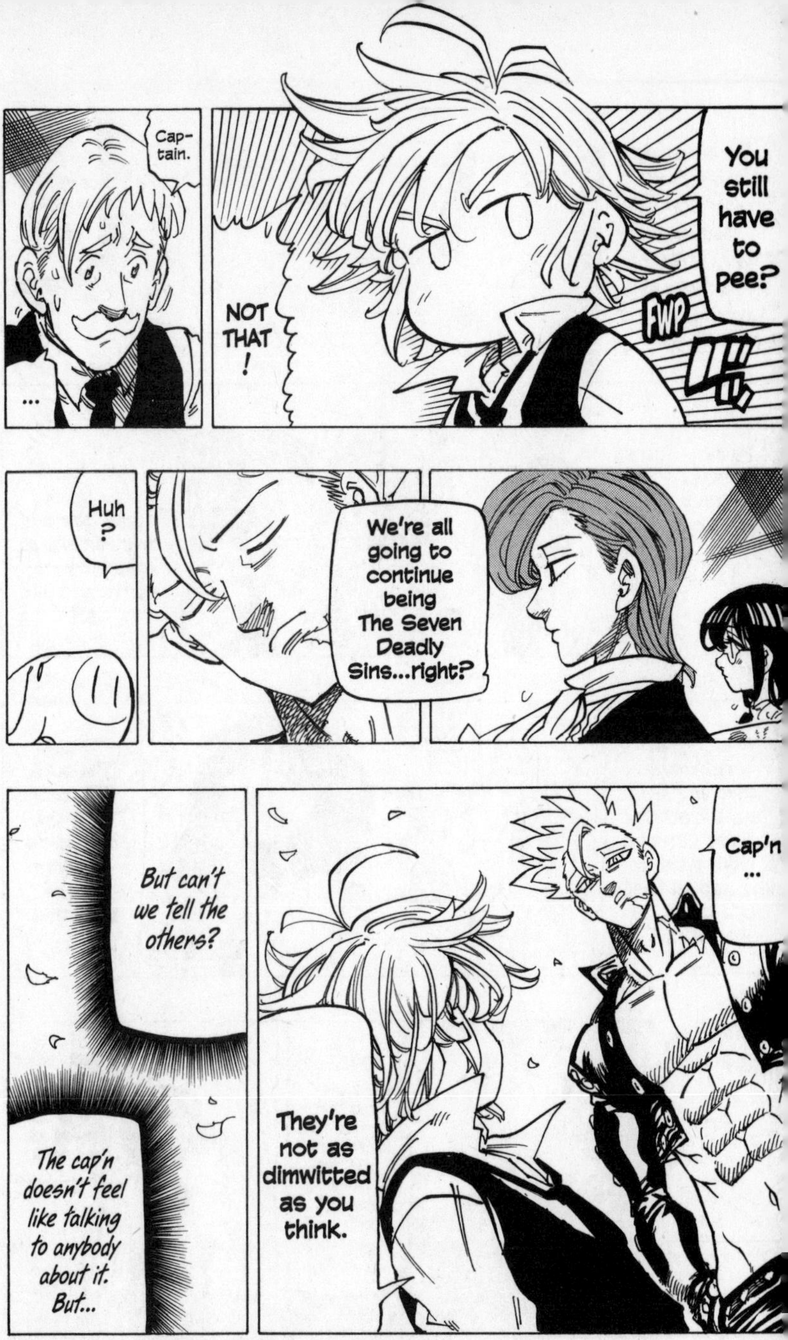
You still have to pee?
FWP
NOT THAT!
Cap-tain.
...
We're all going to continue being The Seven Deadly Sins...right?
Huh?
Cap'n...
They're not as dimwitted as you think.
But can't we tell the others?
The cap'n doesn't feel like talking to anybody about it. But...

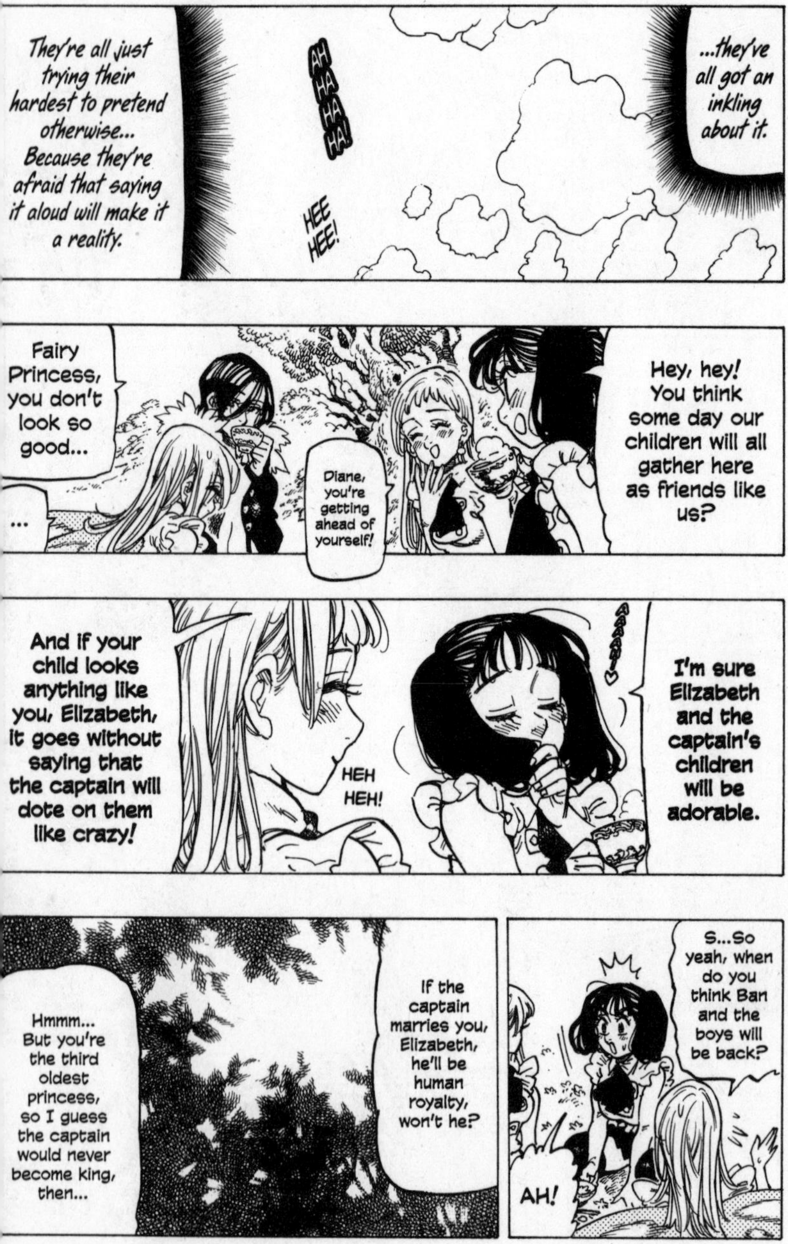
...they've all got an inkling about it.
AH HA HA HA!
HEE HEE!
They're all just trying their hardest to pretend otherwise... Because they're afraid that saying it aloud will make it a reality.
Hey, hey! You think some day our children will all gather here as friends like us?
Diane, you're getting ahead of yourself!
Fairy Princess, you don't look so good...
...
I'm sure Elizabeth and the captain's children will be adorable.
HEH HEH!
And if your child looks anything like you, Elizabeth, it goes without saying that the captain will dote on them like crazy!
S...So yeah, when do you think Ban and the boys will be back?
AH!
If the captain marries you, Elizabeth, he'll be human royalty, won't he?
Hmmm... But you're the third oldest princess, so I guess the captain would never become king, then...

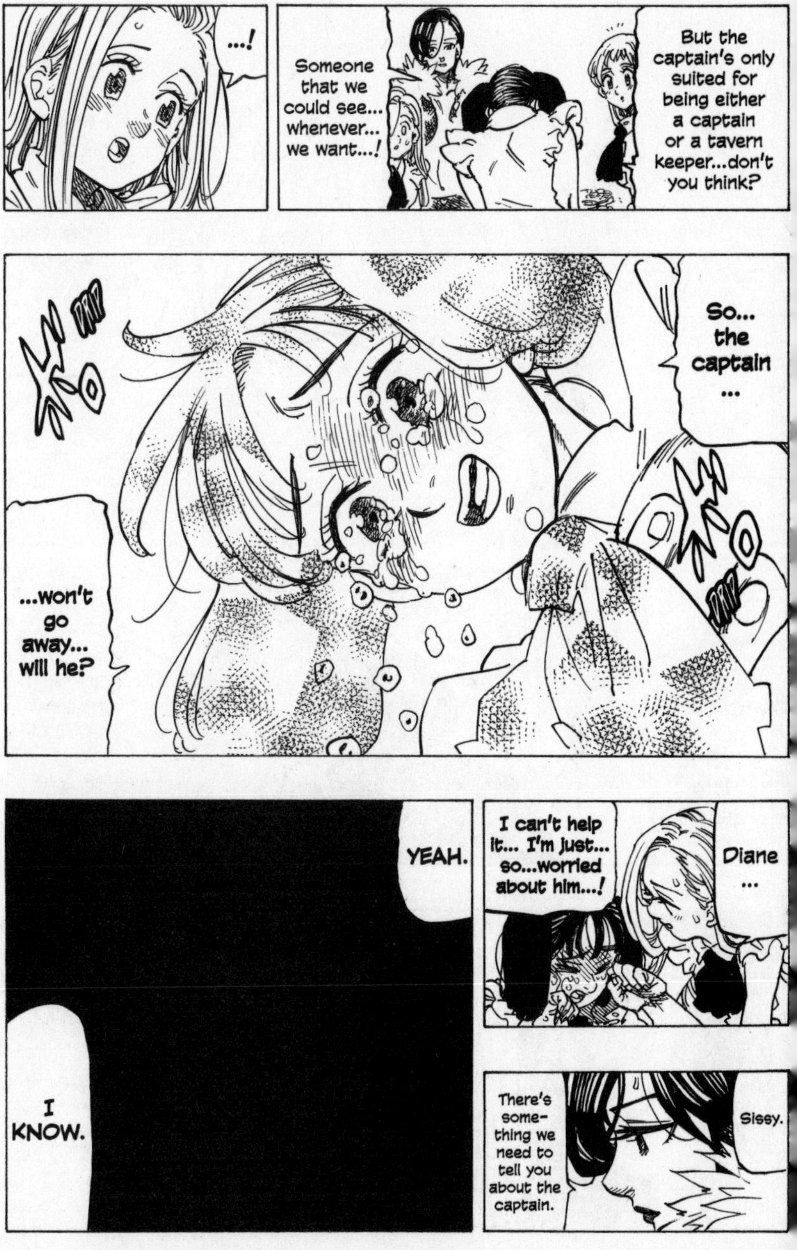
But the captain's only suited for being either a captain or a tavern keeper...don't you think?
Someone that we could see... whenever... we want...!
...!
So... the captain...
...won't go away... will he?
Diane...
I can't help it... I'm just... so...worried about him...!
Sissy.
There's some-thing we need to tell you about the captain.
YEAH.
I KNOW.

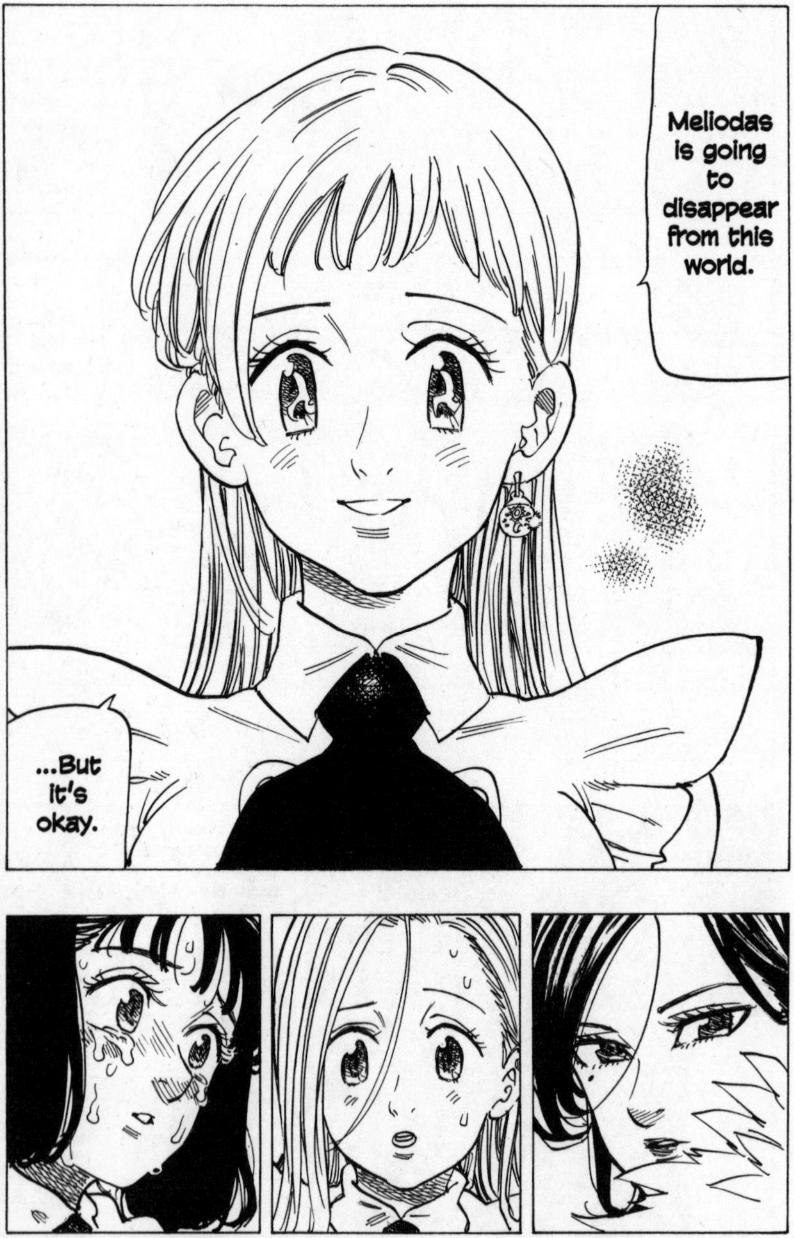
Meliodas is going to disappear from this world.
...But it's okay.

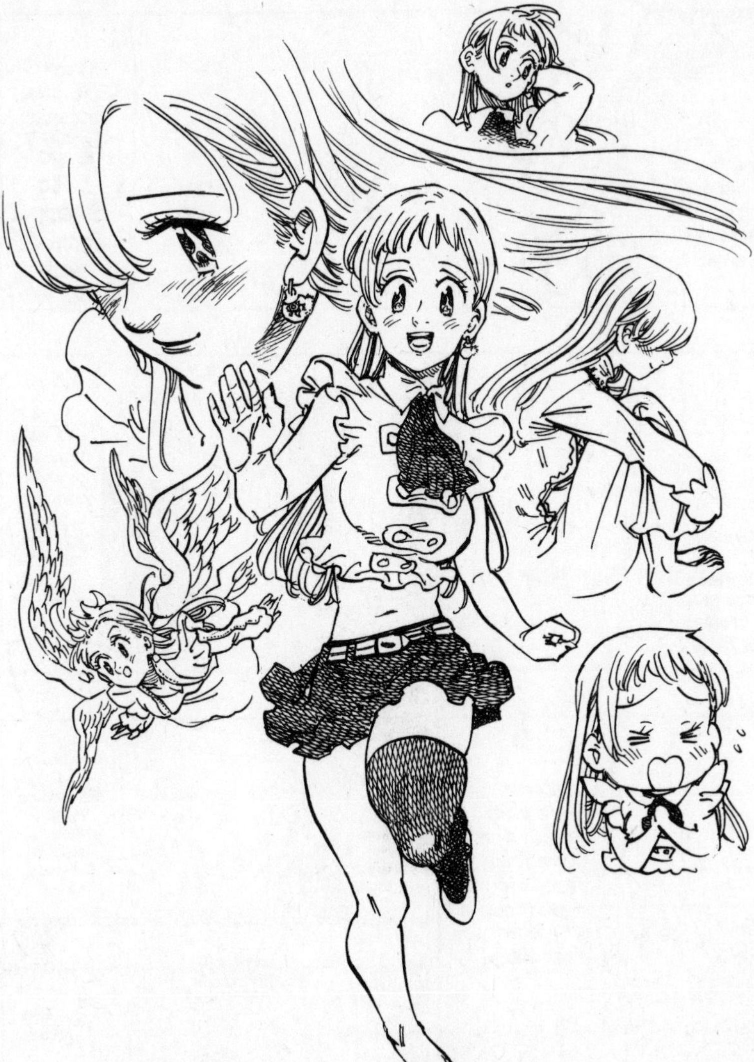

# Chapter 309 - This is the Path I Live

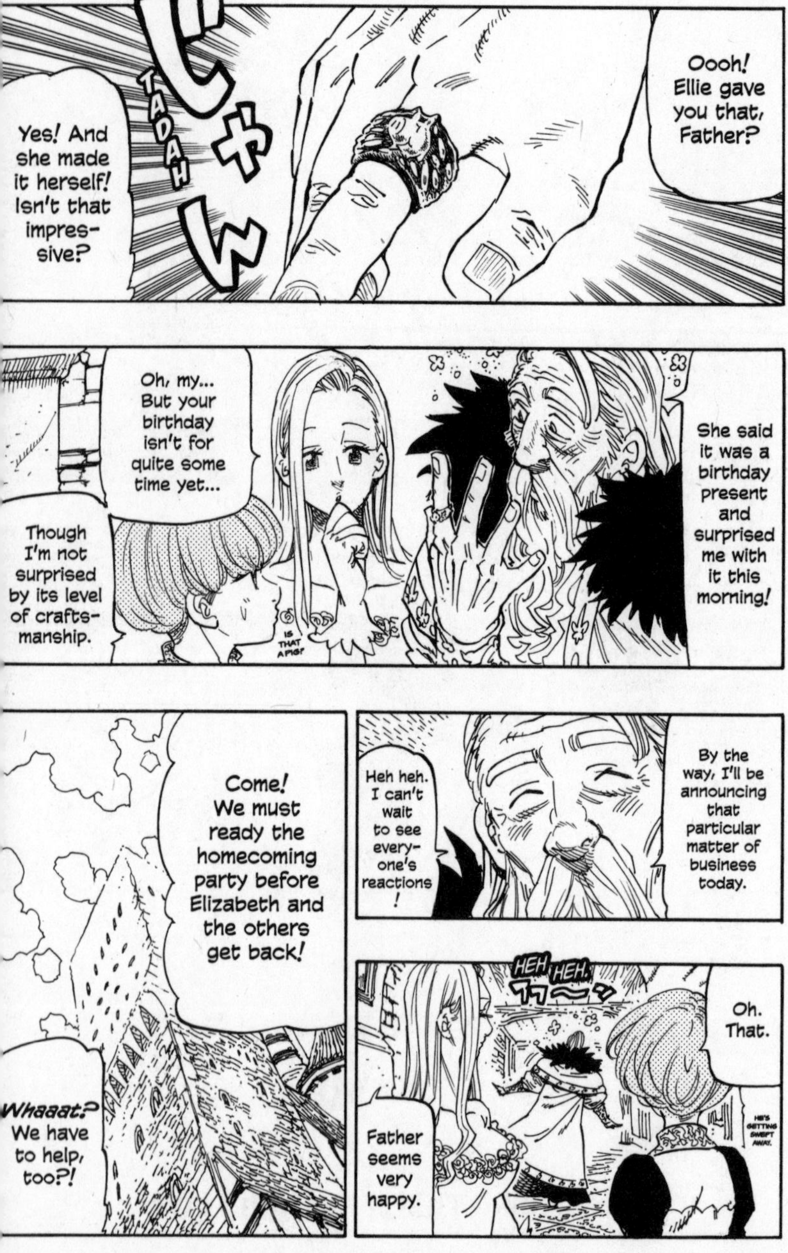
Oooh! Ellie gave you that, Father?
じゃん
TADAH
Yes! And she made it herself! Isn't that impressive?
She said it was a birthday present and surprised me with it this morning!
Oh, my... But your birthday isn't for quite some time yet...
IS THAT A PIG?
Though I'm not surprised by its level of craftsmanship.
By the way, I'll be announcing that particular matter of business today.
Heh heh. I can't wait to see everyone's reactions!
Oh. That.
HEH HEH.
HE'S GETTING SWEPT AWAY.
Father seems very happy.
Come! We must ready the homecoming party before Elizabeth and the others get back!
Whaaat? We have to help, too?!

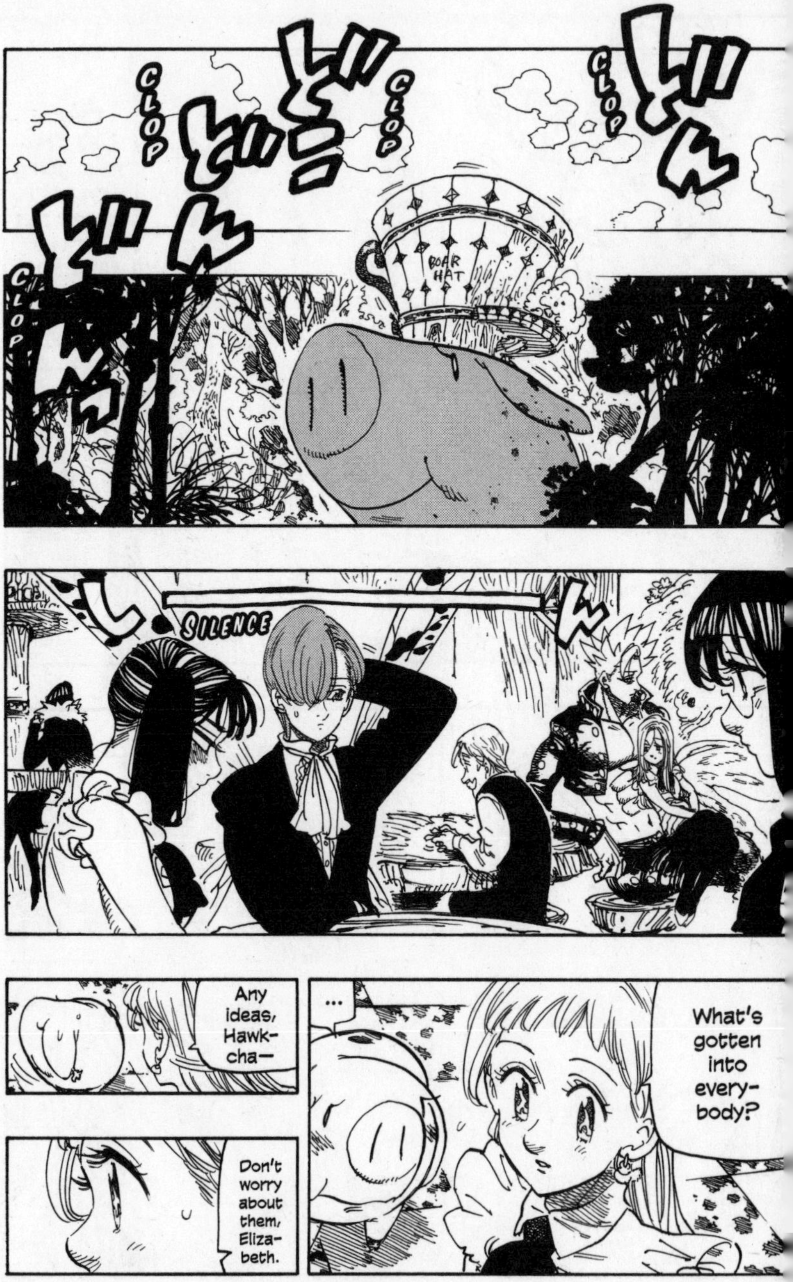

CLOP
CLOP
CLOP
CLOP
BOAR HAT
SILENCE
What's gotten into every-body?
...
Any ideas, Hawk-cha—
Don't worry about them, Eliza-beth.

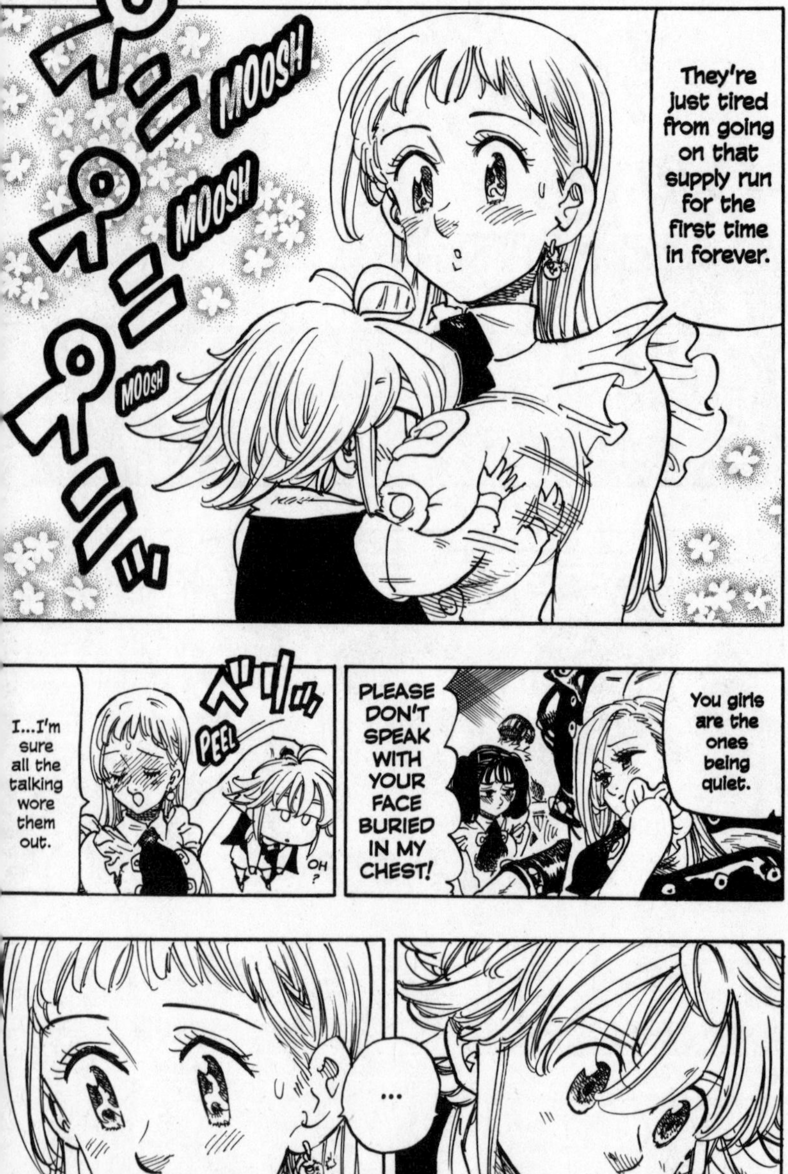
They're just tired from going on that supply run for the first time in forever.
MOOSH
MOOSH
MOOSH
You girls are the ones being quiet.
PLEASE DON'T SPEAK WITH YOUR FACE BURIED IN MY CHEST!
PEEL
OH ?
I...I'm sure all the talking wore them out.
...

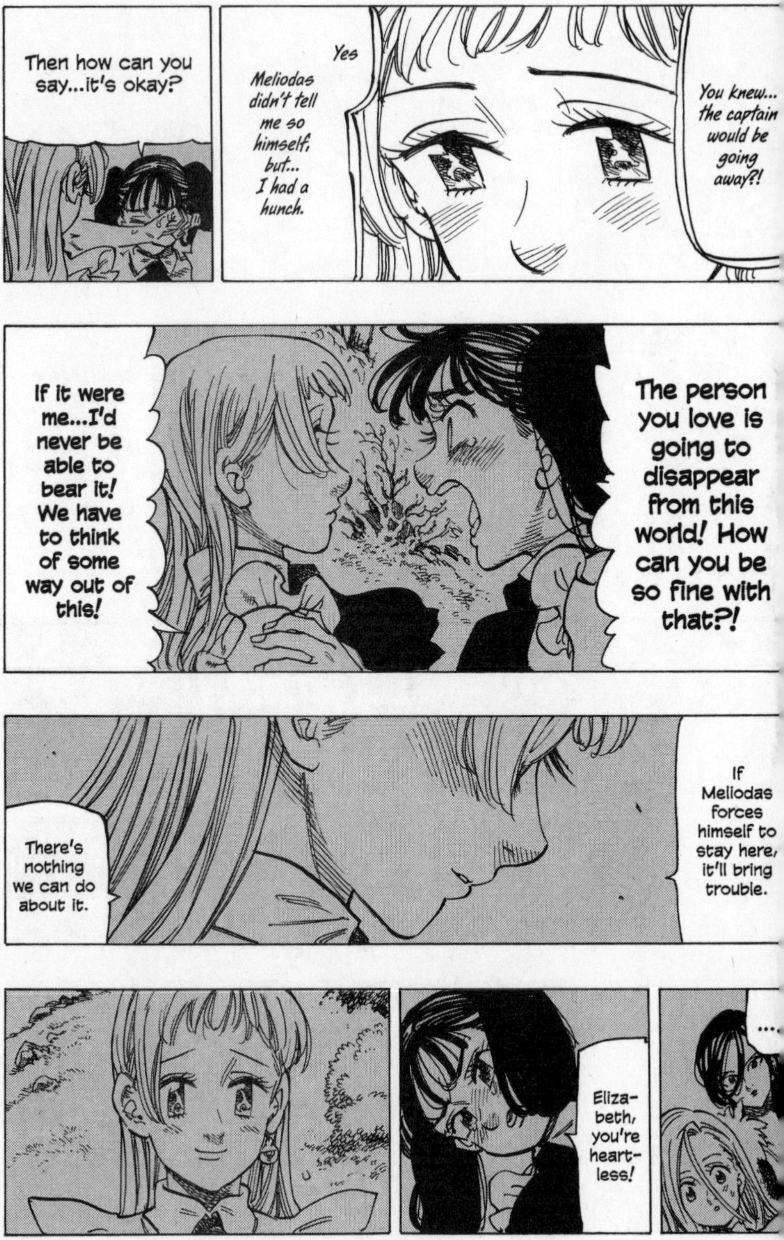
You knew... the captain would be going away?!
Yes
Meliodas didn't tell me so himself, but... I had a hunch.
Then how can you say...it's okay?
The person you love is going to disappear from this world! How can you be so fine with that?!
If it were me...I'd never be able to bear it! We have to think of some way out of this!
If Meliodas forces himself to stay here, it'll bring trouble.
There's nothing we can do about it.
....
Eliza-beth, you're heart-less!

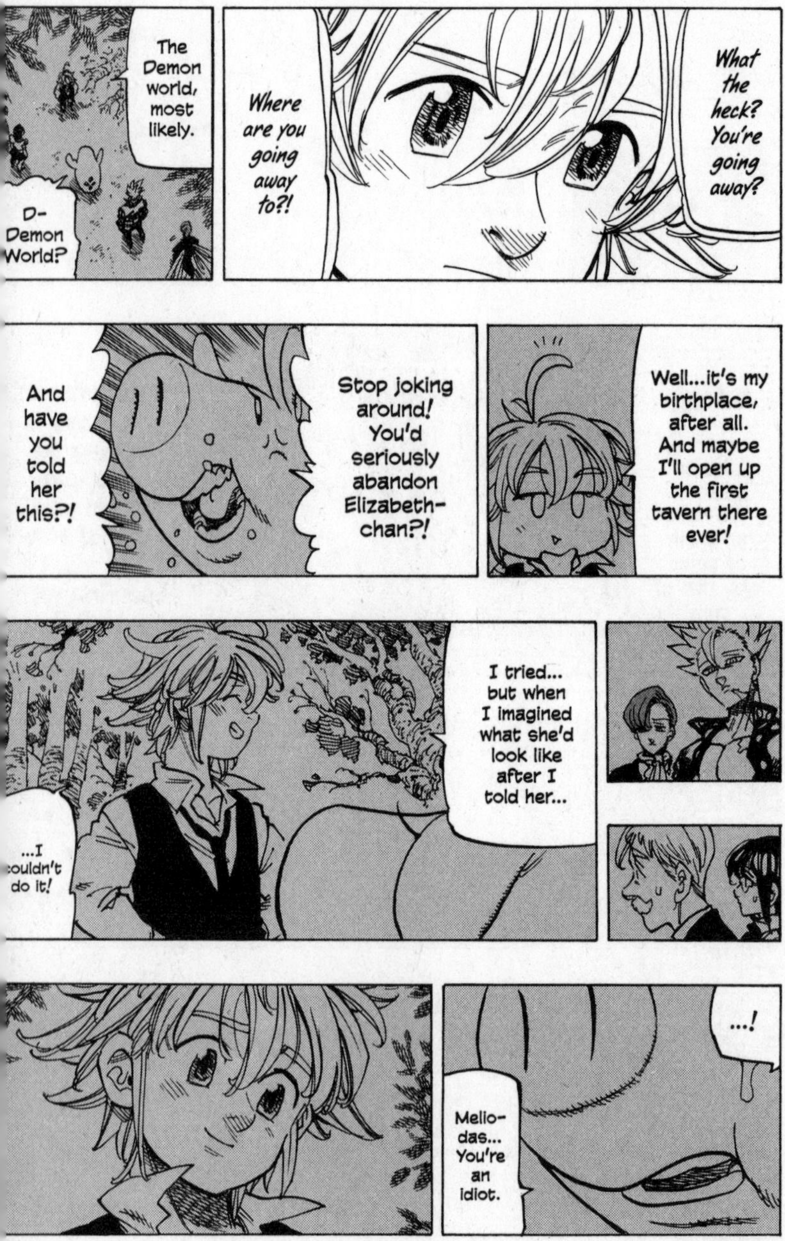
What the heck? You're going away?
Where are you going away to?!
The Demon world, most likely.
D-Demon World?
Well...it's my birthplace, after all. And maybe I'll open up the first tavern there ever!
Stop joking around! You'd seriously abandon Elizabeth-chan?!
And have you told her this?!
I tried... but when I imagined what she'd look like after I told her...
...I couldn't do it!
...!
Melio-das... You're an idiot.

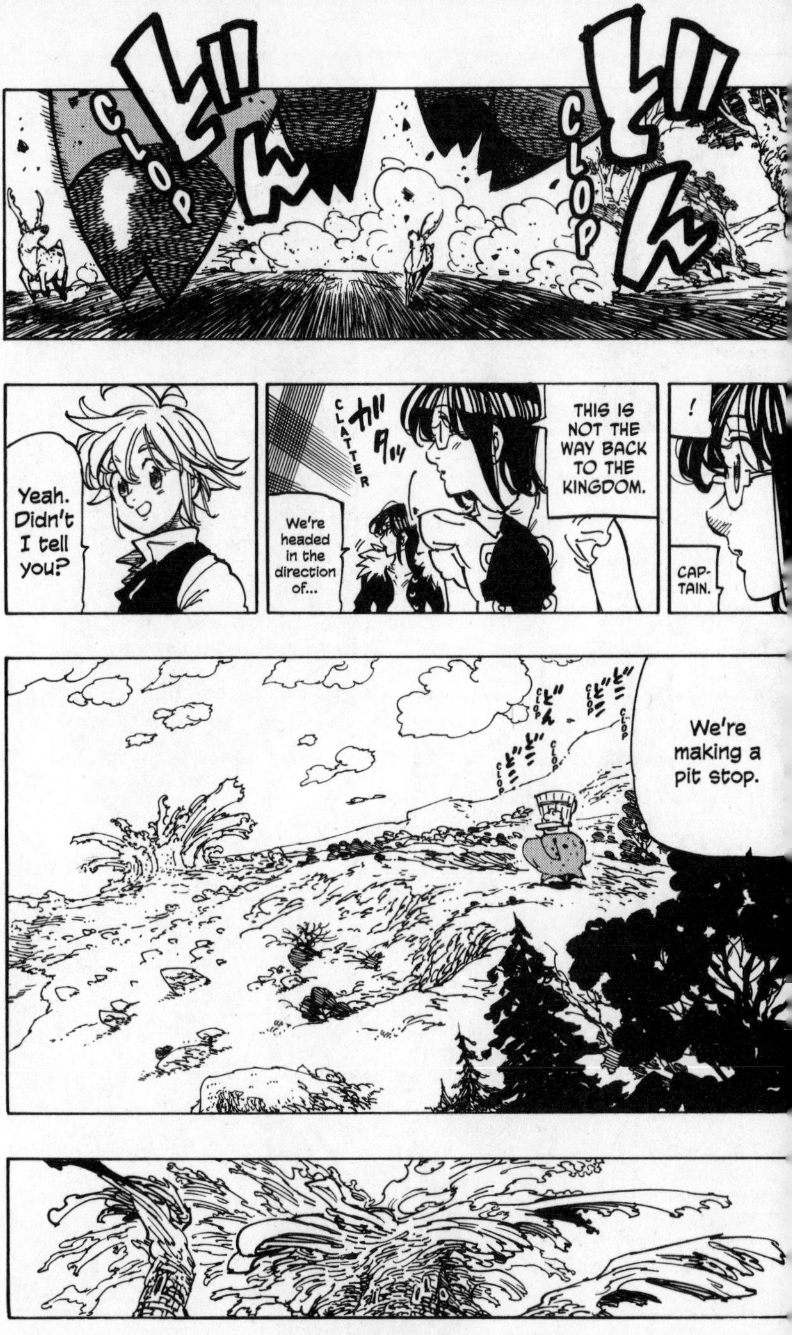
CLOP
CLOP
!
CAP-
TAIN.
THIS IS NOT THE WAY BACK TO THE KINGDOM.
CLATTER
We're headed in the direction of...
Yeah. Didn't I tell you?
We're making a pit stop.
CLOP
CLOP
CLOP
CLOP
CLOP

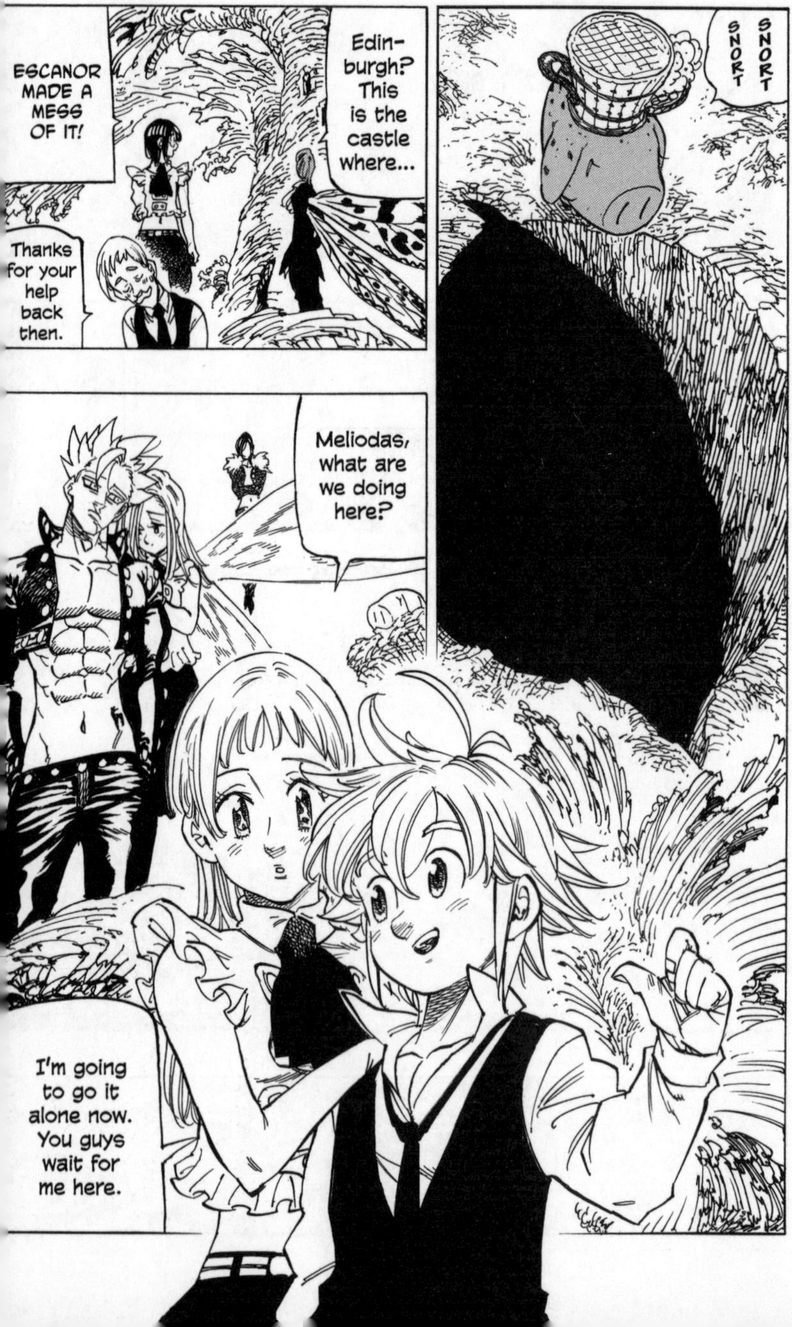
SNORT SNORT
Edinburgh? This is the castle where...
ESCANOR MADE A MESS OF IT!
Thanks for your help back then.
Meliodas, what are we doing here?
I'm going to go it alone now. You guys wait for me here.

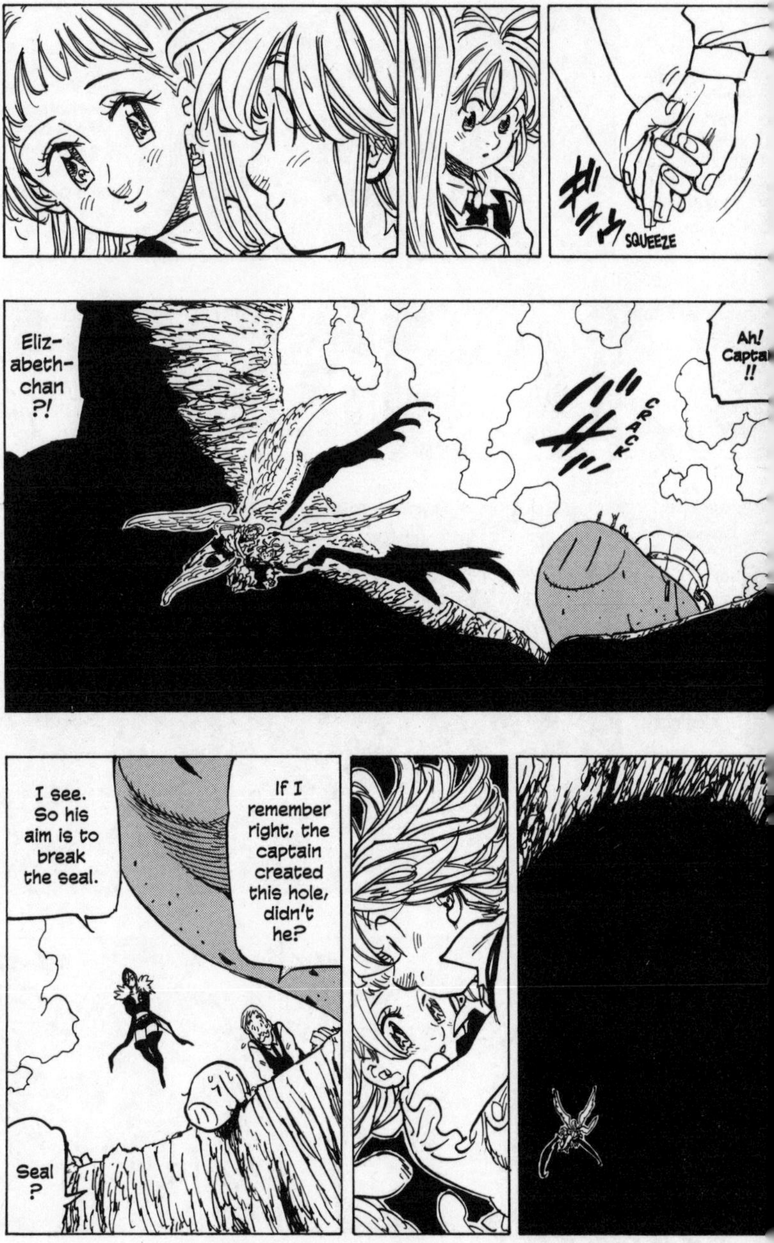
SQUEEZE
Ah! Capta !!
CRACK
Elizabeth-chan ?!
If I remember right, the captain created this hole, didn't he?
I see. So his aim is to break the seal.
Seal ?

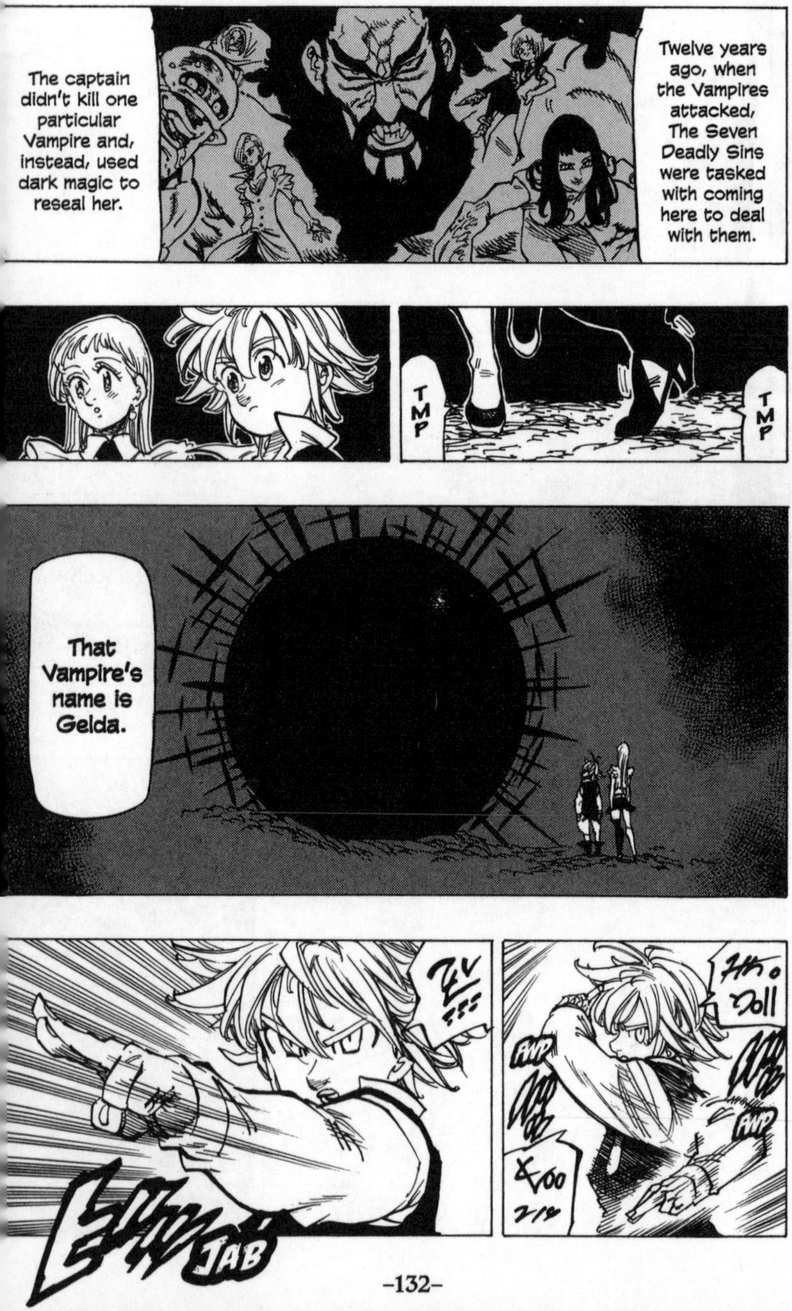
Twelve years ago, when the Vampires attacked, The Seven Deadly Sins were tasked with coming here to deal with them.
The captain didn't kill one particular Vampire and, instead, used dark magic to reseal her.
TMP
TMP
That Vampire's name is Gelda.
FWP
FWP
JAB

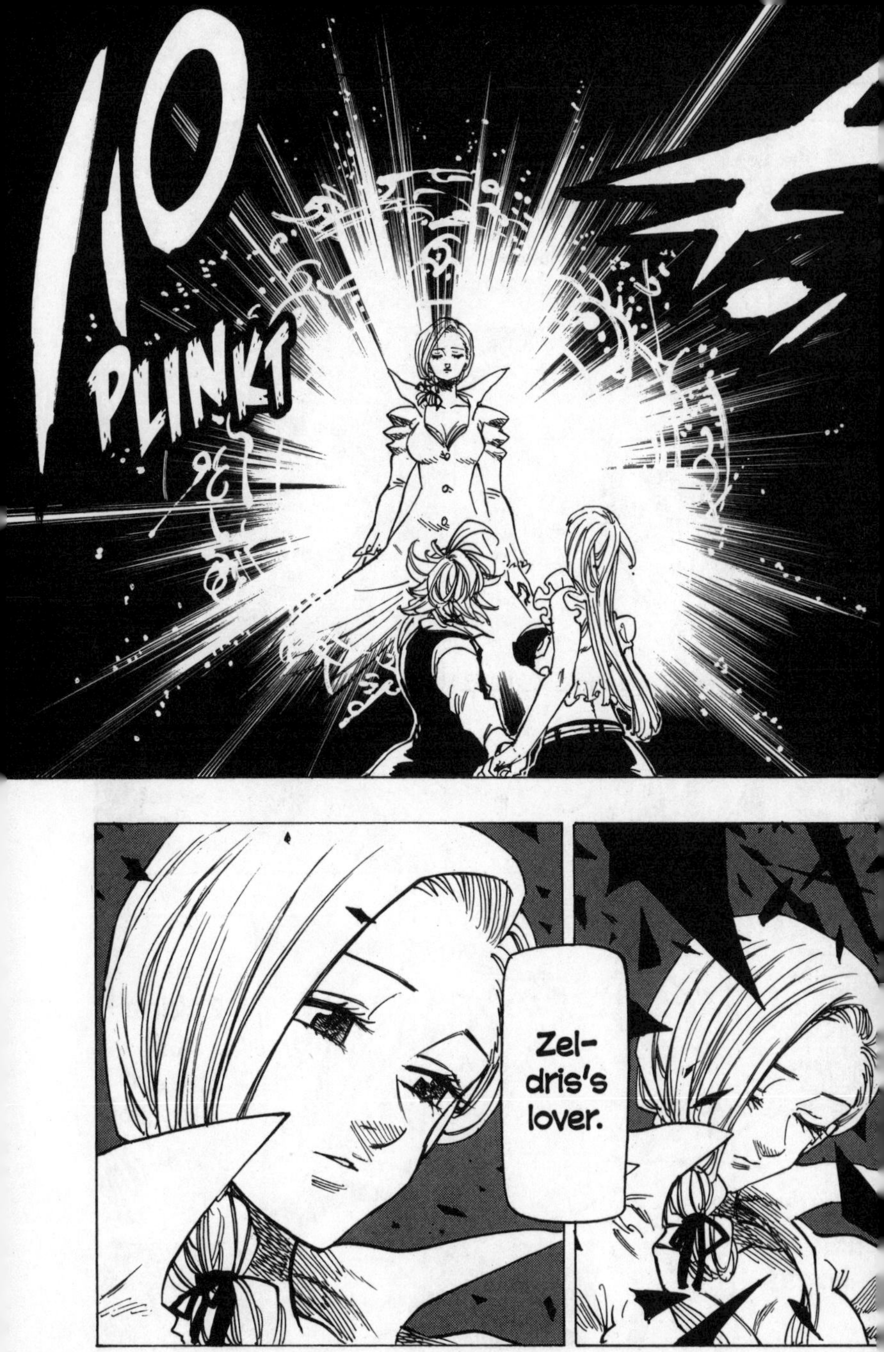
PLINK!
Zel-dris's lover.

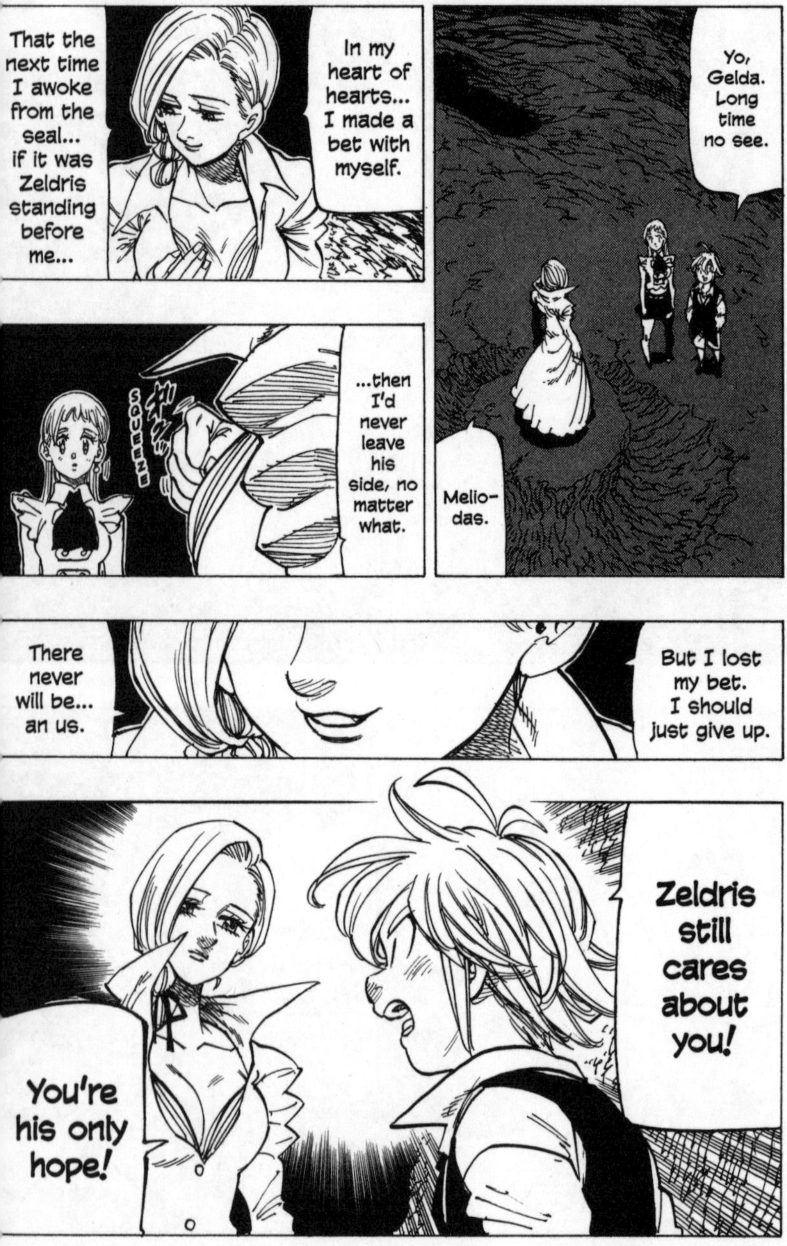
Yo, Gelda. Long time no see.
Melio-das.
In my heart of hearts... I made a bet with myself.
That the next time I awoke from the seal... if it was Zeldris standing before me...
...then I'd never leave his side, no matter what.
SQUEEZE
But I lost my bet. I should just give up.
There never will be... an us.
Zeldris still cares about you!
You're his only hope!

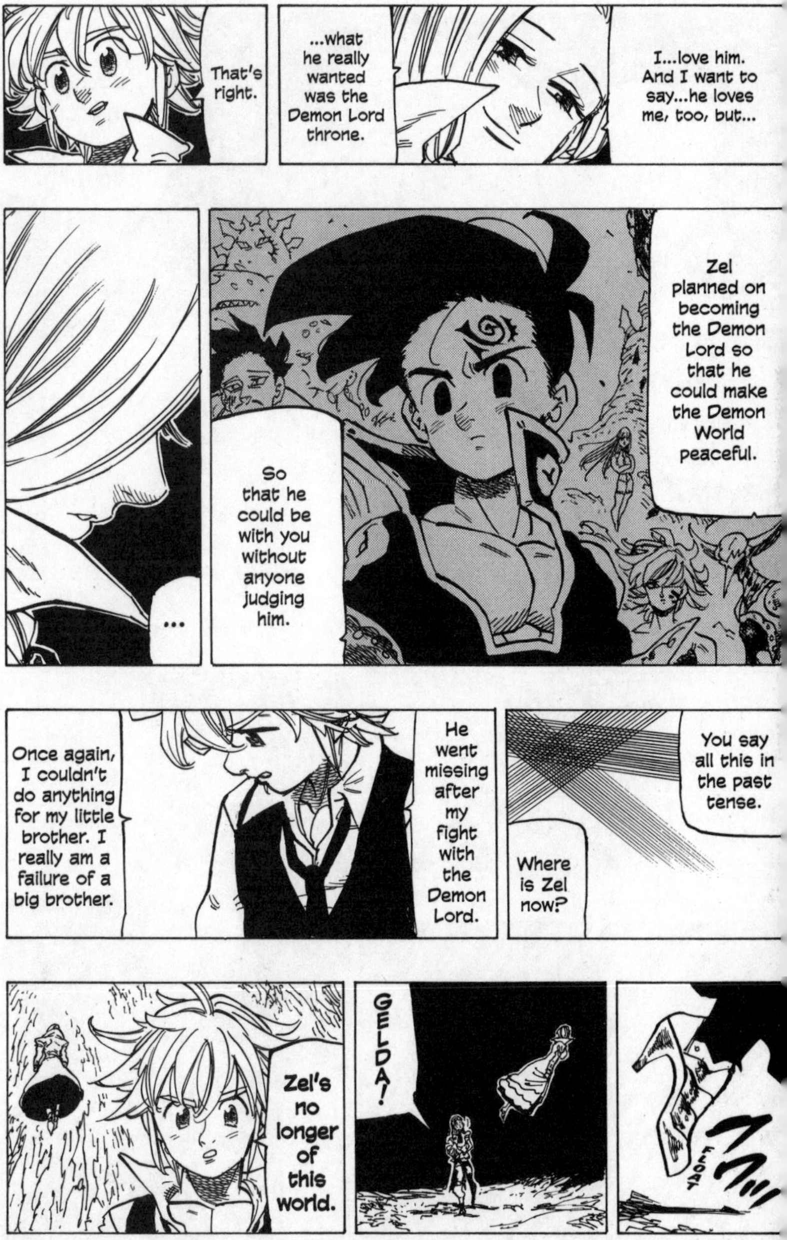

I...love him. And I want to say...he loves me, too, but...
...what he really wanted was the Demon Lord throne.
That's right.
Zel planned on becoming the Demon Lord so that he could make the Demon World peaceful.
So that he could be with you without anyone judging him.
...
You say all this in the past tense.
Where is Zel now?
He went missing after my fight with the Demon Lord.
Once again, I couldn't do anything for my little brother. I really am a failure of a big brother.
FLOAT
GELDA!
Zel's no longer of this world.

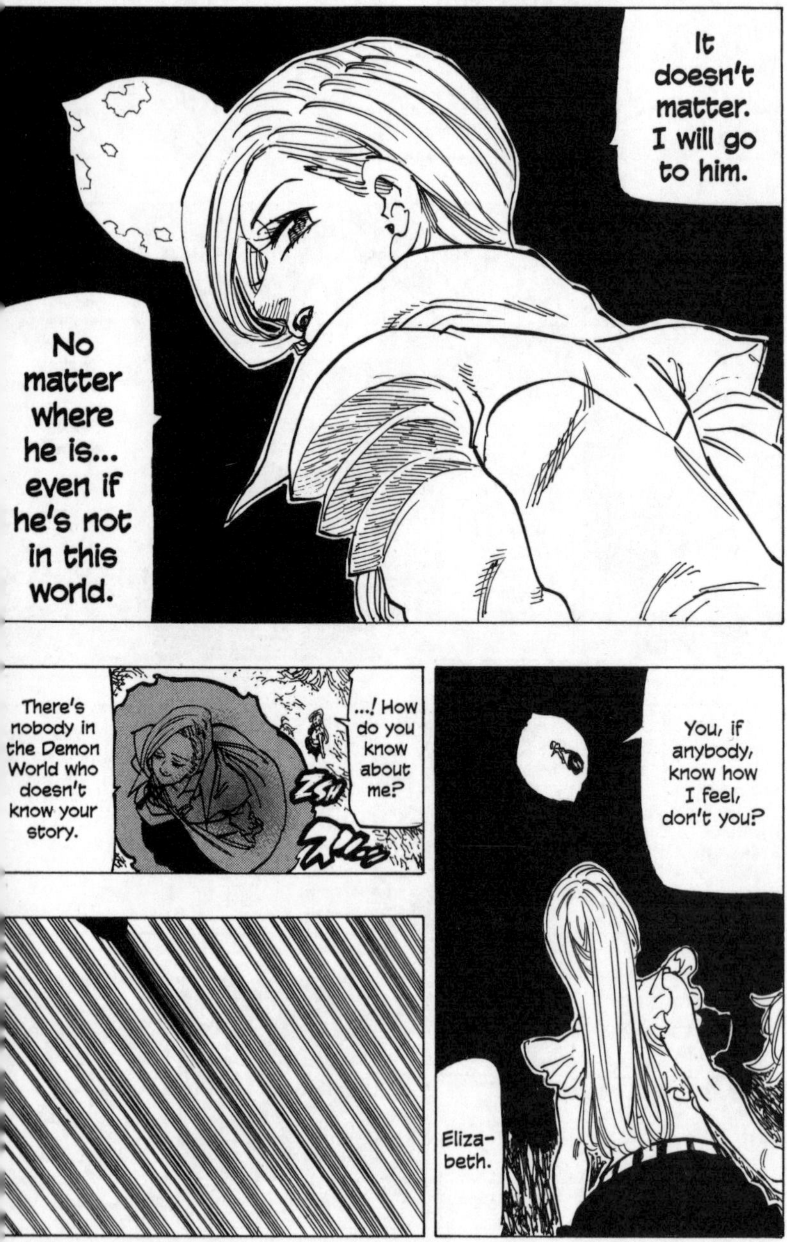
It doesn't matter. I will go to him.
No matter where he is... even if he's not in this world.
You, if anybody, know how I feel, don't you?
Eliza-beth.
...! How do you know about me?
ZSH
There's nobody in the Demon World who doesn't know your story.

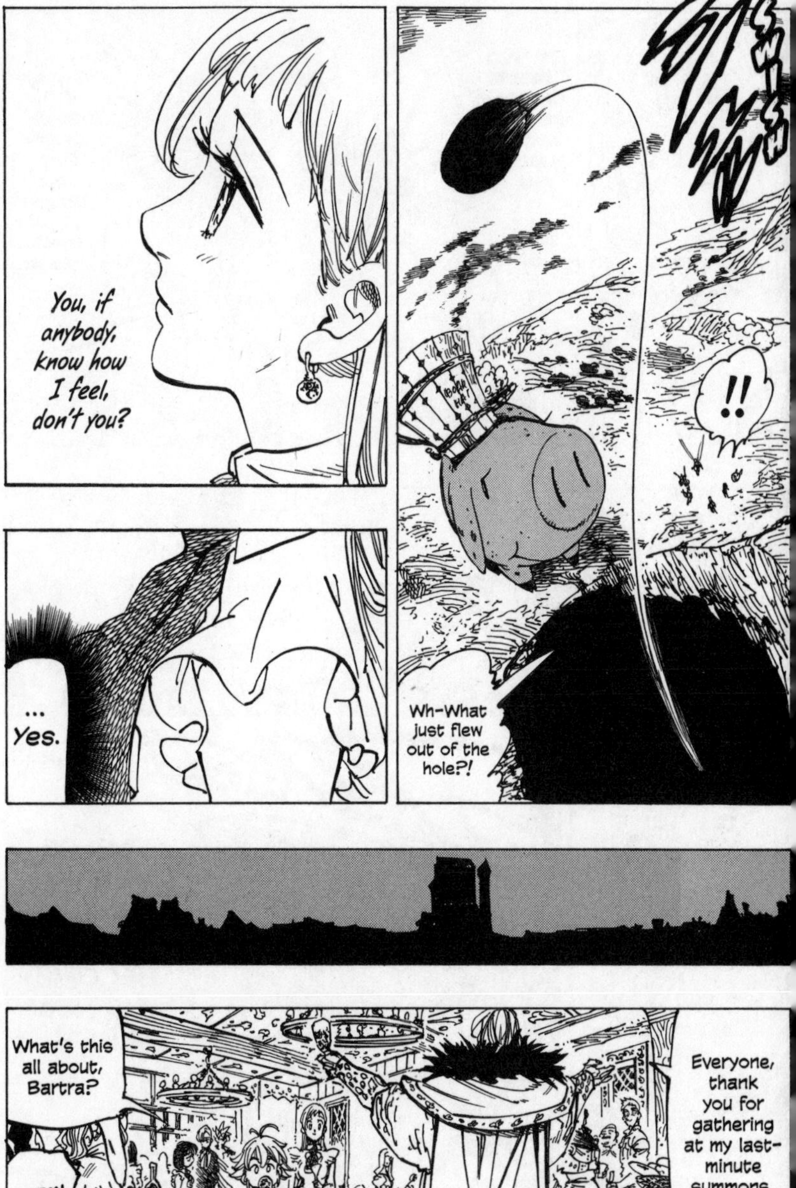
!!
Wh-What just flew out of the hole?!
You, if anybody, know how I feel, don't you?
... Yes.
Everyone, thank you for gathering at my last-minute summons.
What's this all about, Bartra?
AHEM!

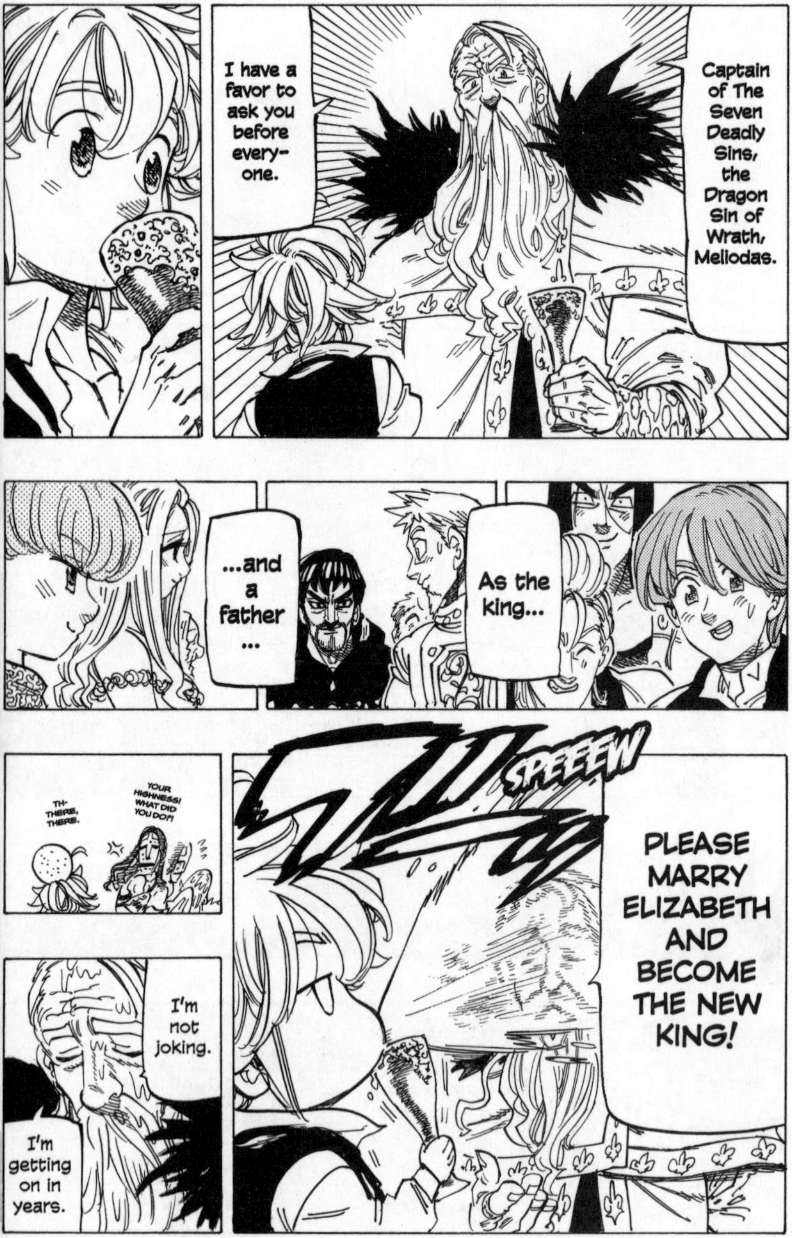
Captain of The Seven Deadly Sins, the Dragon Sin of Wrath, Meliodas.
I have a favor to ask you before everyone.
As the king...
...and a father ...
SPEEEW
PLEASE MARRY ELIZABETH AND BECOME THE NEW KING!
YOUR HIGHNESS! WHAT DID YOU DO?!
TH-THERE, THERE.
I'm not joking.
I'm getting on in years.

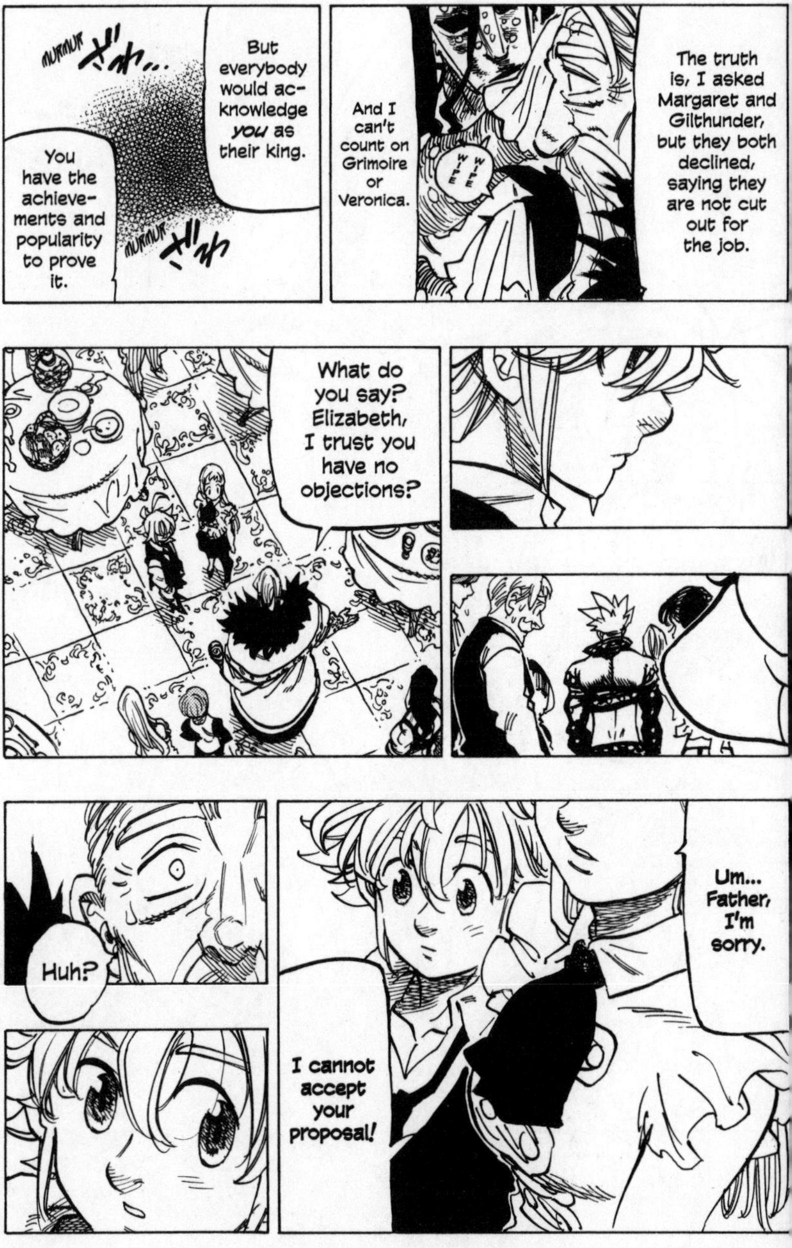
The truth is, I asked Margaret and Gilthunder, but they both declined, saying they are not cut out for the job.
WIPE WIPE
And I can't count on Grimoire or Veronica.
MURMUR ざわ...
But everybody would acknowledge *you* as their king.
You have the achievements and popularity to prove it.
MURMUR ざわ
What do you say? Elizabeth, I trust you have no objections?
Um... Father, I'm sorry.
I cannot accept your proposal!
Huh?

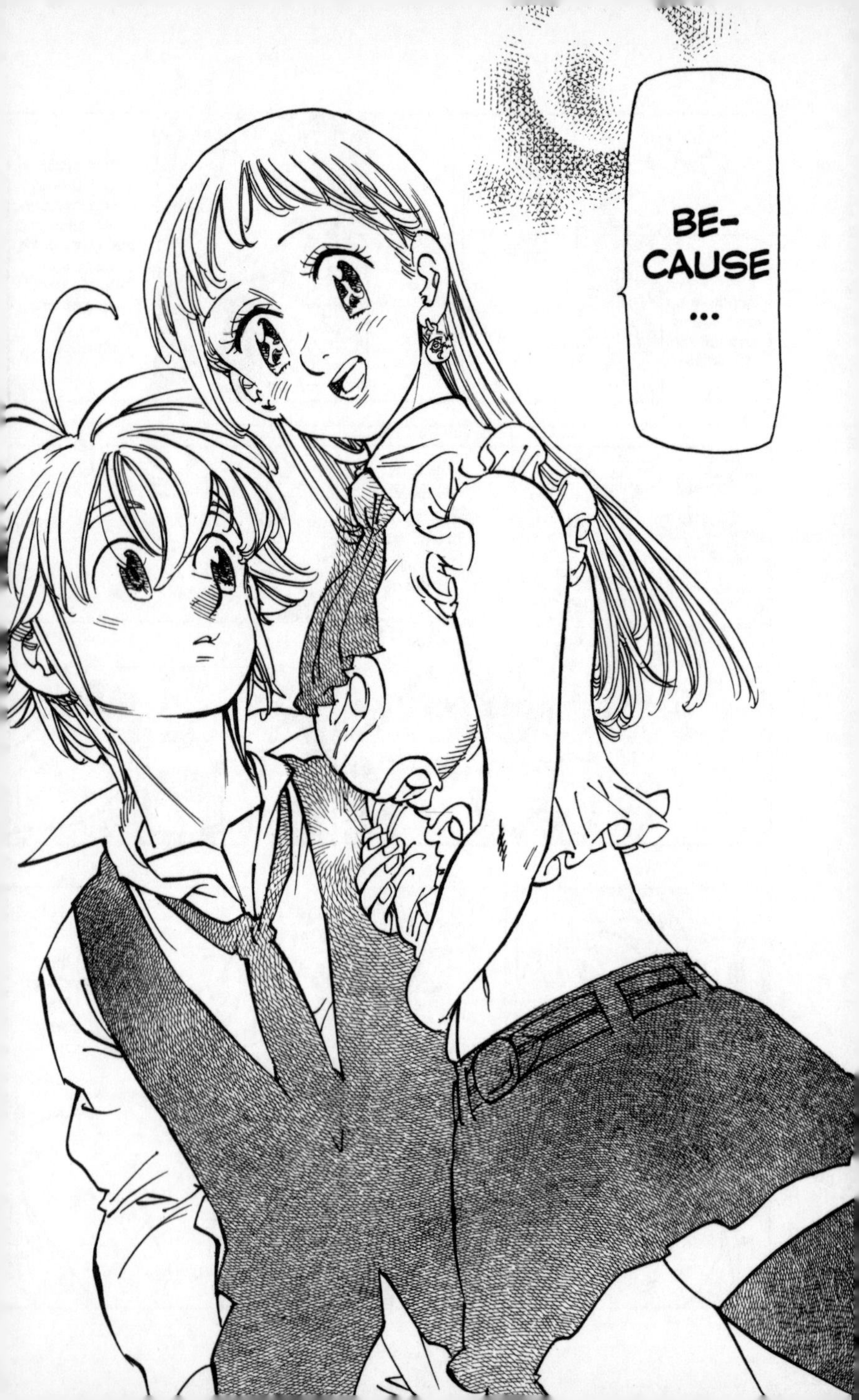
BE-
CAUSE
...

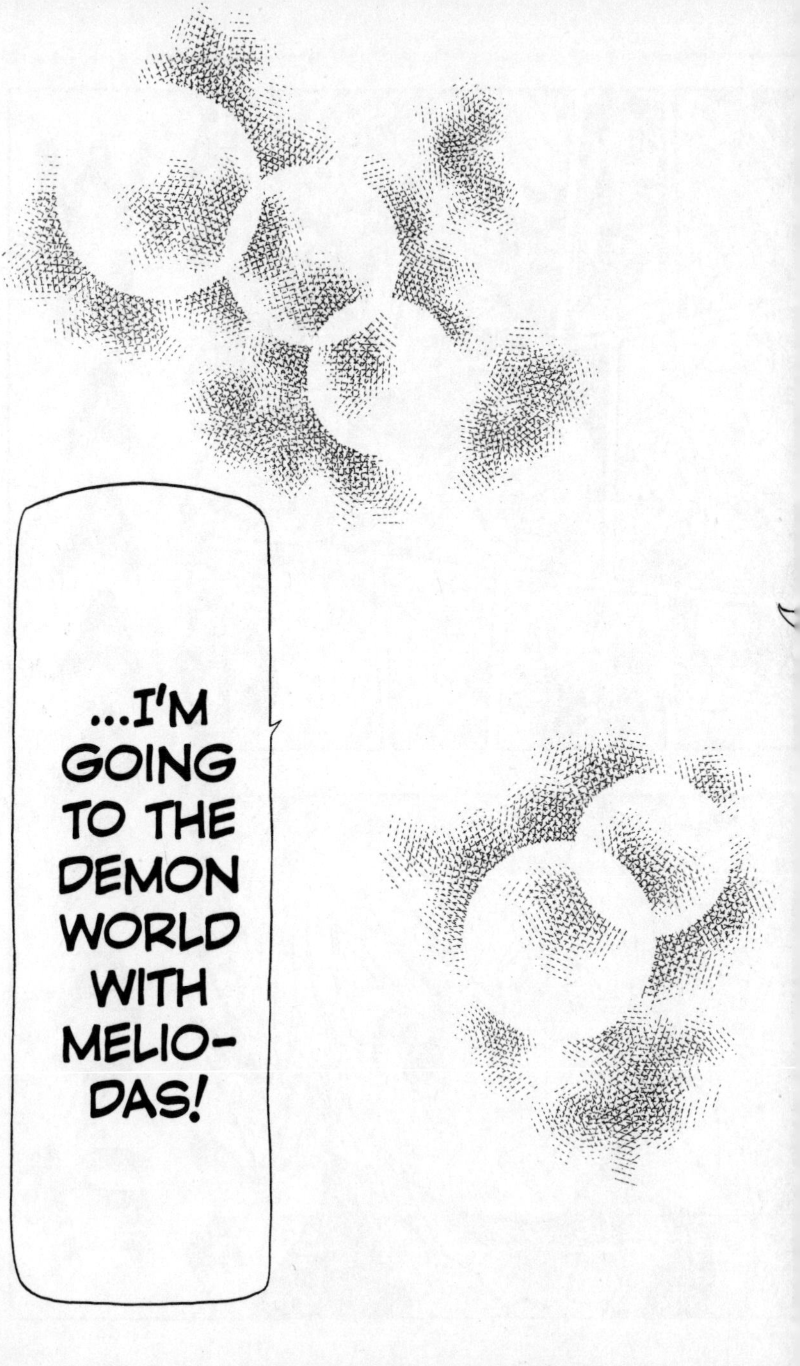
...I'M GOING TO THE DEMON WORLD WITH MELIO-DAS!

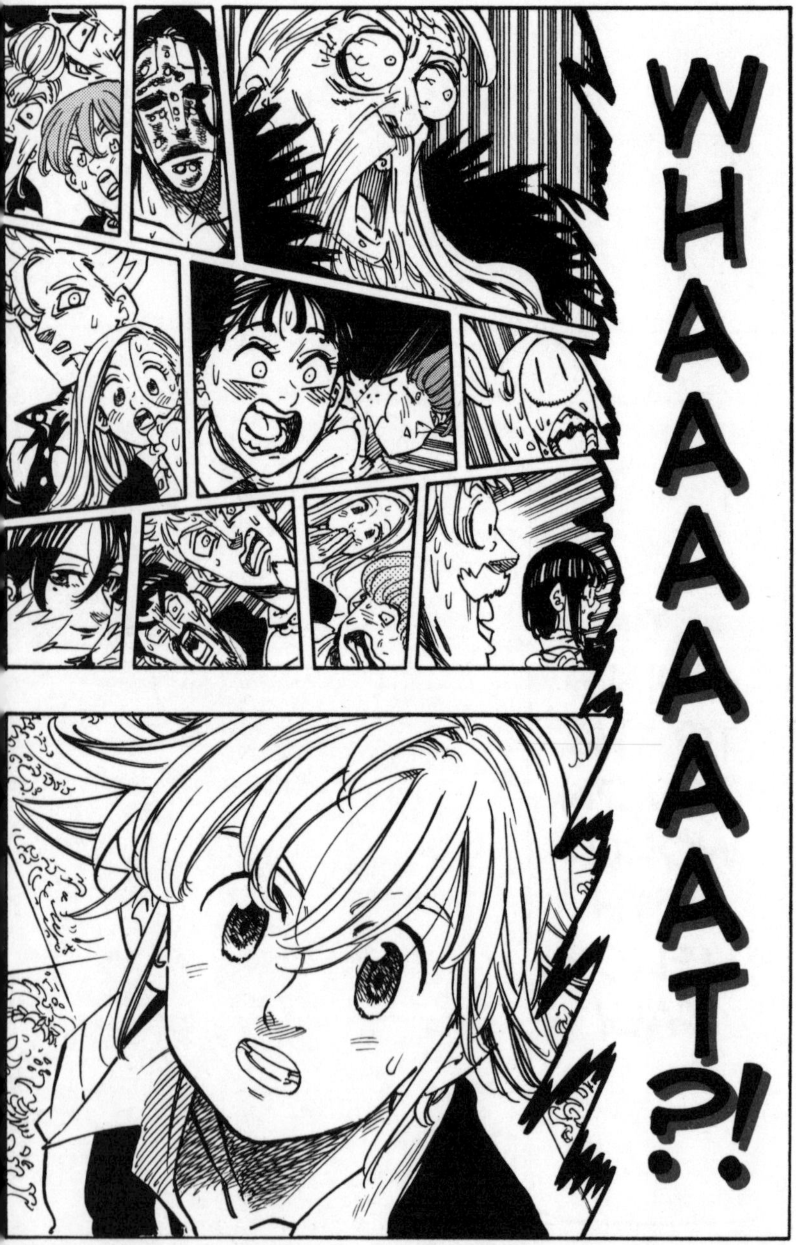
WHAAAAAAT?!

# Chapter 310 - Farewell, Seven Deadly Sins

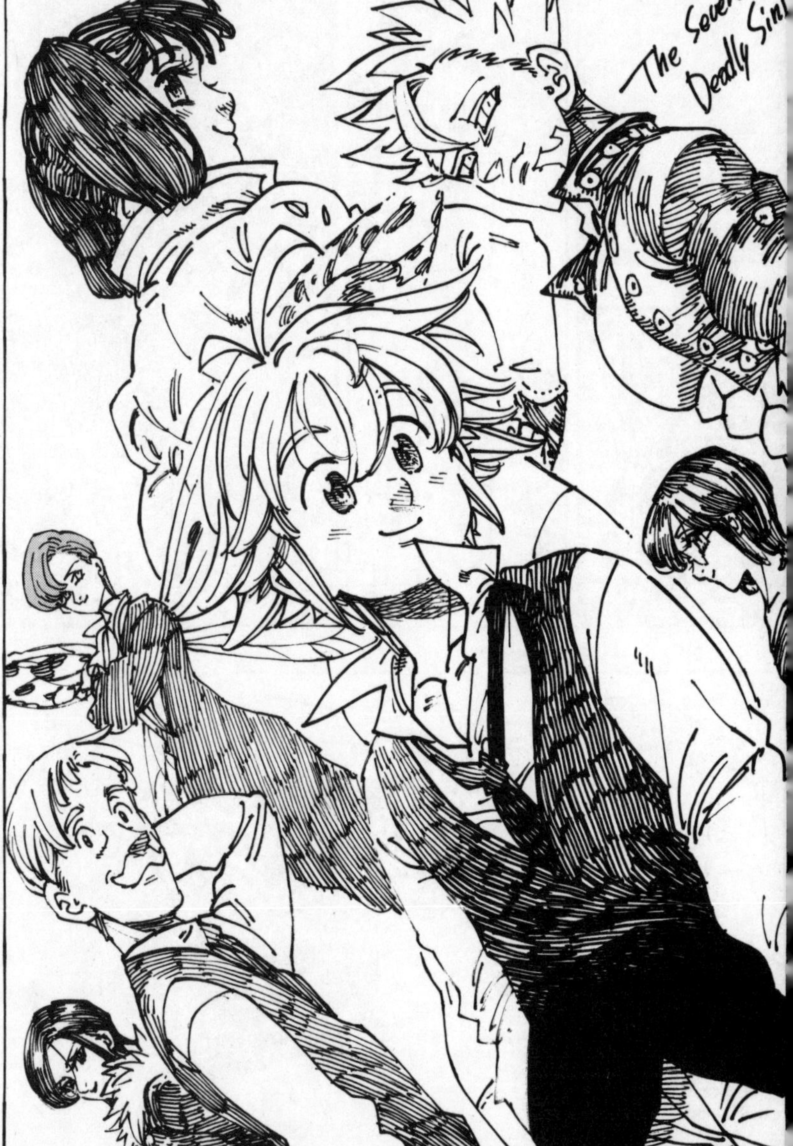
The Seven Deadly Sins

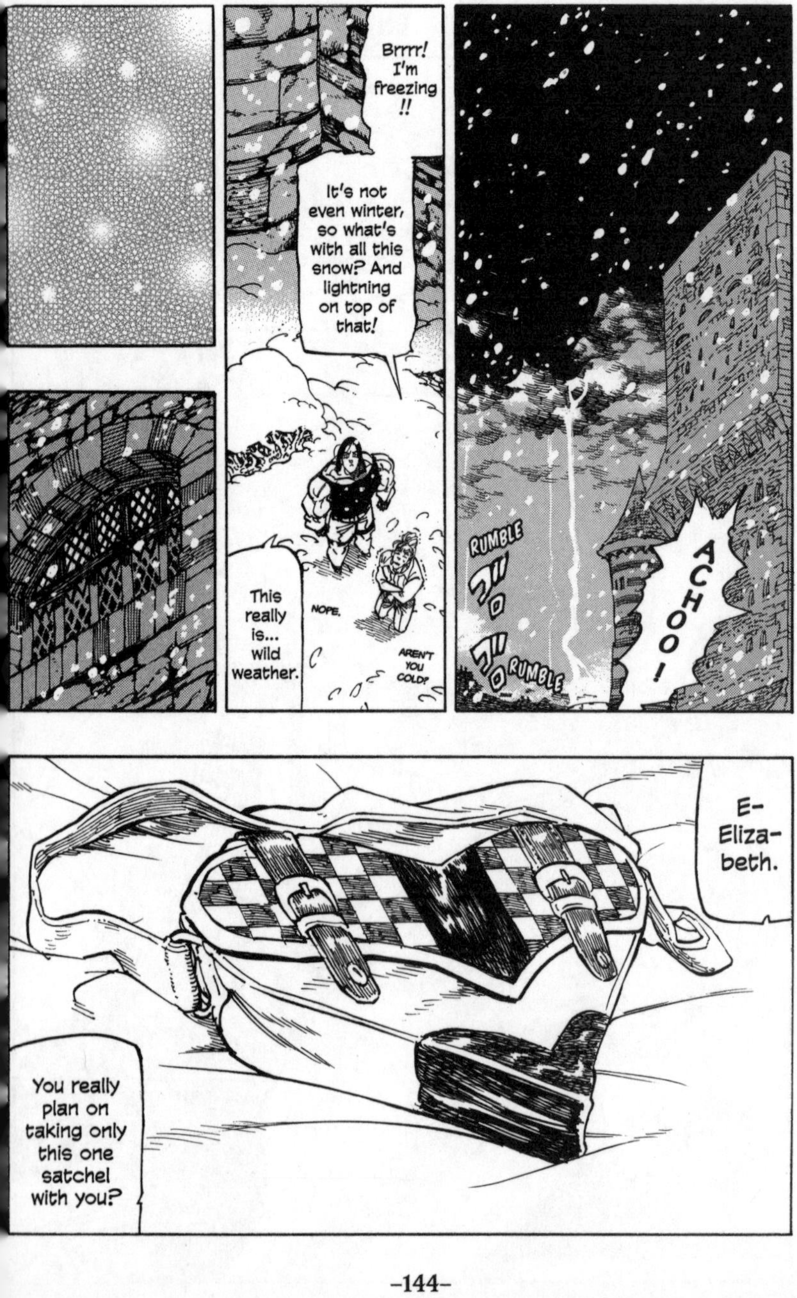
RUMBLE
RUMBLE
ACHOO!
Brrrr! I'm freezing!!
It's not even winter, so what's with all this snow? And lightning on top of that!
AREN'T YOU COLD?
NOPE.
This really is... wild weather.
E-Elizabeth.
You really plan on taking only this one satchel with you?

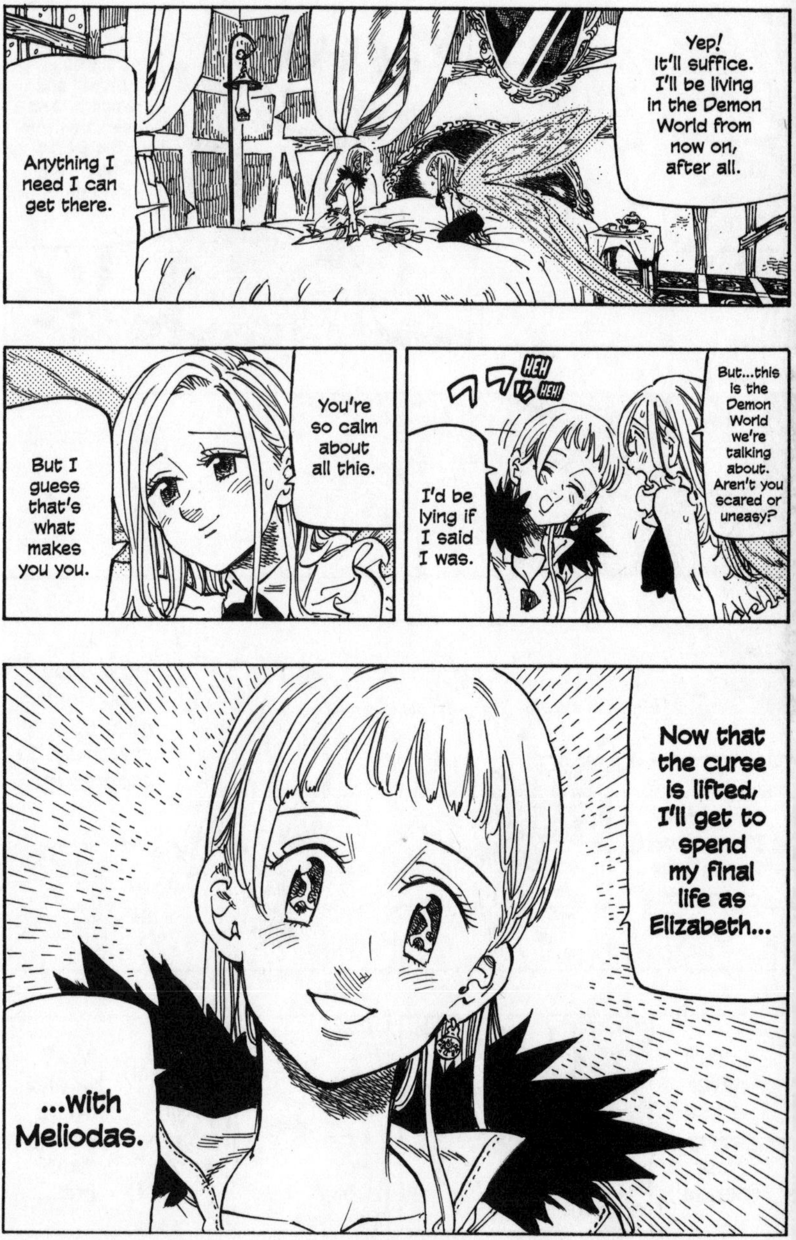
Yep! It'll suffice. I'll be living in the Demon World from now on, after all.
Anything I need I can get there.
But...this is the Demon World we're talking about. Aren't you scared or uneasy?
HEH HEH!
I'd be lying if I said I was.
You're so calm about all this.
But I guess that's what makes you you.
Now that the curse is lifted, I'll get to spend my final life as Elizabeth...
...with Meliodas.

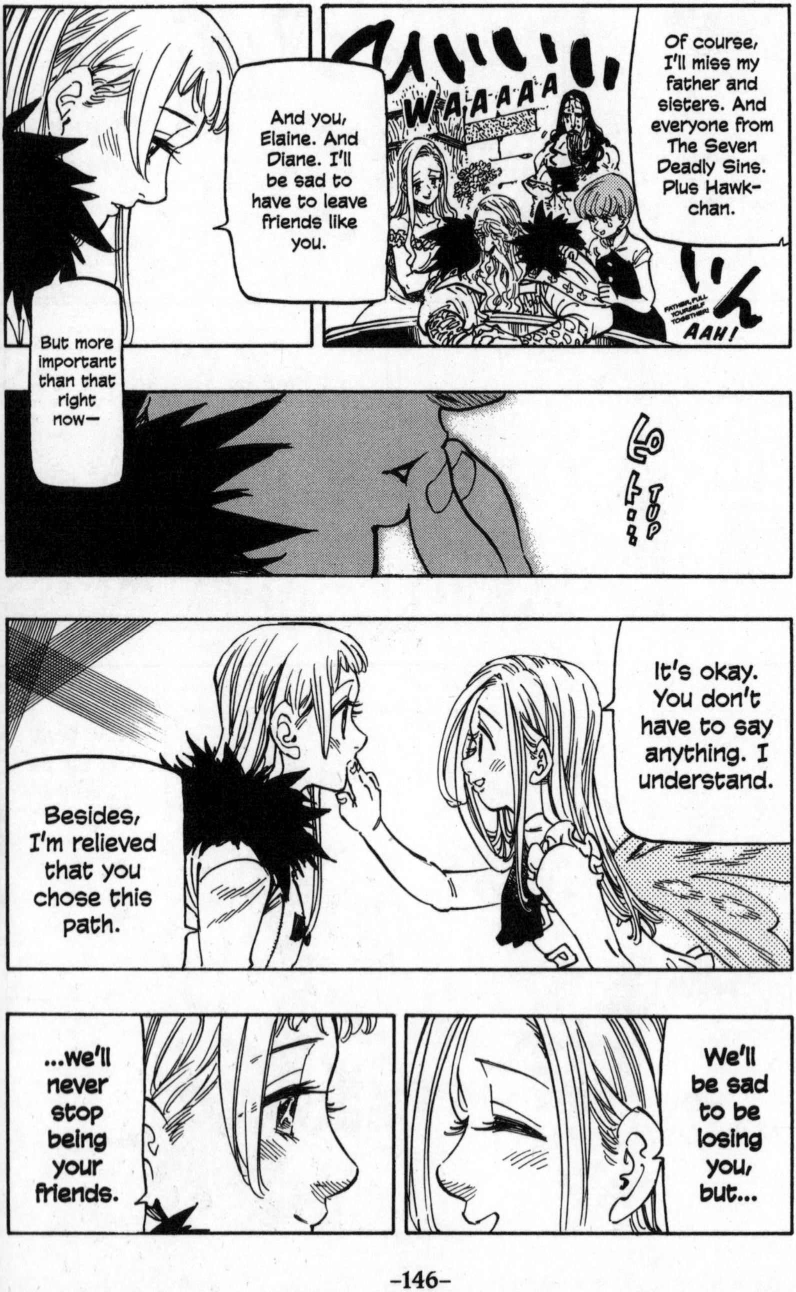
Of course, I'll miss my father and sisters. And everyone from The Seven Deadly Sins. Plus Hawk-chan.
WAAAAA
FATHER, PULL YOURSELF TOGETHER!
AAH!
And you, Elaine. And Diane. I'll be sad to have to leave friends like you.
But more important than that right now—
TUP
It's okay. You don't have to say anything. I understand.
Besides, I'm relieved that you chose this path.
We'll be sad to be losing you, but...
...we'll never stop being your friends.

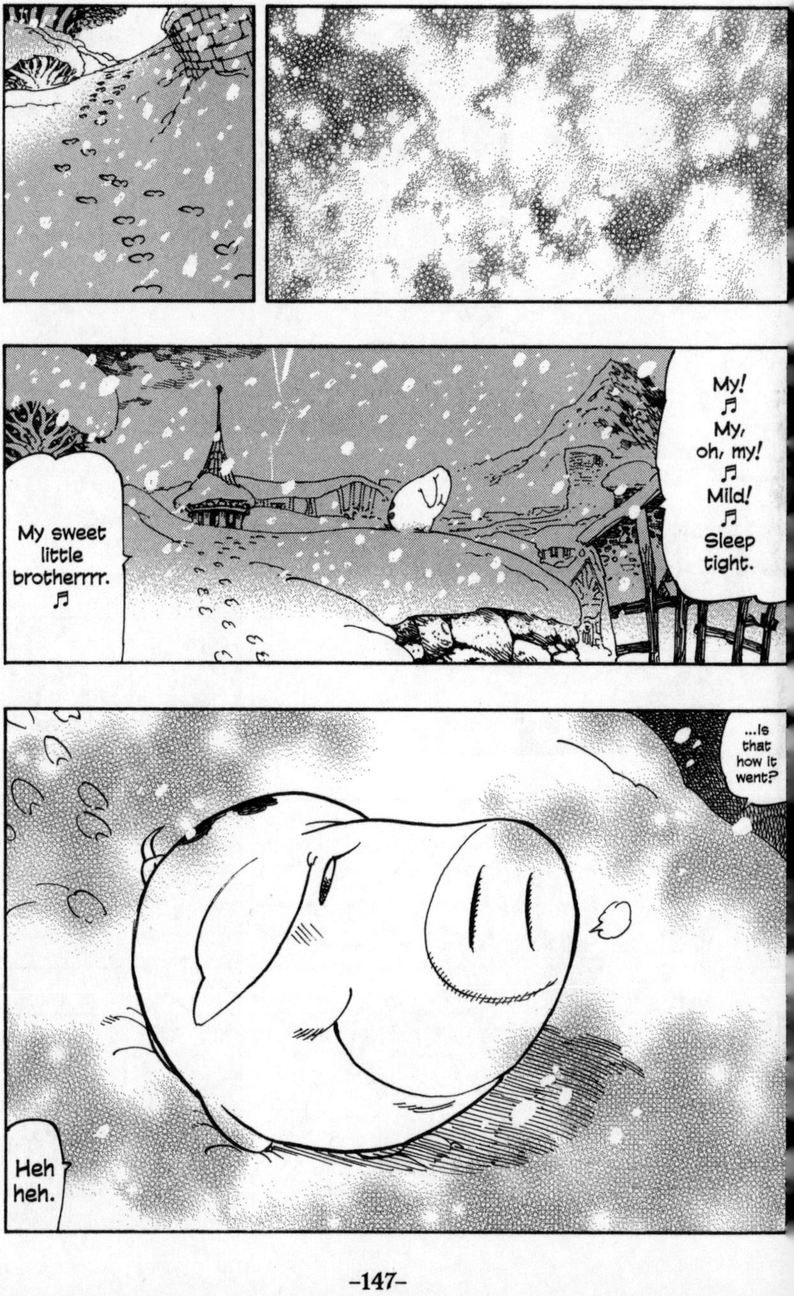
My! ♬ My, oh, my! ♬ Mild! ♬ Sleep tight.
My sweet little brotherrrr. ♬
...Is that how it went?
Heh heh.

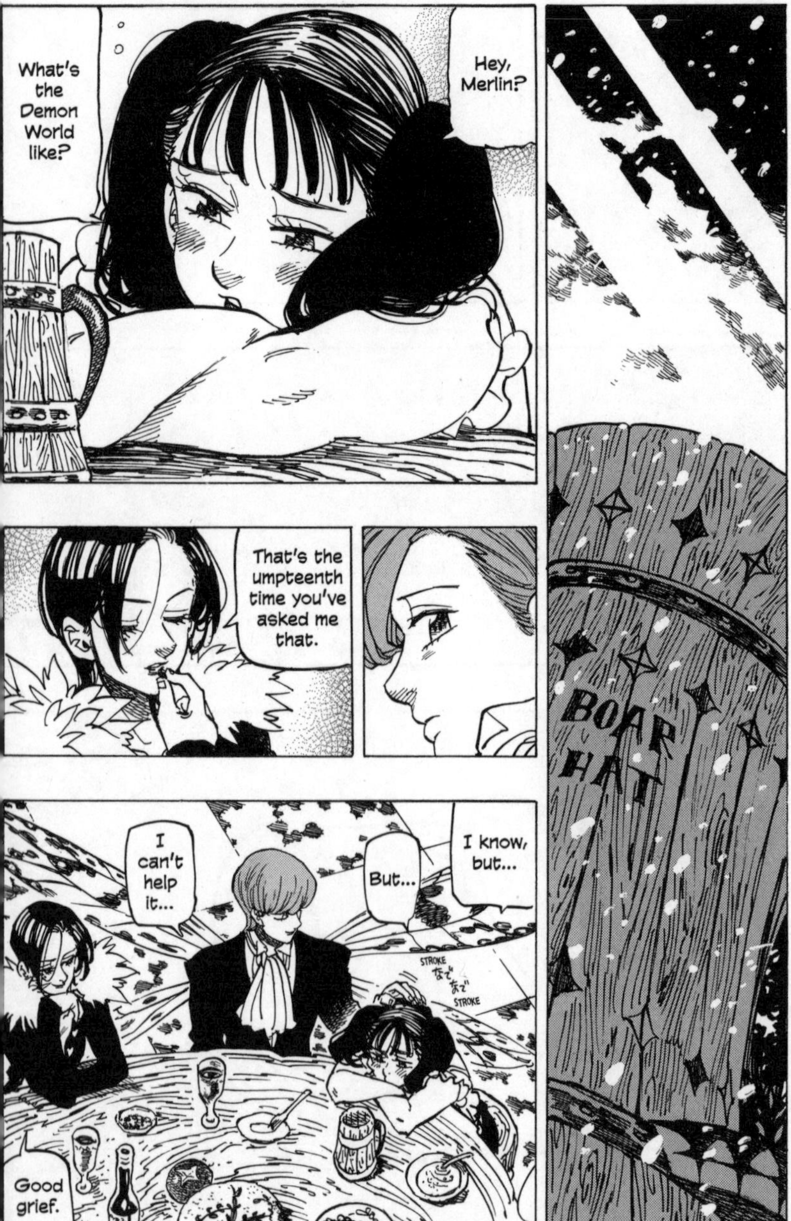
Hey, Merlin?
What's the Demon World like?
That's the umpteenth time you've asked me that.
I know, but...
But...
I can't help it...
STROKE なでなで STROKE
Good grief.

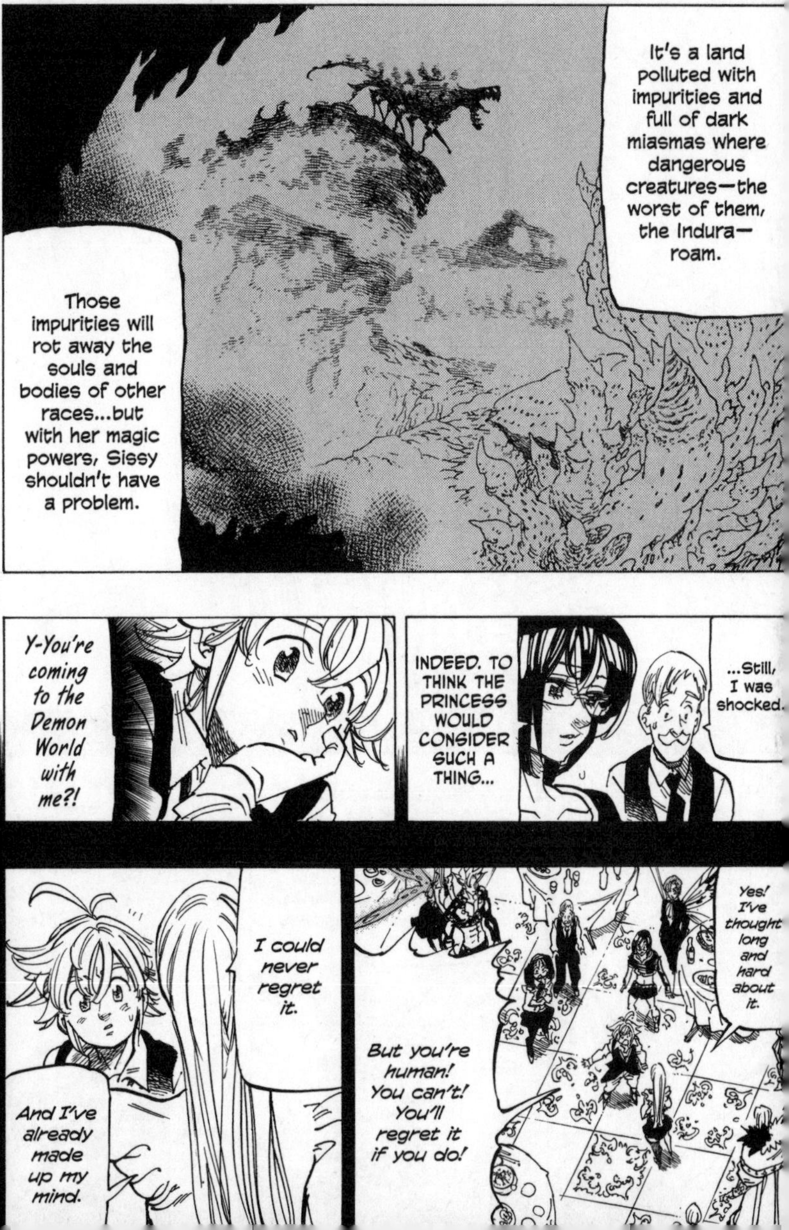
It's a land polluted with impurities and full of dark miasmas where dangerous creatures—the worst of them, the Indura—roam.
Those impurities will rot away the souls and bodies of other races...but with her magic powers, Sissy shouldn't have a problem.
...Still, I was shocked.
INDEED. TO THINK THE PRINCESS WOULD CONSIDER SUCH A THING...
Y-You're coming to the Demon World with me?!
Yes! I've thought long and hard about it.
But you're human! You can't! You'll regret it if you do!
I could never regret it.
And I've already made up my mind.

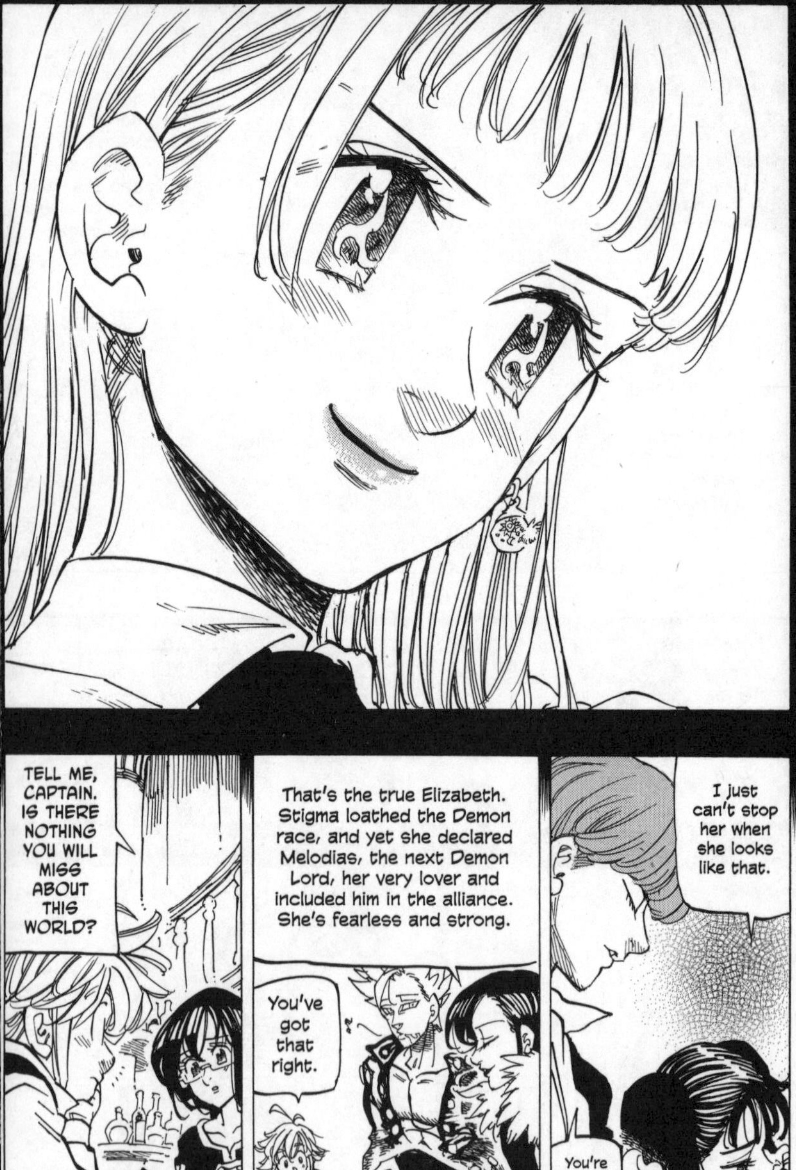
I just can't stop her when she looks like that.
You're not the only one.
That's the true Elizabeth. Stigma loathed the Demon race, and yet she declared Melodias, the next Demon Lord, her very lover and included him in the alliance. She's fearless and strong.
You've got that right.
TELL ME, CAPTAIN. IS THERE NOTHING YOU WILL MISS ABOUT THIS WORLD?

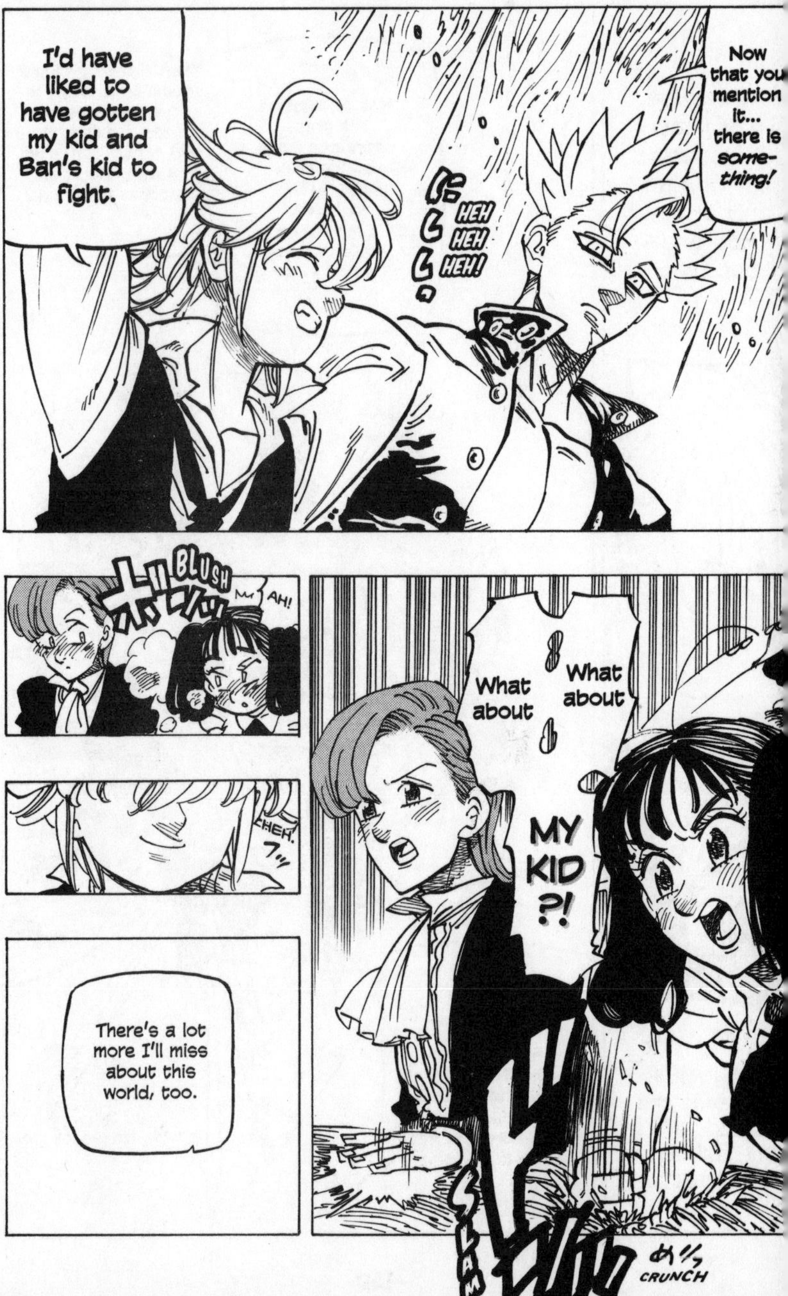

Now that you mention it... there is something!
HEH HEH HEH!
I'd have liked to have gotten my kid and Ban's kid to fight.
What about
What about
MY KID ?!
SLAM
CRUNCH
BLUSH
AH!
HEH.
There's a lot more I'll miss about this world, too.

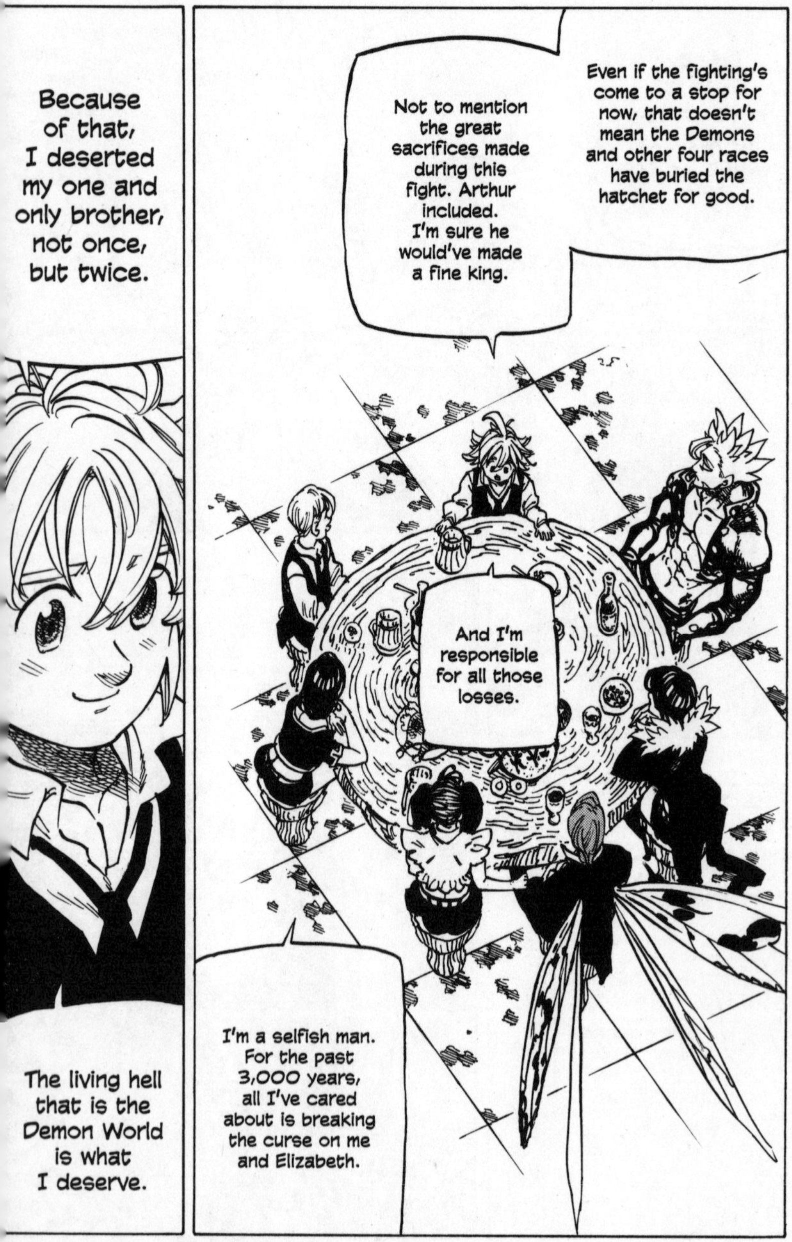
Even if the fighting's come to a stop for now, that doesn't mean the Demons and other four races have buried the hatchet for good.
Not to mention the great sacrifices made during this fight. Arthur included. I'm sure he would've made a fine king.
And I'm responsible for all those losses.
I'm a selfish man. For the past 3,000 years, all I've cared about is breaking the curse on me and Elizabeth.
Because of that, I deserted my one and only brother, not once, but twice.
The living hell that is the Demon World is what I deserve.

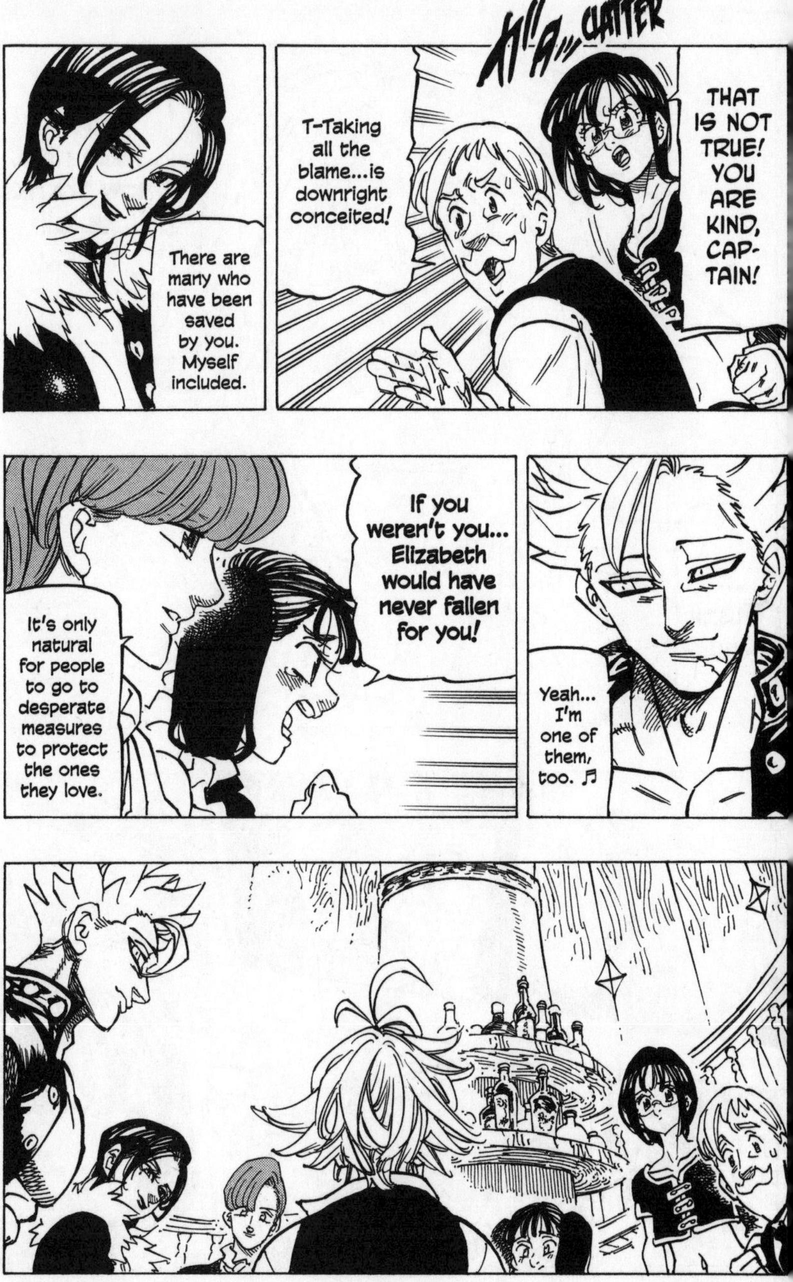
CLATTER
THAT IS NOT TRUE! YOU ARE KIND, CAPTAIN!
T-Taking all the blame...is downright conceited!
There are many who have been saved by you. Myself included.
Yeah... I'm one of them, too. ♪
If you weren't you... Elizabeth would have never fallen for you!
It's only natural for people to go to desperate measures to protect the ones they love.

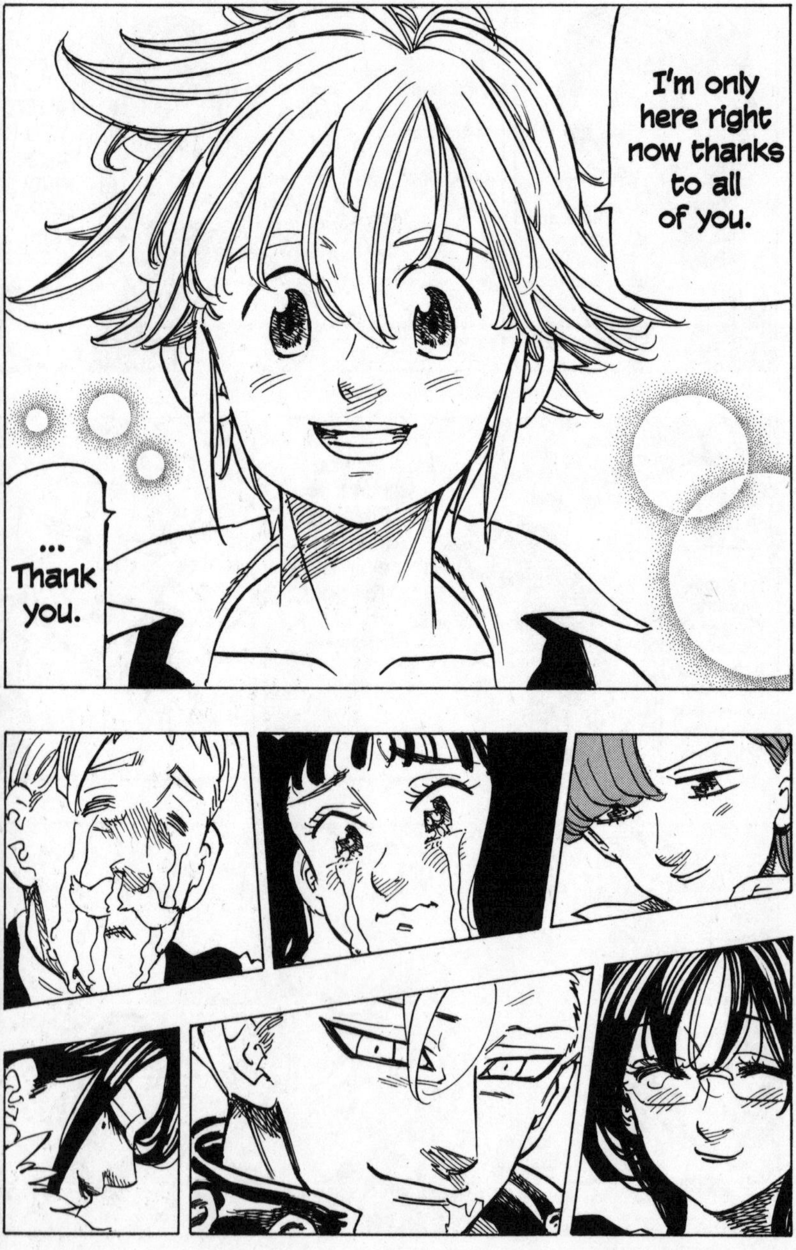
I'm only here right now thanks to all of you.
... Thank you.

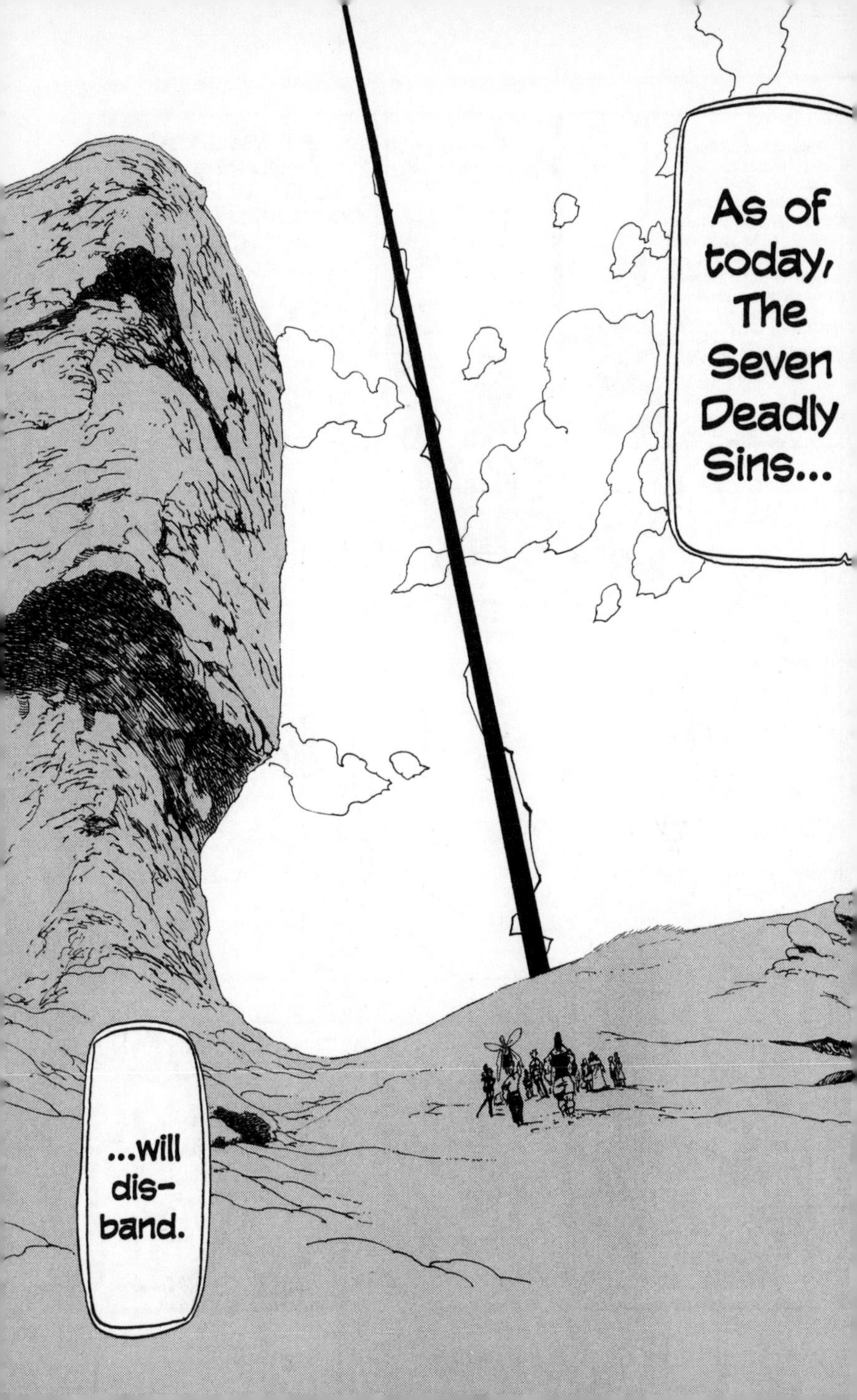
As of today, The Seven Deadly Sins...
...will dis-band.

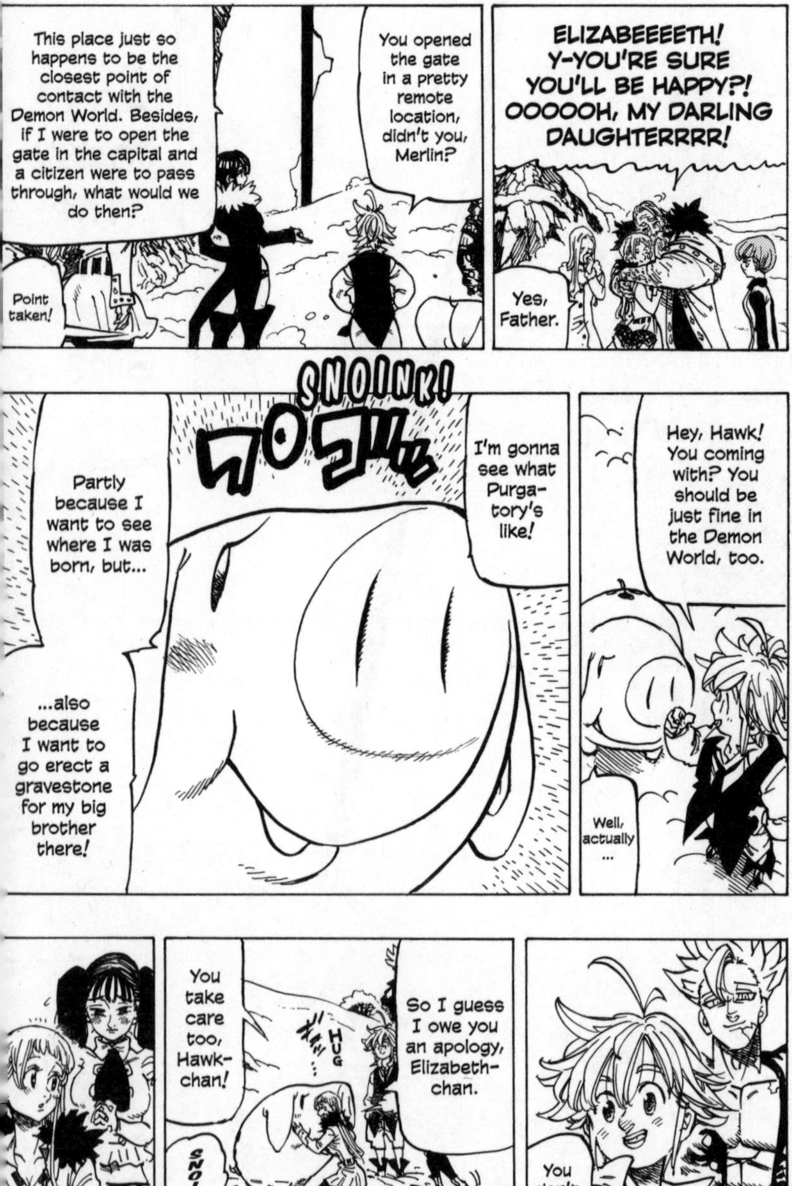
ELIZABEEEETH! Y-YOU'RE SURE YOU'LL BE HAPPY?! OOOOOH, MY DARLING DAUGHTERRRR!
Yes, Father.
You opened the gate in a pretty remote location, didn't you, Merlin?
This place just so happens to be the closest point of contact with the Demon World. Besides, if I were to open the gate in the capital and a citizen were to pass through, what would we do then?
Point taken!
Hey, Hawk! You coming with? You should be just fine in the Demon World, too.
Well, actually...
SNOINK!
I'm gonna see what Purgatory's like!
Partly because I want to see where I was born, but...
...also because I want to go erect a gravestone for my big brother there!
You don't say!
So I guess I owe you an apology, Elizabeth-chan.
HUG
CRUNCH
You take care too, Hawk-chan!
SNOINK!

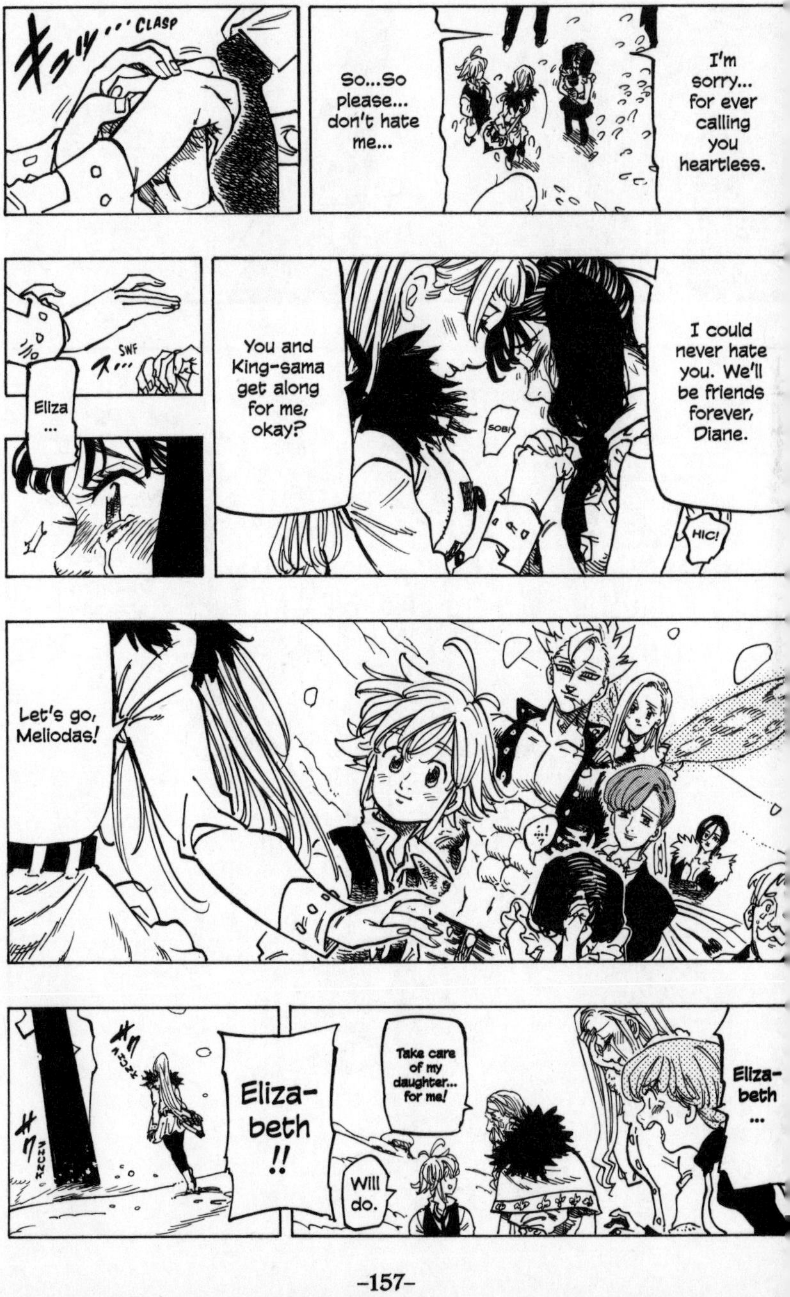
I'm sorry... for ever calling you heartless.
So...So please... don't hate me...
キュッ... CLASP
I could never hate you. We'll be friends forever, Diane.
HIC!
SOB!
You and King-sama get along for me, okay?
SWF
Eliza ...
Let's go, Meliodas!
Eliza-beth ...
Take care of my daughter... for me!
Will do.
Eliza-beth !!
SHUNK

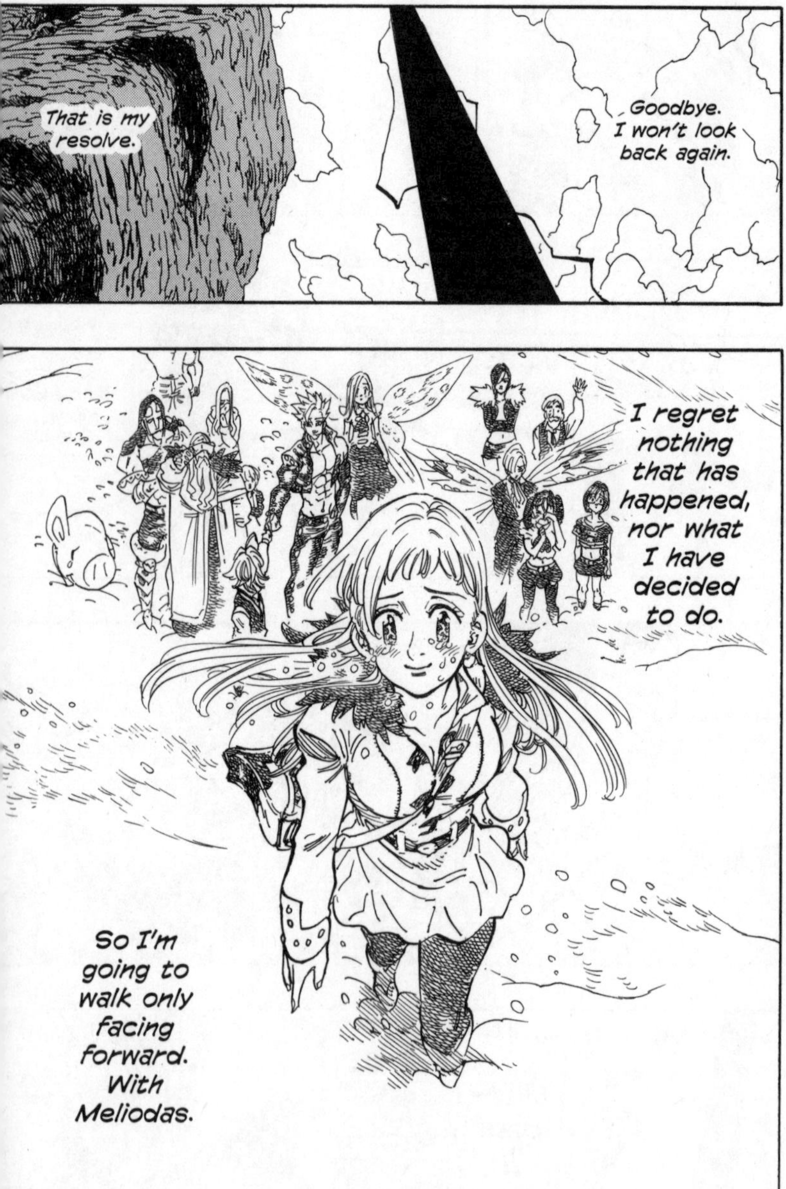
Goodbye. I won't look back again.
That is my resolve.
I regret nothing that has happened, nor what I have decided to do.
So I'm going to walk only facing forward. With Meliodas.

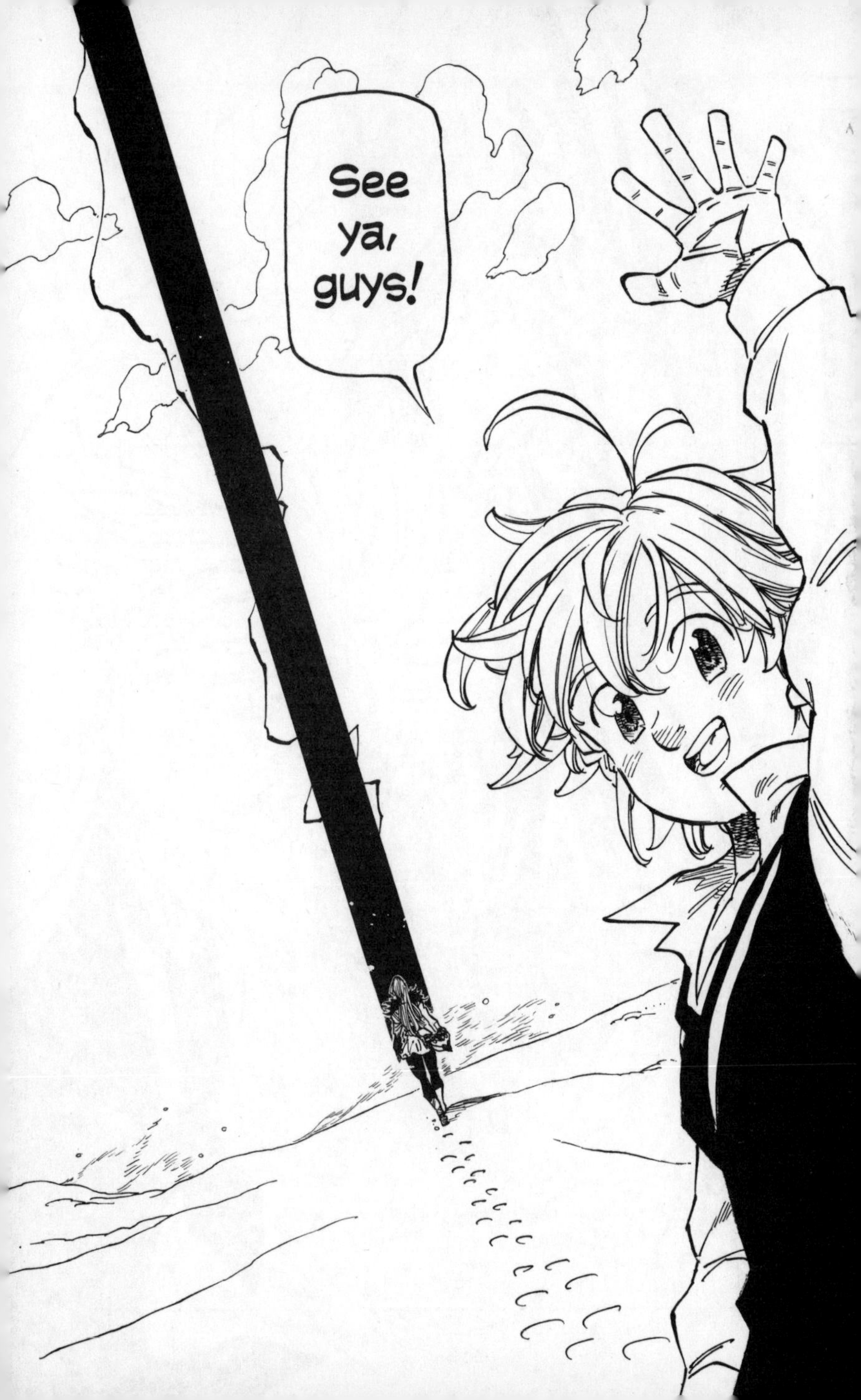
See ya, guys!

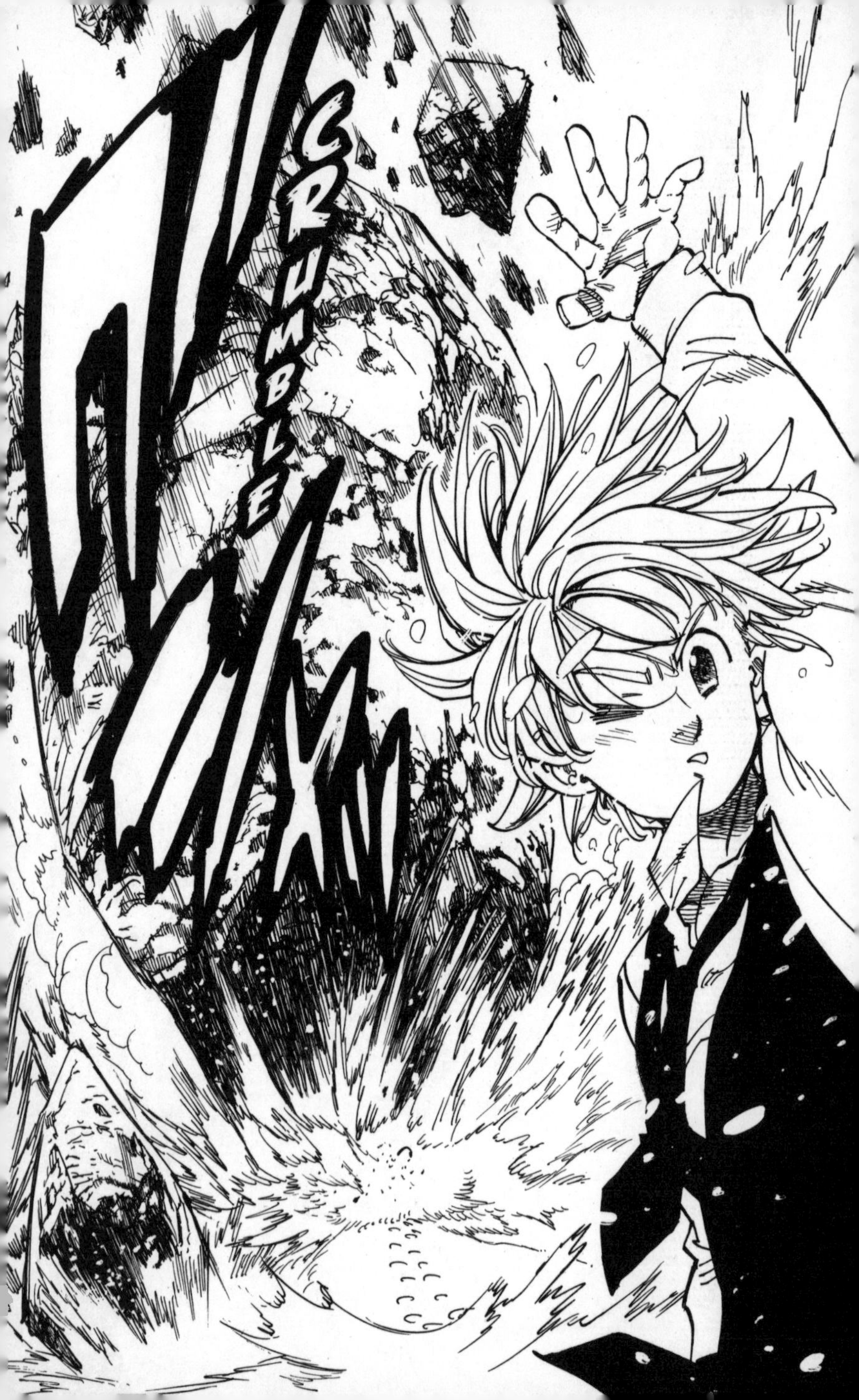
CRUMBLE

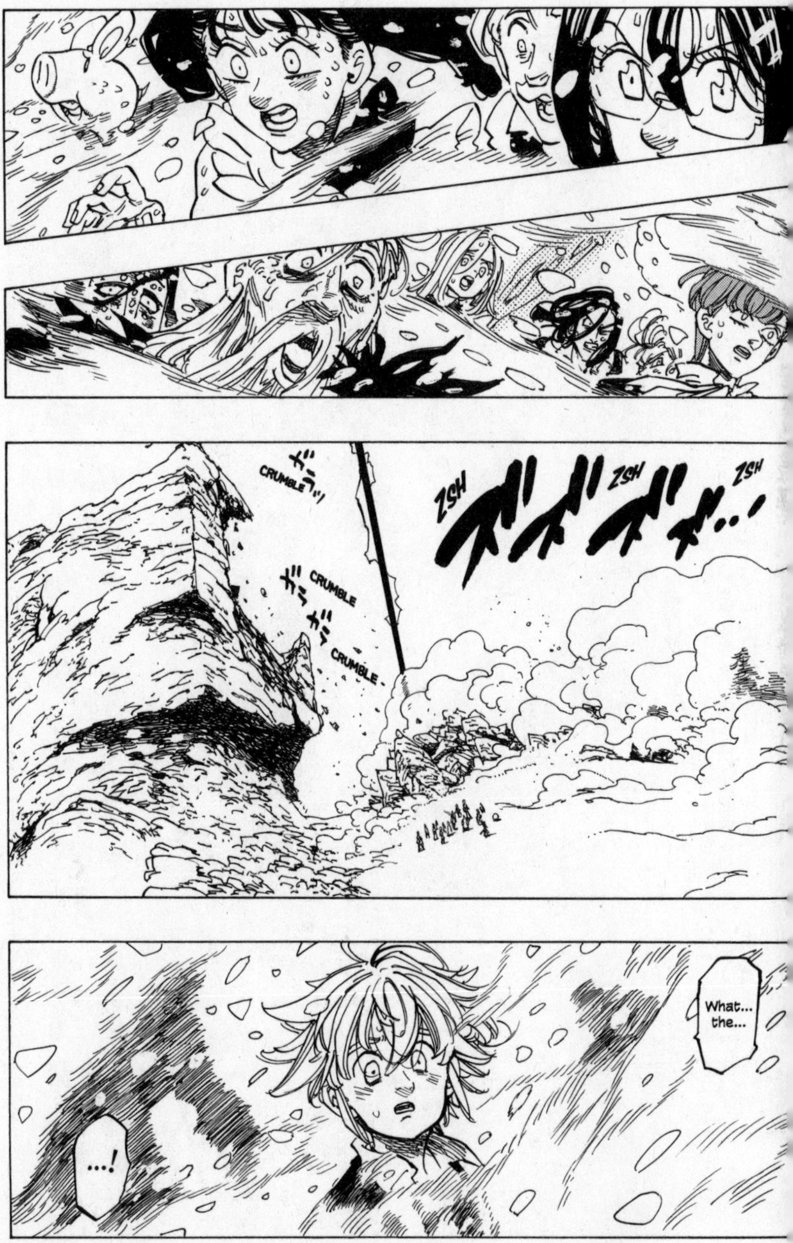
ZSH
ZSH
ZSH
CRUMBLE
CRUMBLE
CRUMBLE
What... the...
...!

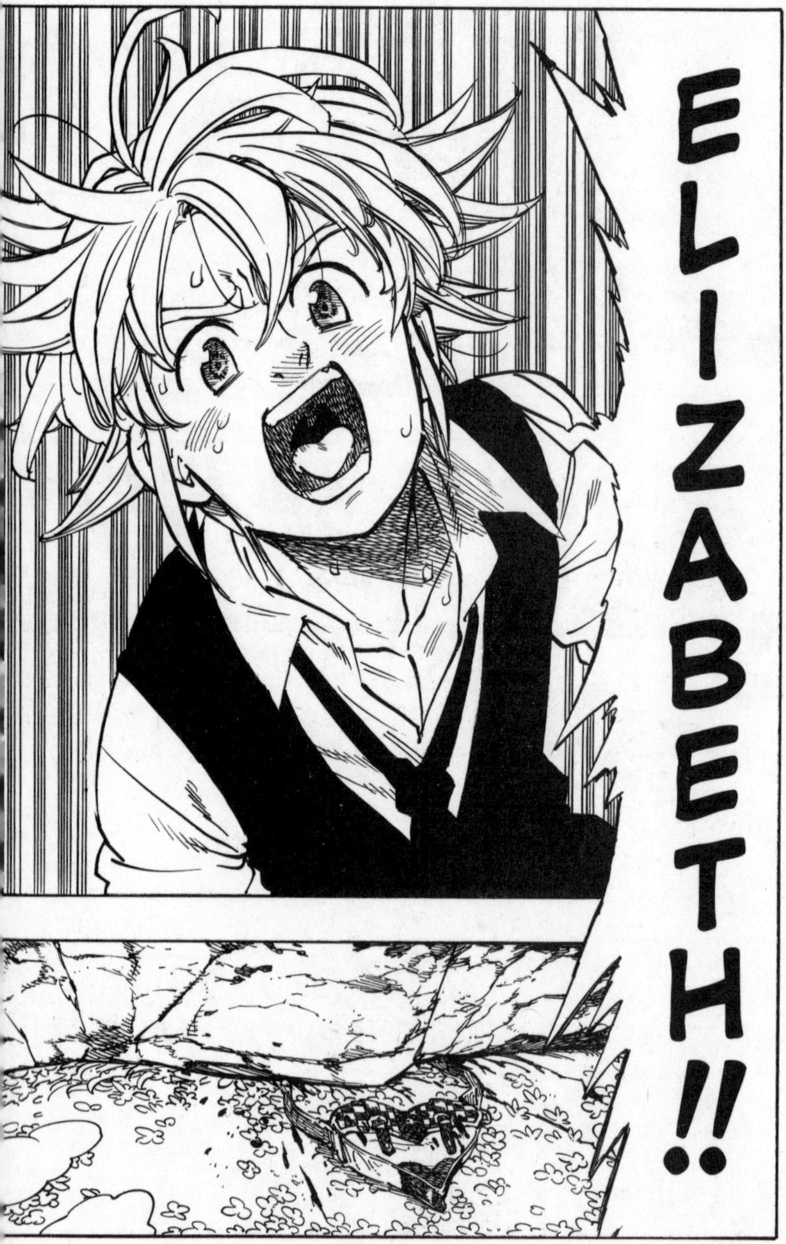
ELIZABETH!!

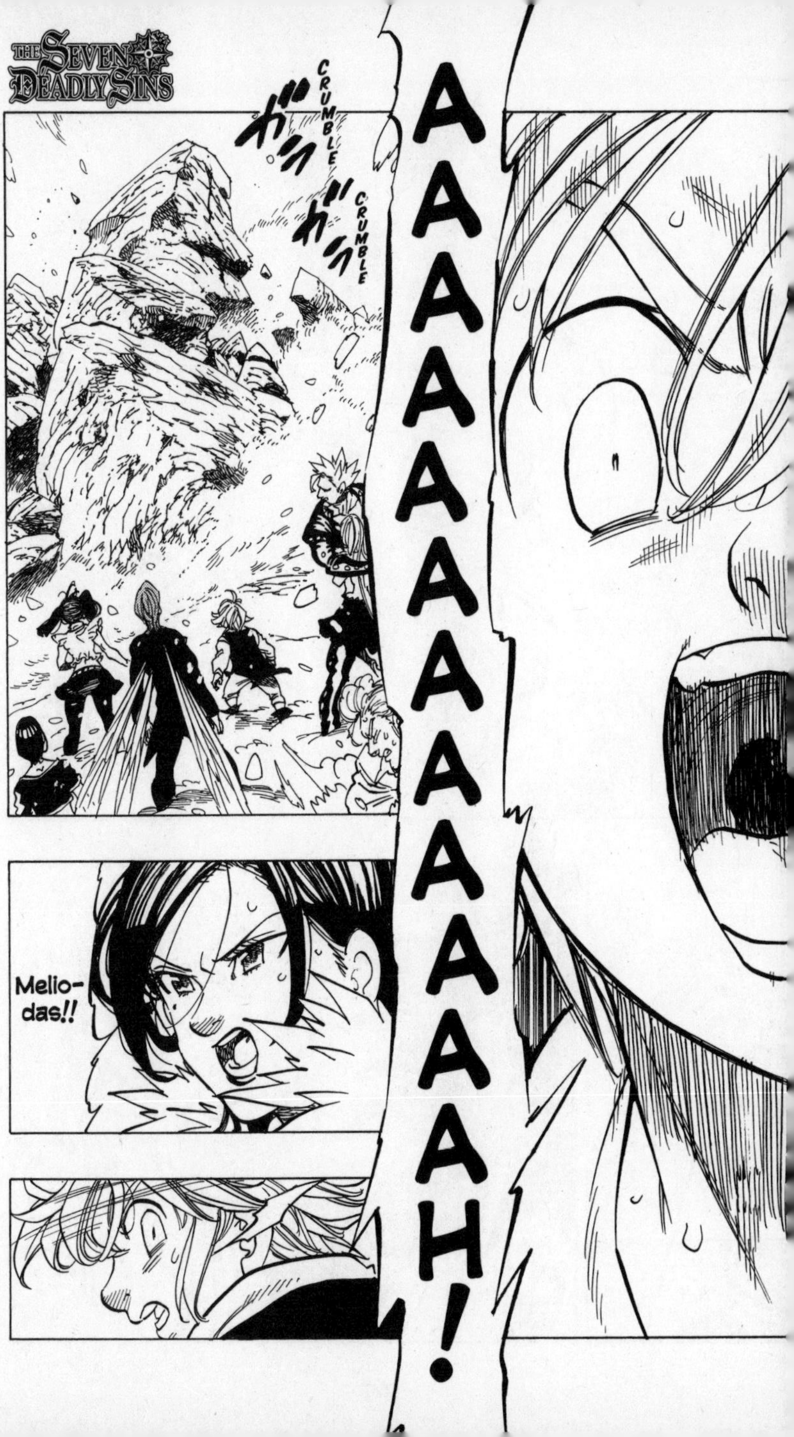
AAAAAAAAAAAH!
CRUMBLE
CRUMBLE
Melio-
das!!

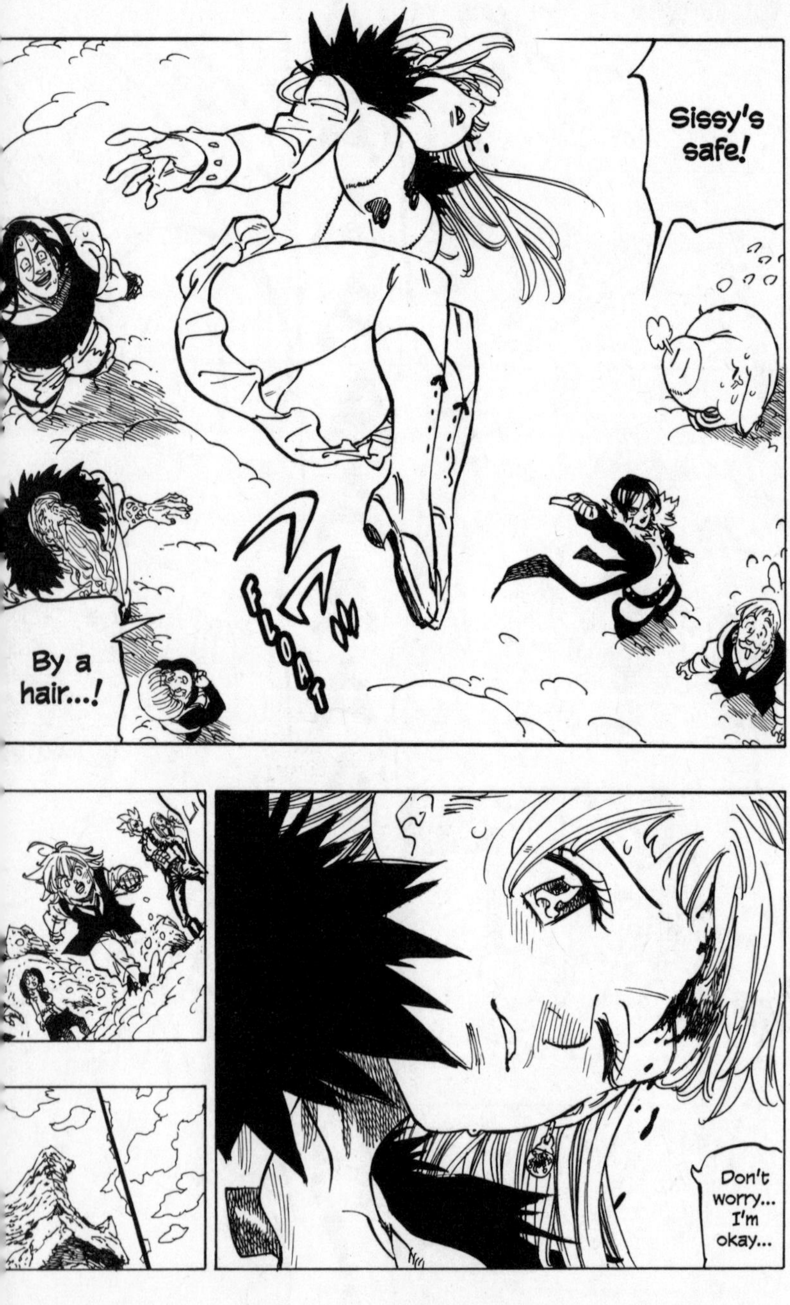
Sissy's safe!
FLOAT
By a hair...!
Don't worry... I'm okay...

# Chapter 311 - It's Not Over Yet

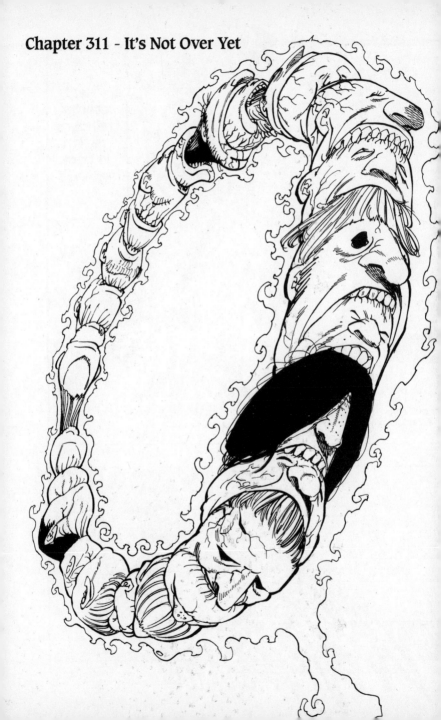

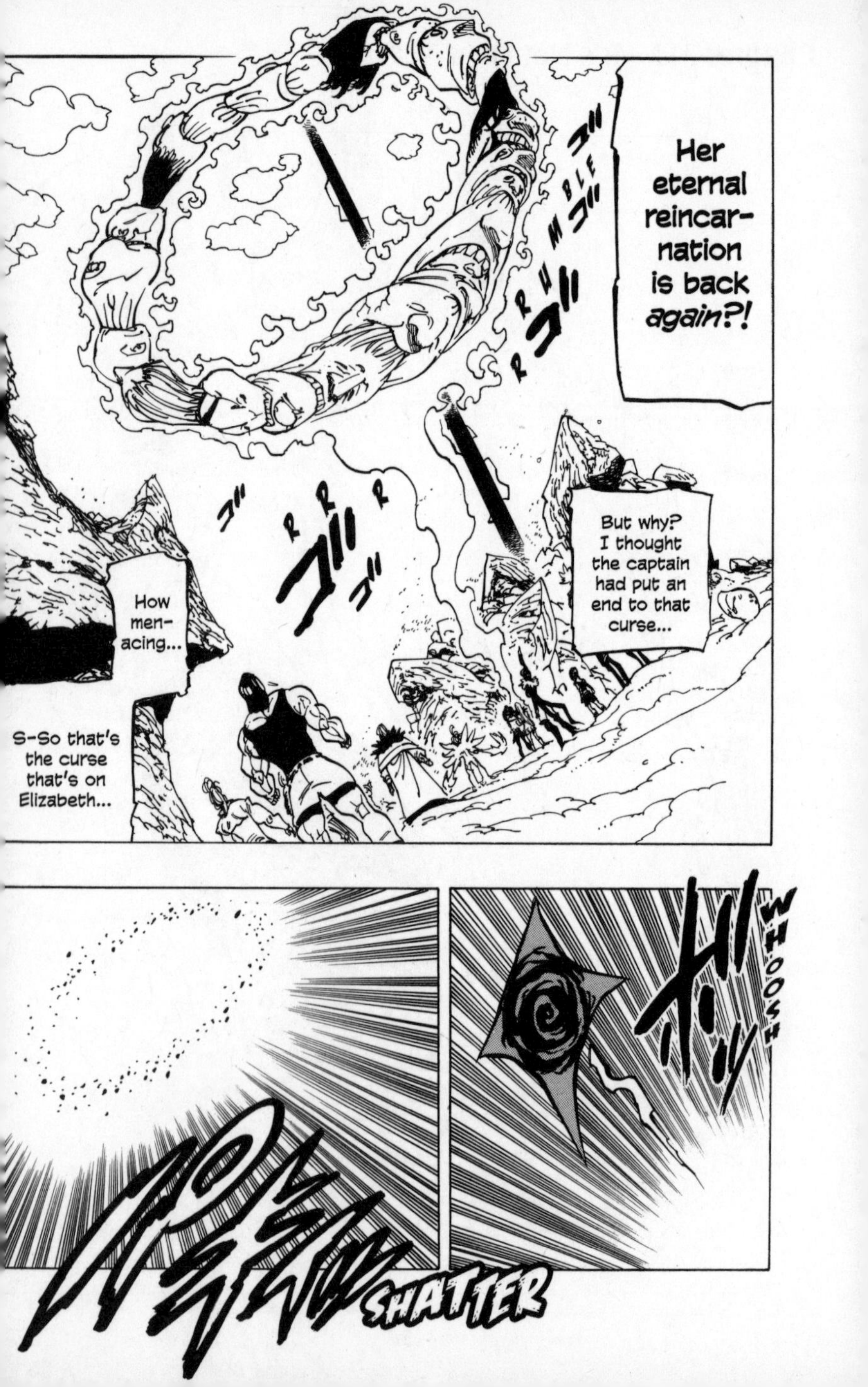
Her eternal reincar-nation is back *again*?!
RUMBLE
But why? I thought the captain had put an end to that curse...
RRR
How men-acing...
S-So that's the curse that's on Elizabeth...
WHOOSH
SHATTER

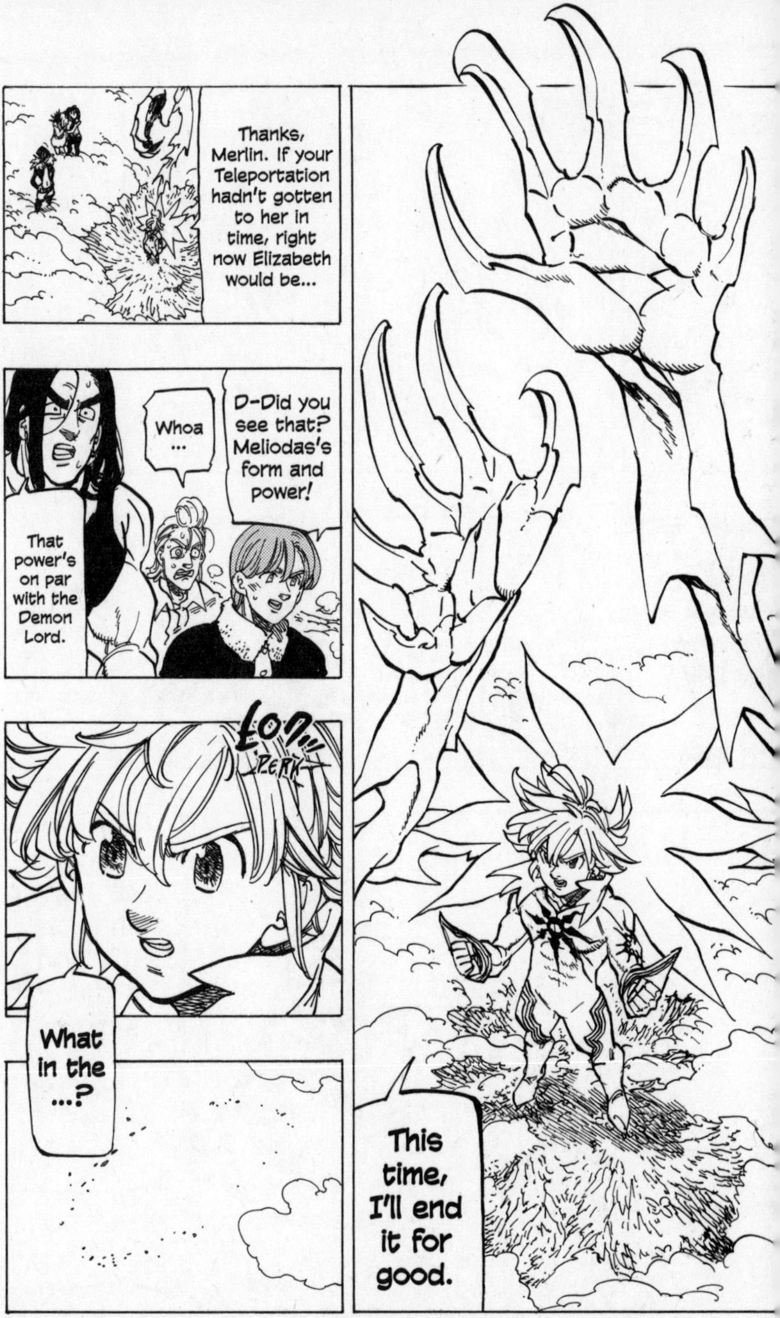
This time, I'll end it for good.
Thanks, Merlin. If your Teleportation hadn't gotten to her in time, right now Elizabeth would be...
D-Did you see that? Meliodas's form and power!
Whoa ...
That power's on par with the Demon Lord.
PERK
What in the ...?

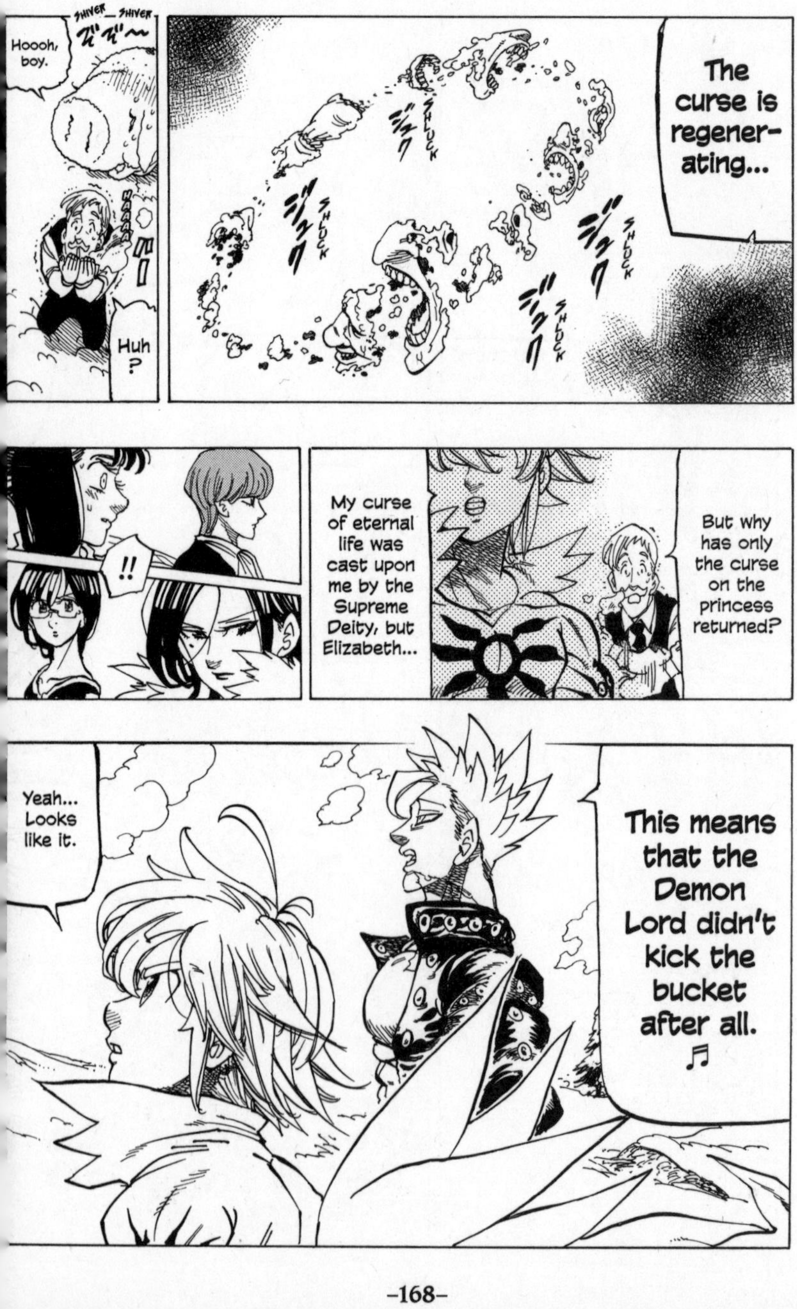
The curse is regenerating...
SHLUCK
SHLUCK
SHLUCK
SHLUCK
SHIVER SHIVER
Hoooh, boy.
Huh?
But why has only the curse on the princess returned?
My curse of eternal life was cast upon me by the Supreme Deity, but Elizabeth...
!!
This means that the Demon Lord didn't kick the bucket after all. ♬
Yeah... Looks like it.

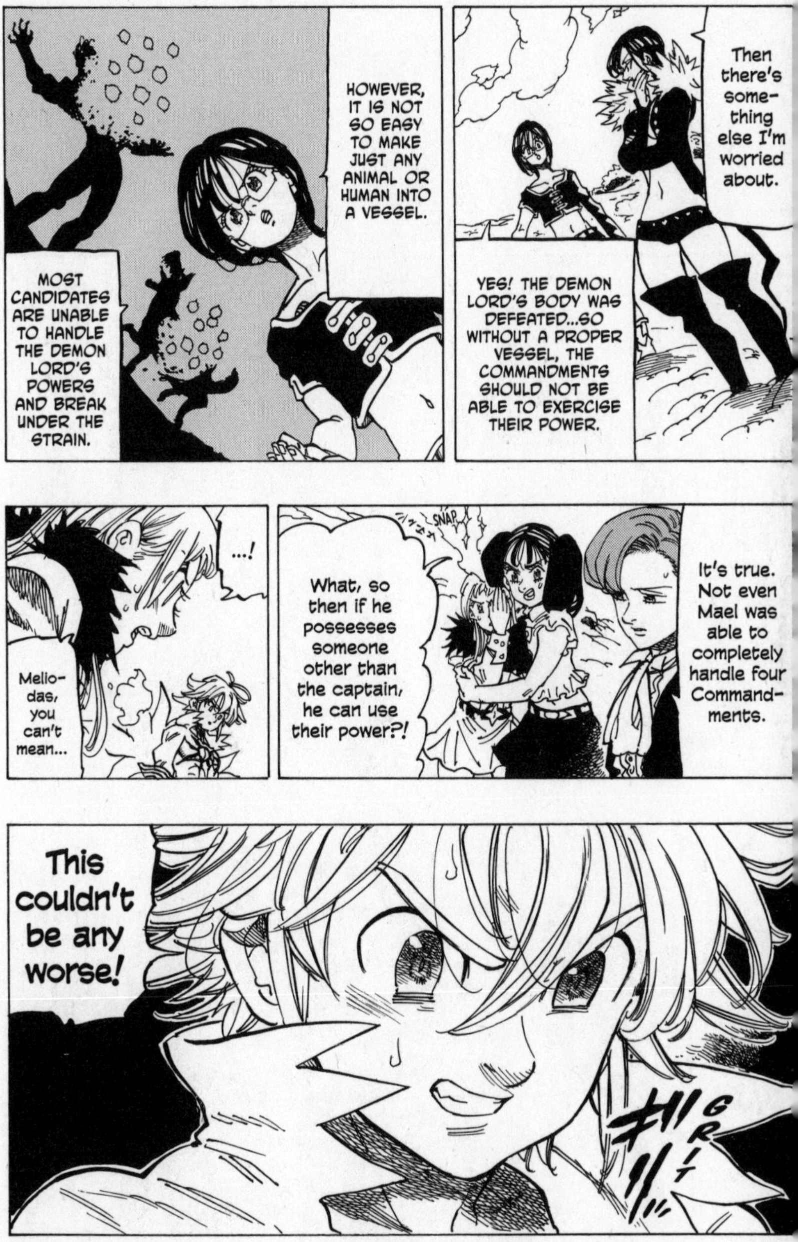
Then there's something else I'm worried about.
YES! THE DEMON LORD'S BODY WAS DEFEATED...SO WITHOUT A PROPER VESSEL, THE COMMANDMENTS SHOULD NOT BE ABLE TO EXERCISE THEIR POWER.
HOWEVER, IT IS NOT SO EASY TO MAKE JUST ANY ANIMAL OR HUMAN INTO A VESSEL.
MOST CANDIDATES ARE UNABLE TO HANDLE THE DEMON LORD'S POWERS AND BREAK UNDER THE STRAIN.
It's true. Not even Mael was able to completely handle four Commandments.
SNAP
What, so then if he possesses someone other than the captain, he can use their power?!
...!
Melio-das, you can't mean...
This couldn't be any worse!
GRIT

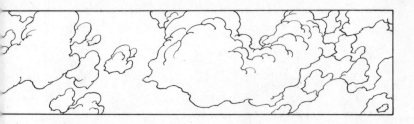

WELL
DONE.

CU-
SACK
....!

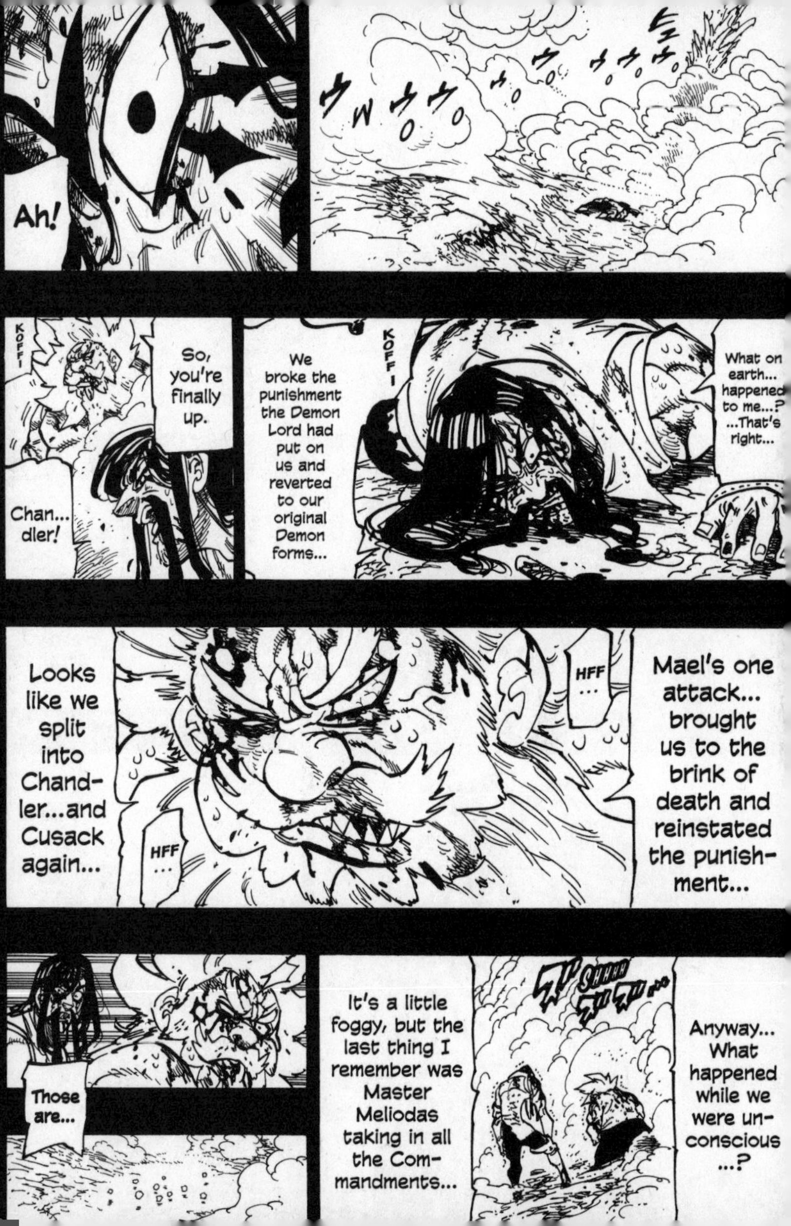

Ah!
What on earth... happened to me...? ...That's right...
KOFF
We broke the punishment the Demon Lord had put on us and reverted to our original Demon forms...
KOFF
So, you're finally up.
Chan... dler!
Mael's one attack... brought us to the brink of death and reinstated the punish-ment...
HFF...
HFF...
Looks like we split into Chand-ler...and Cusack again...
Anyway... What happened while we were un-conscious...?
SHHHH
It's a little foggy, but the last thing I remember was Master Meliodas taking in all the Com-mandments...
Those are...

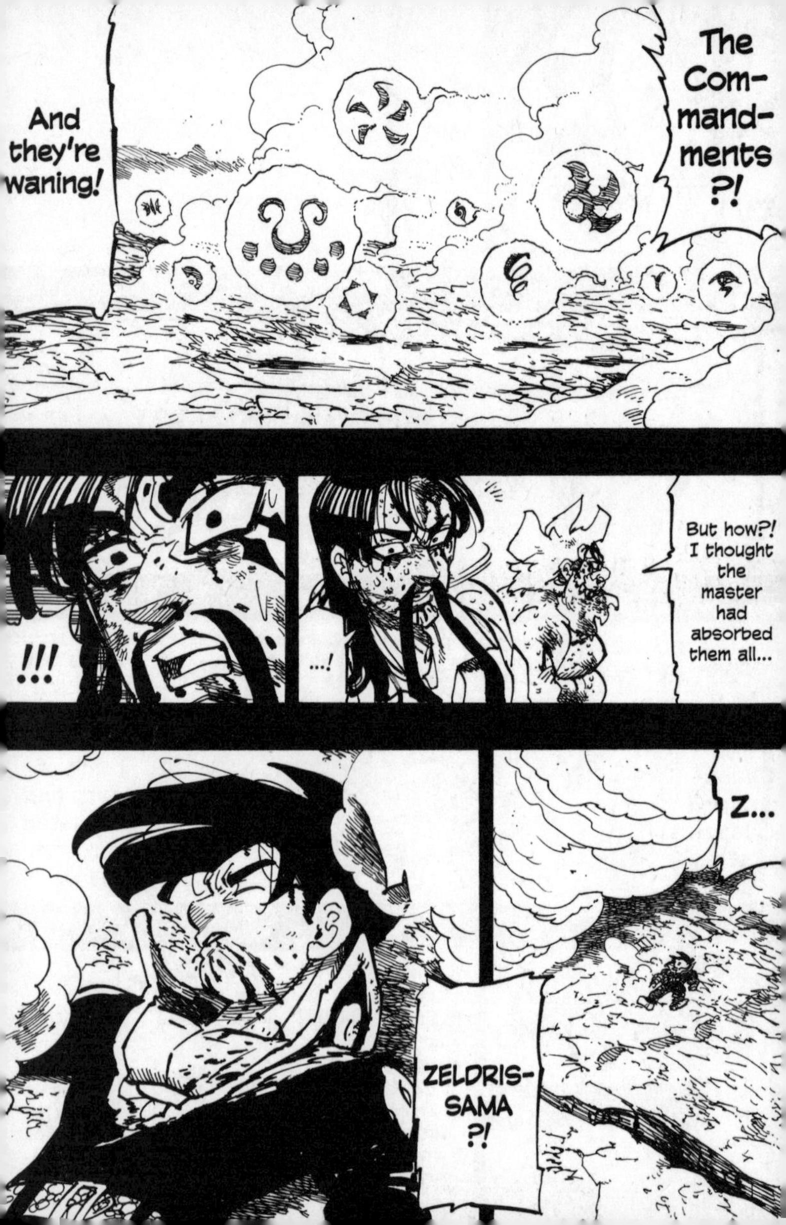
The Com-mand-ments?!
And they're waning!
But how?! I thought the master had absorbed them all...
...!
!!!
Z...
ZELDRIS-SAMA?!

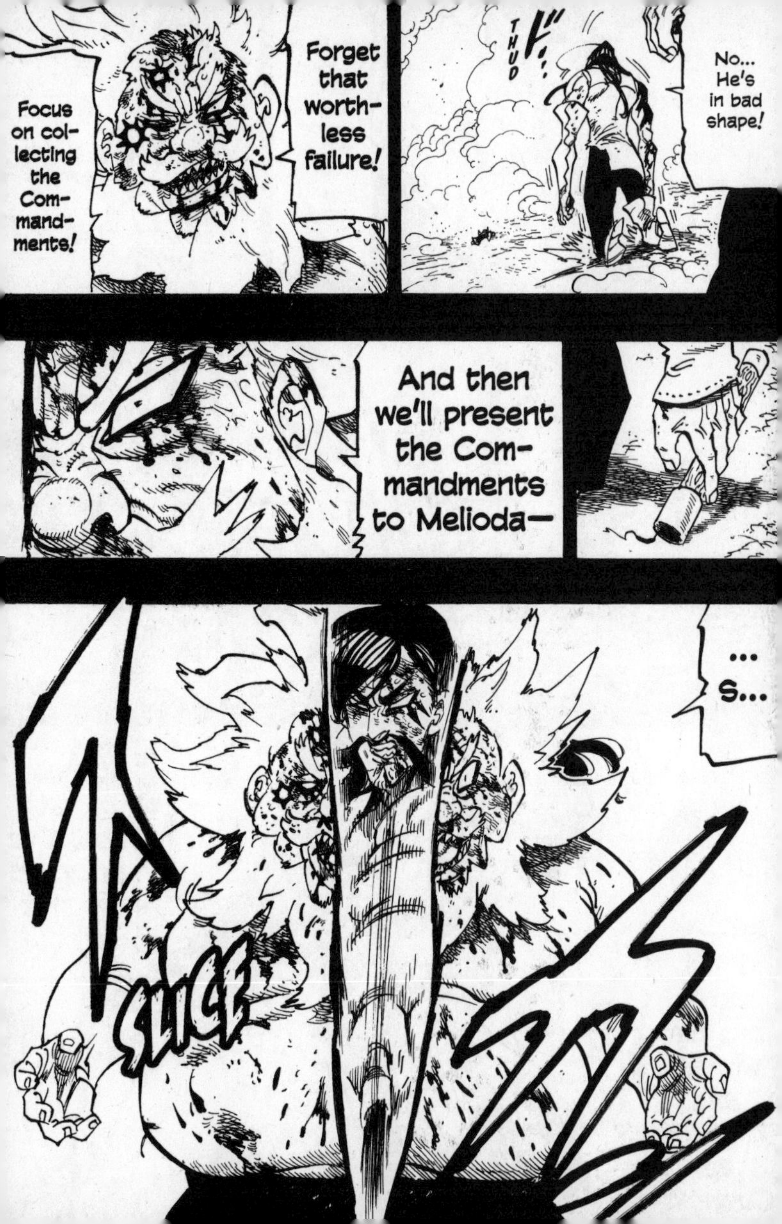
No... He's in bad shape!
THUD
Forget that worthless failure!
Focus on collecting the Commandments!
And then we'll present the Commandments to Melioda—
... S...
SLICE

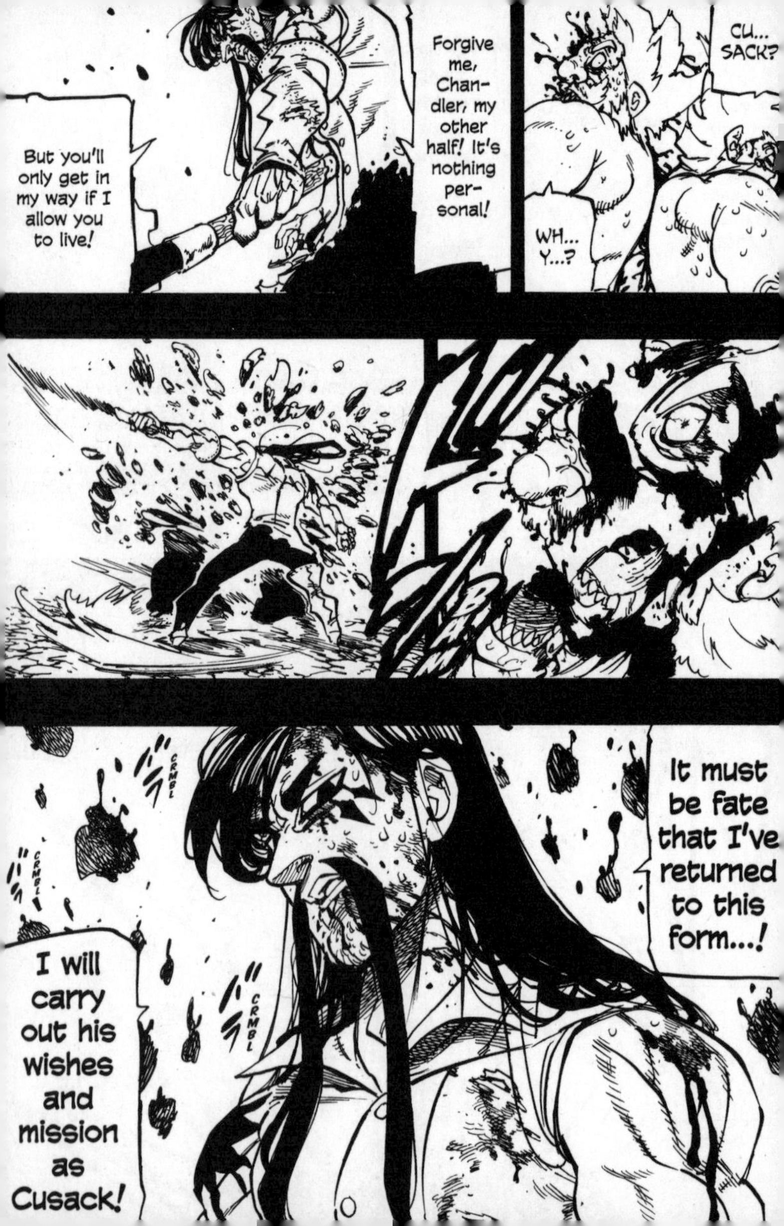
CU... SACK?
WH... Y...?
Forgive me, Chandler, my other half! It's nothing personal!
But you'll only get in my way if I allow you to live!
It must be fate that I've returned to this form...!
CRMBL
CRMBL
CRMBL
I will carry out his wishes and mission as Cusack!

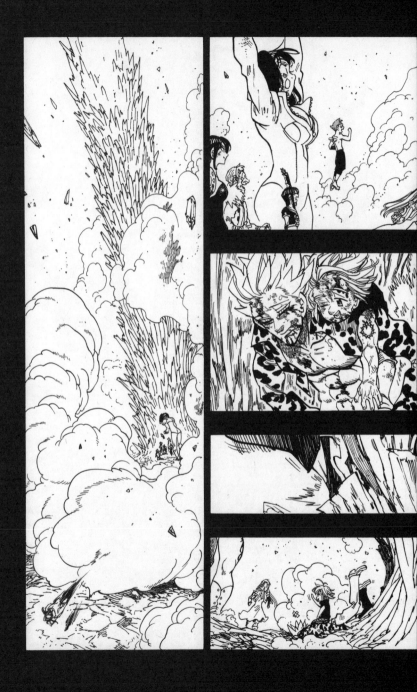

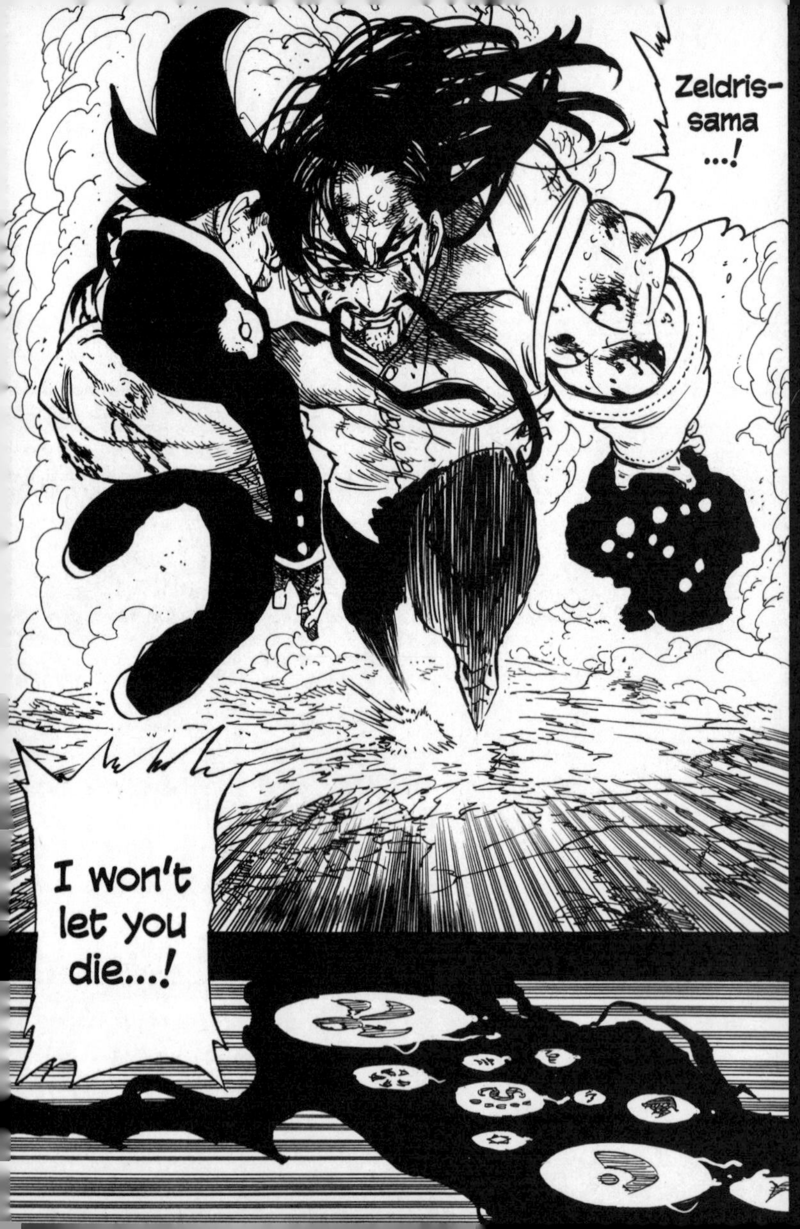
Zeldris-sama ...!
I won't let you die...!

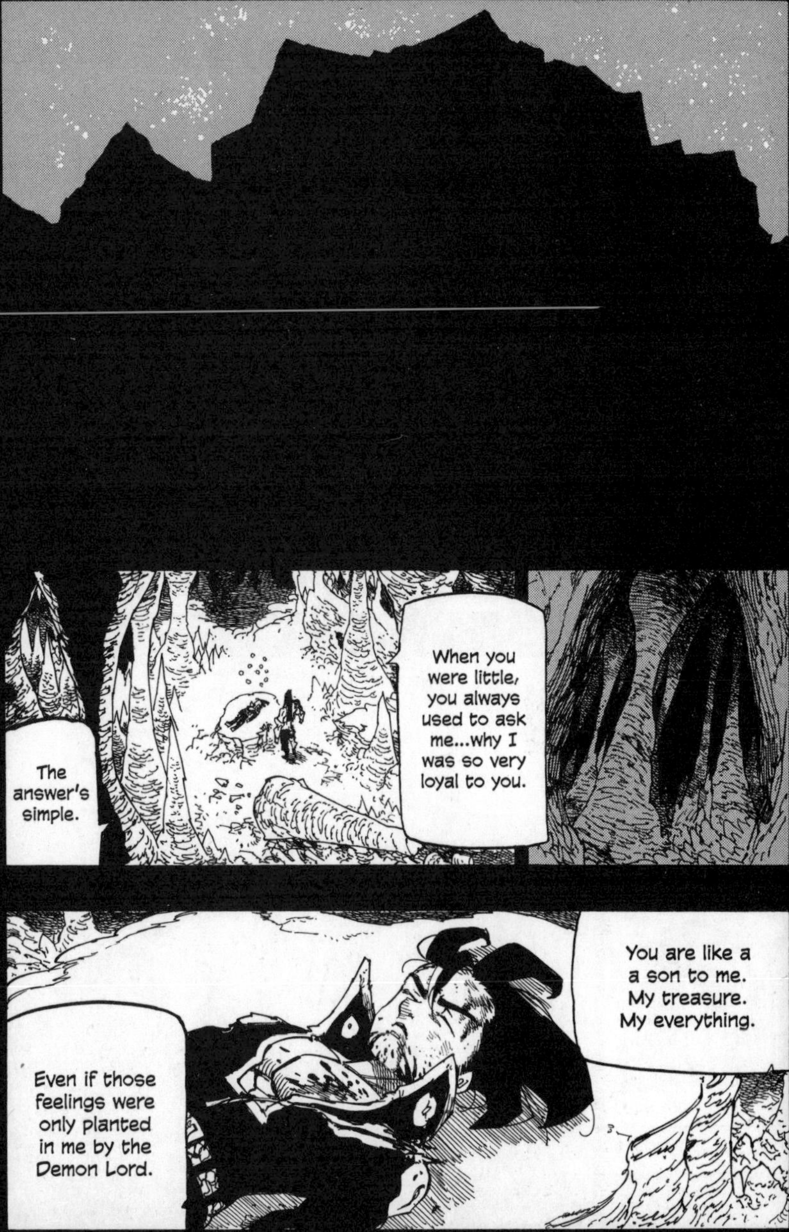
When you were little, you always used to ask me...why I was so very loyal to you.
The answer's simple.
You are like a a son to me. My treasure. My everything.
Even if those feelings were only planted in me by the Demon Lord.

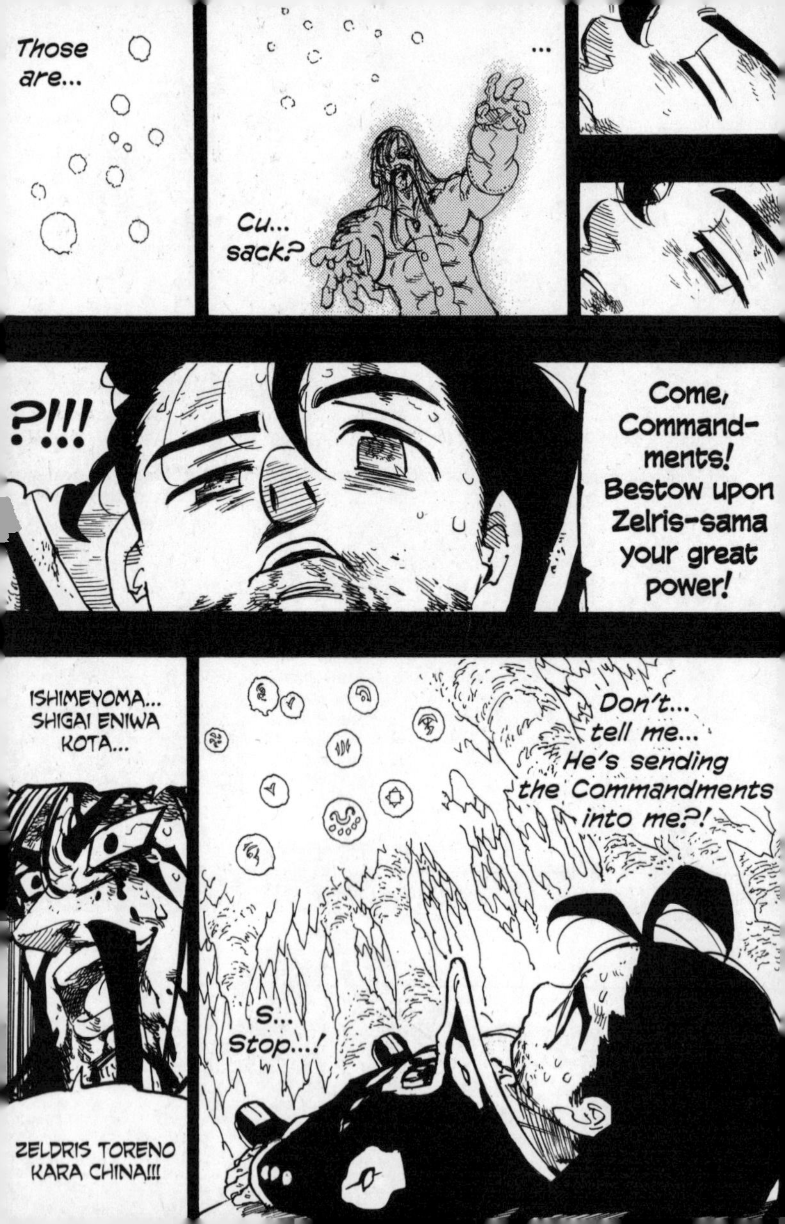
...
Cu... sack?
Those are...
Come, Commandments! Bestow upon Zelris-sama your great power!
?!!!
Don't... tell me... He's sending the Commandments into me?!
S... Stop...!
ISHIMEYOMA... SHIGAI ENIWA KOTA...
ZELDRIS TORENO KARA CHINA!!!

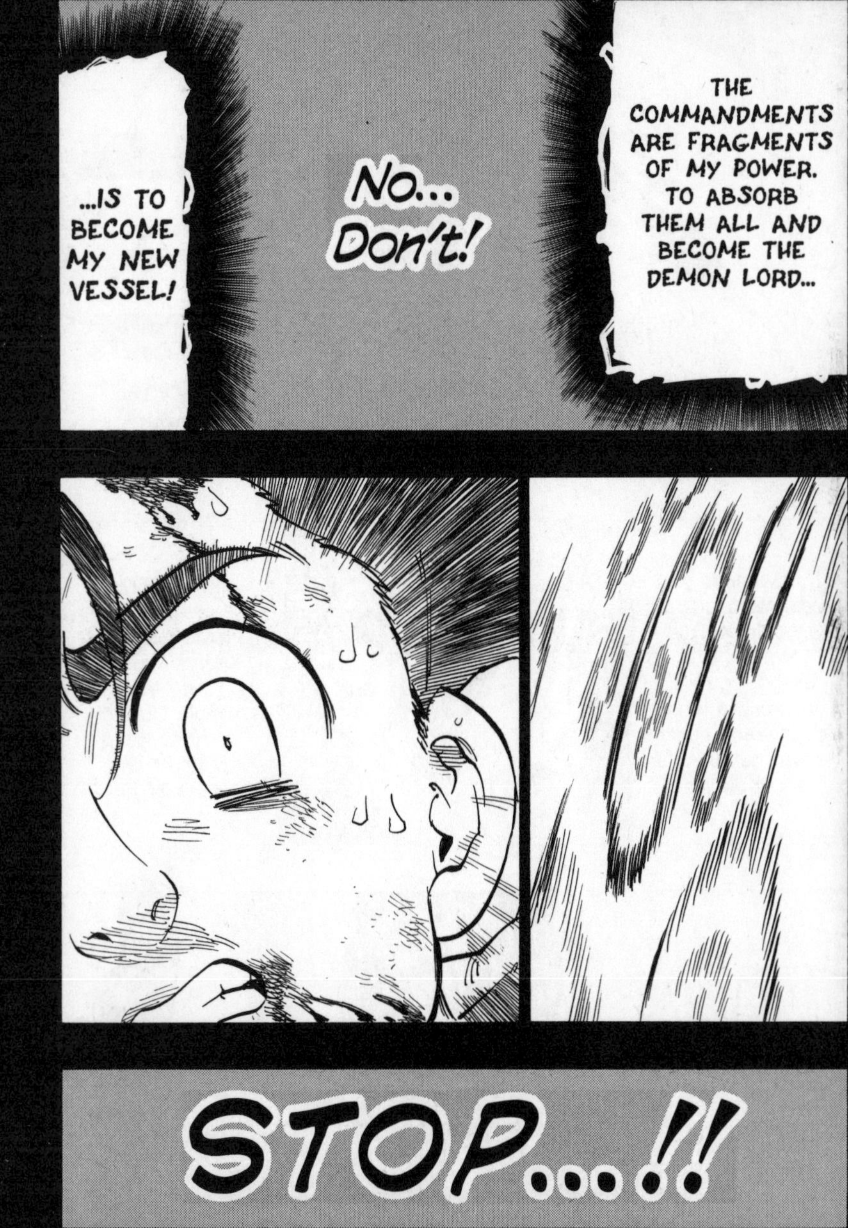
THE COMMANDMENTS ARE FRAGMENTS OF MY POWER. TO ABSORB THEM ALL AND BECOME THE DEMON LORD...
No... Don't!
...IS TO BECOME MY NEW VESSEL!
STOP...!!

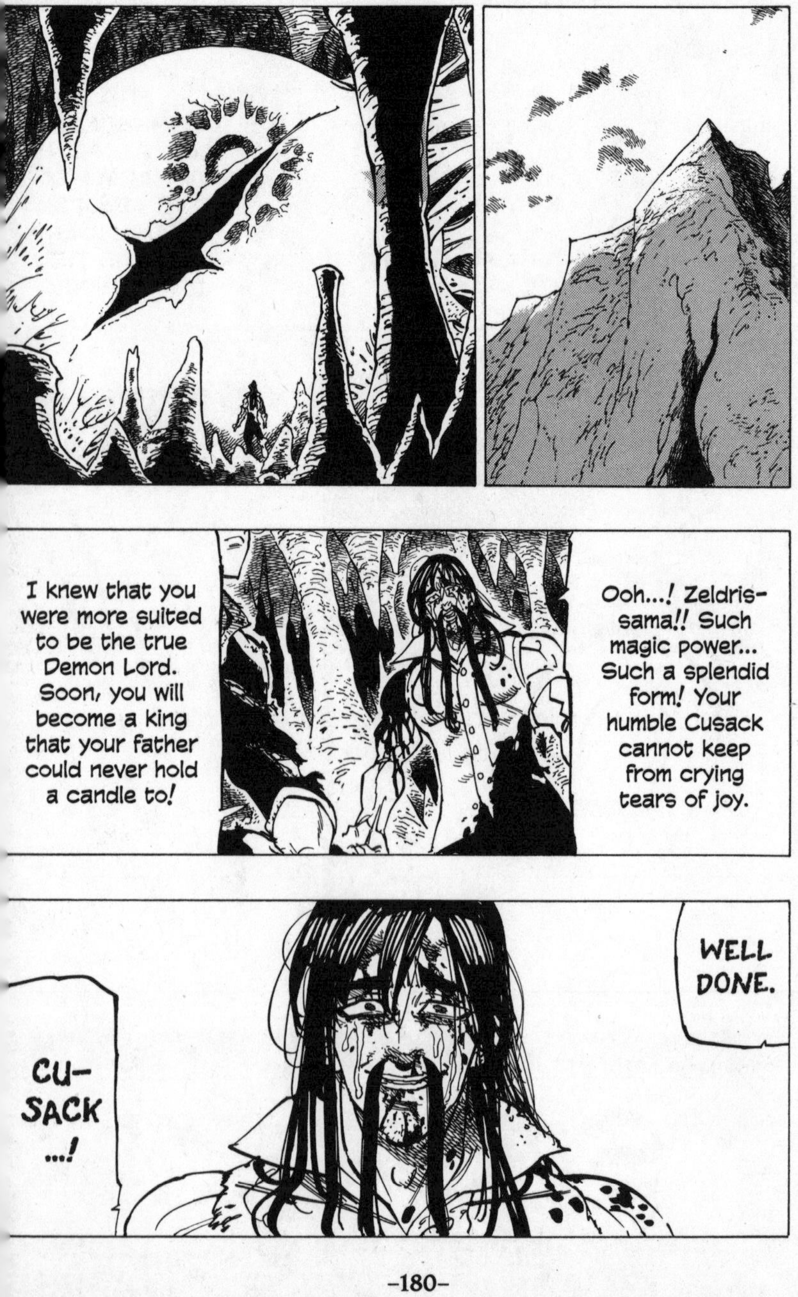
Ooh...! Zeldris-sama!! Such magic power... Such a splendid form! Your humble Cusack cannot keep from crying tears of joy.
I knew that you were more suited to be the true Demon Lord. Soon, you will become a king that your father could never hold a candle to!
WELL DONE.
CU-SACK ...!

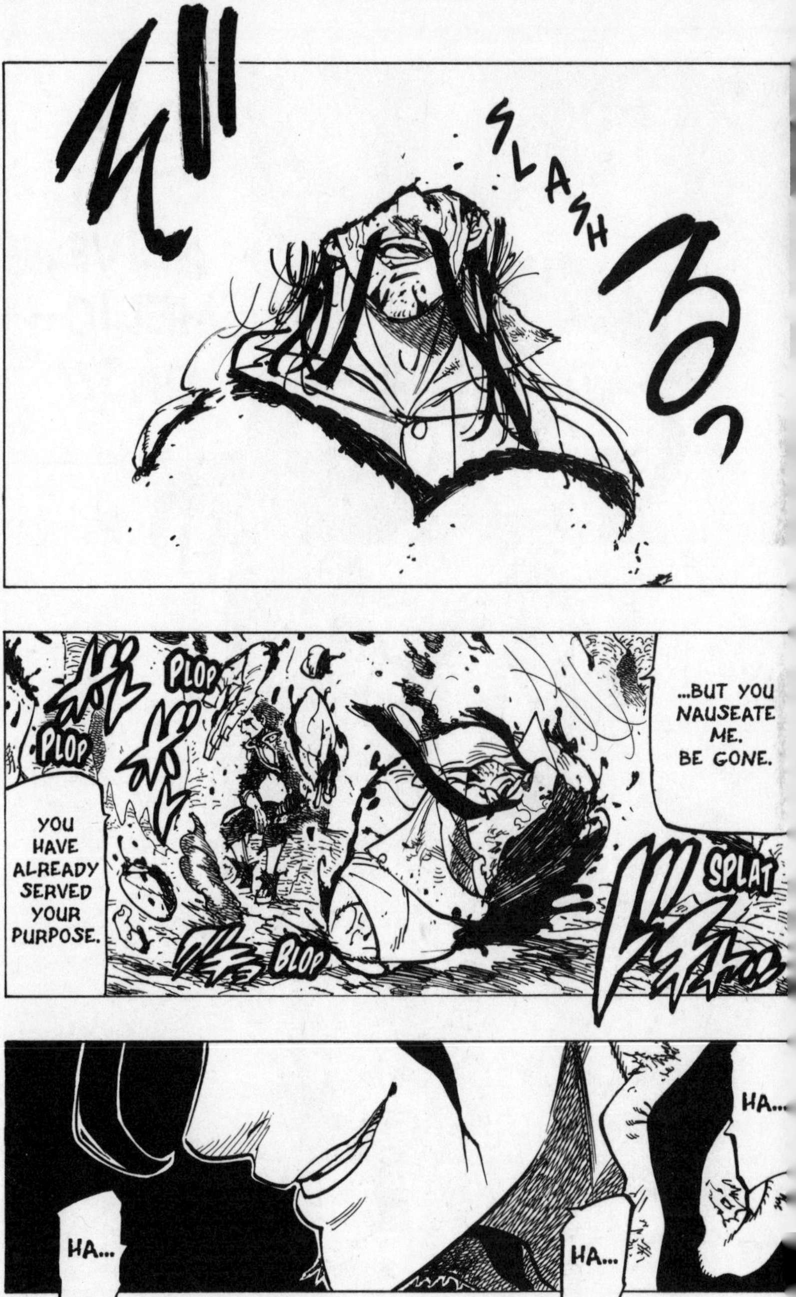
SLASH
...BUT YOU NAUSEATE ME. BE GONE.
SPLAT
PLOP
PLOP
YOU HAVE ALREADY SERVED YOUR PURPOSE.
BLOP
HA...
HA...
HA...

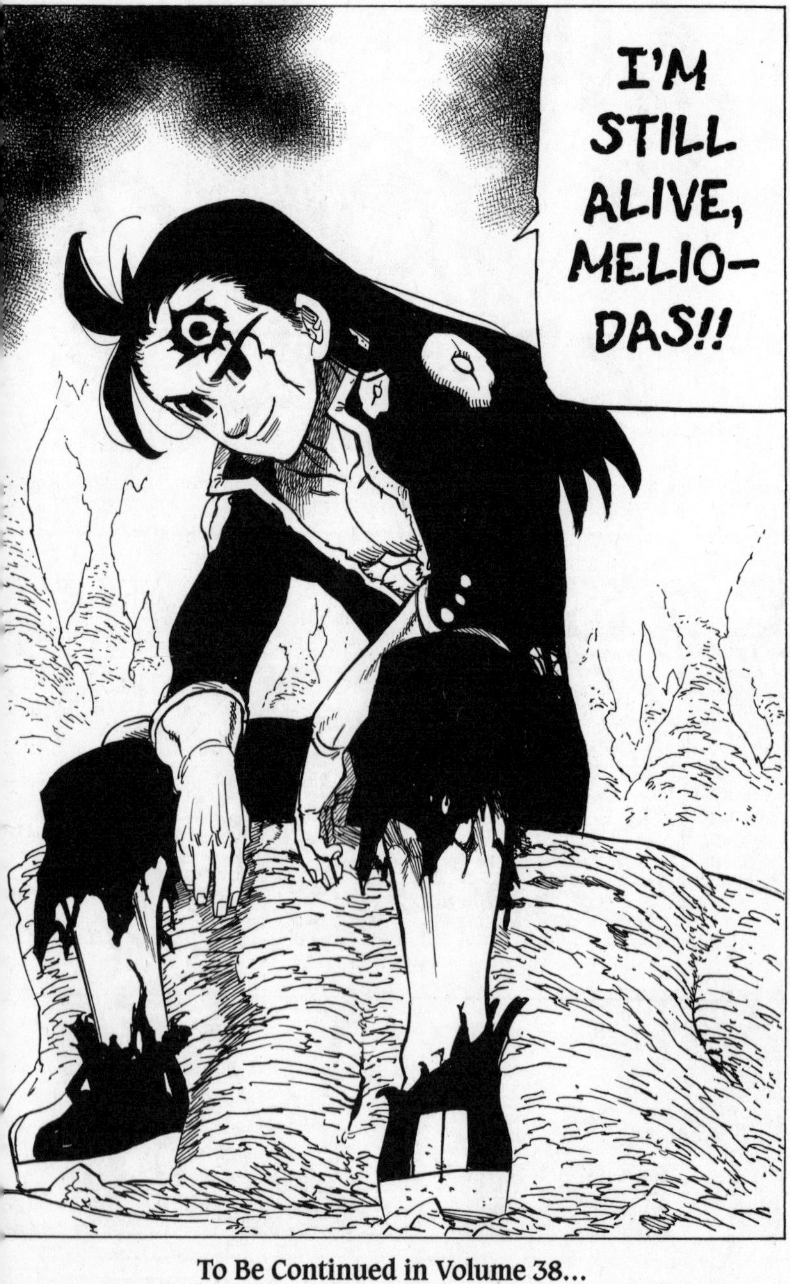
I'M STILL ALIVE, MELIO-DAS!!

To Be Continued in Volume 38...

## "THE SEVEN DEADLY SINS" ILLUSTRATION CORNER

# "THE DRAWING KNIGHTHOOD" SPACE

Be sure to include your name and address on your postcard!

**SPECIAL PRIZE**

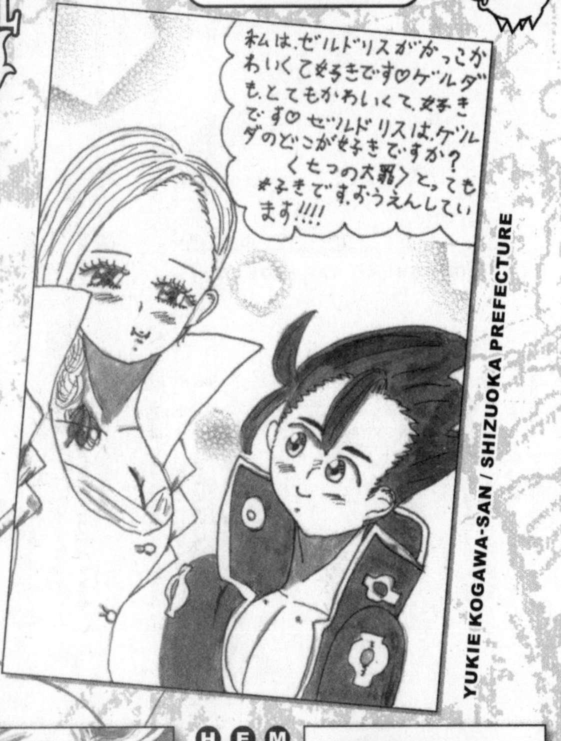

私は、ゼルドリスがかっこかわいくて好きです♡ゲルダも、とてもかわいくて、好きです♡ ゼルドリスは、ゲルダのどこが好きですか？
〈七つの大罪〉とっても好きです。おうえんしています!!!!


Zeldris: "That's right... I love how she says what she thinks and spoils me... Ack! Did I just say that out loud?!"

YUKIE KOGAWA-SAN / SHIZUOKA PREFECTURE

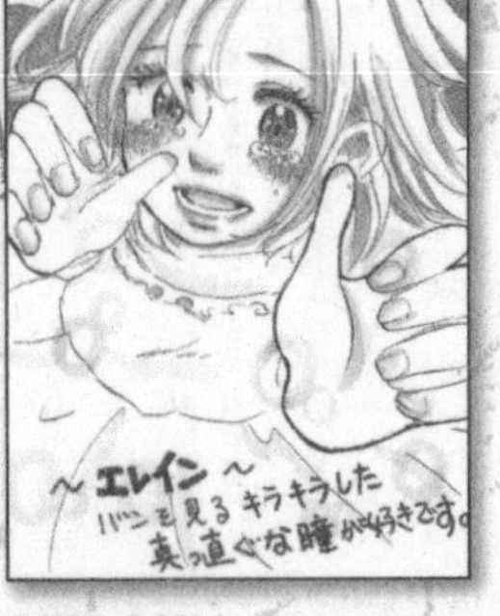

〜エレイン〜
バンを見るキラキラした真っ直ぐな瞳が好きです。


K "Now I understand why Elaine's so head-over-heels for Ban. You won't find another guy like him. I'm happy for you, Elaine."

AIKO-SAN / HIROSHIMA PREFECTURE

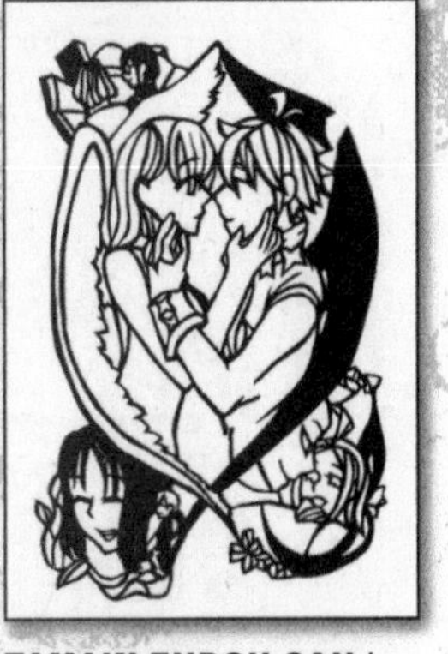

M "We'll overcome our destiny, no matter what!"

E "Yes... No matter what!"

H "I'll help, too!"

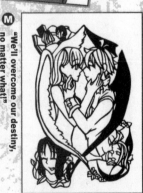

TAMAKI ENDOU-SAN / AICHI PREFECTURE

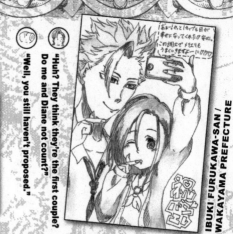

IBUKI FURUKAWA-SAN / WAKAYAMA PREFECTURE

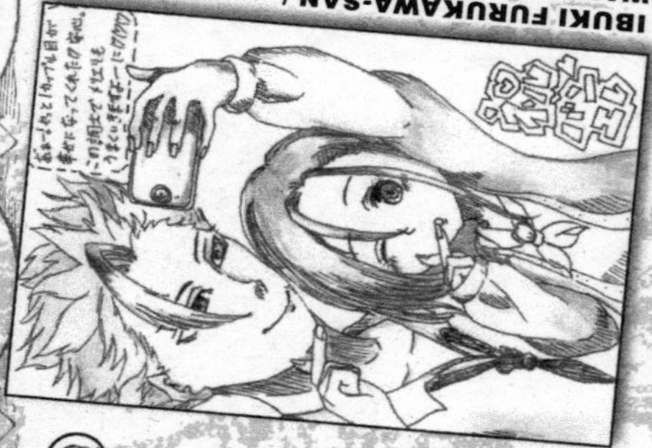

"Huh? They think they're the first couple? Do me and Diane not count?"

"Well, you still haven't proposed."

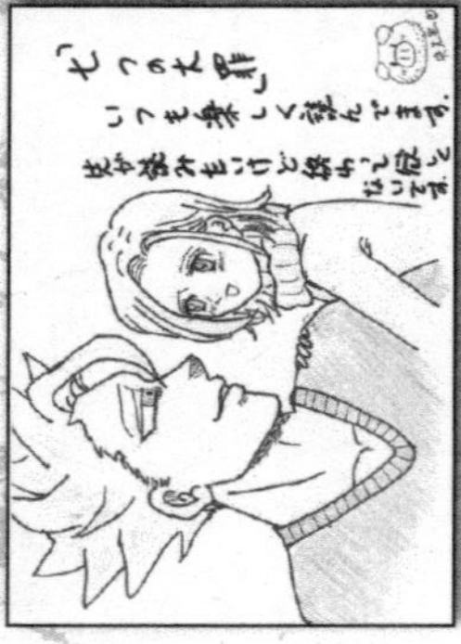
「七つの大罪」
いつも楽しく読んでます。
先が読みたいけど終わって欲しくないです。

GUDENOKO-SAN / TOKYO

B "Now we'll be together forever. ♫"

El "Not just now. My heart's been with you this whole time, Ban."

B "Yeah. ♫"

SARASA WATANABE-SAN / TOKYO

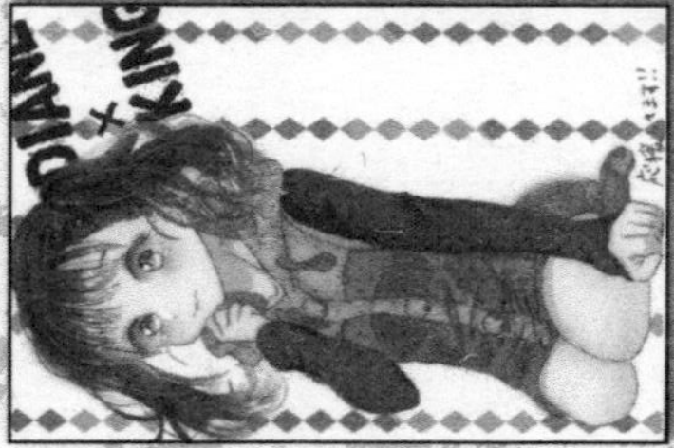
DIANE × KING

K "Huh? Is this Diane wearing my clothes? Or is it...is it my and Diane's...? (blush)"

G "Ah. King has short-circuited."

MOMOKA IGAZAKI-SAN / CHIBA PREFECTURE

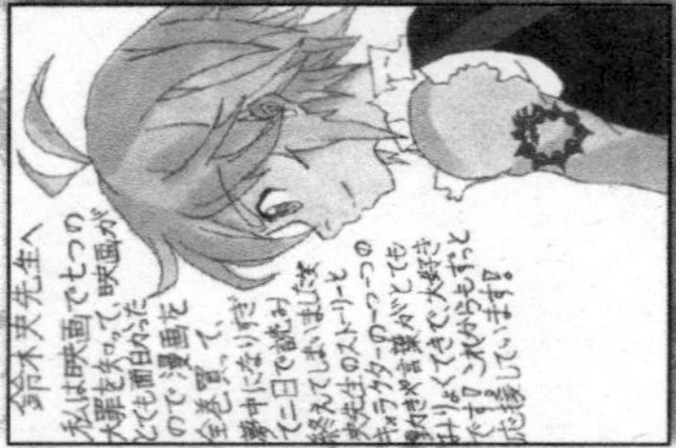
鈴木央先生へ

H "Aw, yeah... I played such an integral role in the movie. In fact, I was pretty much the main lead. I brought the whole pigpen down."

M "What movie are you talking about?!"

TERUAKI YOSHIDA-SAN / FUKUSHIMA PREFECTURE

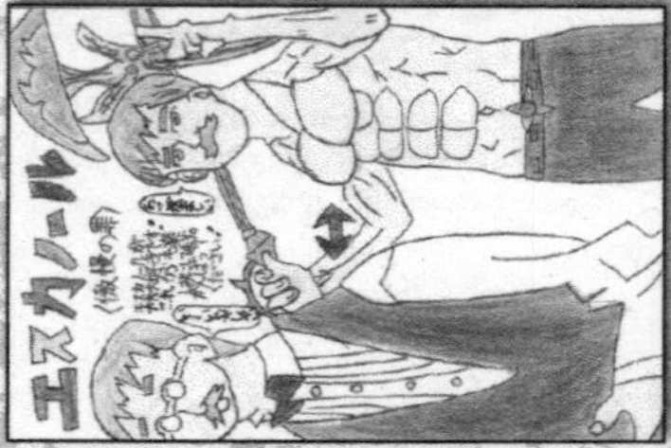
エスカノール
〈傲慢の罪〉

Es "Well now! If you really love my character, you're certainly a bright, young lad. I commend you!"

KING MAGURO-SAN / CHIBA PREFECTURE

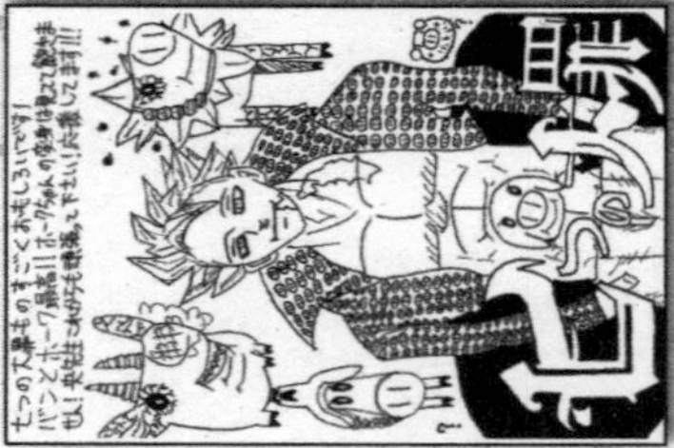
七つの大罪ものすごくおもしろいです!

H "It really is amazing that you got Meliodas back, Ban! Snoink! You always were my best pupil!"

B "Your words honor me. ♫"

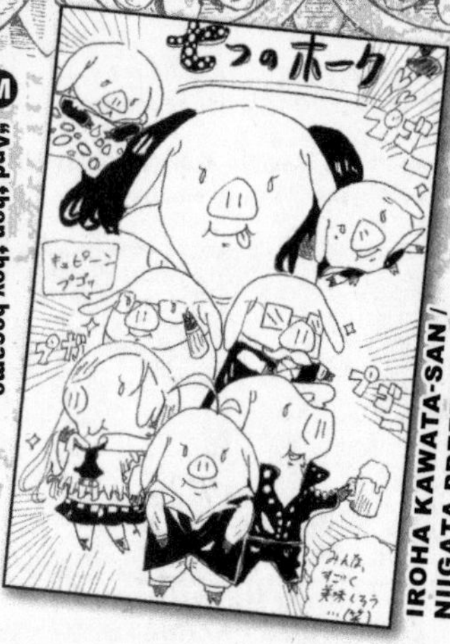
七つのホーク

IROHA KAWATA-SAN / NIIGATA PREFECTURE

**M** "And then they became 'The Seven Pork Dishes'..."

**D** "Uh-oh, Captain. I can't stop drooling!!"

**H** You guys look an awful lot a like. You sure you're not twins?"

**M** "No, no, noooo. Sure we may look alike, but I'm older."

**H** "Yeah, but you're the same height."

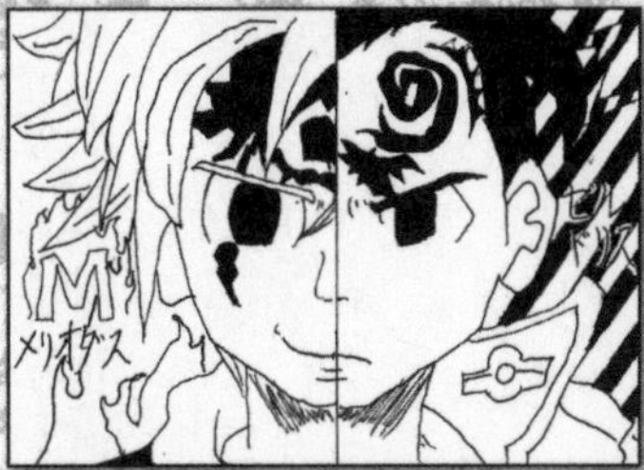
メリオダス

MINATO HAKUYAMA-SAN / SAITAMA PREFECTURE

**K** "Darn it! I also want to awaken! I want to grow fluffy fur and have impressive fangs..."

**B** "That's because that's your brother. ♫"

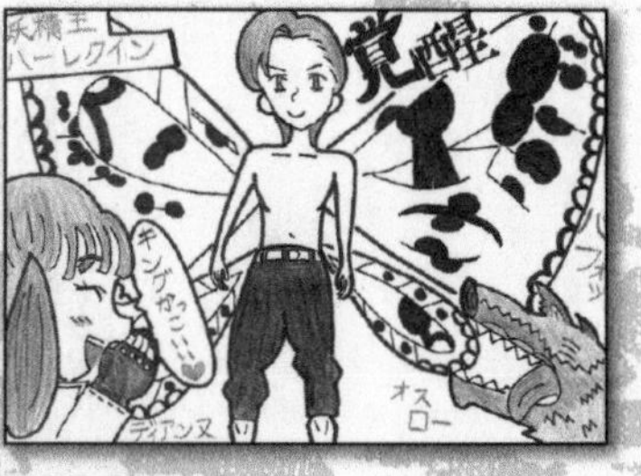
妖精王ハーレクイン
覚醒だー
キングかっこいい
ディアンヌ
オスロー

RINO-SAN / MIE PREFECTURE

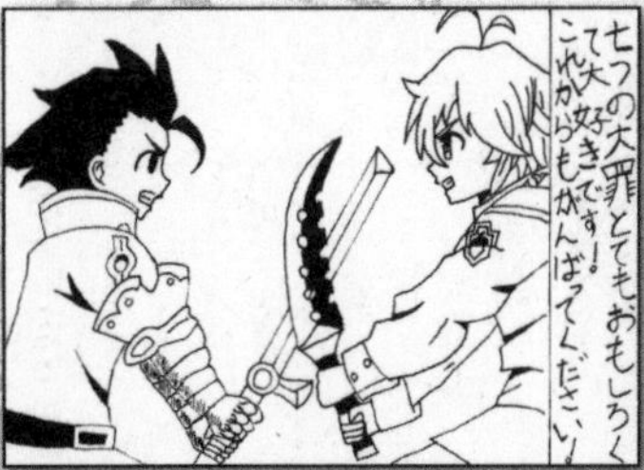
七つの大罪とてもおもしろくて大好きです！これからもがんばってください！

AINA YOKOYAMA-SAN / GUNMA PREFECTURE

**M** "We used to practice with our swords like this a lot back in the day."

**H** "Hmmm. So you guys were actually pretty close."

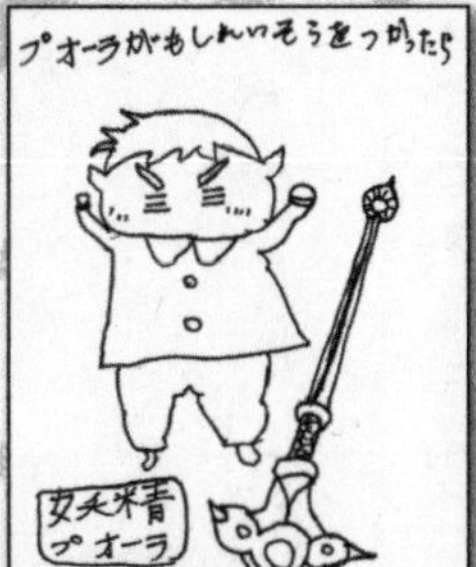
妖精 プオーラ

HISAYA MATSUI-SAN / AICHI PREFECTURE

**Peora** "P-Puoooh! The Spirit Spear's so heavy, I can't move it!"

**K** "Peora... Would you stop playing with my Divine Weapon?"

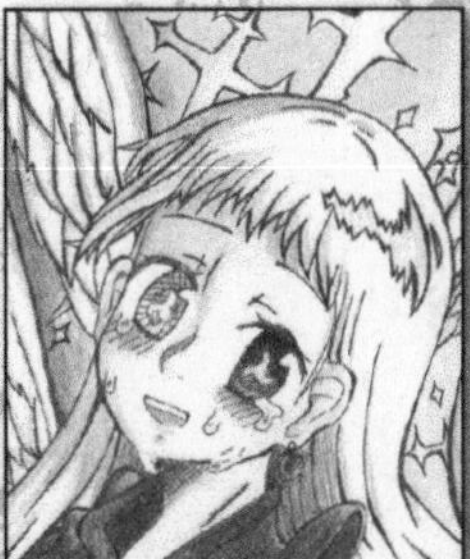

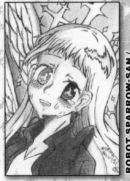

ROBOT SPARROW-SAN / AICHI PREFECTURE

**D** "Just when I thought Elizabeth and the captain could live happily ever after... Aaargh, I'll never forgive the Demon Lord!!"

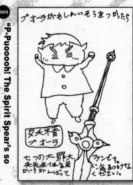

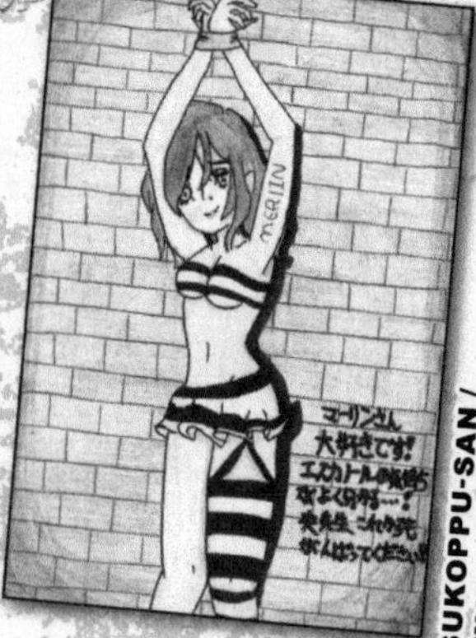
MERLIN
マーリンさん大好きです!

SUKOPPU-SAN / IWATE PREFECTURE

**Es** "Who... Who would dare do this to Merlin-san... (staaaare) I'll never forgive them!! (staaaare)"

**Mer** "It appears you've become the true Fairy King, in name and in reality."

**K** "I won't put Gloxinia-sama's, Helbram's, or Oslo's sacrifices to waste."

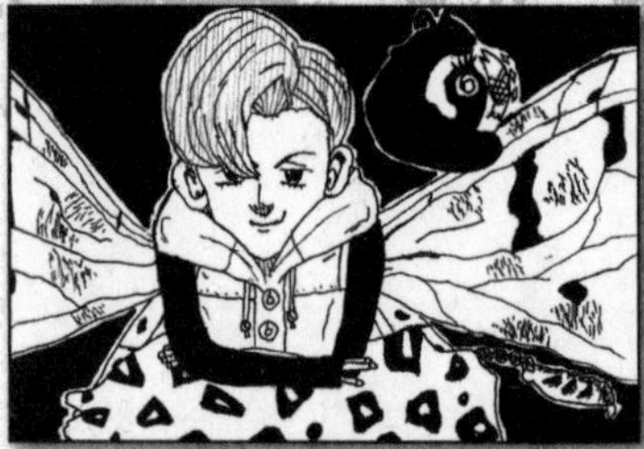

"NIKO MATSUMOTO-SAN / HYOGO PREFECTURE

**Mael** "I want to become the kind of Archangel my older brother would be proud of."

**E** "I know you can do it."

**Es** "I believe in you, too!"

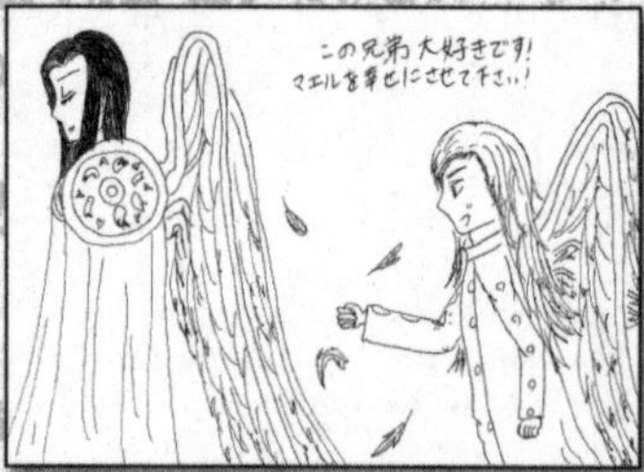
この兄弟大好きです!
マエルを幸せにさせて下さい…!

"RAFAEL-SAN/ AICHI PREFECTURE

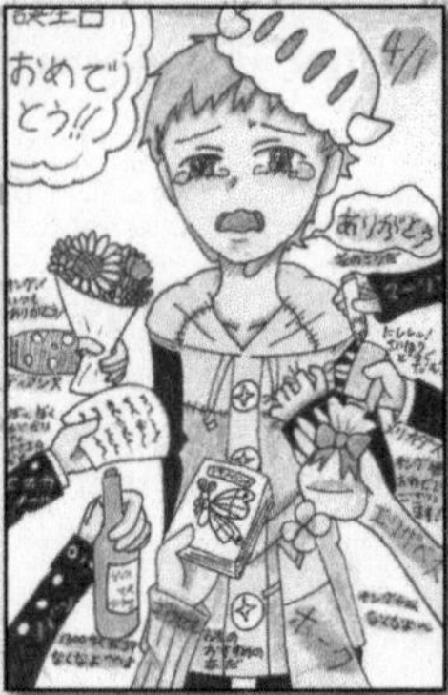
4/1
おめでとう!!
ありがとう

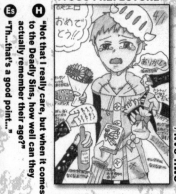

OMU-SAN / UKUOKA PREFECTURE

**H** "Not that I really care, but when it comes to the Deadly Sins, how well can they actually remember their age?"

**Es** "Th...that's a good point..."

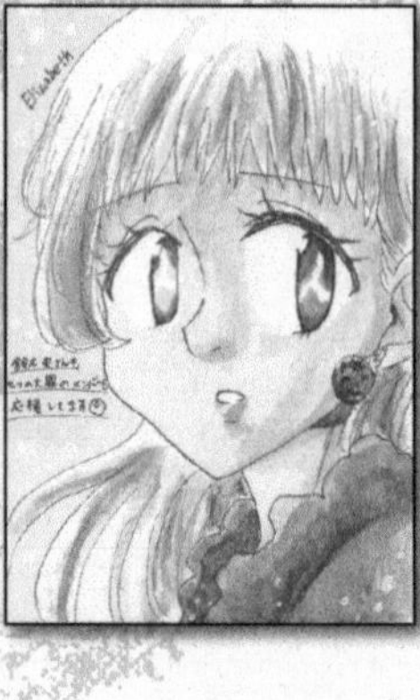
Elizabeth

SARA-SAN / AICHI PREFECTURE

**Mer** "I bet the Demons are thankful that Sissy has such a mild disposition."

**H** "Huh? What do you mean? You're scaring me."

**Mer** "(smirk)"

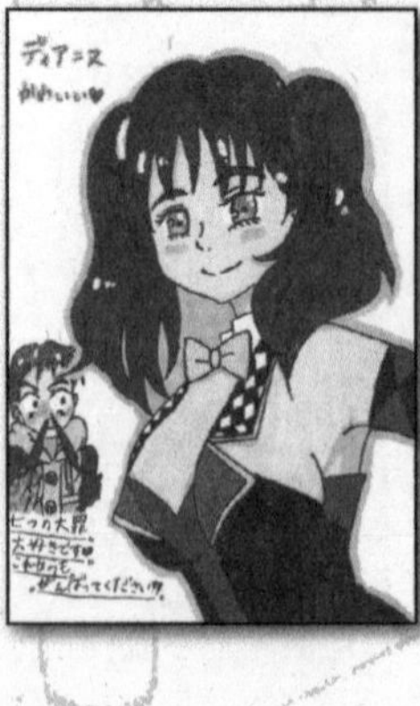
ディアンヌ
かわいい♥

HIYORI KAWABE-SAN / KUMAMOTO PREFECTURE

**K** "Ghaaah! N-no, Diane! I can't take much more of that outfit! (Huff! Huff!)"

RYOTA HORI-SAN / AICHI PREFECTURE

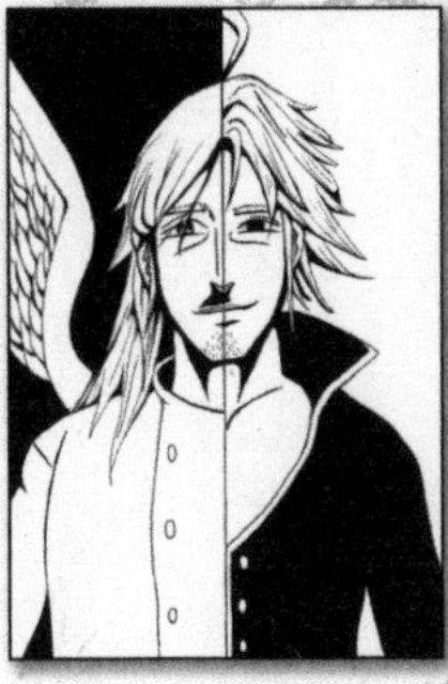

Es "Ooh! It's the man who wins first place in the 'ranking for characters who have had the biggest before-and-after transformation': Mael-san!"

H "That's a long title!"

YUKA TARO-SAN / IWATE PREFECTURE

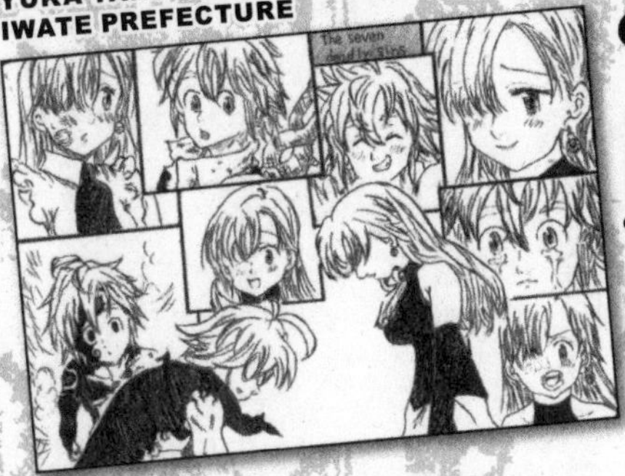
The seven deadly SinS

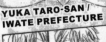

"Even the hardest and saddest past with you are all precious memories to me."

"Thank you, Meliodas..."

YUKINA SASAGI-SAN / KANAGAWA PREFECTURE

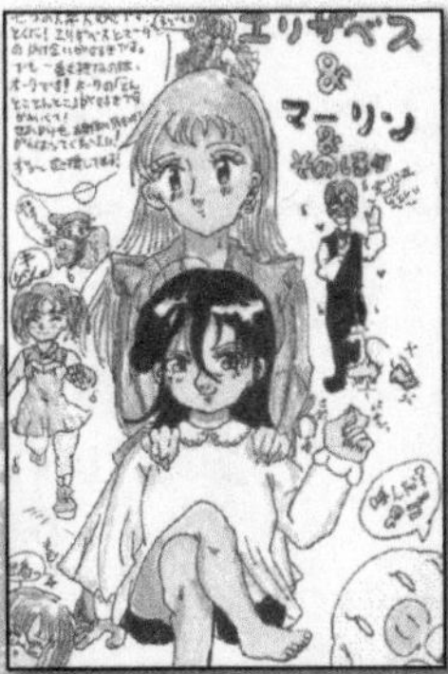
エリザベス
&
マーリン

E "When she was little, Merlin loved to sit on my lap."

D "Aaaw. That's soooo cuuuute! ♡"

Mer "C-cut that out, Sissy!"

YUTARO SHISHIGE-SAN / TOKYO

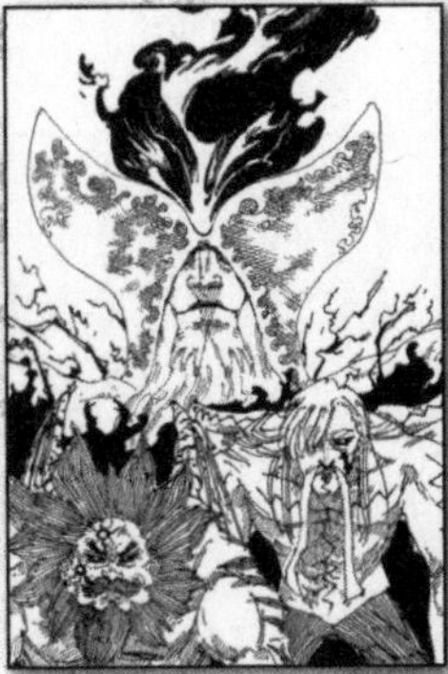

Mer "They were a fearsome duo...but depending on how you look at it, also very pitiful."

M "Yeah. The Demon Lord cannot be forgiven no matter what!"

NATSUMI SUZUKI-SAN / IBARAGI PREFECTURE

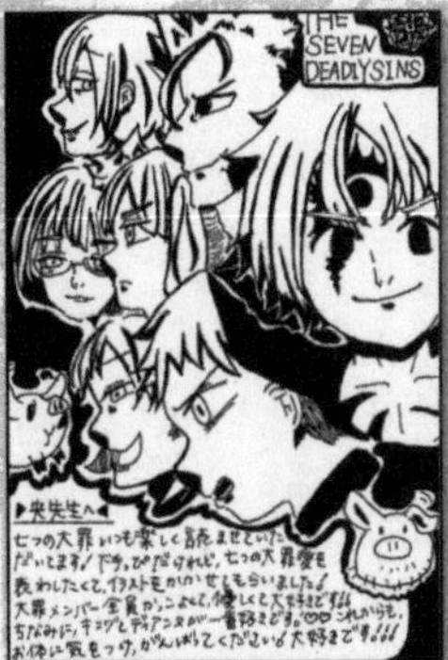
THE SEVEN DEADLY SINS

B "Well! ♫ Sure, we're a ragtag team of members, but...that's what makes us 'us.' ♫"

El "You're so right, Ban-san."

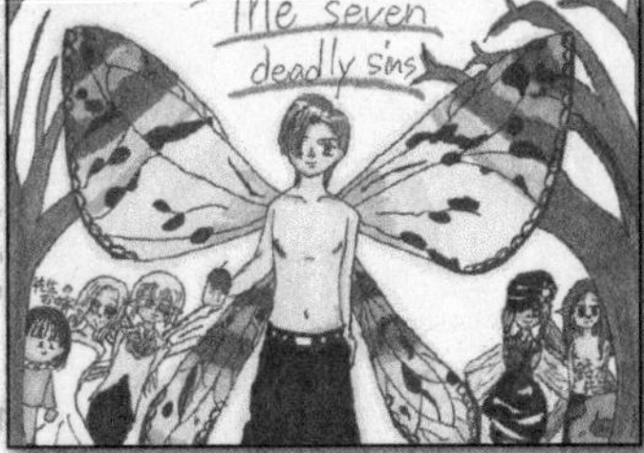
The seven deadly sins

El "B...Brother, there's a weird person and pig behind you..."

K "Oh, yeah. Them. Don't worry about those two."

NANAME-SAN / CHIBA PREFECTURE

I LOVE ICE-CREAM-SAN / AICHI PREFECTURE

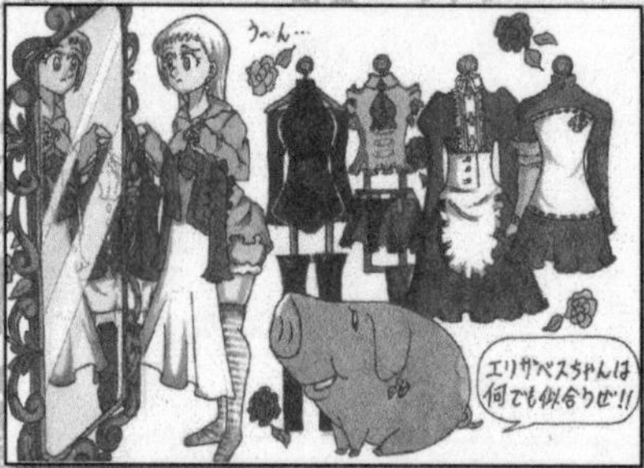

エリザベスちゃんは何でも似合うぜ!!


**M** “Uh-huh. Elizabeth, you look good in anything you wear (grope grope).”

**E** “Eek! ...You perv!”

**M** “Heh heh heh!”

HIYORI KAWABE-SAN / KUMAMOTO PREFECTURE

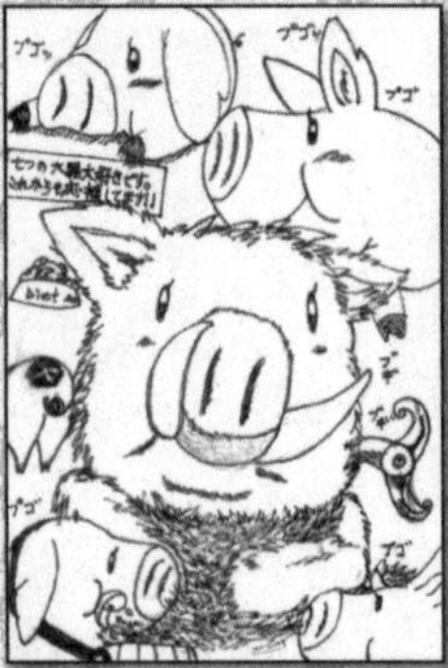

**M** “When the two of them get together, I bet their stink is out of this world.”

**B** “Forget that. I bet they make a delicious soup stock. ♫”

KAZUYUKI SHIJICHOU-SAN / TOKYO

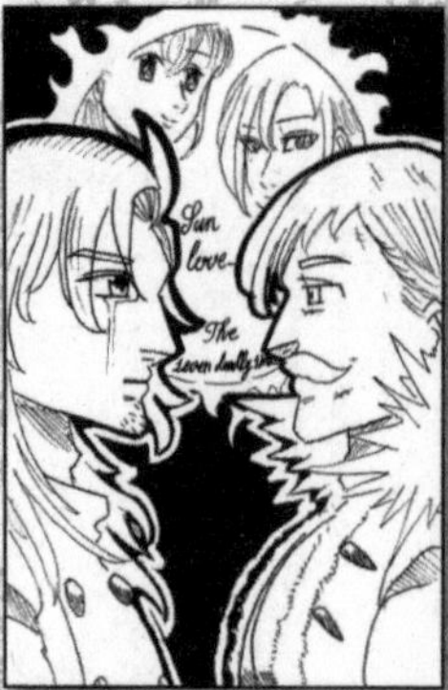

**Mael** “If we'd met sooner, maybe we could've been friends.”

**Es** “Then why don't we become friends now?”

**Mael** “Huh?”

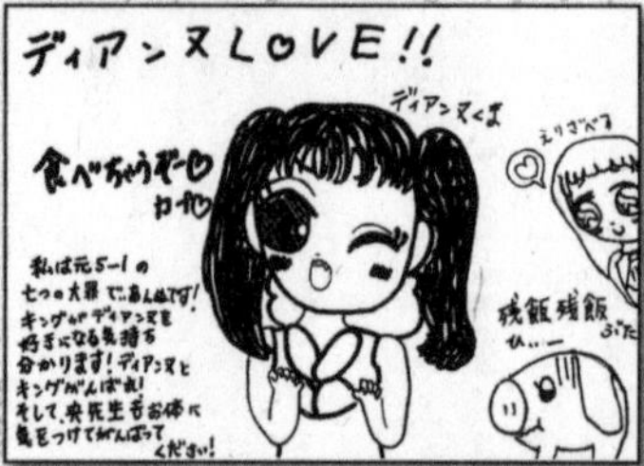

ディアンヌLOVE!!


KEIPYON-SAN / SAITAMA PREFECTURE

**D** “I could eat you up! ♡ Nip!”

**H** “King's been nibbled on!”

**K** “Oh, noooo. Heh heh heh. ♡”

**B** “And he seems pretty happy about it. It's creeping me out.”

NOA SEKINE-SAN / SAITAMA PREFECTURE

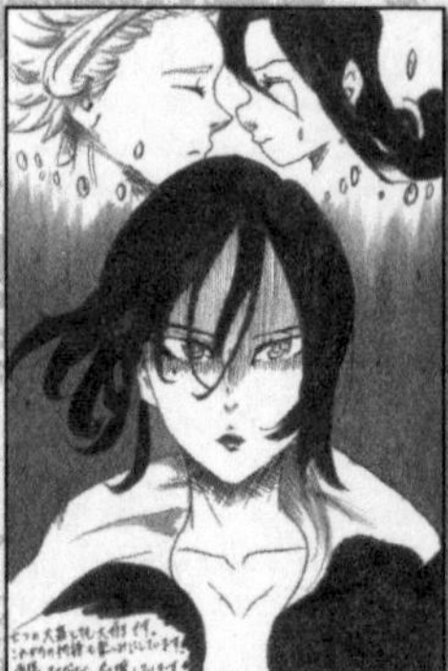

**Mer** “These feelings have nowhere to go... What should I take them out on?”

**Es** “M...Merlin-san.”

**Mer** “...”

KOTETSU-SAN / TOKYO

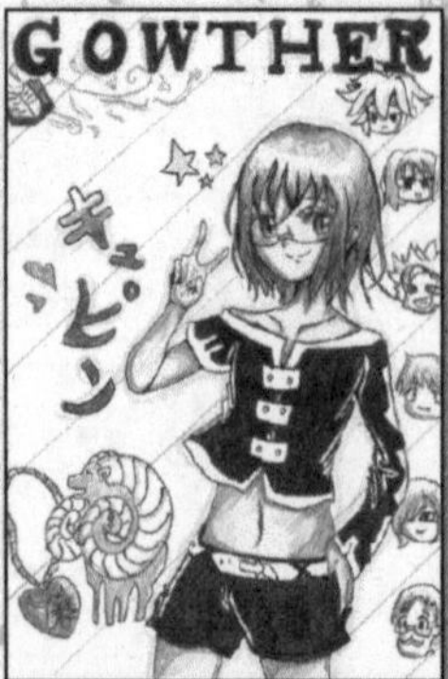

GOWTHER


**K** “No waaaay. I can't believe Gowther knows how to read a situation now. He really is growing up (doting).”

**G** “You are making me blush.

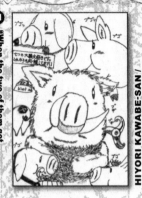

SAKI SUGITA-SAN / HIROSHIMA PREFECTURE

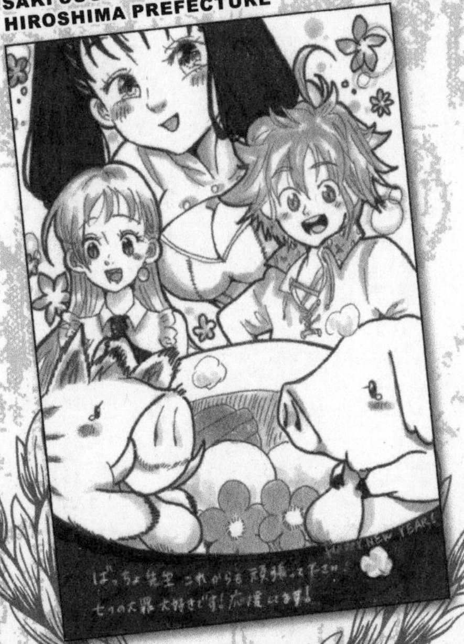

NEW YEAR!
ばっちょ先生 これからも頑張って下さい!
七つの大罪 大好きです! 応援してます!


"You know, there's one more thing I love!"

"Huh?! What's that?!"

"Wild boar stew!"

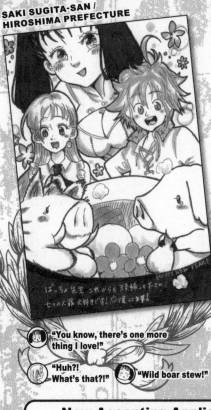

YUMIRII-SAN / AICHI PREFECTURE

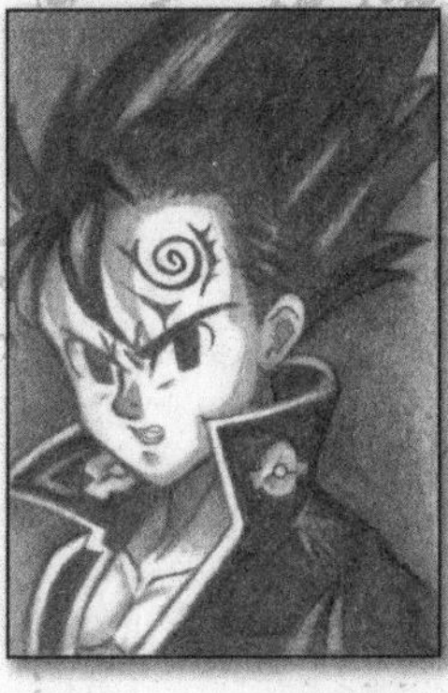

M "If I ever get another chance... then that time for sure...I want to save Zel!"

KUMACHAN-SAN / HIROSHIMA PREFECTURE

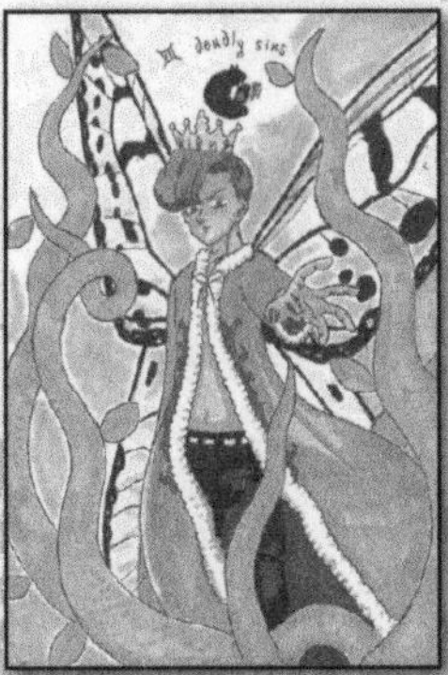

deadly sins


M "Ah! It's King's royal costume!"

G "Ah☆ He shows his belly just like I do!"

## Now Accepting Applicants for the Drawing Knighthood!

- Draw your picture on a postcard, or paper no larger than a postcard, and send it in!
- Don't forget to write your name and location on the back of your picture!
- You can include comments or not. And colored illustrations will still only be displayed in B&W!
- The Drawing Knights whose pictures are particularly noteworthy and run in the print edition will be gifted with a signed specially made pencil board!
- And the best overall will be granted the special prize of a signed shikishi!!

**Send to:**
The Seven Deadly Sins Drawing Knighthood
c/o Kodansha Comics
451 Park Ave. South, 7th floor,
New York, NY 10016

- Submitted letters and postcards will be given to the artist. Please be aware that your name, address, and other personal information included will be given as well.

◀ KAMOME ▶
SHIRAHAMA

# Witch Hat Atelier

A magical manga
adventure for
fans of Disney
and Studio
Ghibli!

Witch Hat Atelier © Kamome Shirahama/Kodansha

## The magical adventure that took Japan by storm is finally here, from acclaimed DC and Marvel cover artist Kamome Shirahama!

In a world where everyone takes wonders like magic spells and dragons for granted, Coco is a girl with a simple dream: She wants to be a witch. But everybody knows magicians are born, not made, and Coco was not born with a gift for magic. Resigned to her un-magical life, Coco is about to give up on her dream to become a witch...until the day she meets Qifrey, a mysterious, traveling magician. After secretly seeing Qifrey perform magic in a way she's never seen before, Coco soon learns what everybody "knows" might not be the truth, and discovers that her magical dream may not be as far away as it may seem...

KC
KODANSHA
COMICS

A Kodansha Comics Trade Paperback Original
*The Seven Deadly Sins* 37 copyright © 2019 Nakaba Suzuki
English translation copyright © 2020 Nakaba Suzuki

All rights reserved.

Published in the United States by Kodansha Comics, an imprint of Kodansha USA Publishing, LLC, New York.

Publication rights for this English edition arranged through Kodansha Ltd., Tokyo.

First published in Japan in 2019 by Kodansha Ltd., Tokyo.

ISBN 978-1-63236-921-5

Printed in the United States of America.

www.kodanshacomics.com

9 8 7 6 5 4 3 2 1
Translation: Christine Dashiell
Lettering: James Dashiell
Editing: Tiff Ferentini
Kodansha Comics edition cover design by Phil Balsman

Publisher: Kiichiro Sugawara
Managing editor: Maya Rosewood
Vice president of marketing & publicity: Naho Yamada

Director of publishing services: Ben Applegate
Associate director of operations: Stephen Pakula
Publishing services managing editor: Noelle Webster
Assistant production manager: Emi Lotto and Angela Zurlo